CW01498728

CONTENTS

POLITICS AND
CIVIL–MILITARY RELATIONS

London and New York

First published 2006 by Oxford University Press for the International Institute for Strategic Studies, Arundel House, 13-15 Arundel Street, Temple Place, London, WC2R 3DX

This reprint published by Routledge
2 Park Square, Milton Park, Abingdon, Oxon, OX14 4RN
For The International Institute for Strategic Studies
Arundel House, 13-15 Arundel Street, Temple Place, London, WC2R 3DX
www.iiss.org

Simultaneously published in the USA and Canada
by Routledge
270 Madison Ave, New York NY 10016

Transferred to Digital Printing 2007

Routledge is an imprint of the Taylor & Francis Group

© 2006 The International Institute for Strategic Studies

All rights reserved. No part of this book may be reprinted or reproduced or utilised in any form or by any electronic, mechanical, or other means, now known or hereafter invented, including photocopying and recording, or in any information storage or retrieval system, without permission in writing from the publishers.

British Library Cataloguing in Publication data
A catalogue record for this book is available from the British Library

Library of Congress Cataloguing in Publication data

ISBN10: 0-415-39880-0 (volume)
ISBN10: 0-415-39813-4 (set)

ISBN13: 978-0-415-39880-0 (volume)
ISBN13: 978-0-415-39813-8 (set)

Publisher's Note
The publisher has gone to great lengths to ensure the quality of this reprint but points out that some imperfections in the original may be apparent

ADELPHI PAPERS

NUMBER SEVENTY-TWO
DECEMBER 1970

Military Manpower and Political Purpose

by Erwin Häckel

THE INSTITUTE FOR STRATEGIC STUDIES
18 ADAM STREET LONDON WC2

ADELPHI PAPER NO. 72

Erwin Häckel is a young German political scientist who is a lecturer at the University of Konstanz. His recent work has been concerned with African Nationalism and with political developments in the Warsaw Pact. Research for the present Paper was carried out while he was a Research Associate at the ISS in 1969-70.

Additional copies of this paper may be ordered from the Institute at the cost of 25p (75 cents) each, post free.

The Institute for Strategic Studies is an international non-governmental research centre concerned with the study of the problems of war, conflict and arms control on an international basis. The purpose of the Adelphi Paper series is to give hospitality to a wide range of analytical work; the papers which form the series are not intended to express the views or the policy of the Institute itself, which is not the advocate of any national position or any particular school of thought.

© The Institute for Strategic Studies 1970

CONTENTS

Military Manpower and Political Purpose

Problems of military manpower are as old as the military function itself. Such problems have basically remained unchanged over time: how many soldiers for the armed forces? how to recruit them? how to keep them? how to train them? how to control them? how to make the best of them?

Attempted solutions to these problems are innumerable and infinitely diverse. But there is one fundamental choice that has always borne and continues to bear on all possible alternatives, and all other choices are secondary to this one: should military manpower rest on the soldiers' own free will, or on compulsion? should soldiers be induced, or coerced? should they be volunteers, or conscripts?

This seemingly clear-cut choice is, of course, rarely perceived in such stark terms. Not one army in history has ever existed on the basis of pure voluntarism or pure coercion. All military manpower systems are a mixture of both ingredients, and it may often be difficult to say where the one ends and the other starts. Were the Mamelukes volunteers or not? Were Germanic tribal warriors coerced into armed service or not? In the modern period of national warfare, is the 'patriot' doing his 'duty' not as much of an incongruity as the 'mercenary' posing as a 'hero'? Even in peacetime armies, coercion and voluntarism go always hand in hand. Once the volunteer has signed up for military service he is subject to the deprivations of military discipline which may be enforced upon him more stringently than upon some conscripts elsewhere. There are, on the other hand, not a few conscripted soldiers who thoroughly enjoy soldiering, and indeed, officers under any manpower scheme are volunteers in one sense or another; no army could afford to rely on officers who did not want to be officers. Moreover, there is today not one conscript army without a hard core, however small, of truly voluntary professional soldiers.

Nevertheless, the difference between voluntary and conscripted military manpower is an essential one, and the decision to base a country's armed forces on one of these two principles or on a combination of both entails a host of problems and alternatives reaching far beyond the limited field of military recruitment policy. It is the purpose of this Paper to discuss these problems and alternatives in the light of recent experience and developments in various European countries. Using a general and comparative perspective it may perhaps help to clarify and put into a broader context some related issues which are all too often seen by national commentators and policy-makers as isolated and bewildering dilemmas due to allegedly singular national requirements or circumstances.

To attempt such an overview should be as timely today as ever. Military manpower problems are, of course, more or less constantly reviewed and discussed wherever and whenever they happen to crop up. But it is obvious in mid-1970 that they are cropping up with more frequency and obstinacy in more instances than in the previous decade, and more people seem to become aware of them now than were used to. The past twelve months alone have witnessed a spate of arguments about military recruitment policies in a wide variety of countries. In the United States, the President's Commission on an All-Volunteer Armed Force came out, in February 1970, in favour of the abolition of the draft system; the Commission's findings, although endorsed by President Nixon, were immediately criticized and thrown into doubt by a majority of Senators. Agonizing second thoughts on the wisdom of the abolition of conscription were voiced in last year's debate on the Defence Estimates in Britain. A reduction

I

of the length of conscript service is being planned in West Germany and Austria and has already taken effect in France. The case for a shift towards volunteer armed forces has been put forward recently by noted parliamentary experts such as A. Sanguinetti in France, Helmut Schmidt in West Germany and H. Kikkert in the Netherlands. Rising numbers of conscientious objectors have added a new element to the debate in several countries, notably in Denmark, West Germany and the United States. At the same time, recently formulated government policy in France, West Germany and Austria explicitly aims at a more comprehensive intake of conscripted manpower. Characteristically, in the general mood for reappraisal, NATO's Supreme Commander in Europe, General Goodpaster, spoke out in a speech in Brussels (10 March 1970) against hasty and fashionable reforms and urged European allies to retain in their armed forces a balanced 'mix' between voluntary and conscripted manpower.

There is no easily discernible trend in the present debate. Discussions of the subject are mostly confined to a national perspective; arguments and experiences in countries with similar problems are rarely taken into account. National policy-makers tend to seek their own solutions for their own problems. While it is impossible within the scope of this Paper to explore individual national problems of military manpower in detail it is precisely the similarity and simultaneity of such problems which facilitates, and indeed calls for, a more general and comparative approach.

The scope for comparison in the present Paper is bound to remain limited for two reasons. First, it would obviously make little sense to compare military manpower problems in countries as diverse as, say, Britain and Congo-Kinshasa. Our focus is, therefore, restricted to 'modern' countries, i.e., those with a level of political, social and economic development similar to that of Britain.

Secondly, there is the dearth of comparable data. It was indeed the most astounding experience to the present writer to find how little reliable information on military manpower is available or accessible to the researcher even if he is prepared to collect his material on a tedious country-by-country circuit. This can be

explained on two grounds. For one, there is the cloak of official secrecy which appears in many countries to be dictated not so much by military necessity but rather by the belief that all substantial information about the armed forces ought to be kept as far as possible among the *arcana imperii*. Not surprisingly, all experts or agencies in Communist countries who were approached in the course of this project proved to be altogether uncooperative. But even in Allied or neutral European countries several seemingly innocuous items of information (mostly relating to manpower shortages and reserves) were withheld on grounds of official secrecy, though often in a curiously erratic fashion: information that was anxiously guarded as classified matter in some countries was cheerfully supplied in some others, and the same happened with different officials in one and the same country. What is revealed here is not only a pattern of bureaucratic idiosyncracies but a serious lack of reflection on the merits of secretiveness within the framework of a strategy of deterrence. Besides, military manpower problems being what they are, they often call for solutions involving a strong measure of publicity; any attempt to shield them from 'outside' attention may only aggravate their causes.

Still more remarkable than the issue of secrecy (though possibly related to it) is the actual shortage of information within national defence establishments themselves. Defence policy with regard to manpower problems seems to be frequently made in a sort of 'black box', with policy-makers groping for solutions to problems whose causes, nature and context remain largely unknown. Officials in a number of defence ministries in Europe, though anxious to be helpful to the inquirer, were embarrassed to admit that basic data about the structure, composition, cost and requirements of their armed services were simply not known. The 'White Paper' which was published by the West German Ministry of Defence in the spring of 1970, has been widely hailed (and rightly so) as an outstanding example of comprehensive data gathering and for its candid appraisal of manpower shortcomings. It remains to be asked, however, why this should be an outstanding example; regular stocktaking of this kind appears to be nothing less than obligatory for reasons of democratic accountability, administrative efficiency and, after all, military security in any country.

Most of the factual material on which the present paper is based was collected in the summer of 1970 through a questionnaire sent to official experts in fifteen non-Communist countries in the northern hemisphere. Ten questionnaires were returned, most of them only partially completed due to the reasons given above. Personal interviews and doublechecks in West Germany, Switzerland, France and Britain served to close some of the gaps thus left open, but revealed also that several items of statistical evidence supplied through questionnaires were either unreliable or not fully comparable to each other.

This Paper can, therefore, attempt only a tentative outline and classification of current trends and problems of military manpower. In the absence of more ambitious studies (devoutly to be wished) it may at least help to raise the subject above the confines of a merely national perspective. Precisely because so little is known or noted about other countries' experiences, it is useful to emphasize the similarity and comparability of national problems of military manpower. National planners looking for specific solutions or experimenting with specific remedies might profitably gain from other countries' experiences. On the other hand, those national planners who are eager to emulate foreign models should pause to examine the full complexities and repercussions of such models carefully; seemingly identical manpower systems may create quite dissimilar problems in different countries. The present Paper seeks to present its findings in a schematic way so as to highlight the different and often contradictory ways in which each of these problems can be looked at.

The findings reported here are derived from the current or recent experience of the most advanced industrial states in Western Europe and North America, i.e., the major NATO countries (Britain, France, West Germany, Belgium, the Netherlands, Denmark, Italy, Canada and the United States) as well as three neutral countries (Switzerland, Sweden and Austria). Specific comparable data is not available for all of these countries throughout but mostly for a varying cross-section of them. While Warsaw Pact countries are not specifically treated they may be assumed to have roughly similar experiences and problems now or in the near future. This assumption is based, apart from sporadic evidence, on the simple reasoning that conditions in Eastern Europe are not so basically different from those in Western Europe as to make a radically different military manpower situation appear probable. All figures given, except as otherwise noted, refer to the situation on or around 1 January 1970; estimated figures are marked 'E'.

One final qualification is in order. The countries whose situation is discussed here are at peace with each other and with the rest of the world (except for the US in Vietnam), though not on altogether amiable terms in many cases. Their armed forces are peacetime forces; some of them have not experienced actual combat for more than a generation; and what is more, they are not seriously expected to find themselves in combat in the foreseeable future. Not warfare but the maintenance of peace is the *ultima ratio* of armed forces according to the doctrine of deterrence. This is, at least in its now almost universal acceptance, a novel if not outright paradoxical function of military establishments, and it creates some specific problems for them. This Paper is concerned with the situation of such peacetime armies, and its findings may have little relation to military manpower problems in time of war.

TYPES OF MILITARY MANPOWER SYSTEMS

No country has a military manpower system which is exactly the same as another's. It is tempting to say that there are as many different types as there are national armed forces; in fact, even among the different Services in any one country there are often widely differing policies of recruitment, training and personnel management. Such a variety seems to confirm

7

those views which regard each nation's manpower problems as basically *sui generis*.

On the other hand, all military manpower schemes have significant characteristics in common, if only in sometimes rudimentary form. For a convenient typology it may be useful at the outset to arrange some basic statistical figures in a rank order according to the proportion of volunteers in national armed force:

Third, there is the 'mixed' type in other countries, relying on a cadre of regulars supplemented by a rotating force of conscripts, or to put it differently, a force of conscripts stiffened with regular personnel. While the third is by far the most common type of manpower systems, combining elements of both 'pure' types, its peculiarities can be studied most profitably by an analysis and comparison of

				Army		
			Volunteers	personnel		
	Total		as percentage	as percentage		Total length
	personnel in	Armed forces	of total	of total	Volunteers as	of conscript
	armed	as percentage	personnel	personnel	percentage of	service for
	forces	of total	in armed	in armed	total Army	Army privates
Country	(1,000s)	population	forces	forces	personnel	(months)
(1)	(2)	(3)	(4)	(5)	(6)	(7)
Britain ..	376	0·6	100	47	100	n.a.
Canada ..	92	0·4	100	n.a.[a]	n.a.	n.a.
United States	3,298	1·6	86	43	69	24
Belgium ..	93	0·9	59	74	53	15
W. Germany	481	0·8	48	70	40	18
France ..	489	0·9	47	65	35	15
Netherlands	121	0·9	42	66	30	16
Denmark ..	43	0·8	41	62	31	12
Austria ..	47	0·6	34	n.a.[a]	n.a.	9
Italy ..	413	0·8	26	71	15	15
Sweden ..	628[c]	7·8	4·5	95	E[b]: 3	11
Switzerland	656[c]	10·4	0·5	n.a.[a]	n.a.	12

Table 1

NOTES

[a] n.a. = not applicable. The Canadian, Austrian and Swiss Armies are incorporated into unified armed forces.
[b] E = estimated.
[c] Swedish and Swiss figures are calculated for the official strengths of the armed forces when fully mobilized. In peacetime active service average figures run as follows:

	(1)	(2)	(3)	(4)	(5)	(6)
Sweden	E: 82	E: 1·0		E: 35	E: 66	E: 33
Switzerland	E: 27	E: 0·4		E: 12	n.a.	n.a.

Column (4) in the above table suggests a threefold typology of military manpower systems. First, there is the all-volunteer ('regular') force along the British and Canadian pattern, relying entirely on the voluntary services of professional soldiers. At the other end of the spectrum is the all-conscript ('citizen') force in Switzerland and Sweden, relying largely or almost entirely on the extracted services of a popular militia.

the extreme and relatively uncommon all-volunteer and militia systems.

'Mixed' forces and militia forces may be lumped together under the heading of 'conscript forces'. But it would be misleading to conclude that these two types have necessarily more in common with each other than with the all-volunteer type. Some 'mixed' forces tend towards the all-conscript type, others towards

4

the all-volunteer type. Italy, with only 26 per cent volunteers, represents the former case, the United States, with 86 per cent, the latter; and West Germany, with her forces made up almost equally by volunteers and conscripts, is most typical of the hybrid form.

Column (6) shows that in conscript forces the percentage of volunteers is significantly lower in the Army (land force) than in the armed services as a whole. Conversely, there is always a higher proportion of volunteers among the other services. In each of the countries under review (except the militia countries), the Navy and the Air Force include more than 50 per cent volunteers, with the proportion reaching 98 per cent in the US Navy (including the Marine Corps) and 100 per cent in the US Air Force.

The naval and air branches are, of necessity, highly specialized and technologically advanced services; their tasks consist mainly in operating complex weapons systems. Land forces, on the other hand, have tasks that call for a lesser degree of sophistication in technical skills and weaponry; they are therefore relatively unspecialized and comparatively personnel-intensive, particularly as regards the infantry which continues to provide the backbone of every modern Army.

This has to be kept in mind in assessing the sequence of figures in column (5) of Table 1 (Army personnel as percentage of total personnel in armed forces), read in conjunction with column (6) (Volunteers as percentage of total Army personnel). The relative size of the Army, as can be seen, tends to be inversely proportional to the percentage of volunteers among total armed personnel. The larger the share of volunteers the more prominent is the role of the Navy and Air Force; the more a country relies on conscripted manpower the more clearly is its armed force dominated by the Army.

The over-all size of any armed force appears to be closely related to this pattern. As shown in columns (2) and (3), volunteer forces are relatively smaller than conscript forces. (The size of the US forces is an obvious exception to this rule.) Volunteer forces, with their emphasis on naval and air weaponry, are relatively compact; conscript forces, with their emphasis on massive land-based soldiery, are relatively sprawling. Thus, the higher the pro-portion of conscripts in the services the larger is the share of the armed forces in a country's total manpower. This is particularly evident, even in absolute terms, in the case of militia armies: Switzerland and Sweden, though ranking among the smallest and least populous countries of Europe, maintain the largest armed forces on the continent beside the Soviet Union.

There is, to be sure, an air of unreality about the vast size of militia forces. Militia forces seem to be barely existent as long as they are not mobilized into active service. As can be seen from the note to column (2) the average strength of armed units on active duty at any given time amounts to only 13 per cent of total force strength in Sweden and to a mere 4 per cent in Switzerland.

But it would be misleading to conclude that a militia is nothing else than what is called the reserve in the armed forces of other countries. Reserves, as the term is generally understood, are supplementary units for reinforcement or renewal of regular force strengths in time of war. Militiamen, on the other hand, continue to serve throughout their period of military obligation as fully integrated members of the armed force, rotating in and out of active service in a succession of prescribed terms of duty.

This, indeed, is the essential characteristic of a militia system. The full body of militiamen *is* the armed force, not an appendix to it. While it would be unreasonable therefore to take as the basis for comparison with other military manpower systems only the small number of militiamen and volunteers on active duty at any given time, it is nevertheless revealing to note that, within this activated core, the role of voluntary personnel is by no means so diminutive as it appears on the scale of the total armed force. Voluntary soldiers, in contrast to conscripted ones, are permanently on active service; their ratio to the total of active troops, as shown in the note to column (4) of Table 1, is no less in Sweden than in the French Army, and not much less in Switzerland than in the Italian Army. Conversely this means that, in a number of European countries, the Army is operated by a small cadre of volunteers, comparable to that of militia armies!

Finally, a word on the length of military service terms. Voluntary soldiers, of course, serve longer terms than conscripts, ranging from a minimum of two years to the maximum of some 40 years (for officers) in most countries. In the all-volunteer British forces soldiers usually enlist for 6-year or 9-year terms, with the option of subsequent re-enlistment; the average length of service of all British soldiers is about eight years.

Minimum terms for conscript soldiers, as shown in column (7) of Table 1, range from 9 months in Austria to 24 months in the United States. It should be noted, however, that these figures apply only to Army privates. Conscripted soldiers entering the Navy and Air Force and/or aspiring to be promoted to the rank of non-commissioned officers or officers are required in many countries to serve for considerably longer periods. Thus, conscripted sailors or airmen promoted to officer rank have to remain in the service for additional minimum periods between three months and three years

in such countries as Belgium, Sweden, Switzerland, Denmark, the Netherlands and Austria. It is evident that in these cases compulsion is superseded by at least a significant degree of voluntarism on the part of conscripted recruits; nobody, after all, can be compelled to incur such additional service obligations if he is not willing to do so.

There is thus an undeniable though sometimes obscured correlation between the length of military service and the percentage of conscripts among the forces. All-volunteer or predominantly volunteer ranks, service branches, or national armed forces are made up mainly of long-serving personnel whereas those ranks, service branches, or national armed forces that rely mainly on conscripted manpower are dominated by soldiers serving only the required minimum term. This must obviously be reflected in different recruitment policies; of which more presently.

PROBLEMS OF PERSONNEL RECRUITMENT

All armed forces are faced with the same dilemma: to get the best possible men, and to get them in sufficient numbers. This is at bottom an insoluble task. High-quality personnel is, by definition, in high demand and in short supply, and manpower planners therefore have to compromise with regard to either the quality or the quantity of recruits, or both. Typically, where such adjustments are necessary, all-volunteer forces tend to sacrifice quantity, all-conscript forces prefer to sacrifice quality, and mixed forces are inclined to seek a middle road between the two.

In all the countries under review, the armed forces today struggle to cope with recruitment problems reflecting this dilemma in typical fashion. Among all-volunteer forces, the British services, ever since the abolition of conscription in 1960, have been unable to meet the recruitment targets set by military planners. These targets now envisage an annual intake of 35,000 recruits, representing about 1·4 per cent of the pool of available young men, but since the end of conscription the figure has never exceeded

1·3 per cent. Thus, in spite of a steady contraction of the total size of the armed forces from 425,000 in 1964 to 376,000 in 1970, in spite of vigorous recruiting campaigns and in spite of recently improving recruitment figures, Britain is still short of more than 10,000 soldiers. Manpower shortages are said to be 'desperate' in the infantry, where Britain has for several years been unable to meet NATO target figures, but the pinch is being felt in other services as well. While Canada does not have similar recruitment problems with her all-volunteer forces, it should be noted that their strength has also declined from 114,000 to 92,000 within the past five years. Canada now has, relatively speaking, the smallest of the armed forces under review: it comprises only 0·4 per cent of the country's total population—an exceptionally low figure. It is naturally much easier to recruit enough men for such a small force.

Conscript forces are faced with a different kind of recruiting problem. They need, of course, not worry about a shortage of infantrymen; they can draw upon their countries' full manpower resources to meet such requirements. But they, too, have their sensitive spots. All conscript forces, as has been pointed out earlier, rely on a core of volunteer soldiers. This core may be very small, as in the case of militia armies. Yet the smaller it is the more vital becomes its function for the life of the armed services as a whole. It is here that conscript systems appear very vulnerable indeed.

Switzerland, to take the extreme example of a conscript army, deliberately restricts the number of full-time military personnel to a bare minimum. All in all, there are only slightly more than 3,000 professional (i.e., voluntary) soldiers in Switzerland, two-thirds of whom make up the staff of the Fortress Guard, the airmen of the Surveillance Squadron and a handful of corps commanders. The rest, numbering 500 officers and 670 non-commissioned officers, form the Instructors Corps, a peculiar Swiss institution charged with the task of training the country's militia officers and NCOs. Target figures envisage a body of 1,460 instructors (630 officers and 830 NCOs), and while the present 20 per cent deficit in strength might appear inconsequential to outsiders it is a severe headache for Swiss defence planners. On the performance of the tiny Instructors Corps depends, after all, the standard of training of the country's entire 650,000-man force, and it is also the reservoir from which most of the highest ranking officers are finally drawn. Yet it has been impossible in recent years to meet the target figures for recruiting new instructors and, perhaps even more seriously, it has also proved impossible to attract applicants of the outstanding quality for which the job calls.

Recruitment problems may be less intricate in other conscript forces but they are often more conspicuous instead. Sweden has an 18 per cent deficit of volunteer officers, Italy one of 10 per cent, Austria one of 31 per cent and West Germany one of 20 per cent. The shortage of volunteer non-commissioned officers is 12 per cent in the French Army, 32 per cent in the Austrian and 21 per cent in the West German. Most of these shortages affect poisitions that require technical training or other specialized skills and experience. Their adverse effects on the performance of the armed forces can therefore be offset only to a very limited degree by promotion of conscripts to higher rank or by the extensive use of conscripted manpower.

What are the reasons for these recruitment difficulties? They are certainly multifaceted and may be altogether different in various countries. Nevertheless, it seems that in all cases one or more of the following factors plays a decisive role.

There is, to begin with, the simple demographic fact that the supply of individuals from which the mass of military recruits are drawn (i.e., the male age group between 17 and 25) varies according to the vacillations of the birth rate. This has obviously affected the scope of volunteer recruitment in Britain where the size of this age group has shrunk by almost 10 per cent during the past five years and is expected to continue shrinking at the same pace during the next five years. It also affects conscript forces, though in a different way. High birth rates during the early 1950s have recently caused, or are likely to cause in the years to come, a marked expansion of the available manpower pool in several European countries. Such a trend must result in an uncontrolled expansion of conscripted armed forces if criteria for the call-up of young men of military age remain unaltered. It follows that these criteria must be modified in the direction of greater selectivity if the size of the armed forces is to remain constant. This problem, which is most acute in militia armies and in countries with mixed forces such as France and West Germany, will be discussed in more detail in a later chapter.

Then there are socio-economic factors which affect military recruitment prospects. Seeking to attract qualified volunteers, the armed forces have to compete with civilian employers on a labour market strained by the demands of full-employment economies, and they are not very well placed to do so. The comparatively low pay of soldiers in many countries, the frequent posting and irregular working hours, the physical stresses, the uncertain career prospects, the unattractive living quarters, the relatively low social prestige of the professional military in some countries (notably West Germany), the stringency of hierarchical subordination and discipline, the inconvenience of long-term service obligations—none of these is likely to appeal to many of today's young men.

The rapid increase of the school and student population is keeping a growing proportion of modern youth in institutions of advanced education at an age when former generations were free to be drafted into the Services; this has the effect not only of increasing the number of deferments and exemptions of potential recruits from military service but also of diminishing the appeal of an officer's career when a university education is now an alternative within the reach of every fairly bright young man.

Hard-pressed military administrations are now turning to a broad variety of remedies designed to get around the recruitment impasse. Most of these remedies run counter to customary practices and hallowed military traditions, and they are clearly disliked by many conservative professional soldiers.

Most notable are the determined efforts made in several countries to overcome the unfavourable public image of military service as being sterile, reactionary, wasteful, unproductive, oppressive, dull, or altogether worthless. The tendency is now to stress the useful contribution of military activity to society as a whole and to the individual soldier's career in particular, and to do this in deliberately 'civilian' terms. Thus, the German *Bundeswehr* now projects itself as 'a service organization producing security', and its Inspector-General, Ulrich de Maizière, is prone to emphasize that 'the officer's profession is an intellectual job'.[1] The British forces in their recruitment campaigns advertise their exciting technical gadgets and stress the quasi-industrial 'productivity' of the professional soldier; their new pay scales, introduced with much publicity as a 'military salary', are openly designed to compete more effectively with civilian incomes. The French forces have taken the lead in offering to volunteers a thorough technical education, tailored to individual tastes, which has come to be appreciated as a valuable asset upon their return to civilian life. Such resettlement training, though expensive, is now being increasingly adopted and expanded in other countries too; in Britain additional efforts are being made to secure the co-operation of industrial organizations in the Army's training activities. Other material incentives include special gratuities and efficiency bonuses, improved social services, sizeable discharge grants, or stipends to officers seeking a university education.

Efforts to improve the attraction of military careers are extended to structural changes in the Services themselves. Thus it is sought to open new opportunities for swift promotion of qualified personnel, to allow greater flexibility of career patterns, to encourage a relaxation of unnecessary discipline and formal subordination, to provide more scope for team co-operation, internal discussion and participation and to relieve soliders as far as possible from drill exercises and the drudgery of routine tasks. Most important, perhaps, there is a tendency to do away with the restraints of long-term service obligations. One method of achieving this is to permit soldiers to quit the service, whenever they please, without material or penal sanctions; such an arrangement may still appear unacceptable even to many progressive military planners but it has been successfully employed by the Japanese armed forces ever since 1954. A more common method is the introduction of short-term engagements. While these are not always popular with military administrations and professional officers (for reasons which will be discussed later) they do have the undeniable potential of improving recruitment. The British Army has met with an encouraging response to its 3-year engagement scheme, re-introduced in 1969,[2] and is now considering offering a 2-year term in the hope of attracting additional recruits who would not enlist for a longer period. In the United States Army a 3-year engagement is the normal term, and in the Navy, Marine Corps and Air Force it is four years; in addition, the Army, Navy and Marine Corps have recently introduced a 2-year scheme. Short-term engagements for four years or less account for 33 per cent of all volunteers in Austria, for 59 per cent in Denmark and for 43 per cent in West Germany. Recruitment of volunteers has improved by 10 per cent since a 2-year scheme, previously abolished, was re-introduced in Germany in 1969. Short-term engagements appeal particularly to private soldiers: 96 per cent of all

[1] *Der Spiegel*, 15 June 1970.

[2] 3-year engagements were available in certain branches of the British Army in the 1930s and during the period of conscription in the 1950s and early 1960s.

volunteer privates in the West German forces have enlisted for a term of four years or less, and half of these for only two years. In addition, short-term volunteers provide a reservoir for further recruitment: 32 per cent of those who had joined the British Army on a 3-year engagement in 1969 have chosen to prolong their term of service for a further period.

When all has been said about possible remedies to recruitment problems the fact remains that such problems persist in many countries despite vigorous efforts to overcome them. It may be that the armed forces will just have to learn to live with them. Shortages in qualified manpower are not, after all, peculiar to the armed forces; they are a universal characteristic of industrialized societies. Maybe there are simply not enough technical specialists available in any country to meet the personnel requirements of large armed forces equipped with complex weapons systems. Maybe no amount of money and no effort of internal adjustment and soul-searching expended by the armed forces could ever overcome the scepticism of large parts of contemporary European youth towards the military profession. Maybe the life of an infantryman is just too unattractive to appeal sufficiently to sufficient numbers of young men. 'Join the Army and see the world!', the famous and time-honoured appeal to British youngsters, is simply a non-starter when its promise has been reduced to the excitement of commuting between Aldershot and the Rhine Army; the once far-flung battle line cannot be held because service recruiters would wish it to be. (Or can it? Was this what Mr. Edward Heath, then Leader of the Opposition, had in mind when he suggested, on 5 March 1970, in the House of Commons that 'a modest presence in the Gulf and the Far East would be effective in securing the recruiting aims' of the British forces?)

Under these circumstances it seems understandable that most countries, trying to make ends meet somehow, are holding fast to conscription. Where enough volunteers are not forthcoming, it seems preferable to substitute them with conscripts as far as this is possible. The idea of abolishing conscription may appear tempting to military planners on many grounds, but the risks involved are such that the temptation is often likely to remain an idea.

The basic risk is that nobody really knows what happens to volunteer recruitment once conscription is abolished. Volunteer recruitment figures may rise, as they actually did in the British case in the early 1960s,[3] but it is conceivable also that they might fall. This is so because conscription, somewhat paradoxically, can help to increase the number of voluntary enlistments for several reasons. First, there is always a small proportion of conscripts (currently 15 per cent in West Germany) who take to military life only after experiencing it and therefore remain as volunteers; these would be lost to the armed forces if there were no conscription. Second, a number of recruits may prefer to enlist as short-term volunteers with full pay rather than having to serve as scantily paid conscripts for only slightly lesser terms; the major part of West Germany's 37,000 2-year volunteers are believed to be motivated in this way, and their services, too would not be available if there were no conscription. Third, in countries with a selective service system, such as the United States, potential draftees may prefer to enlist voluntarily for a short term in the service branch of their own choice rather than run the risk of being called up for what may be a highly undesirable assignment such as combat duty as an infantryman in Vietnam. About half of the 500,000 Americans per year who have in recent years volunteered for military service are believed to be such 'fake' volunteers; and they, again, would not have been available in the absence of conscription.

Recruits found in this way may not provide high-quality manpower but, for military planners, they are preferable to no manpower at all. If only for this reason, conscription is likely to stay. Countries that insist on volunteeer forces, such as Britain, may find it necessary to reduce their manpower targets further and further, but those that remain based on conscription will also have to face modifications of their system.

---

[3] Britain found that many young regular soldiers were unwilling to extend their service while their conscript colleagues were constantly flowing back to civilian life. Once conscription had ended and the conscript, with his natural tendency to dissatisfaction, was out of the way, both regular recruitment and voluntary extensions of service increased.

9

While recruitment is primarily a quantitative problem affecting volunteer forces or the volunteer sections within conscript forces, training is primarily a qualitative problem affecting conscript forces or the conscript sections within mixed forces. This is so because conscripts, as a rule, serve shorter terms than volunteers, and the length of service is directly related to the thoroughness of training and, of course, to the experience of individual soldiers. Volunteer forces or individual volunteer soldiers are likely to be more thoroughly trained, more specialized, more experienced and therefore more efficient than conscript forces or individual conscript soldiers can ever hope to be. Volunteer forces, on account of their superior training and skills, are 'professional' experts when compared with conscript forces, which are liable to remain (or at least to appear as) mere 'amateur' dilettantes.

The gist of this dilemma is reflected in the rate of personnel turnover, as shown in the following table.

Personnel turnover, as should be expected, is lowest among forces with a large proportion of long-term volunteers (Britain) and highest among forces with a large proportion of short-term conscripts (France); combinations of shorter-term volunteers and longer-term conscripts produce intermediate turnover rates (United States, West Germany). This applies to armed forces as a whole as well as to individual services; thus, turnover in every country is higher in the Army than in the Navy or Air Force. Switzerland, as usual, presents an exceptional case, but it is clearly an exception in degree and not in principle.

There are thus several related reasons why training problems are more acute in conscript forces than in volunteer forces, and most acute in those forces with the highest proportion of conscripts. First, because of the shortness of service terms, training programmes can be less thorough and less extensive. Second, because of rapid personnel turnover the armed forces have to devote a very large share of their time and resources to the task of training new recruits in quick succession. Third, also because of the turnover rate, the armed forces have to maintain a relatively large or an exceptionally

---

Table 2

(Base year: 1969; all figures are approximated or estimated)

Country	Annual intake of recruits (1,000s)			Annual turnover[a] (i.e. % of total in category leaving service each year)		
	Volunteers	Conscripts	Total	Volunteers	Conscripts	Total
Britain	29	—	29	8	n.a.[b]	8
Canada	12	—	12	13	n.a.	13
United States ..	500	230	730	18	50	22
West Germany ..	35	160	195	15	66	41
France	27	210	237	12	80	49
Switzerland	<0·2	35	35	<5	6	6

NOTES

[a] Swiss turnover figures are calculated to the Army's full mobilization strength. Militiamen having served their initial term of four months remain technically members of the Army and are periodically recalled into active service. If, however, turnover is measured in the same terms for Switzerland as for the other countries, *viz.* as the percentage of military personnel entering or leaving active service in the course of one year, then the total annual turnover rate in the Swiss forces amounts to almost 100 per cent.

[b] n.a. = not applicable.

competent body of training staff. Fourth, because of the scarcity of experienced career soldiers, training responsibilities have to be entrusted to short-term volunteers or senior conscripts. Fifth, because of the relatively large size of conscript forces, the total amount of training efforts and expenses is much larger than in comparable volunteer armies. Sixth, conscripts are often plainly unwilling or disinterested in military training. Seventh, the training received by conscripts while in service quickly becomes obsolete after their discharge due to changes in tactics and weapons. And eighth, if discharged conscripts are recalled for frequent refresher courses to keep them in practice or to bring their previous training up to date, this can throw a new burden upon already overstrained training staffs.

The paradoxical effect of all this is that conscript forces, although less well trained, have to carry a larger training load than volunteer forces. About 20 per cent of British soldiers are in training (both as instructors and trainees) at any one time; the proportion is considerably higher in mixed forces; and in the Swiss militia system virtually everybody except the tiny core of regular soldiers is engaged in training throughout his military service. Whereas the bulk of the British forces is on permanent stand-by duty the Swiss Army finds its elaborate training schedule in serious jeopardy when a few hundred soldiers are needed for guard duty at airports or international conferences. Increasingly complex weapons require increasingly long and intensive training periods which go beyond the limits of conscript service terms. The tasks of training large numbers of Swiss soldiers in anti-tank warfare tactics or of manning the country's new semi-automatic air-defence system have taxed the capacities of the Swiss militia to the extreme.

There are, of course, drawbacks and problems of personnel training in volunteer forces, too. One problem is the increasingly expensive and time-consuming need for pre-release training for civilian jobs; such training is of no direct military benefit but must be offered as a recruitment incentive. Increased specialization and sophistication threaten to transform over-trained career soldiers into hypersensitive technicians who would be incapable of fighting their way into a nunnery without the support of their advanced weapons systems. Professional soldiers may tend, exactly because of their superior training and experience, to become rigid and unresponsive towards innovation and structural change.

Conscript training systems, on the other hand, do have certain assets. One asset is that all systems of conscription make available to the armed forces men of higher average intelligence than can normally be expected to enlist as volunteers. Such men are easier to train, and can quite quickly fill positions for which a lower grade volunteer might require lengthy training. Another asset is that conscript systems, with their high rate of turnover, produce large numbers of trained reservists; insufficient output of reservists is indeed one of the main criticisms held against the British system of long-service volunteers. The production of huge reserves may, of course, be wasteful and rather senseless if they are never put to any use again, as is actually the case in most mixed manpower systems. But the Swiss show that this need not be so. The entire Swiss militia is, in a sense, a reserve force, but a very active one. Militiamen having completed their initial term of training are recalled into service at least eleven times during their 30-year military obligation not only to be trained and re-trained in refresher courses but, no less important, to serve themselves as trainers for succeeding generations of recruits. The Swiss militia, though guided by the small Instructors Corps mentioned above, is thus basically a self-training and self-maintaining conscript force. Besides, it makes very efficient use of outside knowledge: on the one hand by sending many of its officers and specialists to foreign military training institutions and staff colleges, and on the other hand by making the maximum possible use of civilian skills and experiences accumulated by militiamen during their adult lives and extra-military careers But it is clear that such practices can be adopted by conscript forces in other countries only to a very limited degree.

Recruiting problems and training problems often go hand in hand, but in many cases they seem to urge military planners into different directions. To reconcile or control these conflicting demands calls for the manipulation and application of a bewildering variety of priorities and caveats. It may be useful to summarize briefly the more important of these constraints to the management of military manpower policy.

Defence administrations have to seek a proper balance in each of the following dimensions:

(a) the size of the armed forces;
(b) the rate of personnel turnover;
(c) the distribution of ranks; and
(d) the proportion of civilians in the defence establishment.

Each of these dimensions can determine the volunteer/conscript ratio within the forces, or can in turn be determined by it.

(a) The size of the armed forces is an inverse function of this volunteer/conscript ratio. Volunteer forces can afford to be smaller than conscript forces of comparable capability, but they cannot afford to be equally large.

For reasons of economy and limits to recruitment a country cannot hope to raise and support a large all-volunteer army unless it is (such as the United States) exceptionally wealthy, prepared to pay a very large defence bill, and aided by a strong national tradition of prestigious military professionalism. Volunteer forces are able, however, to carry out their military tasks with fewer men than conscript forces charged with the same tasks. They can equip a greater part of their men with advanced and highly complex weapons that require extensive training and specialization; these weapons again serve to raise the *per capita* effectiveness of volunteer forces far above that of conscript forces. The argument may, of course, be easily turned around: conscript forces by the sheer mass of their manpower can make up for their lesser degree of skills and firepower. This is precisely the reasoning of any militia scheme.

The linkage between size, recruitment and the demographic supply of man-power has already been mentioned. This presents no problem to volunteer forces only recruitment targets have been adjusted to realistic birth-rate projections. For conscript forces, however, it presents the problem of selectivity. A constant selection rate (e.g., all medically fit 18-year old males, or a certain percentage of these) subjects the size of the armed forces to the erratic fluctuations of the birth-rate 18 years before, and this may cause considerable administrative inconvenience. A significant growth of a country's armed force due to the influence of eligible recruits could increase defence costs by a sizable margin, and it could also be politically undesirable. For example, if present selection criteria and service obligations were retained the number of West German conscript soldiers would automatically rise by 38 per cent within the next decade, and the total size of the *Bundeswehr* would swell from the present 480,000 men to no less than 690,000 if the present balance between volunteer and conscript elements were to be retained. To permit such an uncontrolled development is obviously out of the question for economic as well as politcal reasons. Alternatively, if the ceiling of the *Bundeswehr*'s present size were to be retained through an increasing substitution of volunteers by conscripts, the number of West German volunteer soldiers would have to be run down from the present 229,000 to a mere 140,000 during the next decade. Such a development, which would result in a force made up of 29 per cent volunteers and 71 per cent conscripts, is again unacceptable for German military planners. They are already dissatisfied with the present ratio of 49 : 51, and their target is actually something like 60 : 40. Reducing the volunteer element to its bare bones would create immense training problems in the *Bundeswehr*. Moreover, since the Navy and Air Force require an irreducible number of long-service soldiers to run and maintain their complex equipment, this would leave the Army in a state of virtual paralysis. The situation in France and some other countries is basically the same.

The seemingly obvious way out of this dilemma is to adjust the selection rate so as to bring the number of conscripts required by the armed forces into line with the number of conscripts produced by the recruiting mechanism.

16

This can be done either by operating a flexible selection rate or by readjusting selection criteria from time to time. Both methods have been tried out and found to produce highly undesirable results.

A flexible selection rate has been in operation in the United States in recent years. Under the Selective Service system a national draft lottery makes a strictly random choice of recruits from the available pool of eligible young men; only as many are chosen as are actually required by the armed forces. This system, introduced in 1968 to remove the inequities created by the previous system of selection by local draft boards, is now widely acknowledged to be a failure; it has produced new anxieties and uncertainties among American youth and resentment among those who have had the bad luck to draw a number that meant conscription.

Most other countries have chosen the alternative method of readjusting their selection criteria from time to time. Thus, medical screening standards and the statutory provisions for exemptions or deferments from conscript service have been interpreted and handled in such a way as to yield approximately the required number of recruits. This number has always been much smaller than the available manpower pool. As a result, the French forces during the past five years have called up, on the average, only 45 per cent of eligible young men, the rest being exempted or deferred; the percentage is almost exactly the same in West Germany and Italy. While this is a convenient method of keeping the size of the armed forces independent of demographic fluctuations it produces, like the lottery in the United States, bitterness among those who are unfortunate enough to be called up for service. Such unwilling and disappointed soldiers are not good soldiers; officers and training staff frequently complain about being ill at ease with them. Indeed, criticism of the system in France and West Germany has come from professional soldiers as often as it has from dissatisfied conscripts.

In response to such criticism, the French and West German administrations have reversed their policy within the past twelve months and are now seeking to extend the active service obligation to a maximum percentage of the eligible age-groups. The call-up of conscripts with minor physical disabilities and the drastic curtailment of the number and extent of exemptions and deferments is designed to spread the burden of compulsory military service more widely and thereby to reduce the grievance of unequal disadvantage among conscripted youth. In order to cope with the additional influx of recruits the French Parliament, in June 1970, reduced the length of conscript service from 15 months to 12 months, and German defence planners envisage a reduction of the conscript term in the *Bundeswehr* from the present 18 months to 15 months in the near future. Similarly, the Austrian Government is committed to a reduction of Army terms from the present nine months to six months. These are undoubtedly popular decisions, but they are bound to increase the training load of these forces since they both accelerate the turnover and reduce the amount of time available for training.

To complete the list of possible solutions, one more case should be mentioned. Switzerland in 1961 reduced the upper age limit of military obligation from 60 to 50 (officers 55), thereby, in effect, cutting down the Army's total size by almost 100,000 men. But the minimum term of 12 months, to be served in instalments spread over 30 years was retained, and the efficiency of training was indeed increased by the rejuvenation and accelerated turnover of militia personnel. In contrast to what has been said in the previous paragraph about mixed systems this reveals an ability of militia systems to maintain their forces at a specified size, despite the demographic factor and despite the universal service obligation; close to 100 per cent of medically fit Swiss men do actually serve. But this process of adjustment, which is not only painless and popular but even militarily advantageous, is clearly beyond the reach of mixed systems.

(b) The rate of personnel turnover has been shown to be a function of the length of service terms and closely related to the proportion of conscripts among the forces. A high rate of turnover has obvious disadvantages, such as administrative turbulence, the increased burden on training staff, the reduced thoroughness and effectiveness of training and the accelerated demand for volunteer recruitment. Professional soldiers loathe personnel turnover.

But a balanced account should also list the benefits which, though less obvious, can in fact accrue from a reasonably brisk turnover rate.

One of these benefits, already mentioned, is the production of trained reservists: the higher the turnover rate the larger is the supply of reserve manpower. Another is its effect on the forces' age structure. Services with a large proportion of conscript recruits or short-term volunteers are very young forces: conscripts are usually between 18 and 21 years old, and so are most short-term volunteers. Even in the all-volunteer British forces almost 50 per cent of all servicemen are under 25 and 80 per cent are under 35. Such a highly skewed age distribution is unique to armed forces; no other organizations in the public or private sector (with the exception of educational institutions) contain such a massive proportion of young people. While it is true that more and more military tasks – even in combat situations – become less physically exacting the fact remains that for most soldiers a main requirement is still physical fitness; and it is the young who are likely to be the fittest. For this reason no army can dispense with a deliberate turnover of personnel, particularly among the lower ranks.

Another benefit resulting from turnover is that it creates vacancies and therefore opportunities for promotion. A blockage in the promotion channels, caused by excessive numbers at a particular rank level, is apt to affect the morale of the services the more seriously the longer it lasts. Thus, the French Army is now saddled with an over-aged supply of low-ranking officers, now mainly captains held over from the mass of platoon commanders of the war in Indo-China, who impatiently await promotion to higher ranks in which not nearly enough openings are available. Similarly in the West German forces there are not enough major's posts to allow promotion for the already excessive supply of captains in their early thirties. Such imbalances not only create friction between different ranks and age-groups of the hierarchy; more seriously, they serve as an effective deterrent to the recruitment of officer aspirants seeking swift advancement.

There is a problem here intrinsic to all conscript forces. In order to cope with their heavy burden of conscript training they require large numbers of experienced training personnel (i.e., junior officers and non-commissioned officers). But the narrowing upper ranks of the hierarchical pyramid cannot offer an adequate number of openings for promotion. What is necessary therefore is a rate of turnover which is considerably higher among the lower ranks, including the training personnel, than among the higher ranks. In other words, defence administrations face the problem not only of recruiting enough volunteers but of getting rid of many of them after some time. A middle-range service term between 10 and 15 years is considered to be the ideal one for the bulk of volunteers in most armies. But the fact is that volunteers enlisting for a term of this length are hardest to come by; most volunteers prefer to become either life-time soldiers or short-term soldiers. France and West Germany are particularly worried about this problem. In both countries increasing efforts are therefore made to attract such median-term volunteers through additional material and educational incentives and prospects of subsequent employment in civil service positions.

(c) The distribution of ranks among the armed forces is supposedly determined by the requirments of effective administration and command structures, and one might think that these requirements are basically alike in all kinds of modern armed services. But the problems of training and personnel turnover which have just been described certainly have a bearing on the distribution of ranks. The following table (on p. 15) confirms this.

There is a clear correlation between the size of the volunteer element (or else: the length of service terms) and the distribution of ranks. All-volunteer or predominantly volunteer forces have, as a rule, a significantly larger proportion of officers and non-commissioned officers than all-conscript or predominantly conscript forces; the former are made up mainly of higher ranks, the latter mainly of privates. It is hardly possible to say whether one of the extremes or the other represents an 'imbalanced' distribution. There are certainly reasonable criteria for arriving at a balance of ranks in operational units (that is units not concerned primarily with training recruits) and in formations: most armies have arrived at something like the same relationship between leaders and led. Where training units or organizations are concerned, however, the

Table 3

(All figures as a percentage of total forces)

Country	Officers	NCOs	Privates
Britain	14	41	45
United States ..	13	52	35
Belgium	9	31	60
W. Germany ..	7	25	68
France	7	27	66
Austria	5	20	75
Italy	9	21	70
Switzerland[b] ..	E[a]: 4	E: 7	E: 89

NOTES: [a] E = estimated.

[b] Swiss figures are calculated to the Army's full mobilization strength. In peacetime active service, average figures run as follows:

Officers	NCOs	Privates
E: 12	E: 14	E: 74

proportions of officers, NCOs and privates will vary according to the length and type of training for recruits and specialists, and whether or not training is carried out in a reserve organization or even by civilians. So there are bound to be wide variations. One suspects, however, that the large proportion of officers and NCOs among volunteer forces reflects, at least to some extent, a concession to the exigencies of recruitment: whoever would enlist as a private soldier unless he were offered a good chance to be promoted to higher rank? Characteristically, in mixed forces those branches that depend to more than an average degree on the services of volunteers do also have a larger than average proportion of higher ranks; for example, in France there are only 47 per cent of privates in the Air Force as against 72 per cent in the Army, and in West Germany 57 per cent in the Air Force as against 74 per cent in the Army.

Except in militia armies, most non-commissioned officers and almost all officers are volunteers. It is these volunteers who carry the responsibility of training fresh recruits among the private ranks, and obviously the burden of training is much heavier for the small proportion of higher-ranking personnel in conscript

forces than for the much larger proportion in volunteer forces. (The Swiss case shows how a militia can cope with this problem despite its exceptionally small supply of higher ranks: NCOs have to serve about twice as long and officers about three times as long as privates.)

While volunteer forces can offer a large proportion of higher positions to their recruits, conscript forces must (and indeed can afford to) offer them much faster promotion to such positions, as the table below (on p. 16) suggests.

There is obviously much faster upward mobility among junior officers and non-commissioned officers in conscript forces than in volunteer forces. But among senior officers at the rank of major these differences have practically levelled off. Turnover among senior ranks who are not needed for manpower-intensive training tasks is relatively slow among higher ranks in all kinds of forces.

Another effect of the high turnover amongst lower ranks in conscript forces is an increased permeability of the dividing line between officers and non-commissioned officers. In the Swiss militia virtually all officers are drawn from NCO ranks whereas this is relatively rare in the British volunteer forces. Britain has, however, long

15

Table 4

Country	Average length of previous service			
	NCOs attaining rank of corporal (months)	Officers receiving commission (months)	NCOs attaining rank of sergeant-major (years)	Officers attaining rank of major (years)
Britain.. ..	72	40	16	15
Canada ..	84	36	17	15
United States..	25	36	24	14
Belgium ..	12	36	10	17
W. Germany ..	24	30	16	16
France.. ..	6	24	5	16
Italy	6	24	5	16
Switzerland ..	?	12	?	15

NOTE: Figures apply to volunteers only, except Switzerland (militiamen only).

had a scheme whereby suitable young men may join the forces on short-service commissions, normally for three years. The effect of this is that by far the greater proportion of officer material does not appear in the ranks at all, so promotion from the ranks will appear low. A significant number of these short-service officers convert during their service to full regular commissions. Mixed forces are now making increasing efforts to increase their supply of officers on medium-term engagements by promoting capable non-commissioned officers to officer rank. Thus, no less than two-thirds of French Air Force officers are now former NCOs, and the West German Air Force, though less successful so far, is striving to achieve a similar ratio. Such a policy appears sound and reasonable on many grounds. But it is hardly possible to be emulated by volunteer forces. NCOs in these forces are, due to the lower speed of promotion, much older than their colleagues in conscript forces; for example, a British sergeant-major is, on the average, no less than 34 years old whereas his French colleague is only 23. Seasoned middle-aged NCOs may not, in some countries be enthusiastic about an offer of 'promotion' to junior officer's rank.

(d) The proportion of civilians in defence establishments might seem to have little relevance for the manpower problems of the armed forces themselves. But this would be a superficial view.

There is a strong correlation between the size of the volunteer element in the armed forces and the size of the civilian defence administration. This suggests that a bulky civilian 'tail' is not simply a symptom of civilian bureaucratic inefficiency and Parkinson's Law running rampant, as many angry professional soldiers are only too willing to insist; if this were so then the actual correlation should be exactly the reverse, namely, the number of civilian personnel growing with the size of the conscript element.

A large civilian defence administration may in fact be an indicator of high efficiency and specialization of the armed forces, and a very small number of civilians may on the other hand reveal some wasteful and inefficient use of military manpower. Conscripts in many mixed forces are charged with menial duties which – not the least for reasons of recruitment – are left to civilian employees in the case of volunteer forces. More important, the growing trend towards specialization and technological sophistication in all modern armed forces steadily reduces the proportion of military personnel earmarked for actual combat duty. For example, in the United States Army only

16

Table 5

(All figures approximate)

Country	Civilian personnel in defence establishments	
	(1,000s)	(As a percentage of all military personnel)
Britain	330	91
Canada	39	43
United States	1,122	34
West Germany	168	35
France	131	27
Denmark	14	32
Austria	8	17
Italy	82	20
Sweden[b]	E[a]: 30	E: 5
Switzerland[b]	E[a]: 21	E: 3

NOTES

[a] E = estimated.

[b] Swedish and Swiss percentages are calculated to full mobilization strengths. At the average peacetime strength of the armed forces, the appropriate percentage figures are:

Sweden:	E: 37
Switzerland:	E: 43

one soldier out of four is assigned to ground combat duty; the appropriate ratio was one out of three during the Korean War and is expected to drop to one out of five in the post-Vietnam era. The discrepancy between the size of the fighting 'head' and the supporting 'tail' is even larger in those service branches that rely on very complex weapons, as every modern Air Force does. A single jet fighter pilot, for example, is dependent upon a supporting crew of at least ten men on the ground, such as electronics specialists, engineers, technicians, mechanics, craftsmen, administrative and clerical personnel, and other auxiliary hands.

The significant aspect of this phenomenon, as far as manpower policy is concerned, is the growing similarity of the military's skill requirements to those of the civilian sector. This implies, on the one hand, that more and more military tasks can in fact be entrusted to civil servants and civilian employees with appropriate skills, and on the other hand that the military recruitment machinery is in increasing competition with the civilian sector for young men with technical education and specialized skills. The

armed forces in more and more countries may come to realize that they can attract the services of these young men in sufficient numbers only in a civilian and not in a military capacity. Many of these civilians working in defence establishments are, in a sense, military volunteers. In this sense, it is hardly an overstatement to say that the very process of modernization of the armed services enforces a growing degree of more or less covert voluntarism in the pattern of military manpower.

Conservative professional soldiers might be worried by this trend. They might also take comfort, however, from the fact that the Swiss Army, hardly renowned for a leaning towards rash innovation, has been riding on the wave of this trend for some time now, and quite successfully so. Many specialized tasks which in other forces are considered as indispensable prerogatives of military personnel, such as the maintenance of aircraft or the administration of arms depots, are carried out by civilian personnel in Switzerland. The size of the civilian defence administration, compared with the armed forces' average peacetime strength, is therefore as large in the Swiss militia system as it is in the Canadian all-volunteer system. It may appear cumbersome to many critics, but it allows the militia to concentrate on its training tasks and at the same time to maintain even complex and sensitive weaponry in effective combat readiness. This remarkable feat is closely paralleled by the Swedish pattern of defence administration, also a militia system.

To conclude this chapter on problems of manpower policy, it appears that several of the parameters that were discussed seem to point towards one particular model which may avoid a maximum number of disadvantages inherent in different manpower systems while combining a maximum number of possible advantages. Such a model has been discussed independently in several countries in recent years, yet with a significant similarity of considerations and conclusions, particularly in France, West Germany and Belgium; the Austrian and Yugoslav Governments have actually committed themselves to shape their armed forces according to this model.

The model consists, briefly, of a relatively small professional force, made up of volunteers on medium-term and long-term engagements and equipped with the most advanced and powerful weapons, and a complementary and much larger force of conscripts, serving no more than a total of 12 months in several instalments of militia-style refresher courses, trained largely by its own militia training cadre and equipped with light and relatively simple weapons suitable for home-defence tasks. Such a model, which is clearly designed to combine the capabilities of a highly mobile and proficient volunteer force with the massive manpower supply of a large reserve force, may well be on the way to become the dominant form of military manpower systems in Europe. Its actual properties and effects are not sufficiently known to be discussed here; occasional references in the following chapters will have to suffice.

ECONOMIC PROBLEMS

An assessment in economic terms is perhaps the most intriguing aspect in a comparison of military manpower systems. What is the relative cost of a voluntary soldier *vis-à-vis* a conscripted soldier, and of a volunteer army *vis-à-vis* a conscript army? Until quite recently such a question might have been widely regarded as either cynical, for the sacred duty of national defence was to be fulfilled at any cost whatsoever, or as irrelevant, for the actual cost of military manpower was not such that it seemed to call for a choice on the grounds of economy. The same question has assumed vital importance, however, since the soaring costs of military defence, in manpower and equipment as well as in general maintenance, have made themselves felt as an increasingly onerous burden on the shoulders of tax payers. Military budgets in Europe have been levelling off or even shrinking in relative terms during recent years. The double pressure of rising costs and of decreasing public enthusiasm for bearing these costs has made it mandatory for governments to reap-praise existing systems of military manpower in economic terms more critically than ever before.

On the most obvious level volunteers are more expensive than conscripts for the simple reason that they expect – save under exceptional circumstances – to be decently paid for their services whereas conscripts by definition are rendering some sort of forced labour extracted from them with little or negligible remuneration. The 'honorary' pay granted to conscripted recruits in many countries is often not more than a token charity. French conscripts, for instance, have received in recent years a nominal pay of no more than half a franc per day, which is just enough to buy a beer or a cup of coffee. Even in those forces where conscripts are relatively well paid the differential between conscripted and voluntary soldiers' pay is quite considerable: for Army privates the ratio is approximately 1 : 60 in France, 1 : 40 in Denmark, 1 : 15 in Belgium and 1 : 6 in West Germany. Only in the United States forces, where conscripts are drafted in relatively small numbers into the Army and the Marine Corps, are pay scales for conscripts and volunteers identical.

Cash pay alone is, of course, not a sufficient yardstick for assessing personnel costs. Soldiers receive a variety of additional benefits that are usually not accounted for in their pay, such as housing, clothing, food, travel, training, social security, gratuities, allowances, discharge bonuses and similar more or less 'invisible' payments. Most of these benefits accrue to conscripts and regulars alike. Reliable figures covering such comprehensive manpower costs are not easy to obtain as national statistics and fiscal categories differ widely, but allowing for a small margin of error they run as follows, again indicating the ratio between conscripted and regular Army privates: 1 : 16 in France, 1 : 13 in Denmark, 1 : 5 in Belgium and 1 : 1·6 in West Germany. (In the United States the ratio is estimated again at 1 : 1.) Seen in this way the cost advantage of conscripts is reduced significantly by about two-thirds in each country. Still, it is clear that on financial grounds alone a comparative cost analysis weighs heavily in favour of conscription as the most economical manpower scheme, even in the marginal German case. The cited figures reveal, moreover, that to substitute regulars for conscripts would be vastly more expensive to France or Denmark than it would be Belgium or Germany, and more to the latter than to the United States.

On a more sophisticated level, however, such neat costing figures tend to become more and more obscure and indeed almost meaningless. As a total is often unequal to the sum of its parts so the cost of a particular military manpower system may well be different from the cumulative personnel cost of soldiers. An attempt to account for all relevant factors affecting the cost of military manpower on a comparative basis is apt to turn any analysis into a nightmare of uncertainties.

To illustrate, it may be useful again to contrast the extreme forms of all-volunteer and militia forces. Switzerland, with a total defence budget of less than one-tenth of the British, maintains an army almost twice as large as the British forces. But it would of course be nonsensical to conclude that individual Swiss soldiers are twenty times more cost-effective than British soldiers or that the Swiss are militarily twice as powerful as the British. Regulars and militiamen are quite different kinds of fish, and their functions and capabilities differ so widely that individual cost figures, set against each other, may distort more than they reveal. Due to his thorough and always up-to-date training, his experience, his instant readiness and his more sincere dedication a regular soldier is likely to be much more 'productive' in military terms than a militiaman. Although it is impossible to express this kind of productivity in reliable quantitative terms, it may well be that the average regular soldier's 'value' is many times that of the average conscript soldier. This is, of course, not primarily an economic value but it is *also* an economic one. It follows that volunteer armies may be less expensive than conscript armies even though volunteers are more expensive than conscripts.

There are two sides to this argument. On the one side the superior efficiency of regulars makes budgetary expenditure on military manpower more rational and more easily accountable in the case of volunteer armies. Conscript armies on the other side entail a number of wasteful practices and hidden costs that are not evident on the basis of budgetary figures alone.

Thus the rapid personnel turnover in conscript systems not only increases the cost of training and the proportion of available manpower that is bound up in training activities; it also decreases the utility and potential pay-off of such training. The longer the training period the shorter is the remaining part of the conscript's serving time in which he can effectively use his acquired military skills. The more expensive a conscript's training the more wasteful is his subsequent discharge into civilian life. Pure training costs in NATO countries are estimated at some $6,000 for a radar specialist, $7,000 for a parachutist, $9,000 for a tank driver, $20,000 for a guided-missile specialist and more than $600,000 for a jet pilot. All of these jobs are ordinarily done by regulars but in some countries they are also done by conscripts; in militia systems this is the rule rather than the exception. Such specialized training can of course be quite useful to the recipient in his subsequent civilian career, and in this sense all modern conscript armies are rendering valuable services of technical education to their societies, though only as a marginal by-product of military activity and therefore not in the most economical way. Less specialized training, however, is given to the bulk of conscript soldiers, such as infantrymen, and while such training is less expensive it may be practically worthless in civilian life.

Rapid personnel turnover and the massive production of trained conscripts who are subsequently discharged provides large numbers of qualified reservists. West Germany has more than 1·5 million, France more than 2 million and Italy more than 3 million trained reservists. However, if these manpower reserves are not integrated into a meaningful strategic concept their production is indeed a tremendous waste. Military training like any other kind of training becomes obsolete if it is not brushed up in regular refresher courses, and it becomes more rapidly obsolete the more technically specialized it is. Italian reservists are hardly ever recalled for such retraining periods and French reservists only very selectively. West Germany has recently stepped up her reserve training programme, and some 110,000 reservists are now annually being called up for training periods ranging from three days to four weeks. Whatever its military value it needs to be noted that such reservists' training is very expensive again. Not only does it put an additional training load on the regular personnel but it also creates additional turbulence through accelerated personnel turnover. Reservists, in contrast to adolescent recruits, are usually men in their late twenties and thirties with a dependent family and a permanent job. Their military training periods, however short, cause considerable disruption to industrial economies, and the trainees themselves expect to receive adequate compensation for their services. In West Germany this compensation is set at 60 per cent of civilian income for single reservist trainees and 80 per cent for married ones. At DM 12,600 ($3,406) per annum, the average cash pay of German reservist trainees is almost exactly the same as that of the average regular soldier (including officers). Yet their comprehensive personnel costs, augmented by extraordinary administrative expenses, are surely very much higher. Reservists in training are likely, on this basis, to be the most expensive of all kinds of military manpower.

This is indeed the basic economic dilemma of militia schemes. A militia consists largely of reservists in training. The actual cost of such a system cannot be adequately reflected in mere budgetary figures, and the Swiss case for one shows this very clearly. For example, expenditure for training is estimated at 17·6 per cent of total expenditure in the Swiss defence budget of 1970 as against only 9·7 per cent in the British defence estimates for 1970–71; and while it is clear that the Swiss figure, on account of the heavy training load resting on a militia army, must be much higher than the British figure one might be surprised that it is not even higher than it actually is. The fact is that Her Majesty's Treasury has to foot the whole bill for training the British forces whereas the Finance Ministry in Berne gets away with a sizeable discount for training the Swiss Army. A significant share of that burden is carried by numerous sports clubs and voluntary associations offering para-military training and education to Swiss boys and adult men. Such activities are subsidized out of the defence appropriations, and if these subsidies are added to the above figure the share of training costs rises to 19·0 per cent of total Swiss defence expenditure. But the additional value of voluntary services is altogether outside the scope of public accounting. More than 200,000 Swiss citizens (i.e., one-third of the Army) participate in annual rifle competitions. Officers from the rank of captain up are reckoned to spend on the average one hour per day on administrative chores and other work related to their military tasks—unpaid. Farmers make their fields available for Army exercises free of charge. And then there is that unique scheme through which the Swiss people subsidize themselves in order to alleviate the individual burden of conscript service. Organized as a part of the national social security fund to which employers and employees contribute equal shares, it provides compensatory payments to militiamen on active duty as a supplement to their low soldiers' pay. These compensatory payments are staggered in such a way as to make up for any loss of civilian income at least for the lower income groups; total payments out of this fund amounted to Sfr. 215,000,000 in 1969. All of these contributions and services are not carried on the defence budget but they must surely be included in a comprehensive account of Swiss defence economics. Finally, it should be noted that putting the

Swiss Army on alert means a partial mobilization of the population itself and thus a corresponding reduction of the effective labour force. In times of protracted crisis this could entail an acute reduction of the nation's productive capacity.

The Swiss example is an exceptional one in many ways but it is typical enough to demonstrate that a militia system is anything but an easy and painless method of providing military manpower. Conscription has its hidden costs and these costs have to be carried by the national economies in one way or another. 'Conscripton is a tax', as the Gates Commission aptly put it,[4] and this tax is either shown as a public revenue or, more frequently, extracted from the able-bodied male population as a covert tax-in-kind. It is made openly visible as a tax in another peculiar Swiss institution, called *Militärpflichtersatz*; this is a levy imposed on all Swiss citizens who for medical or other reasons do not serve in the Army and who would thus be at an undue advantage *vis-à-vis* their fellow citizens the militiamen. Covertly the tax *qua* conscription is paid by conscripts in the form of compulsory services rendered to the State. In mixed armies this hidden tax amounts to the difference between the pay which the conscripted soldier actually receives and the pay that would be required to induce him to enlist as a volunteer; and this may indeed be a very large sum.

Conscription often leads the armed forces to use manpower inefficiently. The wastage connected with the training of conscripts has already been discussed. Another wastage is the frequent practice of engaging conscripts in manual and menial tasks, such as cleaning or kitchen help, that are not actually military tasks. Auxiliary services of this sort can often be provided more efficiently by machinery or by civilians – and more economically, too, if the real costs of conscripted manpower are taken into account rather than the falsely deflated costs reflected in budgetary expenditure.

Conscription induces the armed forces to call up more recruits than are actually needed. The allegedly low cost of conscripted manpower seems to justify the practice of 'hoarding'

[4] *Report of the President's Commission on an All-Volunteer Armed Force* (Washington, D.C., 1970), p. 23.

conscripts in ample quantities. Young men in conscript armies of the 'mixed' type often complain about having to waste their time (and the taxpayers' money) with apparently useless and senseless tasks. This practice not only causes resentment and disillusion among conscripts who originally had goodwill but may also create unnecessary problems of disciplinary friction. More seriously, it constitutes a significant drain of manpower from productive work in the civilian economy; under conditions of full employment this may add further strains to an already overstrained labour market.

Armed forces in advanced industrial states can no longer rely on a reservoir of cheap unemployed manpower. They have to compete with civilian employers, both private and public, for skilled and well-paid personnel. In addition the budgetary squeeze in several European countries has become so tight that the armed forces can no longer afford to insist on first-rate personnel procurement as well as first-rate weapons procurement. They have to make a painful choice between the two or seek a no less painful compromise. West German and Austrian defence planners now openly acknowledge that they have come to this point, and similar assessments have recently been made though in a more muted vein, by the British and French Governments.

In such a situation the sheer size of any armed force assumes added significance. The larger the force the more expensive is any change in equipment planned for the whole force or major parts of it. The more complicated the equipment becomes the more urgent is the requirement for highly skilled (and thus, increasingly expensive) military personnel. The smaller the force the larger is the amount of money left for new equipment and intensive personnel training.

This is a vicious circle tormenting all military manpower systems but it is clearly more painful to conscript than to volunteer armies. The relative size of an armed force is, as we have noted earlier, directly related to the proportion of conscripts in its ranks. Thus, given a fixed budgetary ceiling a small volunteer army may hope to retain its high level of professional competence *and* advanced equipment by means of a further contraction ('run-down') of its total manpower pool; this is the acknowledged

British policy. A large conscript army, however, cannot hope to attain both goals together. This is most clearly to be seen with regard to reserve and militia forces. Neither France nor Germany nor Italy can ever fully mobilize their huge numbers of reservists because there is not enough serviceable equipment available; and even wealthy Switzerland could not afford to arm the bulk of her 650,000-man force with more than an advanced automatic rifle.

No wonder then that the British model of an all-volunteer force has fascinated many military planners in recent years. The fact that no rush has set in to emulate this model reminds one of the fact that the choice between different manpower systems has usually been made on other than economic grounds; political principles, recruitment difficulties and considerations of military strategy have carried more weight.

Even though there may be a strong case for a switch from conscription to volunteer recruitment it is perhaps a bit unfair to criticize military planners for their reluctance to put it into practice. Any such switch would inevitably entail a net increase in visible defence expenditure. For example, to raise the quota of volunteers in the US forces from the present 86 per cent to 100 per cent would require an additional annual budgetary expenditure ranging, according to various estimates, from two to five billion dollars. This is not a forbiddingly large sum in relation to the total defence budget of the United States. In other countries, however, the corresponding additional expenditure could be relatively much higher because even a small improvement in volunteer recruitment through financial incentives may require a large increase in the pay of *all* volunteers. Such an increase across the board might loom prohibitively large in the defence budgets of those countries which used to rely on 'cheap' conscripted manpower. The experts might agree among themselves that such conspicuous budgetary increases would be more than offset by macro-economic savings or gains in productivity. But the responsible politicians are more likely to let sleeping dogs lie. Why should they ostensibly increase military expenditure when this is clearly unpopular? Why should they try to defy the convenient logic which holds that a burden is not a burden as long as it is not being felt as such? To urge a broader-minded attitude would surely make economic sense, yet it would require more than economic sense. It remains true, however, that defence cannot merely be judged on economic costs alone: if a country could not defend itself with a voluntary army then, whatever the economic advantages of giving up a conscript system, the result of doing so would not be cost-effective.

DOMESTIC POLITICAL PROBLEMS

There is a sacred tradition in constitutional democracies of 'keeping the Army out of politics' and of 'keeping politics out of the Army'. The tradition seems to be a perfectly sensible one for the sake of military effectiveness as well as for the sake of political freedom. But the fact is that politics and the armed forces are always and everywhere in more or less visible interaction, and the real problem for a democratic country is not to keep the two spheres apart but to keep them in harmony. The type of military manpower system to which a country subscribes has much to do with this problem. Military manpower affects politics, and politics affects military manpower.

The discussion about the intrinsic democratic or undemocratic properties of this or that manpower scheme is perennial. Most commentators have leaned towards the opinion that the defence of a democratic country, being the privilege and duty of all the people, should be entrusted to all the people; that a military manpower system is the more democratic, the more comprehensive it is; and that the *levée en masse*, the 'nation in arms', the 'people's army' is therefore the ideal form of democratic defence. In this view the 'citizen in uniform' is contrasted with the 'mercenary', the 'man on horseback' with 'praetorian' ambitions, the hireling with doubtful loyalties and base motivations. To this last

26

insinuation one might object that it is not clearly nobler in the mind to fight for nothing than to fight for money; but the more relevant objection is that to contrast the innocuous conscript soldier with the sinister professional soldier is not only beside the point but dangerously misleading. It suggests a dichotomy which is simply not borne out by reality. Nor would it make sense to reverse the argument, saying in effect that voluntary military force is democratically 'safer' than a conscripted one. No armed force everywhere can be considered absolutely subservient to civilian authority under any conditions. The historical record does not suggest greater democratic reliability of one type of military manpower system as against others. Frequent challenges to civilian control, in Europe before World War II and outside Europe in more recent years, have come from volunteer forces and conscript forces alike. The Greek colonels' *coup d'état* of 1967, the only military takeover in Europe during the past quarter of a century, was carried out by an Army with the highest proportion of conscripts (88 per cent) of all NATO forces, yet it was engineered by a corps of professional officers; if there is a lesson in this, it is not a clear one.

Leaving aside the extreme case of military disloyalty, there are still ample reasons to make a choice between different manpower systems on political grounds. It is safe to say that in fact political reasons, rather than strategic, economic, technical, managerial or similarly functional considerations of a strictly 'professional' character, have always dominated this choice and continue to do so. Although in theory the role of an armed force in democratic countries is simply a function of external defence needs, in practice it is more often determined by political conditions or ideological objectives.

This is most evident in the case of militia schemes. Swiss defence planners do not hesitate to admit that the explicitly non-professional character of their armed force acts as an increasingly painful constraint against programmes of technical specialization and modernization. Yet there is virtual unanimity in Switzerland that the militia principle is to be held undiluted and sacrosanct even if it entails inconveniences and military limitations. It is so closely intertwined not only with the history and political structure of the Federation but with the private life of every Swiss man that to abandon it would mean to abandon the character of Switzerland. The militia has always been the strongest bond of political unity in the country, and probably continues to be. The Swiss Army, it has often been noted, *is* the Swiss nation. This is not just an aphorism. Being a militiaman is a peculiar way of life, it creates a peculiar way of thinking and a peculiar feeling of togetherness. In the absence of a permanent general staff every militiaman is a military expert of his own. If such mutual penetration of the civilian and military spheres means militarism, then Switzerland (beside Israel, another militia country) is surely the most militaristic society in the world. Swiss defence planners believe that the common sense of belonging to a military community is the most powerful asset of their militia which they would be foolish to forsake in favour of more professionalism or more sophisticated equipment, and one finds it hard to argue with them. But it should be observed that Israel is a military community and manages to reconcile this very effectively, under admittedly special circumstances, with high professionalism and sophisticated equipment.

A strong national consensus, and indeed a fierce (though not necessarily aggressive) nationalism, appears to be a regular concomitant of any militia system, fostering and reinforcing each other. This proposition is confirmed in the case of Sweden, despite this country's left-wing image, and in the case of Yugoslavia, where the concept of 'General People's Defence' is explicitly designed to cement the Federation's national unity. Military planners in some West European countries who are fascinated by certain aspects of a militia reserve might ponder the political implications of such a scheme.

Mixed forces have in common with militia forces the claim of representing the 'nation in arms'. But in contrast to the business-like approach which is so characteristic of a militia, theirs is often a strangely unrealistic claim supported by ideological props. 'A standing army', taught V. I. Lenin, 'is an army divorced from the people', and though stretching this point a bit far most Warsaw Pact forces today insist on calling themselves officially 'People's Armies', standing or not; universal military service through conscription is considered to be an indispensable characteristic of any socialist armed force. On the side of conservative thinkers there has always reigned the idea that the armed forces embody the national spirit in a multiple sense: not only by representing the might and unity of the nation, not only by commanding the services of the whole nation, but also by infusing the nation's youth with truly national values. The latter role implies an educational task of character-building to be dispensed by the armed force, exemplified in the Prussian notion of the 'Armee als Schule der Nation', and in the French Army by Marshal Lyautey's injunction to mould recruits as replicas of the model officer (*Du rôle social de l'officier*, 1891).

This national educational role has by now been dropped: explicitly by the West German *Bundeswehr*, silently and rather resignedly by the French Army. But the accompanying notion that the armed forces ought to take into their ranks the whole of the nation's youth has remained in force; it is in fact the major motivation of recent adjustments in French and German recruitment policy. Thus, explaining his decision to seek a maximum call-up rate among French youths M. Michel Debré, the Defence Minister, argued in the National Assembly that it was necessary to 'conserve the national and therefore popular character of the armed forces by means of conscription'.[5] And in West Germany the recent Defence White Paper argued the same case 'in order to ensure the credibility of military service in a democratic community'.[6]

All-volunteer forces, quite naturally, have the most matter-of-fact way of justifying their manpower system. Still, political considerations are at least as prominent as others. Britain and Canada had a variety of reasons to abolish conscription, but the main reason, at least in the public arena, was the belief held by politicians of all major parties that conscript service in peacetime was contrary to national traditions and decidedly unpopular. This belief continues to be held strongly. The intimation of a Labour minister in 1970 that the Conservative Party sought to reintroduce conscription was rejected with significant indignation by Mr Edward Heath, leader of the Opposition as 'a deliberate electioneering trick, false in substance, unjustified in argument, squalid in motivation'.[7]

Whether or not conscription is really unpopular in Western countries is a question that invites argument. Opinion polls suggest that large majorities of people in all major Western countries are actually in favour of compulsory military service. The proportion in favour is, understandably, lower among young people of military age (16 to 24 years) but still remarkably high. For instance, in a recent poll by Opinion Research Centre no less than 65 per cent of British respondents declared themselves 'in favour of bringing back compulsory military service for young men', and among the young men themselves those in favour of the proposition still amounted to 43 per cent.[8] In West Germany according to a recent Ifak poll, conscription is favoured by two-thirds of all adults and opposed by a bare majority of the country's youth.[9] In France an IFOP poll found that supporters of conscription numbered 57 per cent among adults and still 50 per cent among youths.[10]

To assume that these findings are reliable does not, however, mean that to hold fast to conscription or to reintroduce it is necessarily prudent in military or political terms. Half of the young men may be willing or even eager to serve, but if only a small part of the other half prove to be unwilling or recalcitrant recruits the cost in terms of political and military discontent and turbulence may be so high as to outweigh any possible benefits. It is this reasoning which has influenced to a large extent the decision of the United States Administration to seek the abolition of conscription. In terms of domestic political turmoil the use of conscripted manpower by the French forces in Algeria and by the United States forces in Vietnam turned out to be a disastrous blunder. (The same, incidentally, might be said about the use of Russian conscripts in the Warsaw Pact invasion of Czechoslovakia.) Conscript

---

[5] *Journal Officiel*, 10 June 1970, p. 2346.
[6] *White Paper* 1970 *on the security of the Federal Republic of Germany and the state of the German Federal Armed Forces* (Bonn, 1970), p. 630.

[7] *House of Commons Debates*, 5 March 1970.
[8] *Evening Standard*, 13 April 1970.
[9] *Der Spiegel*, 16 November 1970.
[10] *France Soir*, 5 June 1970.

forces – and through them their governments – are much more vulnerable to political dissension than volunteer forces.

There may be a lesson here which military planners could be well advised to study in greater detail. If armed forces in Western countries are in future more likely to be used in police-style internal security tasks than in international confrontations, and there are indeed many indications to this effect, then their reliability in times of domestic political crisis may assume added significance. This is not to suggest that governments ought to look out for the kind of manpower best suited for the oppression of political dissent by armed force, but for the kind that is best suited to contain conflict and dissent within constitutional or, as far as possible, non-violent limits. What seems certain is that conscript forces, and especially militia forces, are particularly badly suited to such tasks – not so much because they are insufficiently trained for them but because they are likely to be too much involved, as individuals, in domestic conflict situations themselves on the one side or the other. The performance of National Guardsmen who violently put down a riot at Kent State University, Ohio, in 1970 will be remembered as an appalling example. Political confrontations, instead of being contained, can easily be escalated into civil strife by the use of conscripted reservists or militiamen in pursuit of 'law and order'.

Again, this does not mean that volunteer forces are necessarily well suited to internal security tasks. The French professional CRS (*Gendarmerie*) units during 'the events' of 1968 were bungling as helplessly as the Italian professional *carabinieri* during the riots of Reggio Calabria in 1970. Things can be handled differently, however, as the British troops in Ulster or the Canadian troops in Quebec, employing a deliberate minimum of force, were able to demonstrate in the same year.

Properly trained, volunteers may be able to cope with internal security problems more effectively than conscripts, quite paradoxically, because they are what military sociologists call 'alienated', 'estranged', or 'not well integrated' in their societies. Such lack of social integration may be felt as isolation and even unpopularity by professional soldiers, and it is certainly something which has to be carefully watched and counteracted by civil societies. In view of his rather anomalous kind of contribution to the welfare of society, however, the professional soldier is perhaps inevitably alienated to some degree. While not putting him into a position of impartial arbitration in political conflict it may still make him sufficiently detached and disinterested to act in an apolitical police role in the service of constitutional authority in time of crisis.

A discussion of domestic political problems relating to military manpower systems would be incomplete, however, without mentioning that the former may in many cases actually result from the latter. One obvious instance is the very fact of conscription itself. Military obligation can be operated deliberately as a repressive instrument by governments; thus, rioting French students were called into military service in 1968, and so were striking Spanish workers in the summer of 1970. More often prospective conscripts on their own take exception to their military obligation. The burning of draft cards has become almost a popular sport in the United States, and there has been a remarkable rise in the number of conscientious objectors in some countries. There were more than 14,000 cases of conscientious objection in West Germany in 1969, amounting to some seven per cent of the *Bundeswehr*'s annual intake of conscripted recruits; in Denmark there were 1,780 conscientious objectors, equivalent to seven per cent of the armed forces' intake, and in the United States 7,260 (more than three per cent). But in most other countries the impact of conscientious objection is insignificant; it is practically nil in those countries where the refusal of armed service is penalized by the obligation to alternative unarmed service of twice the length of military service, as in France or Italy, or by criminal prosecution resulting in jail sentences, as in Switzerland. Even in West Germany, however, the movement of conscientious objection has not assumed the proportions of an organized and consistent political challenge to the institution of universal military service obligation. Popular journalistic accounts may conjure up the existence of a powerful anti-military 'peace movement' among Europe's youth. In reality there is no such thing.

If there is not a broad-based anti-militaristic activity of significant political dimensions, there is undoubtedly a broad stream of a-military apathy of significantly unpolitical dimensions in many Western countries. Such a diffuse mood is hard to nail down in operational terms, but one obvious indication of its existence is the extent of volunteer recruitment difficulties in so many countries. To become a career soldier is clearly not 'the thing to do' among young men in modern Western societies. Even those young respondents who were in favour of conscription in the polls quoted above indicated on further questioning that the roles they envisaged for the armed forces have little to do with the maintenance of national security, but mainly with education, sports, disaster control, aid to the civil community and the like. This corresponds to the low social prestige of professional soldiers particularly in West Germany, France and the Low Countries.

Related to the problem of recruitment is another problem which is apt to result, at least in the long run, in political conflict potential. This is the possible imbalance of certain politically sensitive social groups within the armed forces. Conscript forces with a very comprehensive intake of recruits, such as the Swiss Army, present a perfectly balanced reflection of the social composition of Swiss society. Not so in forces with a selective service system. Secondary-school graduates and students are known to gain an exceptional proportion of exemptions and deferments, either due to their status or to their superior skills in manipulating

the rules, in countries such as France and the United States; instead, lower-class recruits are drawn indiscriminately into the services. This does not create a visible problem, except some degree of cynicism, in a country with an ethnically homogeneous population such as France. It does create a problem in the United States where the disproportionate number of lower-class recruits is visibly identifiable by their black skin. There is some apprehension of the fact that the abolition of conscription might actually worsen this situation: the United States Army could then become largely a black men's force, being the only large-scale organization that offers good opportunities for promotion to underprivileged Negroes.

If Western countries other than the United States do not have significant racial minorities, they have instead linguistic minorities which are as easily distinguishable (but hardly more easy to integrate) than racial ones. Here is clearly the most sensitive problem of military manpower in all multilingual countries. Most of them go out of their way to ensure that this explosive issue remains as unobtrusive as possible. Thus, English as well as French are recognized as official military languages in Canada; French and Italian in Switzerland. (The Yugoslav Army, however, insists on the Russian practice of having the major national language – Serbian – as the one official language throughout the military establishment; this is known to be viewed with growing displeasure by

Table 6

(All figures rounded)

Country	Language group	% of nationals	% of volunteers			
			Officers	NCOs	Privates	Total
Canada	English	77	89	88	80	84
	French	23	11	12	20	16
Belgium	Flemish	63	50	59	60	58
	French	36	50	41	40	42
	German	1	—	nil	nil	nil

NOTE: Bilinguals (12% in Belgium, 11% in Canada) have been proportionately assigned to language groups.

the non-Serbian nationalities.) The distribution of language groups poses no problem among conscripts in Belgium and Switzerland. But what about volunteer recruitment? Volunteers have to be recruited and promoted on their merits, especially if actual recruitment falls short of target figures, and they are unlikely to come forth from the different language groups in neatly balanced proportions. Recruitment of French-speaking officers is acknowledged to be 'unsatisfactory' among the Swiss Instructors Corps; exact figures are not released. In Canada and Belgium as Table 6 shows distribution has been building up in recent years.

There are significant imbalances, most notably among officers, in the Canadian as well as the Belgian forces. In Canada the English-speaking majority is over-represented in the officer corps by about 12 per cent, in Belgium the same applies to the French-speaking minority by no less than 14 per cent. Given the climate of widespread linguistic antagonism and jealousy prevailing in these countries, such figures do have a disquieting ring. Consequently, the Belgian Government, in order to redress the balance at least in the higher ranks, decided in early 1970 to send more than 400 senior French-speaking officers into premature retirement. Painful as such an operation is it may be necessary to save the patient from internal disruptions of a more severe kind. It is likely that the Canadian Government may find itself pressed into establishing a linguistic quota system along similar lines.

MILITARY MANPOWER AND STRATEGIC PURPOSE

All members of an alliance have a plain interest in seeing that each of them adopts and maintains a manpower system which best equips it to meet its obligations and to support its allies. Equally, all have an interest in judging by the same standard any change made in its manpower system by one of their number. If it is accepted, for example, that, at least within Western Europe, an all-militia force trained for territorial defence is exclusively appropriate to a political posture of neutrality, then, to take an extreme case, it is obvious that a proposal by one member of an alliance to adopt such a system would be viewed by its colleague nations as an action of the deepest political and military significance. To take a less extreme case, it has already been pointed out that a change in the West German manpower system which promised to increase the total size of the *Bundeswehr* by a very large amount might well be viewed with some trepidation, even by allies.

An all-militia force is automatically committed to the exclusive role of defending its own national territory; its training, its equipment and its tactical doctrine must all render it singularly inept for any wider commitment such as contributing to the collective defence of an alliance area. It is not inconceivable in theory that a nation possessing only such a force should also be a member of an alliance for collective defence, but it is clear that the nation in question would be able to play only a passive part within that alliance, relying upon its partners to assist in its defence while making no active contribution to theirs. Such a situation is so improbable that, at least within NATO, it can be dismissed from consideration.

The position of an all-volunteer force is more complex. Obviously, as the British and Canadian cases show, such a force can contribute effectively to collective defence. But, as these cases also show, the quantitative extent of its manpower contribution may not always satisfy allies which themselves continue to depend in part upon conscript service. Man for man, all-volunteer forces must apparently always be more expensive than mixed forces of volunteers and conscripts. Given that no nation can afford to maintain forces of unlimited size the tendency will always be for all-volunteer forces to make a relatively smaller contribution to the total manpower requirements of an alliance. More importantly, given that all-volunteer forces do not generate trained reservists as conscript forces do, an alliance made up only of volunteer services would be condemned to a chronic and extreme shortage of reserves. The conclusion seems to be that, while an alliance for collective defence can certainly include a number of nations with all-volunteer forces, and while those forces may even provide a valuable leavening of specialized skill and qualitative excellence, such forces must be regarded, from the manpower point of view, as a type of luxury which can only be afforded if the majority of the partners agree to make up quantitative deficiencies by maintaining mixed forces of volunteers and conscripts.

To reach, thus obliquely, the conclusion that mixed forces are likely to provide the most appropriate foundation of manpower for a collective security alliance (as they do in both NATO and the Warsaw Pact) is not enough in itself. Much will still depend upon the particular form of mixed force concerned, since mixed forces give to their possessors an almost unlimited freedom of choice between international attitudes. It is difficult to see how an all-militia force can stand within an alliance. It is not easy to see how an all-volunteer force, at least in the European continent, can stand outside one. A mixed force can do either, and the view which 'mixed-force' allies have of each other may well, therefore, be influenced by the particular characteristics of a given mixed-force and especially by changes in those characteristics.

It would be impossible to set down in advance a definition of all the ways in which detailed changes in a mixed manpower system can be expected to influence the perceptions of allies. Apart from anything else, the evidence provided by such changes will be interpreted in the context of other evidence from unrelated political or economic areas. In general, however, it is reasonable to expect that changes which tend to increase mobility and flexibility will be taken to improve the 'alliance rating' of the force in question, while those which tend to increase the emphasis on static defence – and especially on the independent defence of the national home territory – will be taken to work in the opposite direction.

In practice, of course, many changes will be ambiguous. At present, for example, a number of West European countries, including France, West Germany, Belgium and Denmark, are all engaged in some re-organization of their military manpower systems. The French have already decided to reduce the term of conscript service to twelve months, in order to allow a more comprehensive intake of recruits (and thus to generate a larger number of reservists). The West Germans are reconsidering their own system, with the object of making more effective use of their vast and growing reserve forces and also, it seems, in anticipation of reducing the term of conscript service to 15 months or less. The Belgians and the Danes (who are examining a reduction of conscription from 12 to 9 months) are involved in reorganizing their manpower systems for what seem to be broadly parallel reasons. In each case, the initial impression is that the effect will be to place greater emphasis upon territorial defence of the homeland by a force of actual or former conscripts. In that sense, the trend may seem to be one which will diminish the 'alliance rating' of these forces. It can also, however, be argued that the net effect is exactly the opposite. By organizing conscripts and reservists into something approaching a militia-type home defence force, a nation may be enabled to relieve the volunteer component in its mixed force structure of any major responsibility for territorial defence and thus to convert it into a highly mobile task force of unprecedented utility for alliance purposes. That, certainly, is the thesis which has already been advanced in West Germany.

In such circumstances, it is clearly impossible to ascribe simple effects to such complex causes. What can be said, however, is that, especially when there are fears about the structural strength of a collective security organization, as there have been in NATO, any change in a military manpower system which argues a growing emphasis on national territorial defence by the conscript component of a mixed force is likely to be taken as running counter to the general purpose of collective security unless it is demonstrably off-set by a directly consequent and proportional increase in the mobility and flexibility of the volunteer component in that force. Inevitably, the onus of proof must be on the author of the change.

It might appear, superficially, that manpower systems appropriate to a collective security alliance would be *a fortiori* those which would provide the best basis for movement towards a genuinely integrated defence. In fact, this is not necessarily the case. All armed forces in the present world are national forces, even if they are assigned to collective security organizations.

Indeed, the simple fact that all nations insist on keeping their armed forces under their own political control, as the *ultima ratio* of national sovereignty, stands as one of the main reasons why attempts to achieve genuine military integration have so far failed. In as far as particular systems of military recruitment constitute a direct expression of national sovereignty or rely upon a concept of nation for their own effectiveness, they are thus calculated to present a barrier in their own right to the submergence of national sovereignty into some wider unit.

Albeit in different ways, this consideration affects all types of military manpower: volunteer, conscript and territorial militia. The militia case is an obvious one. Apart from the specific tactical relationship of any militia force to the defence of a particular national territory, there is a psychological link of even deeper significance. Since militiamen cannot be offered as a primary incentive either public achievement in a military career or the self-esteem which is peculiar to a highly-trained and closely-knit professional force, they are given instead a consciousness of their values which is founded explicitly upon their unique contribution to the defence of their homeland, and thus upon a heightened sense of nationalism. Furthermore, since militia forces for territorial defence tend to involve almost the whole citizenry of a particular country, that heightened sense of nationalism will affect a singularly large proportion of the national population. Clearly, there is no natural progression from this psychological approach to one which is related to the dissolution of national identity involved in political and military integration.

The volunteer case is more ambivalent. In as far as there has been any successful integration within existing collective security organizations, it has been almost exclusively at the staff levels which are dominated by military officers *de carrière*. Within an alliance, indeed, there may well be a growing tendency for the skilled military professionals of separate nations to recognize and respect each other's professionalism and to conceive a joint interest in standing together against what may be seen as the vacillation – or even ignorance – of their political masters. But too much should not be made of this tendency. In the first place, it applies much more strongly at the staff-officer level, and especially within international staffs, than at other levels; professional soldiers serving in their own separate national units do not seem to feel the same sense of common purpose. In the second place, at any level, volunteers commonly share with militiamen a strong consciousness of national allegiance. Their voluntarism has been linked at every stage to the identity and purposes of a particular nation, in whose service their careers have been constructed and by whose standards their personal success will be judged. Even when the political policy of their nation places them in close association with the professionals of allied countries, and even when that association breeds a mutual respect, they are inclined to judge the merit of those other professionals by their own national standards and are certainly not predisposed to subordinate those standards, or the sense of nationality which goes with them, to any supranational aim. Their natural élitist feelings owe almost all their strength to their awareness of being, above all, a *national* military élite.

A predominant sense of nationalism is a less constant characteristic of the conscripted military manpower within a mixed military force. In such a case, conscripts – and thus reservists – tend to mirror the national attitudes of the population from which they are drawn, rather than the artificially heightened nationalism typical of professional soldiers or territorial militiamen. National cases will therefore differ widely. Again, however, they will tend to contain an element of ambivalence. Conscript armies have been found to be powerful nation-building instruments, capable of welding disparate regional or ethnic communities into a new whole with a common loyalty. In that sense, they may also be thought to constitute a barrier to any process of international integration. But there is nothing in this welding process which intrinsically limits its application to the case of a simple nation. Indeed, by the same token, an 'international' conscript army, recruited and organized on the basis of an integrated political unit rather than of separate nation-states, might actually be one of the most powerful instruments of supranational nation-building. In part, the still-born European Defence Community of the 1950s was founded on exactly this line of reasoning. Nor is the implication of this argument

33

necessarily limited to conscript forces. In the future, although the suggestion may seem naïve in present circumstances, it is tempting to speculate that a military force created by 'integrated' voluntary recruitment, on a regional or even on a global basis, might suffer less from the recruitment difficulties which bedevil contemporary national forces. Young men who can find no meaningful career prospect in the profession of national soldier might well think differently on the level of a more ambitious collective security design.

One might summarize the conclusions suggested by this Paper in the following way:

1. From the national point of view, all-volunteer forces offer mobility, flexibility and firepower at the cost not only of heavy *per capita* financial expenditure but also of a shortage of reserves and a partially consequent weakness in combat endurance and 'ground-holding' potential. They are thus more appropriate to nations with diverse or widely-scattered commitments, which may involve limited operations by highly trained task forces or which can back up their conventional capability by a credible threat of escalation to a nuclear level, than they are to nations whose primary concern is the conventional defence of continental territory against threats which may enforce prolonged combat. From the same point of view, all-militia forces provide an economically and psychologically attractive method of mobilizing a nation to the defence of its own territory by relatively primitive military means, at the cost of strictly limited mobility and flexibility within the national territory and none whatever outside it. They are thus more appropriate to nations whose military commitment is exclusively limited to their own defence than they are to those with any wider involvement. Mixed forces can cover the whole spectrum between these extremes, although the ostensibly wide freedom of choice which they offer to their possessors may be more apparent than real, especially given the possible sensitivity of other nations to a form of military force which is more capable than any other of deliberately aggressive action.

2. From the point of view of alliance between nation-states for collective security, all-volunteer forces have the attraction of high quality and high mobility, enabling them to undertake a wide variety of tasks anywhere within the alliance area, but suffer from their quantitative weakness, especially in reserves. All-militia forces, because of the exclusivity of their commitment to home defence, are almost automatically disqualified in practice from membership of an alliance. Mixed forces again offer an indefinite variety of form, and thus of relative 'alliance rating', but changes in their organization or manpower structure will tend to invite doubt on the part of allies in as much as they may be taken to argue a growing emphasis on the territorial defence of a single nation.

3. From the point of view of integrated defence, all-militia forces are once more at a serious disadvantage because of the extent to which they must stress nationalism, as a basis not only for tactical planning but also for psychological attitude. Conscripts, although they must necessarily reflect the general balance of political attitudes within the civilian population, are more likely to be exempt from this particular form of national sentiment. Volunteer forces may also suffer from the heightened sense of national identity with which their professionalism is inevitably linked but in some respects are more suited to the process of international integration in military affairs than all other kinds of forces. If there has been moderate success in specific fields it is, significantly, in the staff work of military professionals. Ultimately voluntary recruitment or, less probably, conscription might both offer – in the name of supra-national nation building – a means of welding disparate national units into an integrated whole.

Having stated the conclusions in that terse form, it only remains to point out that, in as far as any progression from the national point of view through that of alliance to that of integration may be thought desirable, the evidence of military manpower systems does not suggest that the West European wind is blowing in that direction. Although no NATO nation is likely to take any single step which cannot be defended politically as a contribution to alliance efficiency, it is impossible to avoid the over-all impression that there is in Europe an emergence or a revival of interest in military manpower systems which, without marking any overt abandonment of collective security, will best serve the primary purpose of 'territorial defence' for a single nation.

ADELPHI PAPERS

NUMBER ONE HUNDRED AND TWO

Force in Modern Societies: Its Place in International Politics

THE INTERNATIONAL INSTITUTE FOR STRATEGIC STUDIES

18 ADAM STREET LONDON WC2N 6AL

ADELPHI PAPER NO. 102

The Papers printed in this *Adelphi Paper* and in *Adelphi Paper* No. 103 were given at the Fifteenth Annual Conference of the IISS at Travemünde in the Federal German Republic, in September 1973.

Additional copies of this Paper may be ordered from the Institute at a cost of 35p ($1) each, post free.

First published Winter 1973

The International Institute for Strategic Studies was founded in 1958 as a centre for the provision of information on and research into the problems of international security, defence and arms control in the nuclear age. It is international in its Council and staff and in its membership, which is drawn from over fifty countries. It is independent of governments and is not the advocate of any particular interest.

The Institute is concerned with strategic questions – not just with the military aspects of security but with the social and economic sources and political and moral implications of the use and existence of armed force: in other words with the basic problems of peace.

The Institute's publications are intended for a much wider audience than its own membership and are available to the general public on special subscription terms or singly.

© The International Institute for Strategic Studies 1973

CONTENTS

FOREWORD

The Fifteenth Annual Conference of the International Institute for Strategic Studies was held from 13–16 September 1973 at the Maritim Hotel, Travemünde, in the Federal German Republic. It was the second time the Annual Conference had been held in Germany, the last occasion being in 1962, when the venue was Bad Godesberg. As in recent years, the discussion was organized around a single theme, which was 'The Future of Military Forces in Modern Societies'.

'Modern Societies' for the purposes of the Conference referred to the industrial powers. It is plain that in the so-called Third World military power still has a role which is relatively traditional, at least in terms of inter-state conflicts. But in the advanced industrial world it seems to be losing that place in affairs. In part this is due to technological developments such as nuclear weapons and strategic parity between the super-powers. But in part it is also related to the changed acceptability of the use of military force to advanced industrial societies themselves. This raises many questions: Are the changes temporary or permanent? To whom do they apply and if so how may they affect the world balance, world politics and the international system? Can military forces adequate to state purposes be maintained? What type of forces are required and how may they perceive their place in society and be educated to their role? These and many other questions have been impinging more and more insistently on policy-makers and analysts of security problems. They tend to divide into kinds of overriding issues: first, the role of military force in international politics today and in the future; second, the future of the military profession in advanced industrial societies. These were the two themes of the Conference.

Some 210 members of the IISS attended the Conference and in addition to a presentation by Herr Helmut Schmidt, the German Minister of Finance and former Minister of Defence, on the Balance of Power, nine expert papers were prepared either as reports to the Plenary Sessions or as texts for Committee discussion. The main presentations in Plenary Session were given by Professor Laurence Martin, by Major-General Robert Gard of the US Army and by Professor Stanley Hoffman. The Committee papers were presented by M. Jean Laloy, Mr Morton Halperin, Major-General Farrar-Hockley, Mr Gwyn Harries-Jenkins, General Wolf von Baudissin and Mr Adam Roberts.

The five Committees were divided into two groups. The first, of three Committees, discussed the Utility of Force as exemplified in the case of a super-power, the Soviet Union, that of a major economic power, Japan, and in the maintenance of internal order. The second group, of two Committees, discussed the Military Profession, and in particular the problems of Volunteer Forces, and of Officer Education and Alternatives to Existing Forces. Each Committee had a rapporteur whose reports were collated and summarized by one general rapporteur for each group, that for the Utility of Force being Mr Ian Smart and for the Military Profession Dr Theo Sommer.

It has not proved possible to include all the texts in these two *Adelphi Papers* and it has therefore been decided to devote the first paper to the general presentations of the Future of Military Force in Modern Societies, and the second to the issues relating to the Future of the Military Profession, which are less familiar in IISS publications than those on the Utility of Military Force. The Committee papers dealing with the Utility of Military Force have, therefore, with regret, been excluded.

FRANÇOIS DUCHÊNE

The Acceptability of Military Force

STANLEY HOFFMANN

It is a great pleasure for me to contribute to the Conference, but I am in an extremely difficult position. The subject of the acceptability of military force in modern societies is so complex that it is really ideal only for opening statements. It is disastrous to end a conference where one expects a *motion de synthèse*, and I have no synthesis whatsoever. In the second place I think I have much more ability at raising questions than at offering solutions. And finally, as Pascal said long ago: 'Everything has been said already and one comes too late'. But let me try anyhow.

The other side of the problem of the utility of force in the present international system is the acceptability of force to domestic societies, and here we have a whole network of convergent or concordant phenomena including: the abandon-ment of the draft in the United States; the difficulty of recruiting adequate volunteer forces in Britain or the United States; the hostility to things military in countries such as Japan and to some extent West Germany; the revolt against conscription in France only a few months ago. The civilian manifestations of discontent have often led on the military side to bewilderment and even anger. A number of questions are raised by all this.

First, is this a transitory or a permanent phenomenon, an accidental or a long-term trend? Secondly, is this phenomenon in contra-diction to or in conformity with the evolution of the international system? Thirdly, what are its consequences for international relations? And lastly, what is to be done?

I. PAST TO PRESENT

I begin with the first two questions, looking from the past to the present or, if you like, from prophecies to realities. This sudden lack or decline in acceptability can be approached or explained in different ways. One could see in it simply a concatenation of purely accidental circumstances: the post-Vietnam reaction in the United States; the reaction after decolonization in Western Europe; the residues of the impact of World War II on West Germany and Japan; and a general fatigue following a quarter of a century of cold war. In other words, one could see in the present situation essentially a lull, explained by the specific circumstances of each of these countries. One could also envisage the pheno-menon as somewhat less superficial yet still quite reversible: the temporary concentration of most of these societies on domestic problems which were long suppressed while all the top priorities were those of the cold war, or a temporary 'pacification' of the international system in a transitory phase between the bi-polarity conflict and the coming perils of a much more complex world. However, there are also much more sweeping and fundamental explana-tions. It is those I would like to examine. In order to understand any social reality, which is always a chaos of contradictory phenomena, it is always useful to have as a guide the speculations of political philosophy. Of course, political philosophers normally provide one with keys which don't quite open the lock; but the way in which the key does not turn in the lock tells you a great deal about the nature of the lock itself.

It is for that purpose that I would like to examine some earlier prophecies about the evolution of the international system.

Ever since the eighteenth century there have been prophecies about the connection between different types of social order, and war, the most universal phenomenon of mankind; and these prophecies have come essentially in two categories, the pessimistic and the optimistic. On the pessimistic side I can see two main 'streams'. First of all, there are those which assert that the type of social order is fundamentally irrelevant. The decisive thing is the division of the world into separate units and the resulting logic of separateness, competition, glory, which makes of military forces an essential and inherent part of the structure of the international milieu. The origins of this view, of course, go back to Thucydides; one finds traces of it in Rousseau, and today the best expression of this gloomy or sceptical philosophy is in the writing of my friend and master Raymond Aron. It implies that neither any given economic system nor any given class structure can by itself promote or promise the final pacification of the world, because whatever inherent peace-loving qualities any social order may contain can always be negated by the international system. Then, there is a second pessimistic school, quite fashionable these days, which sees modern society as aggravating all the factors which have traditionally led to war. There are, in human nature, aggressive, war-making tendencies which modern society magnifies. Modern society exacerbates friction, frustration and fury; what is denounced here is the impact of urbanization, of collectivized life, or the contributions of modern science and technology to competitiveness, manipulation and greed. A recent representative of that gloomy view is Konrad Lorenz, but there are traces elsewhere in Lewis Mumford or Jacques Ellul – and one can find some origins in Nietzsche or in Spengler.

In sharp contrast to these pessimistic visions, there are two optimistic ones. The first is the whole trend of thought which sees a fundamental opposition between military and feudal societies on the one hand, industrial societies on the other. This is the progressive vision of history celebrated in the nineteenth century by people such as Benjamin Constant or Auguste Comte in France, or by Herbert Spencer in England; one finds earlier traces of it in Montesquieu. They allege that there is something in industrial society which will gradually tame war and eliminate force – because war will become dysfunctional. Industrial society is based on free labour instead of enslavement for war; it is geared to production and commerce, instead of conquest, which is not merely unnecessary for but detrimental to the acquisition of wealth. Industrial societies will also tame war because of a change of values. They are societies in which the citizens want what Constant described as 'le repos et l'aisance' instead of glory, what de Tocqueville called higher status and standard of living instead of turmoil. This is the theme of the opposition between heroic values on the one hand and commercial or bourgeois values on the other.

There is a second, contemporary optimistic vision which is quite close to the first, but which concentrates more on the non-functionality of war in the current international system. It stresses that war has become non-functional partly because of the external consequences of the quest for material development, in other words because of the special nature of the international relations of industrial societies. It emphasizes the strength of the links developed through transnational forces and multinational corporations, which both undermine the integrity and autonomy of the state and heighten the irrelevance of military power to most of the goals such sharply curtailed states must pursue. Partly, the dysfunctionality of war is seen as the consequence of nuclear weapons; the result essentially corroborates the thrust of what, for simplification, one might call the Spencer-Auguste Comte vision. It is directly contrary to the pessimism of Thucydides or Aron, and it emphasizes the fact that international relations are becoming much more like domestic politics.

Let me briefly examine these theories. My own conviction is that the present situation is far more than accidental or superficial. I would like to concentrate on the optimistic, 'pacification' theories. I do not endorse the pessimistic ones. I think that Konrad Lorenz's hypothesis is quite unconvincing; there is no evidence that the tension and turbulence of modern urban life must lead to external war. In fact, one could just as well argue the opposite; people who have been battling with the *métro* all day long have very little energy left for international affairs! Of course, governments have the means, through mass media and political mobilization, to try to whip up chauvinistic frenzy and bellicose enthusiasms. But the calamity of modern war tends to dampen such ardour. As for the Thucydides or Aron view, of course as long as the world is divided into separate units with no superior power and no consensus among them, there is a danger of violence. But one can intellectually construct a world of separate units coexisting in reasonably non-violent competition.

I would now like to turn to the concept of modern industrial society. Even if one accepts the rather mistaken notion of Joseph Schumpeter and Max Weber, who thought that early twentieth-century Germany and Japan were warlike because of the feudal remnants in their societies – in other words that they were warlike despite their industrialization – one must note that some industrial societies have been quite remarkably bellicose. Nazi Germany was far more populist than feudal, and there are very few feudal remnants in the United States which has shown a capacity for war, whether general or limited. In other words, one is thrown back from the concept of industrial society to two different elements: first of all, the nature of the international system itself, and secondly to a deeper scrutiny of the elements of modern society. By itself, the general concept of modern industrial society gets us almost nowhere, because of the profound inherent ambivalence of its main features. In the structure of modern industrial society, one certainly finds the logic described by Spencer or by Comte. There is the international complementarity of all those societies, intellectually and materially linked. They have an interest in peace, from the viewpoint of economic rationality. They exhibit a displacement of threat – one feels threatened by problems like pollution, the population explosion, inflation, perils of unemployment, often more than by external threats. But on the other side of the ledger, one also finds in any industrial society modes of social organization perfectly compatible with what one might call militarism: I mean technocracy, bureaucracy and hierarchy. It is not so long ago that it was fashionable to write that modern industrial societies were potentially ideal garrison states. Fashions change. . . . There is the same ambiguity in the values

inherent in industrial society. All industrial societies have the logic of what one might call consumerism. Consumerism is by itself internationalist: it shifts priorities to welfare, it corrodes community, it erodes borders, which may explain the formidable resistance of China and the Soviet Union to this logic. In other words, there are indeed essential values which go against the military spirit. However, we are in a world in which modern industrial societies come in the national mode, and all of them show also the logic of *collective* power and wealth, inspired by that very sense of community service which makes of an industrial society more than a mere set of services and rationally specialized functions. In other words, there are also values which might just as well lead to war; and they keep interfering with, or distorting, the march of industry towards the peace which Comte had announced. He thought that industry would, at the end, eliminate war altogether, but that was just an act of faith: there is no obvious reason why the 'good' logic must prevail over the 'bad' one.

It is not the industrial essence, therefore, which can by itself explain the current decline of acceptability of military force. The key factors on which we must concentrate are those features of modern society which cannot be derived from the concept of industrial society as such, and yet are crucial because they give to each society its distinctive personality. They are first of all the cultural system, which is only partly tied to the industrial essence of the society, and secondly the political system. One may posit that military force will be more or less acceptable, first of all depending on whether or not the cultural system in the society entails a revolt against imposed discipline – what General Gard in his paper calls 'predictable behaviour' – against the whole system of deference, authority, respect, blind acceptance of leadership, or conformity.* Such a revolt is prominent in the youth culture of today, and it is being fostered by the very deep transformation of family relations all over the Western world. There will also be a decline in the acceptability of force depending on whether the value system entails what one might call a humanistic horror of violence, an increase

* See *Force in Modern Societies: The Military Profession.* Adelphi Paper No. 103 (London: International Institute for Strategic Studies, 1973).

in respect for life, inculcated already in the schools. In other words, anti-militarism will be greatest when there is a coincidence of these humanistic values and of a revolt against traditional authority. (In part of the youth movement of several countries, there was far more of the latter than of the former: leadership was debunked, but violence enshrined.)

The second key factor is the political system. It is the political system which filters the contending forces and values of the society and sometimes compresses them, or consecrates some while repressing others. Here, there are fundamental differences, depending on whether the regime is democratic or not. If it is democratic, the possibility of the state filtering out of society those values or structures which are anti-militaristic will be extremely limited. In democratically governed societies, there is going to be both pluralism and the predominance in the political sphere of those values which prevail in the social order. Moreover, in democratic political systems the main mode of political life is what Aron has called 'satisfaction querelleuse' or, as I prefer to put it, non-cataclysmic permanent dissatisfaction: the politics of universal bargaining. Now, the politics of universal bargaining and incremental compromise is very far indeed from the military virtues, and tends to erode or push down whatever basic consensus exists in the society. It is when the kinds of values I have mentioned coincide with a democratic political system, that the decline of the acceptability of military force is likely to be greatest.

What are the origins of these phenomena? First of all, of course, history and traditions. In modern Western societies, the achievement of the industrial order has been gradual; it has come at least partly through democratic political systems, and it has been shaped by ideological currents which have dominated the society: essentially the currents of liberalism or moderate social democracy. These ideologies are anti-force in essence and inform both the cultural and the political systems of these nations. On the other hand, in Soviet society, the industrial stage has been reached in a forced or hot-house way, through authoritarian and largely militaristic methods, and with an ideology which stresses the usefulness and necessity of force: in other words, under conditions quite contrary to

those which a Comte or a Spencer expected or desired. Another important element has been the impact of the United States. It is the United States which has, so to speak, opened West Germany and Japan to a certain type of polity. And it is also from the United States that the cultural values which I have described above have in the last twenty-five years swept through the whole of the West and Japan. In effect, the United States has made of modern Western and Japanese society an international open-zone in which there is an increasing similarity of behaviour and complementarity of interests, which make the use of force within it quite inconceivable.

Thus, while there may well be an incompatibility between aristocratic or feudal armies and modern society, there is no necessary incompatibility between modern society and some types of armies or military values: it depends on the cultural system and on the degree of democracy. It was de Tocqueville who was right, not Comte: the martial spirit is likely to suffer more from 'democracy' and from 'industrial society' if we want to deal in archetypes. What is happening now in Western countries and Japan is quite simply the full flow of what is the deepest essence of the West. Once the sense of threat, for good or bad reasons, fades or dies, there is at last in a large part of the world an approximation of those conditions of relative harmony and renunciation of force which the liberal and social democratic ideologies of the past have considered to be our promised land. What has happened is simple: the countervailing factors which have compressed those ideologies for so long have been removed, and reinforcing factors have been accelerated. What proves my point is that in those Western, liberal, democratic countries where there exist counter-traditions which still prevent or restrict the full flourishing of the liberal or social democratic ideal of peace without force, or where there is a very strong sense of threat, or which have been more isolated from the international system, there is much less of a decline in the acceptability of force. I am thinking here not only of Switzerland, but also of Israel. But when these countervailing factors are no longer there, we witness the fruition of what we have liked or learned to see as really the essence of our societies.

This brings me to the second question. Is this development in contradiction or in conformity

45

with the evolution of the international system? Is the unacceptable something which remains, alas, very useful? Here we are faced with a basic and very original contradiction: the discrepancy between the domestic and the international systems. This discrepancy was only latent in the past; it is in full bloom now. In past centuries, there were either aristocratic armies which entirely reflected the social order and whose officers, as de Tocqueville pointed out, are members of the élite of society whatever their ranks in the army; these armies fought limited wars – dynastic or predatory – for stakes which corresponded both to the nature of the regimes and to the delicate balance of the international milieu. Or else, as in much of the nineteenth and twentieth centuries there were conscript armies, which not only reflected but also served to unify and consolidate the domestic order, and corresponded to an international system in which war was still a daily possibility to be prepared and fought for, and in which there were such classical objectives as the maintenance of equilibrium, and such modern stakes as the nationality principle, colonial expansion, ideological rivalry and so on. In other words, neither the domestic nor the international order was geared to peace; peace belonged to the realm of exhortation and prophecy.

Today, however, we confront a growing discrepancy. On the one hand there is an international system still divided into rival units, and far more heterogeneous – indeed, heterogeneous in many more ways: ideologically; economically; in forms and levels of power; in the nature and solidity of regimes, and so forth – than ever before. Even though there has been a pacifying impact of the two factors which Kant had announced as the necessary causes of the gradual elimination of war: the horrid destructiveness of modern war and the progress of commerce, i.e., the requirements of survival and of greed ruling out the resort to war; even though there is at present what one might call a decline in the positive productivity of military force, its use is still functional in a number of situations. First of all, there is a residual positive productivity of military force, both in direct use, for the maintenance of a local balance of power or for the preservation of local preponderance, as in Czechoslovakia or the Dominican Republic; and also indirectly, as an instrument of manipula-

tion for influence, either against adversaries (as in the Berlin crises), or in order to control allies (for instance by 'linking' the level of one's protection to the degree of their financial and economic support), or in order to help clients (through arms assistance). Secondly, there is the enormous negative productivity of force, the massive presence of force for deterrence purposes either for one's own protection or for the protection of others. But if one puts these various forms of the utility of force together, one finds, as is very well stated in Professor Laurence Martin's excellent paper, a predominance of the latent over the manifest, of the oblique over the direct, of the limited over the general.* There is no disappearance of the uses of force. But there are shifts, subtle transformations, that tend both to dilute what Clausewitz might have termed war's own grammar – the style and syntax of battle – and to re-enforce Clausewitz' central point: that war does not have its own logic; that war is and ought to be seen as an instrument of policy; and that the logic of force must be that of politics.

However, if we turn to domestic society in democratic polities which are not, or do not feel that they are, under direct external threat, the decline of the acceptability of force is particularly strong with respect to such oblique, latent or indirect uses. One could almost say that the more force is wrapped in political calculations and constraints, the less the citizenry understands or approves its use. It is difficult for democratic societies to accept limited wars, because war in a democracy requires, as was made clear in 1914, the demonification of the enemy; and demonification is quite incompatible with limits, if it occurs – remember 'unconditional surrender' – and is quite unachievable, as was shown by the Vietnam war, if the national interest at stake is felt to be too remote; then the will to win or to face risks is corroded. This explains why it is very difficult for a democracy to mobilize public support for the waging of a balance-of-power policy. As regards indirect uses of military forces, they are difficult for public opinion to accept because of the discrepancy between costs and results, in a world in which the achievements of power often seem quite unconnected to the ingredients of power.

---

* See pp. 20–21.

Finally, as for deterrence, even in the United States, where public support for strategic nuclear forces remains high (partly for economic reasons, partly because these forces are precisely the ones which are most independent from specific political concerns or uses, most unconnected with the logic of politics, most un-Clausewitzian, so to speak, and therefore the easiest to justify in terms everyone can grasp) there is increasing criticism of the credibility of threats of massive, yet suicidal attacks against the adversary's population, and of the horrible results should deterrence fail. Moreover, it is very hard to prove to citizens of non-nuclear or small nuclear states that their security could be enhanced by, or is due to, the costly possession of something which makes sense only if it is not used: it is not easy to demonstrate the negative productivity of limited power against overwhelmingly superior enemy might. All of this leads to a rather bizarre conclusion: that the kinds of uses of force which are still functional are those which would most require cabinet diplomacy, and yet cabinet diplomacy is very hard to wage in the context of socially mobilized democratic societies.

The key to this contradiction is the crisis of democratic nationalism. In the past, there was a very strong link between an external threat and the domestic consensus, between the outside function of the military and its internal role as a school and crucible of citizenship. Consider the French Revolution: the mobilization of Europe against the French Republic turned warring French factions into a nation in arms. This link is still true in Israel. But today, there is both a dissociation and a decline of the roles played by military force in democratic nationalism. As far as the external function is concerned a decline in the sense of an external threat leads quite naturally to the reassertion of the latent pacifism of democratic society. Force is, after all, a blunt instrument, and it is normal that there be a revolt against it when its positive productivity becomes less visible. Moreover, force, deep down, is contrary to Western ideals such as the rule of law. Finally, every Western country has special reasons for this revolt. To many people in the United States, nothing short of direct attack seems to justify the risk of a world holocaust (which explains why they are far more willing to buy a 'sufficient' deterrent, than to keep troops or bases abroad). For Western Europe, and to some extent also for Japan, *any* kind of war would be seen as a condemnation to death, so that everything has to be done to deter war, by every possible means. And since, nuclear deterrence seems to many either unconvincing or even provocative; since conventional means appear inadequate to deter, insufficient to defend successfully, and perhaps even dangerous insofar as they suggest that a conventional war would be possible, there is increasing pressure to rely mainly on non-military means. As for the internal function of the military, its past role as a force of domestic unification is also in decline. To a certain extent, today, it is around economic and cultural phenomena that domestic unification takes place; to put it somewhat irreverently, it seems to me that national television is a far more effective instrument of national unification than is the military, any given external enemy, or any given ideology. Moreover, this internal function cannot be performed unless there is a sense of external peril, and confidence in the nation's capacity to cope with it militarily. To a considerable extent such a military spirit is in decline; in other words the spirit of the democracies is no longer dependent on, nor sufficiently supportive of, what could be called the martial virtues.

This has very important and dangerous consequences. In Western societies, it is difficult to get military force accepted, even though it remains highly functional in the international system, even though, as Ian Smart suggests, the existence of adequate force is essential for the maintenance of national self-confidence in an 'era of negotiation'.* The result of this contradiction in Western societies is a kind of spontaneous 'depolitization' towards force, which exceeds the actual decline of the functionality of military force. But in the Soviet Union, the regime's own domestic need to keep the lid on, so as to preserve its social and political systems from the intrusion of Western ideas, means that, on the contrary, the armed forces are being given a role and kept at a size that go far above and beyond their functionality in the present international system.

---

* See p. 26.

II. PRESENT TO FUTURE

I come to my third question, the consequences of these trends for international relations. I begin with the dilemmas of the Western states. First, they face a world in which there are continuing opportunities for 'traditional' violence: probably not so much in direct military confrontation between themselves and the Communist powers, as through involvement in a violent conflict between third parties (consider the possible effects on Japan of a Soviet-Chinese war, or even of a new Korean war). Also, the temptations to threaten or use force for maintaining hegemony or at least influence over key countries in the Third World will continue – for the purpose of what might be called oblique conquest. Thus, there will be many situations in which national force may still be extremely useful. Secondly, there will be equally enormous opportunities for the kind of chaos against which military force may in fact be of very limited use. For instance, there may be large-scale monetary or commercial conflicts among advanced nations. There could also be tensions between them, and between them and others, over energy supplies, raw materials, sea resources or telecommunications: here, anything like military action or demonstrations would be quite counter-productive either in the long run (by, for instance, producing unwelcome coalitions to prevent any new humiliation) or even immediately through disastrous escalation and contagion. The opportunities for international terrorism, so evident today (and, incidentally, shown by recent poll of French public opinion to be by far the most highly felt threat, whereas the threat of military aggression from the outside was second to last) can be fought far more effectively by police methods than by armies. Thirdly, as if the existence of two very different, but not always clearly distinguishable, groups of cases – those in which force is functional, those in which it is not – did not already risk producing some kind of policy schizophrenia, Western governments preside over societies increasingly pervaded by a sense of the absurdity of using force, which may well encourage those who, elsewhere, believe that they would benefit from violence or chaos.

On turning from the Western states to the world as a whole, one is conscious of a further dilemma. Despite the optimistic prophecies, the world is not yet as peaceful as domestic societies theoretically – although few actually – are. The world is still an arena in which there is no central authority that can order the redistribution of resources, in which people cannot move freely from one place to another even if there is a political or economic incentive for them to do so. It is still a milieu in which there exists no procedural consensus on central institutions. Hence the following dilemma: any large-scale resort to force to resolve deadlocks or to promote change – throughout history, the most effective way of accelerating or achieving change – is obviously either inappropriate, or too dangerous, or unpopular. And yet if our objective is to make the international system more like domestic politics, to eliminate interstate violence from future history, to allow Western values to bloom without danger, to tame and reform trouble-makers, it is hard to see how this can be done without force.

In order to examine the practical effects of these dilemmas, let me pose a double question. If the present decline in the acceptability of force results from the disappearance of countervailing factors, what countervailing factors could be reintroduced that would reverse the trend? And if the trend continues, would it not become a disaster? I will try to answer this question in the most indirect and oblique way. What seems likely to occur in Western societies during the coming years is some combination of the following: continuing reductions of the more unpopular forms of military force – which means, to put it bluntly, men; and an attempt at compensating for this, first of all by increasing reliance on technology, because that is more in line with industry's needs and thrust anyhow as well as less unpopular, and secondly by arms sales to and reliance upon proxies, i.e. feeding the weapons to others. Now, these probable reactions seem to me to be extremely dangerous: there are dangers both in the *consequences* of this combination, and dangers in the *reactions* which states are likely to display if the consequences are as bad as I think they might be.

What will the consequences be? Here, it is necessary to distinguish between states; firstly, between the United States and other modern democratic powers. The United States, like the

Soviet Union, still enjoys a considerable positive as well as negative productivity of her power outside her borders. She is a super-power with global concerns; the world balance, and various regional balances, for instance in the Mediterranean, are dependent on her behaviour. As for the other Western powers and Japan, their nuclear and conventional forces are useful either only in a very limited geographical area or purely negatively for deterrence of direct attacks. This means that if the reductions I have mentioned affect mainly countries other than the United States, if the acceptability of force declines further only in countries other than the United States, the consequences could be rather limited – except insofar as the added burden of responsibility should unbearably strain the resolve and the forces of the United States, as might well be the case. But if, as a result or quite independently, these reductions and this trend should greatly affect the United States herself (or both the United States and all the other Western countries and Japan) then there will be enormous perils, more especially for Western Europe. Then, there is a distinction to be made between the rich countries and the rest of the world. There is a risk of a world divided into two different ages and zones; one in which domestic priorities, the rise in education, the spread of liberal values, will result (to use a fashionable and inelegant word) in a 'decoupling' from the overt use of force; and the other, the rest of the world, in which traditional international relations and stakes of conflict will continue, and in which armies will still play an enormous role, either for the domestic unification of countries torn by ethnic, tribal, religious or class hatreds, or simply for dictatorial rule in lieu of either old oligarchies or the fragile processes and institutions of democracy. If this should be the case, there will be a very great danger that the zone of peace would be gradually affected or infected, either through continuing competition between East and West for advantages in the other zone, or by the chaos that could reign in the poorer parts of the world.

If these are consequences, the reactions which advanced democratic countries are likely to take could also be very dangerous. Of course, those reactions are very hard to describe in advance. Events determine specific reactions. But I think one can make some hypotheses. In domestic affairs, not all democratic regimes are so secure that their collapse, in the event of an acute external crisis that would demonstrate their impotence, has become inconceivable: military rule, or authoritarian rule supported by the army, may still be a consequence of national humiliation. On the world stage, if there should be a crisis suddenly creating an apparent risk of general war, the greatest likelihood would be a hectic collusion of the two super-powers for peace; but the kind of bargaining which would defuse such a perilous situation would give considerable advantage to the power with the greater forces and skill in their manipulation. It is more likely that there would be more limited crises or, even in the absence of crisis, choices and situations in which one would painfully feel either the discrepancy between East and West, or the conviction of Third World states or groups that they can defy advanced, non-Communist states with impunity. This could result in a whole range of reactions. One can imagine a country – Japan, for example – calculating for reasons of general influence, status and prestige, or as an insurance policy against the unknown, that she must remilitarize, especially if in such a country liberal values and practices have not grown very deep roots. Secondly, it is possible to imagine a panic reaction of the strong against the apparently weak, if, for instance, the latter should try to cut off sources of energy or raw materials and the former wanted to show, however inappropriately, that they had not lost their manhood. Suez may be a warning, but there are still those who think that the execution, not the conception, was wrong. And finally, one can picture the West European situation which seems to haunt many observers as well as the French government: in the absence of indigenous and American power, piecemeal appeasement and accommodation to the desires of the stronger super-power would be seen as a necessity, and rationalized as a blessing by the squabbling West European governments. For if the deterrence of war is the supreme imperative, and the revulsion against force leaves only diplomacy as the means to that end, the price to be paid for peace and military security could be Soviet preponderance and political insecurity. This is the plight which is known as 'findlandization', however unfair this may be to Finland, whose only other alternative was not armed independence but satellization. All these reactions would be catastrophic, either because of their external impact or because of their domestic aspects. They would all tend to make the international system much less moderate, for instance because the remilitarization of an important participant could entail or provoke nuclear proliferation, or because of the shock waves caused by a sudden resort to the use of force, or because of the usual effects of appeasement. As far as the domestic aspects are concerned, all the reactions I have described are likely either to result from or to produce sharp internal crises. 'Finlandization' or appeasement is particularly likely to occur in countries which are deeply split domestically or have a strong Communist party. A decision by Japan to re-arm on a much larger scale, or to build a nuclear force, would deepen the polarization of opinion and parties. In other words, if the trend towards the unacceptability of force should be reversed, if a countervailing force should reassert itself, it would often not be a good thing, either domestically or for the world at large; and yet if the trend persists, there will be very high risks, both internally and internationally.

And so I come to my last point: what can be done about this? A first step was discussed in some of the papers submitted to this conference;* it may be called 'making force more acceptable again through military reform'. The point of departure is the recognition of the growing unacceptability of force, but one tries to find a remedy for this by focusing on just one aspect – the relation between the military and their societies in modern democratic nations. But here again the difference, between armies of today and the past creates a formidable obstacle. In the past, the warrior was an expert endowed with a monopoly over his peculiar brand of knowledge (the art of combat, if you like), and as such he was quite apart from all other forms of expertise in society. Even in societies of caste privilege or class distinction, the rigours of military discipline and rank were a second factor setting the warrior apart. But he was also representative, indeed the embodiment, of the dominant values of the social order, whether these were the values of prowess, honour and hierarchy of aristocratic societies or the values of militant nationalism in the modern nation-state. Today, the warrior has lost that monopoly of knowledge. For insofar as part of his expertise is still the art of combat, both the speed of technological change and the fortunately unknown nature of a nuclear war mean that this art remains mysterious even to its practitioners, who have neither code nor compass and must either improvise or guess – just like the rest of us. And in as much as another part of his expertise is general technological knowledge, he shares his information and skills with other broad groups: scientists, engineers, and so on in advanced industrial society. However, neither this loss of his uniqueness, nor the fact that armies tend to become bureaucratic organizations managed along lines similar to those applied to all the other, civilian bureaucracies of modern society, compensate for a new kind of separation. Today, there is a sharp contrast between the dominant social values and those of the military. On the one hand, the ethos of combat and heroism – in increasingly mechanized, dehumanized wars – has lost its appeal. On the other hand, the ethos (if it is one) of economic rationality and efficiency, which informs modern organizations, serves goals of wealth, welfare and economic power, whereas military bureaucracies are inevitably geared to the accumulation, and eventual destruction of unproductive goods.

This does not make any easier the attempts at transforming the relations between the military and their societies. There are two different directions in which this reform can go. Neither direction strikes me as very helpful for the problem we now face. There is first of all the direction of the specialized, highly professional army, in essentials a volunteer force. As we know, such an army has its problems. Externally, these kinds of armies have been well adapted to ages of limited wars; they can be useful for the latent or oblique uses of force and for what the French would call 'ponctuel', piecemeal intervention. However, they risk being quite insufficient to back up nuclear deterrence in those parts of the world where the goal of policy must be not successful defence or counter-attack, but credible deterrence of war altogether. Domestically, such armies tend to be recruited among people of low education and the under-privileged seeking the security and opportunities for

* See Adelphi Paper No. 103, *op. cit.*

ascent which the military offer. Consequently the external efficiency of such armies, even and perhaps, especially, in the non-combat roles which make up much of the usefulness of force, might be quite limited; and there is the grave risk of a loss of domestic support for essentially unrepresentative armies. This problem did not exist in the days of mercenary armies: the King's support sufficed. But in societies dominated by the middle classes, and strongly influenced by the privileged, the political representatives of the electorate are likely either to balk at the costs of making a volunteer army sufficiently enticing, or even to fear the growth of a praetorian 'state within the state'. Without high incentives, there won't be enough volunteers. With such incentives, there will be acute civilian resentment.

Then there is another direction, but exactly the opposite one. De Tocqueville suspected that in democracies armies, ignored by 'the richest, best educated and ablest citizens' might get farther and farther away from the population; he saw the danger of a 'small uncivilized nation possessing arms and the exclusive knowledge of how to use them', amidst the wider nation. He believed that the solution was to make the 'general spirit of the nation' penetrate into the army. But whereas he warned future reformers that what had to be watched and tended to was the general spirit of the nation, and expressed his scepticism about 'finding remedies to the vices of the army in the army itself', we find instead, today, a broad range of proposals aimed at democratizing the army. They range from plans to make the conscript armies more like the society at large (through better conditions of entry and exit, changes in discipline, more meritocracy than traditional hierarchy, more professionalism than combat ethic, closer connections with civilian life), to the advocacy of the militia solution, the Swiss model of territorial defence, which Jean Jaurés had wanted France to adopt before World War I. But there are problems here too. Externally, we know that these armies are quite limited in their functions. They are not satisfactory for the indirect or oblique uses of force. They are most satisfactory for defence or deterrence of a direct yet non-nuclear attack. Moreover, domestically these efforts to close the gap between the people and the army may be anyhow, quite insufficient or counter-productive. The more one tries to make the army like its counterpart civilian organizations, the greater the risk of achieving exactly the opposite: the remaining, inevitable differences will loom large and serve as major irritants, and one may end up with the worst of all possible worlds – an army that will have lost its combat abilities in the very effort to be like a bureaucracy or a corps of engineers, but will not have gained any greater prestige and popularity in the attempt. At best, instead of an ethic of loyalty, there would be, on the part of the conscripts and enlisted men, little more than a very utilitarian calculation, a search for training and for a springboard from which to leap back into civilian life. Such 'improved' conscript armies, or the national militias, may indeed be highly unpopular if there is no very high sense of threat or no tradition as strong and old as Switzerland's. On the other hand, when there is a sense of threat, a system of purely territorial defence may be demoralizing, precisely because it can do no more than resist and defend, and it does not appear compatible with alliances. Thus, these various suggestions for a second direction do not answer the question, which de Tocqueville did not raise: what if the 'general spirit of the nation' is against force? To make this spirit penetrate into the army is not exactly a solution to the problem. In other words, army reform is not the way to overcome the central contradiction between internal attitudes and external requirements. It does not mean that there are no serious choices to be made here. But the answer depends largely on the internal and external situation of each nation – on its past, the strengths and flaws of its polity, its interests abroad and the nature of its friendships and enmities. Also, each choice has its own drawbacks, and none can be a complete solution.

In what direction can we find one? Let me start from a very simple notion. An army which is domestically illegitimate can have no efficiency in international relations; precisely because we are dealing with democracies, there is no substitute for domestic support. The key is the national sense of self-confidence and self-respect. Ultimately, military forces will only be acceptable if the population understands their continuing external functions. This implies two requirements one negative and one positive. The negative is that governments should try to avoid overselling the usefulness of force and forces; for overselling is likely to produce an even more negative reaction in the public. There are attempts at making military force acceptable either by artificially inflating the external perils, which may have the same result as crying wolf too often, or by arguing in nineteenth-century terms that the army is the backbone of the nation and the ultimate guardian not only of its security but of its cohesion and direction, which was much more true then than it is today. Those kinds of arguments are so excessive as to be not just useless but also dangerous. What is necessary, and has not sufficiently been followed through by most governments, is to give a rational and clear explanation of the new functions which force still performs. If force today is misunderstood, it is partly because it is too oblique, but also partly because the change in role has not been well explained. For a government to try to clarify and justify the uses of its forces may well be an essential exercise, for if certain missions or goals cannot be described without either confusion or hyperbole, this would be the signal that there is something wrong with the policy itself.

However, I am under no illusions. Some missions, however rational in policy terms, may be too oblique, or appear too disproportionate to the public (the issue of US troops in Europe appears to be close to the stage where many Americans, even influential ones, find the connection between the burden and the national interest too indirect, or America's share of the burden too heavy for what they see as a primarily European interest). More generally, it is going to be difficult to reverse what one might call the liberal democratic view in which force is always potentially evil, rather than simply an instrument in the orchestra of power – assuming that a reversal of that view would be a good thing in itself. In addition, while I fully recognize that the disappearance of the heroic tradition would be a grave loss, while I recognize the terrible risk that the collapse of national defence traditions would create, I think that we are in a world in which we have to go beyond the simple repetition of the traditional game of power; and if I may quote from an article of mine on the subject: 'However valid or profound classical insights may be about the persistence of force as the *ultima ratio* of politics, a world of nuclear weapons and of problems that cannot be managed within national borders needs something beyond the classical conception. For the game which this conception describes had no other goal than its own perpetuation or its resurrection after breakdowns, whereas today's game must aim both at the avoidance of such a breakdown and at the resolution of the problems which the traditional game can either only exacerbate or at best contain.'

This means that we have certain imperatives. We must start by accepting that, barring international calamities, the loss of faith in the use of force is unlikely to be reversed, and that a reversal, so to speak in the aftermath of calamity, could be dangerous. But we must also realize that this growing or continuing unacceptability of force can create very serious risks in the international competition. However, we must take heart in a number of factors. It is not clear that those competitors who continue to rely very largely on military forces may not have their own problems and their own internal strains. We should not act as if the acceptability of force poses no question either of values or of resources to autocratic governments: even their capacity to shut out humane ideas and to whip up convincing rationalizations may have limits. Moreover, even if we recognize that for a long time to come there will be a discrepancy here between the Western-style democratic societies and the others, we have a number of ways of compensating it. The first one consists of cultivating as much as possible other forms of power. These would, of course, be quite meaningless if there were a complete collapse of military force in the West; but they can go a long way as complements or as partial substitutes. It was Khrushchev himself who saw the East–West competition as primarily an economic race. Among these other forms of power there is, primarily, domestic solidity and national purposefulness. To push force beyond what is acceptable may actually undermine it. While, again, an extreme disproportion of military forces might be disastrous, a modern disproportion may be quite tolerable: as long as the central balance of nuclear deterrence is maintained, such a local or regional disproportion can be offset by domestic efficiency, prosperity and self-respect, precisely because we are in an age where conquest is not very easy, where the risk of escalation exists, and where the political advantage of having superior might can be neutralized both by the risks in using force and by a nation's capacity to withstand blackmail or pressure. Another form of power is organizational capacity. In the case of Western Europe, what it needs most is not rearmament, which would be very hard to sell to domestic opinion, but simply the supplement of self-respect and effectiveness which organized collaboration and division of labour in military procurement and deployment would produce. Concerning these two kinds of power, it seems to me dangerous for West European statesmen to keep repeating that the whole structure of Western defence and resolve would collapse if the United States should withdraw some troops. This can much too easily become a self-fulfilling prophecy. (I can see the function of such a statement in one's dealings with Washington. But even here there are some dangers: for Washington could use its presence as a source of recurrent financial, monetary or trade blackmail, which would in turn perpetuate West European dependence and fragmentation.) I do not think there is any necessity for such a statement to be true unless we make it so, which means that it has something in common with the domino theory.

Secondly, we have to search much more for forms of arms control which could avoid some of the perils I have tried to describe. There is considerable utility in thinking about negotiating freezes and reductions in Eastern and Western forces in Europe, and there is an enormous necessity to regulate and control arms sales to the Third World, a problem which deserves much fuller discussion than I can give here. To be sure, success requires the other side's willingness to co-operate. But this side's own combination of internal strains and fears of escalation or chaos, the desire to enhance its own interests through *détente* rather than toughness, may make such co-operation possible. It is not in the democracies' interest to consent to unbalanced concessions, but a return to the cold war would be even less in their interest.

Finally, it might be useful to start thinking about the long-range problems of international security (which we have wrongly learned to play down or to ridicule) both because of the formidable magnitude of the problem of security in a world full of causes, sparks and powder-kegs, and because there is one kind of use of force which may still be highly acceptable in a democratic society, not tomorrow, not next year, but in a not so distant future perhaps: the limited use of force for general community purposes. The only real hope for our planet is to come to a stage where national security will be seen by each state to have both a 'separatist', defensive, selfish function, and a community or planetary one. One way of combining a renewed acceptability of force and the requirements of the international system is to think of, and gradually institute, what the late Leonard Beaton called the principle of cognizance: what each country does with its forces should be seen as being a legitimate concern of all others. We have to think much more about a problem which we have almost forgotten about: having international forces in readiness either for collective security or for peace-keeping. And in all the new and increasingly salient areas of technology, resources, oceans, space, and so on, we have to think of establishing international regimes which will need procedures of enforcement and even forces for their own protection.

None of this, of course, could ever compensate for a totally disastrous imbalance. But if I am correct, if under ordinary circumstances the acceptability of the purely national uses of force in the contemporary international system is not likely to grow, then we have still quite a number of directions which we can explore instead of wringing our hands, and before declaring that disaster is at hand.

The Utility of Military Force

LAURENCE MARTIN

I

To be set such a topic* immediately implies a good deal about the current climate of opinion. There is a growing consensus that the utility of force has diminished, is diminishing and should diminish further. Intellectuals are always tempted by attitudes that appear both radical and perceptive, but a much wider range of opinion among both the public and political leaders is clearly disenchanted with the military establishment and sceptical of its pretensions. Even such apparently dispassionate publications as the statistical volumes of the Stockholm International Peace Research Institute and, dare one say, the International Institute for Strategic Studies, seem tinged with wonder that so much time, treasure, energy and ingenuity should be devoted to such sterile pursuits. For their part the ministries of defence sustain a certain dogged traditionalism. On appropriate occasions, ministers of defence – Lord Carrington at a British naval exercise in the summer of 1973, for example – assure television audiences how important it is to 'keep our guard up'. The viewer is left wondering whether the military spokesmen are unaware that their fundamental assumptions are rapidly losing credibility, or whether they know it all too well and fear the slightest admission of doubt would bring the whole habit-formed edifice of military expenditure crashing down. Nevertheless, for many Western taxpayers, the military are on the way to becoming latter-day remittance men, given a small slice of the family income on condition they go off and pursue their unsavoury activities quietly where they will not embarrass decent folk.

The position of extreme scepticism is almost certainly unjustified and the bulk of this brief Paper is devoted to reviewing some of the ways in which military force retains its utility. First, however, we must briefly summarize the main sources of this rampant belief that military force has forfeited its place in the arsenal of foreign policy. The argument that force has lost its utility is, of course, closely bound up in a circular relationship with the acceptability of force, discussed by Professor Hoffman (see pp. 6–7), for low utility will diminish acceptability and low acceptability will reduce utility by increasing political costs. Even this simple syllogism, however, would have to be modified if views of both acceptability and utility were changing in an asymmetric way among the nations of the world, for a sense of unacceptability sufficiently high to encourage an attitude of appeasement in one power would increase the utility of force for another. Somewhat similarly, though we must not confuse the continued use of force with its continued utility – for it may be used foolishly or unwisely renounced – we must recognize that if some states do persist in the use of force, others may find that the only effective response is in kind, whatever their own preferences.

Force has, indeed, long been regarded as an instrument that trumps all others and can only be thwarted by countervailing force. Since World War II, however, war between industrialized states has been recognized as an unwieldy tool and in the nuclear age this process has brought about a sharp revision of the perceived relationship between military means and political ends.

On the one hand, so far as purposes are concerned, states have, ostensibly at least, universally embraced the gods of welfare econo-

---

* The title has been interpreted to me as the utility of formally exercised force to the Western powers in the present international system. I therefore try to steer away from the special perspectives of the Soviet Union and Japan and from the topic of the acceptability of force, though this is obviously very relevant.

This is one of two footnotes with which I shall burden my text and I use it also to acknowledge that much of this subject has been ably covered already in a number of books and articles. In the last few years I have found the writings of Messrs Brodie, Knorr, Osgood, Schelling and R. W. Tucker particularly enlightening.

14

mics and rejected those of martial glory. They have also concluded that trade, investment and similar activities are the route to success, rather than conquest and mercantilist rivalry. These conclusions and the type of industrial society that has developed, have led to the adoption of several closely interrelated assumptions: that the chief national purposes are economic; that force does little to attain them; and that exercising force is expensive and increasingly distasteful as a personal activity for industrial man, suiting neither his own preferences for a way of life nor his sense of proper conduct towards others. Moreover, the emergence of societies with mass politics and mass media raises new practical obstacles to success in maintaining and exploiting territorial acquisitions even if they are made. In such a world, investment, production and trade seem the shortest road not merely to economic welfare itself, but also to the less tangible goals of prestige and self respect. All of these assumptions come together in the view that international politics is becoming 'civilianized', that there can be great powers without great military establishments, and that we can cite in evidence the relative decline of the super-powers while they still retain military supremacy.

This leads us, of course, to the second development cited to argue the declining utility of force: to changes in the instruments of conflict and in particular to the self-defeating nature of the supreme nuclear power wielded by the great states. Just as the modern goals of states are no longer to be sought by force, so military means have become incommensurate with any conceivable rational end. Between nuclear powers, it can be said, victory would be neither necessary to destroy one adversary nor sufficient to preserve the other, still less to achieve the victor's purposes. By fear of the process of escalation, the argument goes, the inhibitions of strategic nuclear power reach down to inhibit the use of lesser force for lesser ends. A series of efforts to evade this conclusion by ingenious theories of limited war have failed to win credence and we have arrived at a widespread belief that nuclear power is unusable, and that prudence compels the advanced nations to ensure it remains unused by abstaining from war among themselves altogether.

To these fundamental changes in the nature of ends and means, which are the commonplaces of strategic discourse, even if the consequences can still be debated, we must add some rather more superficial characteristics of today contributing to disillusionment with the role of armed force. The older colonial powers have emerged from decades of rearguard action with little to show for their efforts. World War II has left Germany and Japan with special inhibitions. The United States, having made her own military effort to control the pace of change in the Third World, has suffered a serious humiliation. Vietnam has produced both a widespread, emotional, anti-militarism and a more analytical rejection of both the purposes and methods implicit in the operation. This rejection is facilitated by the waning of the bipolar, cold war confrontation and by a diffused feeling of greater safety produced by the American *rapprochement* with both China and the Soviet Union. This *rapprochement* also encourages the hope that the erstwhile foes of the West are similarly down-grading the utility of force.

The cumulative weight of all these developments leaves little doubt that the use of force is indeed now circumscribed by many new restraints arising from both the international and domestic systems, particularly in the democracies. It remains a question, however, as to how far the present atmosphere depends on fundamental, long-term changes and how far on more transient features of the particular diplomatic and political configuration of the moment. Another – but not quite the same – question is whether the reorientation of views about the relation between political ends and military means ensures that military force can henceforth be safely neglected, or whether the reorientation will persist only so long as a balance of military power is carefully maintained. The distinction is the one inherent in Hobbes' famous dictum that war is any period in which peace cannot be utterly relied upon. It is also the distinction between the conception of security as the absence of all danger, and of security as the state of having recognized and made provision against all the dangers that do exist.* Instinct, common sense

---

* The difference is rather neatly illustrated for those who speak English by recognizing how recently the word 'security' has come to mean safety and ceased to mean complacency. In his entry for 20 October 1674, the diarist John Evelyn wrote 'I discoursed with . . . Colonel Morgan, who undertook that gallant exploit from

and a quick look round the world suggests the latter, more cautious conclusion. The rising tide of domestic and transnational violence, the fact that sheer inertia if nothing else will ensure that today's vast military establishments will not melt away tomorrow and that their mere existence will arouse defensive anxieties in others, the inherently adversary nature of the overarching nuclear balance, – all these factors and more offer *prima facie* evidence that the real debate must not be whether military force still has utility, but what are the more essential manifestations of this utility in the changed circumstances of the present.

II

A brief but more detailed examination of these manifestations must begin with the hackneyed but inescapable topic of nuclear deterrence. An increasingly dominant view holds that the strategic nuclear forces of the super-powers do nothing but deter the use of each other by making it suicidal. This view is enshrined in the Strategic Arms Limitation agreements, which institutionalize mutual vulnerability. Even some official American statements suggest that the role of the nuclear forces is essentially negative and that they are consequently of declining relevance to specific diplomatic issues. For some it is a short step to regard the detailed design of deterrent forces as of little further interest, so long as they preserve a minimal state of mutual assured destruction.

This is not the place to pursue the debate about the future of strategic nuclear forces. Even if the purely self-sterilizing function is the only one they perform, the forces are not, of course, devoid of utility, for no-one has yet found a alternative basis for the stalemate that underlies the whole structure of super-power relations. But if we cannot pursue it in detail, we must at least recognize that a debate still exists as to whether some nuclear postures may not be better than others. It is too early to dismiss altogether, for example, the merits of seeking superiority or, at least, an absence of inferiority. This problem is implied in President Nixon's much quoted four criteria of deterrence, with

their rather cryptic insistence on being able to wreak no less (not merely 'adequate') destruction on the Soviet Union than the latter can inflict on the United States. What presumably underlies this principle, and equally President Nixon's worry expressed elsewhere about being left with only suicidal responses to a major strategic challenge, is a continued conception of intra-war deterrence and of effective use of strategic postures to bargain in crisis. Closely related to this notion is the problem of whether vulnerability is really a policy psychologically acceptable for the long run and whether, as a consequence, methods of strategic defence may not yet come to play a part in super-power arsenals.

Safety under mutual vulnerability depends uncomfortably on assumptions of rationality on both sides. Even within what might be regarded as rational conduct, the outcome of mutual deterrence may depend on perceptions of risk and interest which are sensitive to changes in political situation and national leadership. The possible volatility of Soviet and Chinese leadership is obvious and recent scandalous upheavals in Washington have done little to reassure critics of American decision-making processes. Nuclear multipolarity adds another complication and the sum total is a world in which one can yet imagine high levels of strategic armament rather than low, or force postures including a substantial defensive rather than purely offensive component, appearing a useful hedge against political and technological surprise.

III

The point of rehearsing these familiar arguments is simply to emphasize that even if super-power strategic nuclear forces are regarded as doing no more than inhibit each other and preserve their owners from direct attack, they have not become irrelevancies that can safely be left to ossify. In practice, of course, nuclear forces are not regarded as purely negative elements and assiduous efforts are made to extend their deterrent utility over a wide range of interests. It is true that so long as the super-powers are content with being immune from direct attack, foreign territory has lost most of its strategic significance. But nations, certainly great ones, commonly have a more extensive conception of self, just as most of us would regard living as more than not being dead. This, then, is what

Nombre de Dios to Panama ... he told me 10,000 men would easily conquer all the Spanish Indies, they were so secure.' *The Diary of John Evelyn* (London: Dent (Everyman's Library), 1952), vol. 2, p. 97.

underlies the notion of seeking to preserve a 'compatible' world in both cultural and economic terms. Moreover, while foreign military bases may have lost their relevance to the core of super-power safety, the extension of a hostile hegemony may nevertheless affect security by allowing opposing ambition to feed on itself.

It is very true that there is much less confidence today in military methods of preserving access to a compatible world. On the other hand, the danger in Europe, which is still the central American concern overseas, is conceived chiefly in military terms. The overhanging presence of the Soviet Union which gives rise to the fear of finlandization is almost entirely related to Soviet military power. Certainly it is not due to Soviet economic or cultural pre-eminence; these are the areas in which the Soviet Union is on the defensive. Moreover, by all the signs, the Soviet Union is thoroughly convinced of the value of her own local military predominance, particularly to discipline her Eastern European glacis, which is itself in large part a military conception. In maintaining this policy the Soviety Union may, of course, be behaving anachronistically, but by doing so she arouses an inevitable Hobbesian anxiety in neighbours. Here is a reminder that even were military force to decline as an instrument of foreign policy, the considerable domestic security requirements of large states would perpetuate a military capability that neighbours could never wholly discount. Some of what the British government has called, in quite another context, a 'general capability' for military action is inherent in remaining a state. When the state seeks to discipline neighbours under a conception like the Brezhnev (or Monroe?) doctrine, the effect is considerably magnified.

In Europe today one can see many hints of the kind of deference military preponderance buys the Soviet Union. There is not only the double standard applied by much of Scandinavian opinion to East–West behaviour and the nervousness of some NATO members about the possible provocative effects of military exercises, but also the tendency to approach questions of East–West trade, and even the new European arms control and security negotiations, with a certain readiness to accept the worse end of a bargain in order to placate a Soviet Union that might otherwise rattle her sword.

By common consent some array of Western countervailing military force is necessary to preserve for the Western Europeans that minimum freedom of action that constitutes independence. Having long abandoned the idea of matching Soviet power level for level, the essence of European defence (which applies to Japan too) is to mark Western Europe off as an American sphere of influence. In this way Europe profits from the shadow of the American deterrent. So far, however, the maintenance of a capability for local defence has seemed the most effective way to mark out the sphere of influence. The forces deployed by the Western coalition serve a variety of interrelated purposes. They put the Soviet Union on notice that aggression will meet at least a modicum of violent response and thus they attempt to arouse all the inhibitions against acts of war today. The American presence assures the involvement of the United States in crisis management from the start; and this does something to affect the degree of super-power *interest* in disputed issues that is probably the main determinant of success in confrontation between nuclear super-powers whose ultimate military *capability* is unlimited. The Europeans' own contribution buys them a degree of self-respect and a certain access, if limited, to American planning and decision-making. It also gives them some standing in such super-power military dealings as affect European interests.

There has been considerable speculation as to whether these mechanisms, which are the germ of realism in the flexible response, could not be supplanted by more civilized linkages. On the one hand, American economic involvement in Europe might be regarded as sufficient earnest of commitment, as the full-scale economic integration of Western Europe itself may be reducing the credibility of picking off the Europeans one by one. On the other hand, it is sometimes said that as the essential military forces are American, the European contribution might be more and more by way of economic concessions and direct subsidy to the United States. This would complement the belief that generous commercial relations with the Soviet Union give her a vested interest in not being aggressive.

Broad American hints that continued military support may be dependent on accommodating European commercial and monetary policies certainly remind us that economic relations are of increasing importance, and can play a part in security relationships. But these hints are not, of course, inviting the substitution of European economic for military efforts. There are several reasons for believing that any attempt to do that would be unwise. These reasons include: a complete absence of any evidence that either American diplomacy or actual American military action has been at all closely correlated with economic stakes in the past; the difficult psychological implications of mercenary status for both payer and payee; the bearing of these implications on the element of 'bring our boys back home' which plays a part in the movement to withdraw American troops from Europe, even though the economic arguments are more commonly stressed; and the inability of an economic contribution to provide Europe with its own military option in the future.

Military force thus retains a very plausible utility when deployed for the security of the lesser Western powers. Of course, it need not be deployed exactly as it is at present. Its essential function is to actuate all the inhibitory deterrent influences inherent in the present international configuration of power. There is no reason in principle why this should be incompatible with agreed force reductions. Even considering Western military dispositions in isolation, it is possible that the doctrine of flexible response harks back too much to the age of conventional warfare and tries too hard to simulate World War Two. Admittedly there is a great dilemma between containing any outbreak of hostilities that arises from the unintended course of events, and deterring anyone contemplating deliberate aggression. For the latter purpose one should perhaps try not so much to help the enemy limit the consequences of his actions, as to force him to ponder the outrageousness of what he contemplates. This perspective might suggest reconsidering the balance between such elements of defence as speed of reaction and staying power, conventional and tactical nuclear response, national deployment and functional specialization. The coming restraints on resources will inevitably require a good deal of such reconsideration.

Any discussion of the role of force in preserving the security of the leading allies of America must contain at least a paragraph or two on the lesser nuclear forces. Despite all the counter-arguments, the case for preserving and extending the nuclear options in European hands remains formidable and in the course of time it may well appear more compelling for Japan, which is, however, at least spared direct contiguity with a super-power. For reasons of space and not of unimportance, the main arguments are merely listed here. There is the belief that multiple centres of decision complicate the calculations of would-be aggressors or 'blackmailers'. There is the danger that ultimately the American guarantee must prove infirm under mutual vulnerability; this, it is said, requires at least a European option on the future. There is the prospect of more genuine multi-polarity and perhaps of wider proliferation, so that lesser nuclear forces may perform deterrent functions outside the bipolar alignment. There is the hoary old idea of access to the Top Table of strategic discussions. After the Strategic Arms Limitation Talks (SALT) no-one will be inclined to exaggerate the last notion. Nevertheless, the lesser nuclear powers, if not a party to SALT, have been a factor in the talks and will become increasingly so if their purview widens. Would the Europeans have received even as much consultations as they did if none of their number had some ability to rock the boat, be it ever so slightly?

It will be said that the European forces are too insignificant to carry weight. But the advocates of strategic arms limitation cannot have it both ways. Such restrictions as the super-powers place on themselves make the technological tasks of the lesser somewhat more manageable. More to the point, as the super-powers testify to their dread of nuclear war and assign their nuclear weapons increasingly to mere mutual deterrence, they both erode their credibility as nuclear guarantors and suggest that anyone who can pose a limited nuclear threat should compel respect. The less one is content with mechanistic analysis of complex strike plans, and the more one accepts that deterrence works largely by the permeation of diplomatic situations by a rather crude but politically powerful sense of risk, the better appears the case for being in the nuclear business if you can afford it. A special argument for this will arise if the United States tries to retain a tactical nuclear element in the escalatory mechanisms of Europe, while progressively decoupling her strategic force from all but deterrence of attack on American territory.

IV

The above topics require discussion, for it is in these realms that the Western powers testify to their belief in the continued utility of force by spending most of their military budgets. But Europe and Japan nevertheless seem fairly safe from aggression over a wide range of military postures because the deterrent vested interests of the powers are so high. This is not the case in the so-called Third World.

Since 1945 the Western powers have spent a great deal of money and conducted most of their active military operations in Afro-Asia, trying to project their influence and exclude that of others. This process began in the rear-guard action of European colonialism, and was continued by American efforts at containment. Western motives can be summarized as:

(a) a desire for access, here not so much in terms of cultural 'compatibility' as of access to materials and markets. This was thought to require a degree of order, stability and regimes friendly to the West;
(b) the hegemonial rivalry with the Soviet Union and/or China gave a value to denying them access and synthesized all the local issues by the fear of a domino effect in which Communist successes would feed on each other. The two motives obviously intertwined.

Western enthusiasm for this game has somewhat diminished. The colonial rearguard action has been fought out with dubious advantages for those who sought to delay change. The United States, which took up the torch, burned her fingers several times and in Vietnam has just beaten a hasty retreat from the fire. More fundamentally, the disillusionment reflects a sharp reassessment of both the costs and the advantages of military force as a tool of policy in the Third World.

On the cost side, local forces have greatly increased their capacity for action, both by the perfection of guerrilla techniques and by the acquisition both as states and insurgents of modern military equipment, much of which, with packaged maintenance, suits them surprisingly well. Moreover, as the price of intervention has risen, declining faith in both the utility and the acceptability of force have fed on each other. So far as the benefits of intervention are concerned, the decline in enthusiasm has been related to a complex argument which can only be summarized here. First, the decline in the hegemonial quarrel between 'East and West' and the Sino-Soviet split have deprived the Soviet Union and China of any certain expectation of profiting from local situations and raised Western hopes that the Communist powers will pay a price in good behaviour for the sake of the global balance, The West's own experience and the Soviet record in the Third World have aroused greater confidence that Communist penetrations will have a high propensity for self-sterilization. Secondly, the assets of the Third World seem somewhat less essential as the West observes the profitably incestuous nature of trade among the developed countries. Thirdly, greater faith is now placed in non-military methods of preserving access. In part, this is a more sensitive conception of the Third World's own interests – 'they can't drink the oil' – and in part a belief that the inevitable pluralism of the Third World will facilitate the erection of local balances and thwart any would-be hostile hegemony, indigenous or external. For all these reasons and others, including simple disgust and boredom, we have recently seen a precipitate withdrawal from Afro-Asia. This has been most marked in the main practitioners of intervention, Britain and the United States, and the theory and even language of the Nixon Doctrine is remarkably reminiscent of the British flight from East-of-Suez.

It is far from easy to prophesy what policy the Western powers will adopt toward military action in the Third World after what might be called the era of competitive meddling. One option is for the great powers to let the Third World stew in its own juice. Another, the germ of which can sometimes be seen, would be for the superpowers to police spheres of interest. There is room to doubt, however, whether the Communist powers could really resist the temptation to intervene or whether the West – which must mean chiefly the United States? – could successfully define a sphere of interest without a military presence or at least a capacity to project one. One danger that comes to mind is what one might call the 'Korean illusion' recalling the way in which an apparent but false American lack of interest encouraged Communist aggression and a consequent East–West collision.

Doubts about a policy of mutual abstention are increased, of course, by the rising use of military, particularly naval, forces by the Soviet Union to pursue her interests in the Third World. As the West has often found, a military option can become something of a compulsion and it is therefore not impossible that Soviet forces will become a more active instrument of Soviet policy, extending, perhaps, even to direct military intervention in local crises. Moreover there will inevitably be a great deal of local strife and a high level of local armed force. These forces, whether spontaneously or as the proxy of other powers, might create situations affecting Western interests. Of these the two most popularly mentioned are oil supplies and the security of sea-routes. The so-called energy crisis ensures that oil is one Third World asset access to which cannot be lightly dismissed. Arabs may not drink oil but their revenues are already so high they may decide to sit on it or interrupt its flow.

What answer the Western powers will find for these conceivable but not inevitable problems remains to be seen. It may not, of course, be the best answer. Many writers have argued the powerful reasons for not expecting a wrecking policy on the part of either the Communist or Third World powers. Any Western policy will be cautious for some years to come. The preferred solution would probably be mutual abstention of the great powers and the West will doubtless use all the leverage it can derive from the global diplomatic balance and its local economic and political influence to avoid military action. Nevertheless, theory as well as experience suggests that sometimes the violent card is a powerful one to play, and all the more so if there is no countervailing capability. This can be seen in many superficially dissimilar cases: the Icelandic gunboats and the New Zealand frigate off Mururoa would have had a quite different significance had they not the latent (not always latent in Icelandic waters) power to use force. The entry of Soviet naval forces into Middle Eastern and Indian Ocean waters is said to have inhibited Western options. Presumably the inhibitions are reciprocal and to abandon a military role altogether would confer on the Soviet forces precisely the monopoly the West once enjoyed.

Insofar as such considerations impel any of the Western powers to sustain a military presence in the Third World – both British and American policy contain a pledge to do this at present – we may expect it to act as indirectly as possible. Supplies rather than troops, proxies rather than self, professionals rather than conscripts, are likely to be the preferred style. For many purposes direct intervention would be counter-productive abroad and politically unacceptable at home.

There are, however, still instances in recent history where intervention is widely considered to have been constructive – the confrontation between Malaysia and Indonesia for example – and not until the later stages of the Vietnam War was a consensus achieved against military action. Blazing in with guns and *Phantoms* is unlikely to recommend itself as a way to get oil. But where Western military forces can find a local balance to influence and some local client to stiffen and support, the answer might well be different. The most powerful combination to overcome Western inhibitions would be one in which a material Western interest such as oil or maritime security could be coupled to the aid of a plausible local victim of aggression. Moreover American policy in the recent Middle Eastern war has reminded us their interests cannot be calculated in a narrowly materialistic way. All in all, it is too soon to say that Western military force has lost its use or its utility even in the Third World.

V

A general conclusion must recognize that the two fundamental sources of doubt about the continued utility of military force are the nuclear stalemate and the pre-eminence of economic, welfare-oriented goals. Along with these go far-reaching changes in public attitudes in the West and the perhaps more transient chastening lessons from some recent Western military experiences. The pre-eminence of economic goals, however, does not eliminate the possibility of conflict by error or the emergence of leaders having other purposes or who are simply irrational. Equally, the strategic nuclear balance provides only an uneasy security, it is not to be maintained without effort and cannot be effective over a wide range of issues without some complementary military structure. Something akin to the military balance sought in Europe thus retains its utility and there is a much more tentative case for not wholly abandoning more distant military capabilities, at least on a minimal scale. Indeed, so long as the other purposes are pursued, it would be difficult for the Western powers to divest themselves of all capability for intervention, though they need not, of course, exercise it. But if military force remains useful, it will generally be much inhibited at all levels and will exercise its influence typically in latent ways. These ways may be more difficult to analyse than older, more overt forms of military activity. They may, however, be even more pervasive in world politics, because their manifestations are more subtle and the ultimate stakes are higher. The probability of major war may have declined, but one instance will be enough to endanger the whole system.

Because military force may be most effective when merely latent and because it must now be more intimately orchestrated than ever before with the whole range of foreign policy instruments, it is more difficult for the armed services to explain their role. Feeling perhaps that it is difficult to sell themselves as general insurance against the unlikely and the unpredictable, they tend to cling to outdated scenarios which the public instinctively greets with scepticism. Not the least difficult or important task of Western governments is therefore that of preserving in times of complacency the capabilities to which the public will turn for reassurance at moments of crisis.

Committee Discussions on the Utility of Military Force in Modern Societies: Report to the Conference

IAN SMART

The three committees in Stream A were called upon to consider the utility of military forces for two great nations – Japan and the Soviet Union – and for one vital function – the maintenance of internal order.

As the discussion proceeded in all three committees, the contrasts between these issues became more apparent than did the connections between them. Far from a pattern of satisfying coherence, what emerged was an incoherent fecundity of views about the relevance of different military forces which did much to justify General Farrar-Hockley's quotation of Solon, on being asked to state the best form of government for men. 'For whom', he replied, 'and in what circumstances?' Certainly, no agreement was reached on generally applicable criteria by which the utility of any military force may always be judged. Instead, the tacitly shared conviction was evidently that the utility which nations – and even individuals – will ascribe to the military arm must depend upon their particular domestic or international situations, and even more upon the expectations which they have derived from their separate cultural and ideological histories. Thus, at every turn of the discussion, it was the idiosyncracies, rather than the consistencies or the paradigms which multiplied.

Japan, indeed, has been offered by some as a paradigm: a paradigm of the economically potent nation which aspires to pursue the currently advertized goal – whether distant oasis or mirage – of uniquely 'civilian' power. Despite (or perhaps because) of its argued vulnerability to direct assault and its undoubted vulnerability to indirect strangulation through the interruption of external trade, Japan is allegedly intent upon that alchemist's 'grand experiment': the transmutation of great economic into great political power without the use of any military catalyst. All

recognize the difficulties of the journey to that goal, not the least of which is the lack of any map. At the same time, all are bound to acknowledge the impressive failures of others to challenge Japan with any set of countervailing arguments which emerge from reason rather than intuition. The Japanese experiment may fail. And, even if it succeeds, it may prove to have no application to other states in other situations. It has been made apparent, however, that Japan's choice will be based not only upon ethical or idealistic grounds – nor upon a mere naïveté. 'To those who are good to me', said one Chinese philosopher, 'I am good. And to those who are not good to me, I am also good. And thus all men get to be good'. So the Japanese may hope, as they renounced military status. But they might – and do – add that the available alternative options in any case lack obvious attraction. To defend Japan's maritime trade or foreign investments against a major and co-ordinated onslaught is a task which might well defeat armed forces ten times the size of the far from insubstantial military strength which Japan, largely at American behest, already maintains. Yet to move even a fraction of the way towards the construction of such vast military strength might be exactly calculated to provoke those fears and hostilities elsewhere in Asia which would enforce the further elaboration, or even the use, of that strength.

The option of reinforcement can be held open, perhaps, and the present Japanese Self-Defence Forces constitute a potential cadre on which much greater strength, whether only conventional or nuclear as well, might be founded. Greater pressures to take up that option of reinforcement are possible in the future: if conflict over resources should erupt in the China Sea, if the United States should turn her back, if the Soviet Union, which Japan fears, should become more imminent, or if China, which is imminent, should come to be more feared. Meanwhile, Japan, with a historically-founded psychological diffidence which overshadows her material vulnerability, and with no current examples of the translation of military strength into political power which she finds persuasive, looks to protect her great economic interests through diplomacy, through import diversification and through the avoidance of entanglement in the affairs of others. 'And thus all men get to be good'. As to the parallels between Japan's prospects and those of other highly developed countries, their frailty has, on the whole, been seen during the discussion as so great that all which has clearly survived is the conviction that West European states such as Germany must like Japan count any radical change in the present security situation, with its vital element of American guarantees, as a change for the worse.

There remains, therefore, a most uncomfortable sense of uncertainty, with rational arguments against the construction of much greater Japanese military strength standing beside intuitive expectations that such reinforcement will, after all, prove necessary. Are we sure that intuition will prove a better guide than reason to the future? Or is it that this intuition concerning the ineluctable utility of military forces for a 'great' power is itself founded not upon the greater wisdom of others, in Western Europe or North America, but upon their unconscious assumption of a general convention on the point in international affairs? Military strength commensurate, by historical measure, with economic wealth and with political aspirations may seem to them to be a part of some natural law. And so, of course, it may be. Yet the contention that it is may also be akin to the defensive irritation with which some in the more narrowly Western world might regard a neighbour who ostentatiously rebuffs the insurance salesman shortly after they have themselves paid out another heavy premium. If Japan should succeed in her 'grand experiment', she may be felt to stand not only as an example to others but also as a reproof.

Of those powers least likely to follow a Japanese example of 'civilian' power, should it in fact be offered, the Soviet Union has unanimously been identified as one. The contrast is ostensibly extreme. With an empire to guard in Eastern Europe, with another super-power to match and with China perceived as both physically and ideologically malevolent at the eastern gates, the Soviet Union has no lack of easy justification for great military strength. And even were their superficial reasons less obvious, it would be widely accepted that Soviet leaders would persist in ascribing a high utility to the maintenance of equally large military forces. They form, it has been said, an integral part of a composite foreign policy mechanism: protecting both territory and system, providing the ingots from which decisive political influence may be forged and, in any case, proving to all, including herself, the Soviet Union's right to be reckoned as the equal of one and the superior of all other in the world.

No consensus was available in the discussion on the exact balance between design and chance in constructing Soviet military forces or policies. At the same time, no contradiction was offered of the argument that the image of Soviet political power, in the eyes of the leadership in Moscow as in those of others, is closely intertwined with the fact of Soviet military strength. To that extent, military forces were seen to have an undoubted utility for the Soviet Union. Indeed, as the Soviet economy falters, as the Soviet empire murmurs and as the Soviet ideology ages, reliance upon that remaining military pillar of national power may grow. If Western nations and Western societies judge, as that happens, that the utility of their own military forces is progressively less self-evident, the result may be a growing asymmetry of both strength and perception between East and West, especially in Europe, which will be calculated to breed alarm and even, perhaps, excursion from the solidarity of close alliance. Already, after all, the Soviet Government may see the defensive need for a favourable asymmetry of strength in Europe and, in seeking, on that ground, to secure her empire against both external and internal threat, may present an apparent threat to Western Europe and a clear obstacle to the mutual reduction of forces towards any new symmetry. If West European states then perceive Soviet military strength as a ground for their own political conformity to Soviet desires, can the Soviet Government be expected to contradict them?

And yet, how solidly is the military pillar connected to the edifice of international political power, even for the Soviet Union? Some have argued that the junction is well-made: that the Soviet Union, armed with a set of co-ordinated policies clustered around a coherent idology, is peculiarly equipped to translate her military strength into usable political power. From that argument has arisen the contention that the Soviet political aim is now to secure wide international agreement to ostensibly truistic statements of general principles, in order that military preponderance may thereafter be used to obtain the specific interpretation of those principles in ways directly favourable to the Soviet interest. Yet it has also been judged that the Soviet Union will wish to avoid actual combat in any cause short of the survival of her own state and system. Moreover, although the Soviet Union retains more characteristics of a monolithic state than any country in the West, her government cannot be entirely insensitive to the pressures for non-military resource allocation which exist within her society, the repulsion of which may affect not only national morale but also international standing as a technically and economically advanced nation. And, perhaps above all, the Soviet Government has chosen to commit herself openly and increasingly to a policy of judicious political and economic accommodation with the developed market-economy countries, and especially with the United States.

All of those factors serve to constrain Soviet ability to convert freely between the military and the political currencies of power. If the Soviet Union has always chosen, on one level, to stand alone in the world, she has now also chosen, on other levels, to join a wider trans-ideological community to a slowly but steadily growing extent. That choice is not without a price in terms of freedom of action, including the freedom to impose political policies on others outside the Soviet empire by military means. The Soviet Union is not immune to such constraint. Nor does Marxist-Leninist doctrine contain any attempt to show how King Canute might have succeeded in turning back the tide; instead, it provides a list of reasons for his inevitable failure. It has not been, and it cannot, I think, be argued that the Soviet Union will rapidly devalue the perceived utility of her military

forces. In that respect, the contrast with Japan is clear, and possibly revealing: in one case, no generally accepted rational arguments have been advanced for building up military strength from a low level; in the other case, no decisive rational arguments have been advanced for cutting it down from a very high one. Yet both countries seek political power on the international level – and both may face greater difficulty than some have assumed in finding that elixir which would convert military strength to that positive end, as distinct from the end of negative deterrence which the forces of each more clearly served. In the final analysis, the positive international influence of each – and, with it, the external political utility of military strength – may prove to be, like Keatsian beauty, in the eye of the beholder. In other words, it will not be they themselves but the remaining countries of the world which will decide how much international weight should be attached to the relative military strength of the Soviet Union and to the relative military weakness of Japan. In many important respects, the difference between the degrees of political and economic influence thus accorded seems likely to be somewhat less than the order of magnitude which separates the sizes of their military establishments, or the two orders of magnitude which separate their respective military budgets.

In turning inwards from external influence to domestic order, echoes of the Soviet-Japanese contrast have persisted in the discussion. In one case, little hesitation has been evident during the last 50 years in using military units to enforce order within either the nation itself or its satellite territories. In the other, the very idea of using regular military forces in such a manner has been dismissed, since 1945, as a political impossibility (despite the specific provision for it in law). That persistent contrast marks the extent of a spectrum of variation which embraces all countries, democratic, developed or otherwise, despite the fact that it is on the developed democracies that the principal attention has here been focused.

The problem of internal disorder itself, whether actual or potential, displays admittedly 'global' features. On the one hand, a relatively small number of determined people is everywhere capable of exhausting the resources of the normal 'daily' police force within a relatively short time. On the other hand, at least in the democracies, there is a general, if varying, reluctance to employ military forces internally except as a final alternative to anarchy. And, when military forces are employed within a democratic state, there is a general inclination to confine their involvement to the shortest possible period and their role to the containment of violence in order that others may seek a political resolution of the conflict.

Where the differences occur is, above all, in the attitude to the use of *regular* military units, as opposed to units of specially trained and equipped policemen. The employment of the army itself in the restoration of internal order has been described as an Anglo-Saxon quirk, variously attributed either to specific considerations, such as the tradition of unarmed police and the habit of military action within colonial territories, or simply to the general and well known idiosyncrasy of Anglo-Saxons. Other races employ specially-constituted, para-military police formations: the CRS in France, the Riot Police in Japan, the *Celeri* in Italy, the *Policia Armada* in Spain or the new units of the *Bundesgrenzschutz* (BGS) in West Germany. The argument over respective merit has raged back and forth. Its only clear outcome has been a renewed demonstration of the extent to which, internally as externally, the utility ascribed to military forces varies less with objective circumstances than with the subjective prejudices which constitute the crowning glory of every community's cultural history. The depth of the feelings which attend national preferences concerning the exact institutional identity of the hand which fires the rubber bullet or throws the tear gas canister is as impressive as it is, presumably, ennobling. The British, we have been told, would not tolerate a para-military police force. The Japanese would not tolerate a regular army trained or deployed for internal security. The typical views of a Frenchman employed by a Japanese firm in Northern Ireland have not been explored. Patently, however, the utility of military forces in this context is to be measured, above all, in terms of criteria which reflect the same sort of international variation as the criteria applied to their external utility.

That, indeed, is the message which has emerged most clearly from the whole discussion: that

there is no single currency in terms of which the value of any component of military strength may be stated to universal satisfaction. In the first place, utility may not be measured in the abstract, 'For whom,' asked Solon, 'and in what circumstances?' Utility for what purpose? In relation to which adversary? On whose behalf? In the second place, the measurement of utility, given the lack of any objective and universal scale, must always be at least dual. The utilities ascribed to a particular force by its commanders, on the one hand, and their potential adversaries, on the other, will notoriously be different – whether the dichotomy is international or domestic. In the third place, there is a visible tendency to attach a special increment of utility to that type or size of force which actually exists. Japan finds a high utility in a force which bears no proportional relation to that level of force with which the Soviet Union is uniquely content. In the fourth and final place, cultural, historical and psychological predilection plays a greater part than any universal logic in determining the utility of particular forces.

Here, it may be said, the developed Western countries face a particular difficulty. If the tendency is indeed, as many have suggested, for Western societies to find progressively diminishing utility in military forces, there is likely to be no universal law of valuation by invoking which that tendency can be checked. Moreover, if there is, as some have suggested, an additional tendency for Western *societies* to adopt systems of valuation in this and other fields which diverge increasingly from the systems employed by Western *governments*, as the embodiments of the state, that problem will be compounded. That implies a danger for the West which may be more serious, in present circumstances, than any danger that the Soviet Union will indeed convert her military strength into effective political power. If Western governments believe that some level of military capability is an essential precondition of confident political negotiation with the East, and if their societies increasingly decline to acknowledge the utility of such a level of strength, the result may be an unwillingness on the part of governments to take what they see as the greater risks then involved in flexible negotiation. The discussion in Stream A has considered the physical utility of military forces within their own borders and both their physical and political utility beyond those borders. If there is one question left more open than others, it is exactly that which concerns the *political* utility of military forces within a domestic context – and especially their utility as sources of that political self-confidence without which nations will not feel able to explore prudent modifications of the international environment. Despite the dangers of internal violence or external threat of which we are all conscious, it may, in fact, be that last utility of military forces – as a condition of self-confidence in negotiation – which will have the greatest importance in an era of political manoeuvre between East and West. Men, in desperation, have gone naked on to the battlefield or towards the barricades, but they have not commonly gone unclothed into the halls of diplomatic conference – in Helsinki, in Vienna, in Geneva or in New York.

ADELPHI PAPERS

NUMBER ONE HUNDRED AND THREE

Force in Modern Societies:
The Military Profession

THE INTERNATIONAL INSTITUTE FOR STRATEGIC STUDIES
18 ADAM STREET LONDON WC2N 6AL

ADELPHI PAPER NO. 103

The papers printed in this Adelphi Paper and in Adelphi Paper No. 102 were given at the Fifteenth Annual Conference of the IISS at Travemünde, Federal Republic of Germany, in September 1973.

Additional copies of this Paper may be ordered from the Institute at a cost of 35p ($1) each, post free.

First published Winter 1973

CONTENTS

The International Institute for Strategic Studies was founded in 1958 as a centre for the provision of information on and research into the problems of international security, defence and arms control in the nuclear age. It is international in its Council and staff and in its membership, which is drawn from over fifty countries. It is independent of governments and is not the advocate of any particular interest.

The Institute is concerned with strategic questions – not just with the military aspects of security but with the social and economic sources and political and moral implications of the use and existence of armed force: in other words with the basic problems of peace.

The Institute's publications are intended for a much wider audience than its own membership and are available to the general public on special subscription terms or singly.

© The International Institute for Strategic Studies 1973

Printed by Adlard and Son Ltd, Bartholomew Press, Dorking, Surrey

FOREWORD

The Fifteenth Annual Conference of the International Institute for Strategic Studies was held from 13–16 September 1973 at the Maritim Hotel, Travemünde, in the Federal German Republic. It was the second time the Annual Conference had been held in Germany, the last occasion being in 1962, when the venue was Bad Godesberg. As in recent years, the discussion was organized around a single theme, which was 'The Future of Military Forces in Modern Societies'.

'Modern Societies' for the purposes of the Conference referred to the industrial powers. It is plain that in the so-called Third World military power still has a role which is relatively traditional, at least in terms of inter-state conflicts. But in the advanced industrial world it seems to be losing that place in affairs. In part this is due to technological developments such as nuclear weapons and strategic parity between the super-powers. But in part it is also related to the changed acceptability of the use of military force to advanced industrial societies themselves. This raises many questions: Are the changes temporary or permanent? To whom do they apply and if so how may they affect the world balance, world politics and the international system? Can military forces adequate to state purposes be maintained? What type of forces are required and how may they perceive their place in society and be educated to their role? These and many other questions have been impinging more and more insistently on policy-makers and analysts of security problems. They tend to divide into two kinds of overriding issues: first, the role of military force in international politics today and in the future; second, the future of the military profession in advanced industrial societies. These were the two themes of the Conference.

Some 210 members of the IISS attended the Conference and in addition to a presentation by Herr Helmut Schmidt, the German Minister of Finance and former Minister of Defence, on the Balance of Power, nine expert papers were prepared either as reports to the Plenary Sessions or as texts for Committee discussion. The main presentations in Plenary Session were given by Professor Laurence Martin, by Major-General Robert Gard of the US Army and by Professor Stanley Hoffman. The Committee papers were presented by M. Jean Laloy, Mr Morton Halperin, Major-General Farrar-Hockley, Mr Gwyn Harries-Jenkins, General Wolf von Baudissin and Mr Adam Roberts.

The five Committees were divided into two groups. The first, of three Committees, discussed the Utility of Force as exemplified in the case of a super-power, the Soviet Union, that of a major economic power, Japan, and in the maintenance of internal order. The second group, of two Committees, discussed the Military Profession, and in particular the problems of Volunteer Forces, and of Officer Education and Alternatives to Existing Forces. Each Committee had a rapporteur whose reports were collated and summarized by one general rapporteur for each group, that for the Utility of Force being Mr Ian Smart and for the Military Profession Dr Theo Sommer.

It has not proved possible to include all the texts in these two *Adelphi Papers* and it has therefore been decided to devote the first paper to the general presentations of the Future of Military Force in Modern Societies, and the second to the issues relating to the Future of the Military Profession, which are less familiar in IISS publications than those on the Utility of Military Force. The Committee papers dealing with the Utility of Military Force have, therefore, with regret, been excluded.

FRANÇOIS DUCHÊNE

69

The Future of the Military Profession

MAJOR-GENERAL ROBERT G. GARD, JR., US ARMY*

I

It has become conventional wisdom to acknowledge that the advent of the nuclear era has had a revolutionary impact on the military profession. There are, of course, obvious implications for strategic deterrence, super-power confrontation and general war; but the claim seems exaggerated otherwise, particularly in a period of effective nuclear parity between the United States and the Soviet Union, and the growing nuclear capability of China. To a significant degree, these developments have neutralized the utility of nuclear weapons except for their deterrent role. Recent social and political changes appear to have greater implications for the profession of arms in democratic societies.

We know little more today about the functions of power than did Hobbes or Machiavelli, but we think differently about its use. Along with other factors, modern communications in combination with a new emphasis on human values have brought about widespread questioning of the morality of the use of force, especially as it affects non-combatants. The military appears to many as a blunt, insensitive and immoral instrument; to some this not only invalidates the employment of armed force, but it raises questions concerning the legitimacy of military service and even the maintenance of an active military capability in a period of growing belief in the termination of the cold war.

In the minds of relatively large and influential segments of the populations of Western democracies, there also are fundamental doubts concerning the effectiveness of military power in achieving political objectives. This is related not only to the potential destructiveness of general war, but also to the loss of ability of modern nations to exercise relatively easy control of less-developed entities through selective, but potentially unlimited, application of power. In addition to the lack of domestic support for 'colonialism', and concern for the indigenous population, developments have improved significantly the ability of 'Third World' countries to resist. The growth of nationalism and the spread of modern medicine and public health, with the consequent multiplication of youth sufficiently healthy to bear arms, make it possible for an underdeveloped society to stalemate the armed forces of more advanced nation-states. A relatively primitive military force armed with light but modern weapons, often supplied by a third party, can inflict on modern formations a level of casualties unacceptable for sustained involvement, given contemporary Western cultural values. Various combinations of these factors apparently were operative in the cases of the Dutch in Indonesia, the French in Indo-China and Algeria and in the 1956 Suez affair, as well as the more recent conflict in Vietnam.

Changes within modern Western societies, while by no means uniform, have been so rapid and pronounced that the term 'social revolution' often is used to describe the composite effect. Although it may be too soon to identify longer-term trends with certainty, it seems clear that at least for the immediate future the effects will place the style as well as the functions of the military profession under general attack, as mass media spread these views throughout the social structure.

There are deep-seated doubts, especially among youth, concerning the effectiveness of our larger institutions to respond to individual and social needs. Many are disenchanted with what they regard as outmoded practices and insensitive, and even dishonest, officials; and they perceive a wide gap between declaration and performance. This in turn leads not only to a cynicism concerning bureaucracies but also to a tendency to challenge the very concept of authority, especially when it is perceived as arbitrary.

* The views expressed are those of the author, not of the Department of Defense or any other agency of the US Government.

I

70

In the relatively affluent 'post-industrial' societies, particularly in the United States but probably increasingly elsewhere, employment and income are regarded by youth to a much greater extent than ever before as means rather than ends. As larger economic enterprise is well aware, young people are generally hostile to being regarded principally as factors of production. Also, there is a prevalent desire for more privacy and less formality, and for greater personal identity, freedom and opportunity for self-expression.

By no means is this 'anti-establishment' outlook focused exclusively on the military institution; but combined with other anti-military attitudes, both traditional and more recent, it presents a unique challenge to the military profession. Whereas earlier military service was regarded generally as a somewhat disagreeable but necessary and wholesome occupation, its current standing is significantly lower. Many perceive the military not only as reactionary and oppressive but also as a wasteful, unproductive drain of substantial resources better used to meet pressing social problems. It has become popular to criticize the military institution, and those who are members of it, as the personification of what is wrong with society.

Despite these political and social developments, however, the world situation will require modern Western societies to maintain substantial active military capabilities for the foreseeable future. Interdependence in a variety of forms clearly is increasing; but international society has not yet become a community, and force remains the final arbiter in the absence of a general consensus on the means of achieving peaceful change. World politics is becoming in some ways more dangerous and certainly more complex. Along with greater equality between the two superpowers, greater disparity is developing among nations regionally. Also, in an increasingly multipolar world, it is important to recognize that there are differences in forms and amounts of power.

General war appears extremely unlikely in an era of nuclear parity, and the Vietnam experience has reinforced strong inhibitions against unilateral commitment by Western democracies of military force in situations with a high degree of political, economic and social instability. But there remains a wide range in between. It is imprudent either to assume that states will abandon the threat or use of military force, or to ignore the essential relationship between military capability and international politics in an era of negotiation.

It is apparent that the Soviet Union is enhancing her already substantial capability to project her sea and land power globally, and that recent increases in Soviet strength in Central Europe provide significantly more than enough military capability in amount and kind for continued domination of Warsaw Pact countries, or defence against NATO forces. The principal issue is not the current likelihood of aggression, but rather the need during periods of crisis for a military posture adequate to deter by confronting an opponent with risks he is unwilling to incur. Disregarding this requirement could undermine the very basis for optimism concerning *détente*, for moderation may be a product of deterrence, and intentions may be born of opportunity.

Concerning strategic forces, there is little dispute about the need, at the least, for retaliatory capability that is survivable and adequate to ensure unacceptable destruction of potential enemies after absorbing a surprise attack. There is less agreement, however, on the strategic forces that are needed to preclude the Soviet Union from perceiving such a sense of superiority as might encourage attempts to coerce the United States or her allies. But even more controversial is the requirement for general-purpose forces. It has become popular to discredit the validity of conventional deterrence because the concept evolved as the handmaiden of a containment policy now considered to be outdated.

Yet international relationships are increasingly important for the survival of nation-states, and world security in general depends upon a reasonably orderly and peaceful environment. Beyond the need to deter direct attacks on the United States and her allies, it remains essential to prevent a major hostile power obtaining by military aggression exclusive domination over areas vital to our national interests. This requires what Samuel Huntington recently called a 'counter-intervention' capability.[1] To perform this task, credible counter-forces must be

[1] Samuel P. Huntington, 'After Containment: The Functions of the Military Establishment', *The Annals of the American Academy of Political and Social Science*, March 1973.

maintained in addition to those committed to the NATO defence. Assurance to allies, as well as deterrence of potential enemies, requires that such forces must be capable of controlled response to meet threats on the level posed in order to permit a conventional defence at least for enough time to indicate resolve, and to produce a substantial pause without resort to nuclear weapons. In discussing the need for local military equilibrium, Professor Shulman reluctantly concluded: 'If we wish to move toward a world in which force does not dominate politics, we cannot escape the painful conclusion that a balance of conventional forces is needed.'[2]

II

The fundamental task of the military profession has not changed. In general terms, that task is to provide the nation with a trained armed force, skilled in applying military resources in support of national policy. But now, and for the foreseeable future, it is essential that members of the military profession develop a greater appreciation of the relationship between means and objectives. In the nuclear era, deterrence of military aggression is a more important objective than ever before; and if deterrence fails, the conduct of military operations calls for containing outbreaks of violence and controlling, not exploiting, force.

Although the generalization may not apply to the same degree to the armed forces of nations with a history of extensive colonial involvement, or to those with experience in peace-keeping functions, until recently the expertise of the military profession was focused principally on preparations for, and the conduct of, combat operations, to include the administrative and logistic functions required for support. The criterion, although never easy, was simple: destruction of the enemy's capacity to resist, in the shortest possible time with the fewest possible friendly casualties. There was a more or less well understood division of labour between civilian authority, responsible for politics and diplomacy, and the military professional who fought wars with minimal interference from his political superiors. But events following World War II forced an intertwining of what had formerly been

essentially separate military and civilian functions. Conceived in the early cold-war period, and born during the Korean conflict, a concept of national security policy and strategy replaced the less complicated arrangements for national defence. There was a new requirement in both peace and war to orchestrate the military with other instruments of statecraft.

It is essential that the military professional appreciate the implications of Clausewitz' admonitions that war is a continuation of politics, not a substitute for it, and that war has its own grammar, but not its own logic. Yet, it must be emphasized that the grammar of war continues to be the conduct of combat operations. The 'management of violence' in inter-state relations is the uniquely military function that is central to the concept of the military profession. Ensuring proficiency in this skill, therefore, remains a primary obligation of the military profession to the society it serves. Nor has this mission changed in the nuclear era, with its required emphasis on deterrence and control of combat operations, although it has become more difficult. To be credible, a deterrent force must be capable of performing the military task for which it is designed; and in the current international configuration, it must be ready for immediate employment. Developing a flexible, responsive and effective combat-capability calls for extensive and precise training that remains a continuing challenge to the military professional.

But it is more important than ever before to ensure that armed conflict does not create its own logic. The battlefield has lost its virtual autonomy. The traditional concept of military victory must be redefined as the achievement of a satisfactory political outcome. This significant change must be fully understood and accepted by military professionals, including those at the lowest tactical level.

Moreover, the demands of national security preclude the military professional from restricting his peacetime activity to preparation for war. No longer can he abstain from, or minimize participation in, policy formulation; nor can he limit himself to traditionally narrow considerations. The military profession cannot escape the requirement to attain high-levels of capability in analytical, technical and managerial skills not considered until recently to be primary military responsibilities. And in applying military re-

---

[2] Marshall D. Shulman, 'What Does Security Mean Today?', *Foreign Affairs*, July 1971, p. 618.

3

sources, the military professional must learn to integrate operations more effectively with political, economic, social and psychological measures. Military force must be employed in a manner consistent with societal values; for in modern democracies, legitimacy of means has become a paramount factor.

Probably the most challenging task of the military profession is ensuring sensitivity and responsiveness to societal change, while retaining values essential to success in combat. At the very time the popularity of the military is at a low ebb, Western societies are increasingly relying on volunteers and reducing terms of conscription, or in some cases eliminating compulsory service altogether. Periods of compulsory service are being cut to the point at which little more than individual training can be accomplished; for example, Denmark and Belgium are requiring only six months. The United States recently embarked on an uncharted course: maintaining both substantial active forces and a sizeable reserve and national guard on a volunteer basis. Some in the US military believe that by simply restoring stability in command positions and re-emphasizing discipline, law and order will be sufficient. But the experience of other Western democracies is instructive; attracting volunteers has proved a most difficult task even without the negative effects of direct involvement in the Vietnam conflict. This is not to imply that essential discipline should be sacrificed for the sake of recruiting, but rather to recognize that the gap between values held by a large percentage of youth in Western democracies, and those essential for effective functioning of military units is probably larger today than ever before.

Vital to combat operations, and therefore essential to the military profession itself, is a set of precepts, often summarized as 'Duty, Honour, Country', which are somewhat different in essence, and certainly in degree, from those held by liberal civilian society. Military organization is hierarchical, not egalitarian, and is more oriented to the group, or unit, than to the individual. The stress is on discipline and obedience, rather than freedom of expression, because military operations often require immediate decision and prompt action, not thorough analysis and extensive debate. The military, therefore, must rely more on training, simplification and predictable behaviour, and less on education,

nuance and empiricism. Until relatively recently, civilian society generally was inclined to tolerate, and even support, the syndrome of corporate values of the military profession as necessary to the combat function. Yet these precepts have come under attack as a result of societal changes and disillusionment with the results of military operations, exacerbated by unpopular conscription and frustration with large military budgets.

Current difficulties in attracting volunteers probably will persist, at least in the short run. Although less serious than with other ranks, there are some problems with officer recruitment. For example, despite innovation within the military institution and additional incentives, Britain has reportedly experienced difficulty in obtaining a sufficient number of qualified volunteers for the officers' academy at Sandhurst. The military academies in the United States once again have more than enough applicants considered to possess adequate leadership potential, but there are fewer now with top-flight college entrance attainment and an increasing number with scores below the minimum usually required by our more prestigious academic institutions. The majority of officers for the US forces are obtained from the college Reserve Officer Training Corps programmes. With the reduction in enrolment, it has been necessary to increase the number of programmes and to offer generous scholarships in return for a commitment to service of a shorter period than required of service academy graduates.

III

The recruitment of young enlistees presents far more difficult problems. Beyond the issues of social prestige and comparatively low pay in some countries, there are related but separate disincentives: living conditions frequently are perceived as unattractive; working hours often are irregular; discipline is relatively stringent and there usually are varying degrees of physical and mental stress. In the current environment, it is likely that the young soldier of middle-class background will disappear from the ranks of the ground combat arms. Early American experience with exclusive dependence on volunteers has produced shortfalls in total ground force enlistments, even with a relaxation of the ceiling on enlistees without a high school education. All military services, but particularly the Army and

Marine Corps, undoubtedly will be required to rely to a significant degree on recruitment of young men from disadvantaged backgrounds, with all the problems this will pose for technical training. A partial solution may lie in the greater use of women in support tasks not involved directly in the combat function. The United States has been able to meet her increased recruiting objectives for women while maintaining the requirement that they have a high-school diploma.

Concurrent with extensive social change and relative affluence there is a new emphasis in modern democratic societies on domestic problems and social justice. Although anti-military sentiments may become increasingly amilitary, substantial increases in resources for armed forces are highly unlikely. With inflation, and more than proportional increases in equipment costs due to racing technological developments, there will be insufficient residual funds to maintain the same strength levels while financing the increased per capita costs necessary to attract and retain volunteers. The choices are difficult, and the premium on efficient management is higher than ever before. Executive and legislative leadership will provide guidance and set the limits, but the willingness of military leadership itself to respond positively and imaginatively to the situation will determine to a significant extent the ability of modern democracies to maintain viable armed forces. Attempting to revert to past practices which may have been adequate for a different situation will be self defeating; but as Basil Liddell Hart cautioned in his *Thoughts on War*, 'The only thing harder than getting a new idea into the military mind is to get an old one out'.

Although probably more prevalent in the US armed forces than in other Western democracies, there developed a tendency during long periods of mass conscription to emphasize institutional objectives, even unimportant ones, with minimum regard for their impact on personnel. To attract sufficient volunteers, military service should be perceived not only as professionally challenging but also as personally rewarding, as a continuation rather than an interruption in one's personal development. While priority must continue to be accorded to organizational effectiveness, greater attention must be given to the effect of practices and procedures on the individual soldier.

The concept of a contract, although unwritten, may be useful in establishing an equitable relationship between what the soldier is expected to give the military institution, and what he or she receives from it. The armed services reasonably can expect from the soldier job-proficiency and disciplined behaviour, while the soldier in return is entitled to respect as a person, work satisfaction and the opportunity for development. There must be a reasonable balance between the institutional requirements of mission and role behaviour on the one hand, and the needs and desires of the individual on the other; these are by no means inconsistent, but they are not necessarily the same.

Careful force planning and programming are necessary to establish the pre-conditions for professionally rewarding peacetime service in units with a mission of combat readiness. There is an inclination to maintain in the active force more combat-type units than can be supported adequately or manned at or near full strength. Also, it must be appreciated that extensive administrative and logistical activities are required to support military installations and units. Excessive economies or the arbitrary reduction of military or civilian manpower result in the detailing of men from tactical units to perform essential functions. Such diversions of personnel – and what is even more damaging, programmed shortages of manpower, equipment and spare parts in units – not only preclude purposeful training relevant to the military mission, but also create the commonly perceived environment of frustration and make-work which discourages enlistments and makes it difficult to retain quality personnel. Those volunteering for military service desire and expect a vigorous and challenging experience and proper utilization in furthering the objectives of the organization. Contrary to frequent allegations, often from within the ranks of the military profession itself, genuine volunteers do not appear to be seeking 'permissiveness' in the sense of toleration of failure to meet established standards; in fact, the evidence is quite the contrary.

Fundamental to maintaining first-line, ready forces is a willingness to reduce force structures to provide the necessary professional environment. The argument is often advanced that it is better to have a larger number of active units, even at lower stages of manning and readiness, which can be filled out in times of emergency. But this ignores the demands of a volunteer force for meaningful and rigorous training opportunities. Also, in addition to the essential capability for immediate employment, a smaller number of more highly-trained units can provide personnel to form additional forces with greater effectiveness than if they had to upgrade the training of entire organizations, to include those in positions of leadership, after filling units maintained at cadre strength.

Equally essential for proper force-structuring in order to create an environment conducive to a rewarding military experience, is the ensuring of highly professional small-unit leaders in both junior officer and non-commissioned officer ranks. This requires not only investment in appropriate education and training, but also a wide latitude for local initiative. Senior leadership, all the way up to the civilian secretariat, must be alert to opportunities to relieve the lower echelons of non-essential harassment and over-supervision, and to provide necessary support and assistance. Such factors, difficult for the subordinate to articulate and easy for the superior to overlook, are important in the career decisions of the brightest and most effective young leaders.

IV

Recent changes have made it difficult to maintain the traditional cohesiveness of the professional officer and non-commissioned officer corps. Revolutionary technology and bureaucratic imperatives have required the development within the uniformed services of a far greater number of specialized skills more comparable with civilian occupations, and not related as directly to the combat function, thereby depreciating the motivating function of the military mystique. Increased contact with civilians has a diluting effect on some of the values which could be relatively easily maintained within a more isolated military community. Strict discipline and the Spartan life become less attractive, and the sense of commitment that engenders an over-riding dedication to duty is eroded in the absence of a more direct sense of responsibility for combat readiness and the lives of one's soldiers. This has increased the traditional tensions within the professional ranks between the tactical and supporting forces, as it has become apparent that modern armed forces require a larger proportion of administrative and technical specialists. It has been suggested that it would be useful to apply different standards to ready combat forces and to the rest of the Army.[3] Whatever one's views on this, the previously accepted tenet that an effective tactical commander inherently possesses the necessary initiative and capability to cope successfully with the full range of assignments is obviously outdated. Career patterns must permit the development of applicable skills, and ensure a reasonable prospect of reaching higher positions of responsibility and rank for those who contribute effectively to functions other than those of troop command.

Leaders in the armed forces of modern democratic societies must understand better the nature of individual, group and institutional behaviour. No longer can primary reliance be placed on authority and command. Positive motivation, job satisfaction and self-discipline are increasingly important for the effective functioning of military units. Leaders at all echelons must be sensitive to the impact on their personnel of policies and procedures. This involves matters such as the elimination of unnecessary sources of dissatisfaction and frustration, or the mitigation of effects of those measures that are required; distinguishing between what is important and what is pressing, then allocating time and other resources between them; and trying to see to it that activities are pointed toward useful ends, rather than being ends in themselves.

The military profession can be made highly challenging to those in positions of leadership; but under current and foreseeable circumstances, the professional rewards of military service alone are unlikely to counter disincentives sufficiently to attract the volunteers necessary for the ranks of a substantial peacetime active or reserve force. Military organizations, therefore, must place increased emphasis on recognizing each soldier as an individual and as the possessor of both immediate and ultimate potential. His legitimate expectations now go beyond minimum physical requirements to higher rungs, than ever before, on the ladder of satisfaction. Placing too great an emphasis on short-term low priority organizational goals and ignoring or short-changing the desire for personal development will preclude attainment of the fundamental long-term, high

---

[3] William L. Hauser, *America's Army in Crisis*. Baltimore: The Johns Hopkins Press, 1973.

priority institutional goal of a viable armed force. The best recruiting device is not the cleverest advertisement in the media, but soldiers who return to their communities with the conviction that they have found in their military service a personally rewarding experience that they can endorse to others.

The nature of many military positions ensures that the serviceman will have an opportunity to learn a skill that he can afterwards use in a civilian occupation. This has proved to be a strong incentive for enlistments in the US Air Force and to a lesser extent the Navy. But there are also many functions, particularly concerning the ground forces, that do not provide this advantage. Even the offer of generous cash bonuses has failed so far to attract a sufficient number of high school graduates into the ground combat arms of the US Army.

Given the likely source of the majority of enlisted recruits for low-skill military occupational specialties, there should be an explicit commitment to provide the opportunity for remedial education and technical training especially for those who volunteer for a long enough term to make such investment worthwhile. According to reports, Britain has found it profitable to permit selected young enlistees to continue their education under military sponsorship, and France has enjoyed considerable success in guaranteeing technical training to volunteers. The US armed forces currently offer general education development and the opportunity to learn a marketable skill before discharge from the service; but the effort is sporadic and subject to local decision. The potential of a more extensive, systematic and integrated programme is evident from the polls and samplings of American soldiers who invariably list the opportunities for education and training as their principal incentive for joining the Army.

Essential to the maintenance of sizeable active forces is the question of re-enlistment. Whatever the initial motivation for entering the armed forces, a satisfying experience should promote organizational commitment and a positive motivation for dedicated service. This should ensure an adequate number who desire to elect military service as a career, while others may prefer to take advantage of an option for a more limited term. Personnel policies must be developed to cope with important questions of tenure.

Cadre organizations, designed to accept fillers in times of emergency, can accommodate a proportionately larger number of higher ranks and therefore provide greater opportunities for a lifetime career for the military professional. But in any event, to prevent stagnation and allow reasonable prospects for promotion, there must be adequate provision for shorter terms of service without discouraging enlistments beyond the minimum period. This requires providing opportunities for a second career. Tying in transition to a civilian governmental position following a certain period of voluntary service in the armed forces, as has been instituted by the Federal Republic of Germany and France, is one example. Similar arrangements could be made with other governmental, or even private, agencies. The point is that military service will be far more attractive to short-term professionals, as well as potential enlistees, when they can be assured of an opportunity to lay the groundwork for continued employment if their services are no longer required, or if they choose not to continue with a military career. Careful and flexible management of such programmes with proper structuring of incentives should be effective in encouraging the necessary spectrum of terms of service.

In the armed forces of relatively affluent democratic societies, wage structures are unlikely to be set high enough to provide the primary incentive for required enlistments or re-enlistments. Nevertheless, adequate financial compensation and living standards are necessary, if not sufficient, conditions to attract volunteers. Military institutions must keep pace with the new emphasis in civilian communities on life-style and human welfare by furnishing a wide variety of personal and community services to care adequately for servicemen and their dependents. A far higher proportion than ever before of those serving in the military are married and therefore expect to be able to provide a decent living for their families.

To summarize, the military profession in modern democratic societies is faced with a set of conditions that make it more difficult than ever before to fulfill its obligations. The nuclear era has not eliminated the traditional mission of combat operations; in fact, in addition to broadening the military mandate, the current and foreseeable international situation places an

7

even greater premium on ready forces which must be more highly skilled in the application of military resources. But at the same time, Western societies have evolved in ways that complicate the ability of the military to accommodate social change with the requirements for effective military forces. The challenge is greater for the army than for the more technically oriented services, the air force and the navy. Within the US Army, limited experience to date in relying on volunteers indicates that the combat arms present the most serious difficulty. Sustained inability to recruit sufficient numbers of qualified personnel could have implications for deterrent strategy, to include forward deployments. It does seem clear that the combined active military forces of Western democracies will be significantly smaller than those of our potential adversaries. Adequate national and collective security will depend upon higher quality to offset superiority in numbers. Military professionals have a major share of the responsibility in ensuring that service in the

armed forces is the sort of rewarding experience which will attract and retain the necessary personnel. But in a democracy, much depends on active participation in the dialogue by the influential public in the clarifying of issues and the prompting of necessary action by executive and legislative leadership.

Despite the difficulties, the military profession has much to offer. War is rarely an ennobling experience, but preparation for it requires the development of diverse and interesting skills along with physical, mental and moral attributes. The current situation provides an opportunity to revitalize the military profession by capitalizing on the positive values of human dignity, subgroup identity and personal and social development held by an increasing proportion of our youth, and by accepting as a constructive challenge their calling institutions of democratic societies to account to fulfill the ideals we long have espoused.

AIR VICE-MARSHALL F. B. SOWREY COMMENTS:

I propose to develop three aspects of this subject. These are: the changes that are occurring in the military profession of their own volition; the prospects of attracting men to join the armed forces in the future; and the way in which armed forces must, in my view, develop if they are to maintain the confidence and support of the social communities that they serve. One difficulty is that the title 'The military profession' is itself a generalization – it embraces the three elements of operating on Land, Sea or Air and the wide spread of executive, leadership and technical functions within each of them.

Spontaneous Changes

The first point to make is that the military profession is not a growth industry in developed societies – although there have been exceptions in Germany and Japan. Over the past 20 years the total armed forces of the United States, Soviet Union, France and Britain have declined from a figure of 2·6 per cent of their population down to a figure of 1·3 per cent. The Armed Services are thus in a state of change and the fact that this is recognized and accepted is at least a major step in the right direction. It is generally accepted that repressive discipline is counterproductive in societies where acceptance of hierarchical patterns of authority is now no longer the norm. One extreme example of this is the appearance amongst some conscript armies of a form of Trades Union. In parallel with this is the fact that money spent on military objectives has virtually stabilized world-wide. Even if it is broadly pegged to a proportion of the Gross National Product, inflationary pressures and the need to improve the quality of

human life have resulted in a rising proportion of defence monies being spent on personnel – their pay, allowances, housing, clothing and the like. In Britain this has increased from under 30 per cent of the Defence Vote 20 years ago to about 50 per cent and a number of countries are around this figure. It can go even higher – notably I gather in Canada. (One wonders how long the Soviet Union can keep hers at the reported rate of 30 per cent.) Part of this, of course, is a measure of the penalty one pays in financial terms for all-regular forces and the need to make the profession financially attractive in comparison with others in society. In addition, there is the rising cost and complexity of equipment, and the pressures of personnel and equipment costs on defence monies is one of the major management problems.

Although the military do not in fact have a profit motive, they are none the less deeply concerned with costs and this is perhaps one of the greatest changes that has occurred. Attitude surveys carried out by D. J. James[1] in the British Services showed that officers have long since ceased to regard themselves as gentlemen retained to be prepared to fight, but tend to see themselves as being individuals engaged by the State to do professional tasks at appropriate rates of pay. The attitudinal and managerial changes that this is beginning to bring about are considerable The modern serving officer is more and more required to have a financial knowledge of what he does – to contribute to the choice between various defence options which may be offered in terms of cost benefit

[1] *The Officer Concept*, D. J. James – A principal psychologist, MOD London. Privately circulated draft.

8

or cost effectiveness. This pre-supposes a knowledge of economics, a familiarity with the tools of modern industrial management in financial terms, and an organization within the Services to enable those with the ability to put this into effect.

The Armed Forces themselves are broadly sensitive to changes occurring in society around them. They are aware that decisions on defence in the future are going to be increasingly complex, because of the complexity of the theology of deterrence, because of the practical military aspects of defence and because of the wider purview required of current military leaders. In political and sociological terms, the increasing world-wide trend towards higher educational standards, particularly at university level, may mean that armed forces are attracting a greater proportion of the well-educated to their ranks. Currently all three British Services are recruiting over 400 men and women graduates annually as officers, and graduates below this level are not unknown. A university graduate entering the service of his country at 22 with contacts and friends outside the service and his formative years spent in a heterogeneous society is less likely to perpetuate a form of organization where the means have become ends in themselves, and the end product has been lost to view. Moreover, a greater proportion of modern society is orientated towards supplying services rather than production, and the armed forces increasingly see themselves as suppliers of a service even though they may never perform the ultimate service in practice. In fact to be ready to fight so as not to have to fight.

A further facet of inflationary pressures is certainly producing changes in the pattern of British Services. For instance, the unlikely case of the forces becoming largely introspective and living apart from the remainder of the community in garrison areas has already been eroded by rising house prices. The young serviceman has realized that he must pay for his house throughout his working life rather than leave it until retirement to be bought with the terminal grant or savings from a military career. A recent small but significant sample in one of our Services showed that of the 35 per cent of officers and servicemen who owned their own homes the majority were under 40 years old. The effect of such developments as this is that progressively greater numbers of British servicemen are living as part of the community and identifying themselves with local problems. However, this presents problems in providing the 'round-the-clock' management that is part of the military structure. In parallel has been the erosion of the traditional 'family cohesion of military life. Before the advent of the Welfare State, the military community provided medical, dental and hospital facilities free as of right to servicemen and their dependents as well as low-cost housing and a wide range of welfare facilities. Although this underlying paternalism is still of great worth, particularly when the husband may be away from home for long periods of time, it is less necessary as the intelligence levels of service families improve and more of these facilities are taken for granted as being state-provided. Thus the character of armed services will change as their own members and their families become less dependent and more inclined to exercise freedom of what is now a very wide choice in many fields. Furthermore, the British serviceman can in effect decide on the length of his own voluntary engagement by giving 18 months notice at, virtually, any time.

Attracting Recruits

Having mentioned some of the changes and pressures which are with us, what are the prospects of developed industrialized societies attracting sufficient men to join the armed forces? I have purposely avoided any mention of quality because one of the major contributions that armed forces can make is in the training of military manpower and in bridging the gap between the enthusiasm of the recruit and the skills he needs in productive service. Demographic trends in Britain over the next 10 years and forecast needs for the Services show that, depending on the assumptions we make, between one in every 7 and one in every 11 young men at some stage between the ages of 16–24 has to join the armed forces for some period if we are to meet our requirements. The Royal Navy and Royal Air Force have been attracting something like the right proportion of people in this age group, but the Army's 'extraction rate' (as it is termed) is not at present good enough. The Services are the largest employers in many countries and if a significant part of the forces is made up of volunteers, they need a fairly highly developed understanding of what is wanted to attract the young men to join. Attitude Surveys in Britain have shown that the conscious motivation is principally a chance to learn a trade and the career opportunity that this brings, with a chance to travel and an exciting life as next in order. The negative motivations may well be that a man is dissatisfied with his present situation either at home or in his job. Certainly in Britain a desire to join the Forces usually results from a conscious wish on the part of the individual to change his life-style fairly radically.

General Gard mentioned the difficulty that the officer academy at Sandhurst faces in attracting the right men but to put this into perspective the current short-fall numbers 15 per cent and organizational changes in training are expected to redress this.

The diminishing returns from the greater use of civilians was mentioned. However, possibly Western attitudes may change to the jobs that women can undertake in the armed forces and this may be a way of partially redressing any man-power shortage.

If the existence of the state is threatened there is seldom any difficulty in raising citizen armies. However, the aim is to avoid reaching this crisis position. How then are volunteer armed forces to find a meaningful place in a society whose attitudes may well be antagonistic and who may regard the values and trappings of the Services as being socially irrelevant?

independence but satellization. All these reactions would be catastrophic, either because of their external impact or because of their domestic aspects. They would all tend to make the international system much less moderate, for instance because the remilitarization of an important participant could entail or provoke nuclear proliferation, or because of the shock waves caused by a sudden resort to the use of force, or because of the usual effects of appeasement. As far as the domestic aspects are concerned, all the reactions I have described are likely either to result from or to produce sharp internal crises. 'Finlandization' or appeasement is particularly likely to occur in countries which are deeply split domestically or have a strong Communist party. A decision by Japan to re-arm on a much larger scale, or to build a nuclear force, would deepen the polarization of opinion and parties. In other words, if the trend towards the unacceptability of force should be reversed, if a countervailing force should reassert itself, it would often not be a good thing, either domestically or for the world at large; and yet if the trend persists, there will be very high risks, both internally and internationally.

And so I come to my last point: what can be done about this? A first step was discussed in some of the papers submitted to this conference;* it may be called 'making force more acceptable again through military reform'. The point of departure is the recognition of the growing unacceptability of force, but one tries to find a remedy for this by focusing on just one aspect – the relation between the military and their societies in modern democratic nations. But here again the difference, between armies of today and the past creates a formidable obstacle. In the past, the warrior was an expert endowed with a monopoly over his peculiar brand of knowledge (the art of combat, if you like), and as such he was quite apart from all other forms of expertise in society. Even in societies of caste privilege or class distinction, the rigours of military discipline and rank were a second factor setting the warrior apart. But he was also representative, indeed the embodiment, of the dominant values of the social order, whether these were the values of prowess, honour and hierarchy of aristocratic societies or

the values of militant nationalism in the modern nation-state. Today, the warrior has lost that monopoly of knowledge. For insofar as part of his expertise is still the art of combat, both the speed of technological change and the fortunately unknown nature of a nuclear war mean that this art remains mysterious even to its practitioners, who have neither code nor compass and must either improvise or guess – just like the rest of us. And in as much as another part of his expertise is general technological knowledge, he shares his information and skills with other broad groups: scientists, engineers, and so on in advanced industrial society. However, neither this loss of his uniqueness, nor the fact that armies tend to become bureaucratic organizations managed along lines similar to those applied to all the other, civilian bureaucracies of modern society, compensate for a new kind of separation. Today, there is a sharp contrast between the dominant social values and those of the military. On the one hand, the ethos of combat and heroism – in increasingly mechanized, dehumanized wars – has lost its appeal. On the other hand, the ethos (if it is one) of economic rationality and efficiency, which informs modern organizations, serves goals of wealth, welfare and economic power, whereas military bureaucracies are inevitably geared to the accumulation, and eventual destruction of unproductive goods.

This does not make any easier the attempts at transforming the relations between the military and their societies. There are two different directions in which this reform can go. Neither direction strikes me as very helpful for the problem we now face. There is first of all the direction of the specialized, highly professional army, in essentials a volunteer force. As we know, such an army has its problems. Externally, these kinds of armies have been well adapted to ages of limited wars; they can be useful for the latent or oblique uses of force and for what the French would call 'ponctuel', piecemeal intervention. However, they risk being quite insufficient to back up nuclear deterrence in those parts of the world where the goal of policy must be not successful defence or counter-attack, but credible deterrence of war altogether. Domestically, such armies tend to be recruited among people of low education and the under-privileged seeking the security and opportunities for

---

* See Adelphi Paper No. 103, *op. cit.*

From Conscription to Volunteer Armies

GWYN HARRIES-JENKINS

It is increasingly apparent that industrialized democracies which seek to maintain a viable military posture in contemporary society, are faced with a number of seemingly insoluble problems. In most countries, the traditional forms of military organization have been subjected to considerable criticism. The crisis of legitimacy, opposition to the perceived dominance of the military-industrial complex and a refusal to endorse the moral worth of conscription, are indicative of public opposition to the continuance of historical types of armed service establishments. In short, the rejection of the goals and styles of the military suggests that we are witnessing the end, or at least the transformation, of the mass army.[1] One effect of this is that conscription, it is argued, can no longer be relied upon as the main source of future military manpower. A transnational rejection of compulsory military service, variously attributed to factors such as the decline of nationalism, highly personalized opposition to military institutions, the impact of a youth sub-culture and the growth of neutralism, apparently predicts an inevitable end within the next decade to traditional methods of raising armed forces.[2] The fundamental question which arises is: With what can conscription be replaced?

In examining this question further, some analysts have gone beyond a simple consideration of possible alternatives to conscription, to discuss the more fundamental issue of the role and place of the military in modern society. Thus Biderman,[3] in seeking to formulate new and alternative models of armed forces, has raised the important question: What *is* military? This is a very pertinent consideration in any discussion of civil-military relationships, but most of the debate which has taken place has not proposed any radical alternative to the existing military. Instead, it has emphasized that the alternative to conscription is the all-volunteer armed force. The emergence of volunteer armies seems, following the examples of Britain and the United States, to be inevitable.

This postulated solution to the problems faced by the contemporary military is to many people an attractive one. Much of the debate about the relevance of the conscripted mass army in modern warfare is based on ideological arguments. Condemnation of conscription thus comes from groups whose attitudes range from a belief that it is unnecessary and undesirable because the element of compulsion interferes with the liberty of the individual, to those who reject conscription because the widening of recruitment limits the attempts of the military to preserve the occupational mystique which is the basis of their claim to differential privileges. Concomitantly, the apparent validity of the more moderate argument that universal military service has some advantages for society is limited. The rationale of the thesis which is advanced is often founded not on the manifest benefits of conscription, but on its latent advantages, such as the function of the military as a training and educating institution, as the promoter of egalitarianism or as an agent of socialization.[4] Since the critics of conscription can rightly point out that non-military forms of national service can equally promote the furtherance of these elements of distributive and substantive justice, it is difficult to accept as valid the thesis that conscription has an important societal function. Consequently, a vehement opposition to compulsory military service appears to be more indicative of universally held valid opinions. The inevitable alternative to conscrip-

[1] Charles C. Moskos, Jr., 'The Emergent Military: Civil, Traditional or Plural', *Pacific Sociological Review*, April 1973; J. van Doorn, *The Decline of the Mass Army: Sociological Essays* (London: Sage Publications, 1974).
[2] Morris Janowitz, *The US Forces and the Zero Draft*, Adelphi Paper No. 94 (London: International Institute for Strategic Studies, 1973).
[3] Albert Biderman, 'What is Military?' in Sol Tax (ed.), *The Draft: A Handbook of Facts and Alternatives* (Chicago: University of Chicago Press, 1967).

[4] Gwyn Harries-Jenkins, 'The Mass Army: A British Reaction', in J. Van Doorn (ed.), *The Decline of the Mass Army: Sociological Essays, op. cit.*

II

tion thus seems to be the politically and morally acceptable one of volunteer armies.

It is questionable whether this rejection of conscription is a dominant attitude at the mass level, or whether it is characteristic only of the attitudes and opinions of a vociferous cultural and intellectual minority.[5] Equally, the assumption that the emergence of the volunteer army is inevitable in all advanced industrialized societies, is a hypothesis which does not take into account a number of important factors. It presumes, for example, that armies in these societies are representative of the democratic competitive model of military professionalism in which conscription is a dysfunctional characteristic. It can, however, be argued that no such single model exists in reality, and that a contemporary national military must be analysed against the historical and cultural orientations of the parent society. From this, it is evident that in the majority of advanced industrialized societies, the traditional use of conscription as a means of recruitment to the military will not readily be displaced. In short, it is far from certain that the conscript mass army *must* and *will be* replaced by the volunteer armed force. Here, it is dangerous to extrapolate from the insular examples of Britain and the United States where anti-militarism has traditionally opposed not only the existence of a conscript military, but has also been highly critical of the existence of a standing army in peacetime.

If we accept, however, for the purpose of further analysis that the emergence of a volunteer army is a possibility, then we must note that this postulated solution to the problem of establishing a viable military posture raises further social and political issues. In particular, the number and social composition of the military become questions of fundamental importance.

Numbers

The initial problem is whether the enforced phasing-out of conscription can be followed by the recruitment of an adequate number of volunteers. Cross-cultural comparisons have to be made with care, but the British experience since 1961 with an all-volunteer force suggests that the manpower problem can only be solved if cumulative cuts are made in quantitative and qualitative

requirements.[6] Similarly, the report of the West German Commission for a New Force Structure predicted that, in the absence of conscription, a shortfall in volunteer recruitment would be inevitable. Conversely, the Gates Commission in the United States concluded that an all-volunteer force would be feasible at relatively low cost.[7] Although these conclusions differ, it is evident that these and other countries face common difficulties. No one is prepared to suggest that the recruitment of volunteers will be an easy task. Indeed, it can be seen that the basic features of an advanced industrialized society generate complex military recruitment problems.

The primary difficulty faced by the military establishment is that it must compete with other public service and commercial organizations for the skilled manpower which it requires. This supply is not inexhaustible. The narrowing of the skill differential between the armed forces and civilian organizations increases the degree of competition. No longer can it be presumed that the bulk of the armed forces will be recruited from a residual civil population. Officers cannot be selected on the basis of ascriptive criteria which do not take into account the required level of technical and intellectual ability. Concomitantly, the supply of potential recruits is affected by a number of external factors. Improved educational opportunities in civilian life, a decline in the traditional advantages of a military career and improved social security benefits are among some of the factors which make life in the armed services less attractive than hitherto. Now the military must compete with civilian organizations for the recruits which it requires.

One way of competing in this economic market place is to reintroduce the traditional method of paying a recruiting bounty. In adopting this policy in July 1973, South Africa announced that she would pay a bonus of R. 3,000 (US $4,350) to white citizens if they would sign up for two years instead of the compulsory twelve months' national service. In announcing this step, the South African Defence Department forecast a

---

[5] Jerome Johnston and Jerald G. Bachman, *Young Men Look at Military Service* (Ann Arbor, Mich.: Institute for Social Research, 1970).

[6] Maurice A. Garnier, 'Some Implications of the British Experience with an All-Volunteer Army', *Pacific Sociological Review*, April 1973.

[7] Stewart W. Kemp, 'The British Experience with an All-Volunteer Force', *Studies Prepared for the President's Commission on an All-Volunteer Force* (Gates Commission) (Washington, DC: 1970).

'stampede' of volunteers and suggested that strict selection would have to be imposed since it was envisaged that there would be more volunteers than would be required.

The payment of a bounty has a number of apparent advantages. It is relatively cheap, for, as a once and for all payment, it does not necessarily affect longer-term costs which are inherent in the provision of a career pattern or a pensionable engagement. To the potential recruit, the pecuniary advantage is readily apparent. But there is no guarantee that a bounty system will be accompanied by a satisfactory retention rate. There is the very real problem of recruiting for a permanent cadre of highly skilled and trained personnel. Nor is it certain that the payment of a bounty will attract the type of recruit which the military requires, and it can be suggested that the bounty is most attractive to that part of a residual population which the armed forces are least likely to want. A more pungent criticism of the bounty system, however, is that it identifies the military, in the eyes of the general public, as a force of mercenaries, so that it has dysfunctional consequences in terms of any projected military self-image.

For this latter reason, it is preferable in terms of civil-military relationships for the armed services to compete with civilian organizations by increasing the level of extrinsic reward to a point where military rates of pay are seen to be comparable with those paid to civilians of a similar skill-level. This overcomes the criticism that the military is a force of mercenaries. In addition, the emphasis placed on comparability which suggests that the military task is similar in form to the civilian one, has the subsidiary effect of strengthening the validity of the convergence thesis of civil-military relationships. But a number of problems still arise. How can a similar skill be defined? This is a difficulty which has taxed the Prices and Income Board in Britain. Similarity can be seen where the military professional or tradesman carries out a function which can be clearly defined in terms of a civilian profession or occupation. Yet this may be difficult, if not impossible, where the exercised skill has a purely military relevance. How can a bureaucratic rank-structure which ensures that officers and soldiers of a similar rank-level enjoy similar rewards, accommodate the wide variations in rates of civilian reward? Inevitably, some military skills will be under-rewarded in comparison with civilian standards; others will be overpaid. To what extent does a basis of comparability which stresses secondary features of the military role such as skill in management, or which emphasizes status characteristics such as the possession of academic qualifications generate dysfunctional consequences?[8]

The most pertinent problem which arises is that the payment of a strictly comparable rate of reward is not an adequate incentive to recruiting. Yet, if the pay of a serviceman becomes visibly superior to the extrinsic reward which is available in civilian life, then, although this may improve recruiting, the military is again open to the charge that it is a force of mercenaries. In addition, it is clear that most tax-payers are reluctant to approve the large increases in military expenditure which would inevitably result from the higher rate of military pay. The armed services, too, are reluctant to solve their recruiting problem by economic incentives alone, for these do not guarantee the required mix of numbers of qualified personnel. So to satisfy the demands of a democratic society and to meet the professional needs of the military, we are forced to accept the premise that a volunteer force can only be raised with the payment of a rate of reward comparable to that of civilian occupations.

Although conclusions drawn from British experience may not be universally applicable, current trends in recruitment suggest that the adoption of this premise generates a number of problems.

From the following table, which coincidentally reflects the reduced intake requirements of the Navy and the Royal Air Force, it can be seen that the Army recruited less than half as many men in April and May 1973 as during the same period in 1972. This showed a considerable slump, even though increases of pay from 1 April 1973 maintained the attractiveness of service pay, in comparison with what could be earned in civilian life. Moreover, this slump was part of a continuing pattern which followed two exceptionally good recruiting years, and it can be argued that there are no favourable factors in sight which would reverse this trend. The conclusion which must be

---

[8] Gwyn Harries-Jenkins, 'Dysfunctional Consequences of Military Professionalization', in M. Janowitz and J. Van Doorn (eds), *On Military Ideology* (Rotterdam: Rotterdam University Press, 1971).

Enlistment and Total Strength of the British Armed Forces				
	ENLISTMENT		TOTAL STRENGTH	
Service	*April/May 1972*	*April/May 1973*	*1972*	*1973*
Royal Navy	1,368	793 ⎫	78,534	77,748
Royal Marines	207	205 ⎭		
Army	5,651	2,393	174,476	172,618
Royal Air Force	651	416	103,941	98,918
	7,877	3,807	356,951	349,284

drawn is that economic incentives do not produce the required number of recruits. This again suggests that extrinsic reward, in the form of increased military pay, is not an adequate form of activation and that alternative solutions must be sought.

The very real problem faced by the military is that it is difficult to isolate the type of reward which makes a career in the volunteer force attractive to potential recruits. One hundred-and-forty years ago, the Duke of Wellington suggested that the core-trait of military reward was the 'honour' which men obtained. This, and their conception of national need, provided adequate personal motivation. In contemporary society, however, such interpretations of reward are no longer sufficiently persuasive. A large part of the age-cohort from which future recruits must be drawn is highly critical of all aspects of military life, particularly those characteristics which appear reminiscent of neo-feudal styles of honour. The combination of these factors suggests that the normative involvement of the recruit with the military, an involvement which for so long was a corner-stone of recruiting policy, no longer has any validity. What, however, can it be replaced with?

If the alternative cannot be a high rate of extrinsic reward which meets the calculative needs of the potential recruit, then the ideal-type of reward must be related to re-definitions of the military career. At one level, this necessitates the identification of the military as a constabulary or fire-brigade force.[9] At another level, a level which is more immediately attractive to the potential recruit, this means that the military

career must be seen as another form of the public service career. A strengthened civil service basis to the military career must recognize that for the majority of recruits, their military experience will be one part of an occupational life-cycle and that it is an interlude in an essentially civilian existence. Even for those officers and men whose service covers periods in excess of twenty years, it must be recognized that their military career is but one phase of a two-phase career which is primarily a life-time career in public service. Hence, transfer to the civil service establishment must be made the mandatory right of retiring military personnel. At the same time, a flexible system of lateral movement between the civil and military sides of the public service establishment will not only make it possible to draw on a larger and already trained pool of manpower, but also broaden the basis of recruitment in both spheres.

Such a solution will inevitably meet with opposition from vested interests both in the military and in the civil service. But it is a solution which must be considered in detail, for a failure to achieve military manpower targets can severely affect the strategic capabilities of the armed forces, and the effects of this are more serious than the effects of modifications to the traditional relationships between the military and the civil service.

Public Images of the Military
One effect of this proposal is that it will modify the accepted public image of the military. But it is also inevitable that the introduction of volunteer forces modifies hitherto existing images. On the one hand, the absence of personal involvement with the military encourages an evaluation of armed forces based on 'ideal' or 'pure' types of

[9] Morris Janowitz, *The Professional Soldier* (Glencoe, Ill.: Free Press, 1960); John A. Jackson, 'The Irish Army and the Constabulary Concept', in J. Van Doorn (ed.), *Armed Forces and Society* (The Hague: Mouton, 1968).

the image. Here, five models can be isolated, so that the military is seen by the outsider to be either aristocratic, heroic, bureaucratic, professional or managerial. These 'ideal-types' of the public image are not mutually exclusive, and, in reality, the boundaries between them are blurred. In the context of external evaluation, however, there is a tendency to assume that the volunteer army must be totally identified with one of the five models. On the other hand, the marked selective social characteristics of volunteer armies and their reliance on occupational self-recruitment contributes to the social isolation of the military. This, in turn, apparently reinforces subjective external evaluation of the public image, and seemingly confirms the validity of reached conclusions. This reliance on occupational self-recruitment is no new phenomenon. It is traditional in the cultural context of the armed forces where father–son succession promotes the transmission of basic values and postulated loyalties. It is apparent in conscript armies. In France, some 40 per cent of St Cyr entrants originate from military families.[10] For the United States, it has been suggested that the last decade has seen the growing unrepresentativeness of the officer corps.[11] In Britain, recruitment figures for the volunteer army show how even more reliance is placed on young men from military families.[12] Between 1961 and 1970, 59 per cent to 69 per cent of successful candidates for a regular commission had a father who held a commission in the armed forces. An analysis of the 1970 applicants showed that of those who were finally selected for officer training, 72 per cent came from a family in which the father was serving in the armed forces.[13]

The British experience is not necessarily a valid prediction of future trends in other volunteer armies. It must be evaluated against the traditional patterns of recruiting for the British military. Yet, this reliance on special groups at a time when the national educational system is producing an increasing number of individuals who would objectively qualify for entry to a career in the armed forces, suggests that a volunteer army tends to be unrepresentative of the broader social structure. Such a conclusion is strengthened by reference to the previous experience of other countries having volunteer armies, as with the United States before 1940 where the officer corps had a strong element of selected social characteristics.

The importance of this conclusion is that, if it is confirmed by the future experience of countries with volunteer armies, such social selectivity will considerably modify the public image of the military. Once again, the armed forces will be seen to be a caste with caste privileges, a criticism frequently levied against volunteer armies of the past. In this situation, it is considered that links with civil society are attenuated; military values are thought to differ from those of the parent society. The resulting public image will be one of an aristocratic or heroic military where the institutional autonomy of the armed forces encourages the redefinition by the military of its role. The validity of this public image can be justified on a number of grounds. The components of the military mind, particularly its nationalism, political conservatism and authoritarianism, validates the aristocratic public image.[14] The military ethic which accepts the nation-state as the highest form of political organization, and which holds that the security of the state depends upon the creation and maintenance of strong military forces, endorses the applicability of the heroic image.[15] The consistent emphasis placed on the importance of power in international relations and on dangers to state security, an emphasis which is the rationale for the retention of traditional forms of military organization, further confirms the validity of these public images.

The military mind and ethic are equally present within the conscript mass-army, but their effect on the public image of the military is largely offset by the apparent democratization and civilianization of the military establishment. Moreover, positive steps taken by the armed forces to promote the managerial and professional military self-image also counteract the effect of the outlook and reactions of the military

[10] Raoul Girardet, *La Crise Militaire en France 1945–1962: Aspects Sociologiques et Ideologiques* (Paris: Libraire Armand Colin, 1964).
[11] Charles C. Moskos, Jr., *Public Opinion and the Military Establishment* (Beverley Hills: Sage Publications, 1971).
[12] *Westbury Analysis* (London: Central Office of Information, 1971).
[13] Maurice A. Garnier, 'Some Implications of the British Experience with an All-Volunteer Army', *op. cit.*

[14] Bengt Abrahamsson, *Military Professionalization and Political Power* (Beverley Hills: Sage Publications, 1972).
[15] Samuel P. Huntington, *The Soldier and the State* (Cambridge, Mass.: Harvard University Press, 1957).

15

establishment. It is clear, however, that even within the conscript army it has become increasingly difficult to continue stressing these elements. The trend toward civilianization probably reached its limit some years ago. The concept of the military manager has lost much of its attractiveness within the military organization. Thus in the volunteer army of the future, attempts to counteract the public image of the military as an aristocratic and heroic institution, by stressing the managerial and professional characteristics of armed forces, or by emphasizing its civilianism, are unlikely to be successful. Indeed, persistent references by the military to its professional and managerial attributes have dysfunctional consequences. This encourages, *inter alia*, a critical evaluation of the military which, based on civilian standards and definitions of professionalism and managerial ability, produces an unfavourable subjective assessment of volunteer armies. Not only are the claimed military self-images rejected but the apparent validity of the aristocratic and heroic public images seems to be confirmed.

Conclusion

In this short paper, it has been possible to consider briefly two specific problem areas which are associated with the transition from conscript to volunteer armies. A large number of other problem areas need further examination if a more comprehensive picture of the relationship between the volunteer army and its parent society is to be obtained. Certain tentative conclusions, however, can be drawn from the two areas which have been examined.

In general terms, the outlook for volunteer armies in the field of recruitment and the public image is a pessimistic and expensive one. If the style, role and form of the military remains unchanged, it is highly unlikely that a sufficient number of suitably qualified recruits can be obtained. A shortfall in recruiting seems to be inevitable in a period of general anti-militarism. Minimum manpower requirements could be achieved, but the cost of this in both social and economic terms would be too high a price for a democratic advanced industrialized society to pay. But irrespective of the precise numbers recruited to a volunteer army, it seems inevitable that such a military force would, if raised by traditional methods to carry out traditional tasks, find itself in a position of considerable social

isolation. A fundamental turning inward would be associated with a reversion to tradition, characteristics which are indicative of a military force divergent from civilian society. The associated aristocratic and heroic public image of the military would then confirm the perceived division between the volunteer army and the parent society.

A number of alternatives to the traditional form of volunteer armies can be envisaged, alternatives which, in taking into account the political and strategic requirements of a specific society, can still permit the maintenance of a viable military posture. For instance, the *segmented* military may be a more viable proposition. This model recognizes that from an institutional standpoint, new organizational forms are required. Basically, the tertiary level of functions such as clerical administration, education, medical care and other support and administrative elements can be completely civilianized. At the second level of technical functions, such features as lateral entry into the military system, enhanced opportunities for the employment of military personnel on non-military tasks and conditions of employment which reflect marketplace standards, will produce a convergent sector which operates on principles common to civil administration and corporate structures. For the combatant arms, the traditional mode of military organization will be retained. To compensate for the strains associated with the functions of these arms, the level of differential privilege will be considerably increased. This, in turn, produces many of the problems to which reference has been made, but the stresses associated with the creation of an élitist, highly paid and privileged group which forms one part of a *plural* or *segmented* military, are part of the price which has to be paid in the establishment of all-volunteer forces. The style, role and form of the volunteer army are not pre-determined. Options are still open to political leaders, and the volunteer army of the future can be adapted to meet the demands of the parent society. Equally, military professionals can make adaptations to ensure the maintenance of a viable military posture in contemporary society. The danger, however, is that neither the politician faced with the demands of an electorate, nor the military leader under pressure from traditionalists within the armed forces, is prepared to consider change.

Alternatives to Existing Forces[1]

ADAM ROBERTS

To accept a brief to write a paper on a subject so enormous, and so strewn with pitfalls, as alternatives to existing military forces is risky. One is bound to take note of George Kennan's confession of error in having very briefly touched on this question in the 1957 Reith Lectures: 'I was very foolish to say these things. Either they were wholly misconceived and had no value, in which case the statement of them was the expression of some real intellectual failure on my part, or they were so much ahead of their time as to be unintelligible. In either case, they should not have been said.'[2]

Before proceeding into so dangerous an area, it is necessary to define clearly the limits of this enquiry. This paper is about possible alternative means of achieving at least some of those declared objects (e.g., deterrence against foreign attack) to which national armed forces today are in the main ostensibly committed. Since existing forces come in almost as many shapes and sizes as there are sovereign states, it would be rash and pretentious to claim that, in a single paper, it was necessary or desirable to discuss alternatives to all of them. Indeed, one of the weaknesses of much strategic writing is precisely that certain key notions, such as cost-effectiveness or limited war, have been elevated into a strategic theory; general applicability in space and time has been claimed for them, they have been divorced from political and economic realities and the possibility of failure has been honestly faced. This paper is therefore deliberately restricted to the subject of possible alternatives to cadre-conscript or all-volunteer armies; it is also restricted

geographically – dealing largely, though not exclusively, with the problems faced by the Western European members of NATO.[3] It may be that the questions raised in this context have some general relevance to the larger problem of the role of armed forces in modern urbanized industrial societies, whether East, West or neutral – and whether or not new security arrangements or alliances emerge in Europe in the next few years.

The suggestion that it is worth looking at alternatives to existing armed forces in Western Europe does not spring from any dogmatic assumption that present forces in Europe and present external military guarantees have no function. Nor is it assumed that war or major aggression is inconceivable in Europe in the remaining years of the twentieth century, nor that a restructuring of the defences within NATO countries is necessarily the most important contribution they can make to their own security and that of others. One could no doubt argue that 'the creation of an all-European system of collective security' could be a substitute for existing defence arrangements, or that NATO might best be strengthened by 'the participation of the USSR in the North Atlantic Treaty'.[4] There might be substantial scope for UN or other observer forces to see that the peace is kept between European countries. Such radical proposals, whether or not within the realm of possibility, are beyond the scope of this paper.

One could argue, perhaps more plausibly, that the diplomatic initiatives summed up in the word

---

[1] This paper has been revised in response to criticisms and suggestions made at the IISS conference. The revision was completed before the 1973 Middle East war broke out, and although that war will no doubt have implications for many matters touches on here, to have jumped to conclusions about them while hostilities continued would have been unwise. Hence no further changes, apart from two footnotes, have been made.
[2] George F. Kennan, *Memoirs 1950–1963* (London: Hutchinson, 1973), p. 257.

[3] Mr Malcolm Muggeridge, when asked in a television interview in the autumn of 1973 what was the most boring topic for an article he could imagine, said 'After NATO What?'. The reader has been warned.
[4] The two quotations are from a note issued by Molotov in Moscow on 31 March 1954. The Soviet Union was of course anxious at the time to stop West German rearmament and the proposal for a European Defence Community.

17

Ostpolitik have contributed more to European security in recent years than any military re-arrangements could have done. But there is a danger of over-simplification here. The frequent statements to the effect that international *détente* in no way removes the need for national defence largely miss the point. If such statements are meant to imply that the aim of *détente* policy is to lower the defences, they are misleading. Indeed, an important element in the *détente* is the mutual understanding of security interests. The condition of apparently reduced threat of war which Europe enjoys seems, perhaps paradoxically, to be based on an assumption of keeping the two major alliances in Europe in something resembling their present form, and there have been many indica-tions, over the last twenty years at least, that the Soviet leadership is anxious to preserve some level of American presence in Western Europe. A case in point is the timing of General Secretary Brezhnev's speech at Tbilisi on 14 May 1971, in which he suggested that the wine of talks on mutual force reductions in Europe be tasted. This was made immediately before one of Senator Mansfield's resolutions to cut American force levels in Europe unilaterally came up in the Senate; the White House opponents of the resolution had an ally.

However, if statements implying that the aim of *détente* is disarmament are too simple, so are any which imply that no defence questions are changed at all. *Détente* does unavoidably affect the nature and context of defence problems and how the public and governments think about them. It may do so increasingly if some written or tacit East–West agreements are reached on force levels in Europe, or if proposals for a European security system are made more precise and realistic than they have so far been.

There are some factors which might seem to make the question of alternatives to existing forces entirely irrelevant. Western Europe is perhaps more likely to be undermined by a failure of multi-party democracy in the face of processes such as pollution, inflation, corruption, property speculation or unemployment than by any overt foreign military attack; and the issue of the structure of the armed forces may seem, and even be, largely irrelevant to these latter problems – like worrying about the fence while the house has dry rot. One can only conclude, however, that even if the system of defence has no connection

with these other challenges (and that would be hard to sustain), it may nevertheless need some attention in its own right, because a number of developments are making some change in the defences inevitable anyway.

Seven Problems of West European Defence
The following, briefly and crudely summarized, would seem to be the principal reasons for con-cern about the existing structure of defence arrangements in NATO Europe. The points are in no particular order of importance, and there is a good deal of interconnection between them.

(1) *Political Character of Modern Armies*
The prevailing liberal democratic ideology of Western Europe has a strong built-in suspicion of standing armies, and it is not surprising that this should find some manifestations at the present time. The most extreme fear – and, one hopes, groundless – derives from the fact that tradi-tional armed forces have been a common instru-ment for conducting *coups d'état*. Apart from various exceptions in France, Turkey and Greece, this tendency has been held in check in NATO Europe. But allegations that a NATO plan was used in the conduct of the Greek coup, and that the CIA gave the green light – whether or not correct – only strengthen public appre-hensions that armed forces and alliances can easily become the instruments of minority or alien control of a state.[5] Though it is true that most coups have occurred elsewhere in Europe, it is still possible that a coup anywhere in the world may tend to discredit the military every-where – especially, perhaps, in countries where attachment to constitutionalism is strong.

It is certainly true that much of the use of armed force since 1945 has been largely irrelevant to the perceived threats or needs of the popula-tions of Western European countries. It has often been used in distant colonial or post-colonial situations – as at Suez, in Algeria, or in Indo-china – where it has been surrounded by both moral ambiguity and the taint of failure, and this is bound to lead to a certain remoteness between armed forces and the societies which employ them. The American crusade in Vietnam in which a cadre-conscript army engaged in a long

---

[5] Such allegations about Greece are made in Andreas Papandreou, *Democracy at Gunpoint: The Greek Front* (Harmondsworth: Penguin Books, 1973), p. 27.

war for questionable reasons and with atrocious means, has probably contributed to this remoteness, even in European countries not directly implicated in Vietnam at all, and it may have stimulated the (admittedly modest) increase in the number of conscientious objectors during the last decade in West Germany, Denmark, and even in neutral Sweden.[6] Any distancing between armed forces and society may lead to a poor intake of volunteers, either in quantitative or in qualitative terms.

It is possible that nuclear deterrence, too, has heightened the distance between societies and armies. If the choice offered by the realities of the nuclear age really was between being Red and being dead, many would no doubt prefer the first alternative – especially if being dead seemed to threaten the survival of the values fought for anyway. Moreover, the fact that there are numerous defects in Western capitalist society has, of course, led some people to go further and conclude either that the imposition of Communism from outside would be no disaster or that it makes little difference whether one lives in Washington's or Moscow's sphere of influence. All governments, the argument runs, are tarred with the brush of repression or exploitation. Such views, which are by no means synonymous with traditional pacifism, may in some respects be simplistic but they are not necessarily unreasonable.

Political isolation could have other causes. The idea that armies should be the principal guardians against subversion, or that they represent a set of values or a style distinct from those of civil society, contains some dangers which may not have been adequately perceived. Also, the very process of invoking foreign threats, which seems inevitably to be part of the business of most armed forces, produces its own problems. There is a serious possibility that either governments in general, or the armed forces which serve them, may prefer the simplicities and certitudes of an earlier period to the complexities and ambiguities of the present. This is of course not exclusively a Western danger. The Marxist belief that capital-ism knocks at every door, while not necessarily devoid of truth does represent a fairly sweeping generalization. The same applies to the equivalent Western notion: that if you leave a door open the Russians will pour through it. If military or political élites in the West make a fuss about such notions when these are not widely shared in their societies, this is only likely to exacerbate the political isolation of Western armies. To base the entire rationale for the existence of armies on the invocation of a single danger is clearly fraught with political risks; more cautious claims might be more convincing.

(2) Nuclear problems

The present NATO strategic doctrine can best be characterized as flexible escalation. It is based largely on a nuclear bluff which, if called, could mean the gruesome sacrifice, not merely of everything being defended but also of a good deal else besides. That there are no simple solutions to the dilemmas posed by nuclear weapons is accepted, as is the fact that mutual nuclear deterrence has proved more stable in Europe than some pessimists, myself included, expected. Nevertheless, numerous well-known strategic and political developments in the last ten years do raise a number of difficult questions about the plausibility of external nuclear guarantees – especially at a time when, as the 1972 SALT agreements made very clear, the strategic forces of both the United States and the Soviet Union appear to be based on the notion of Mutual Assured Destruction. There are also problems connected with the deployment and intended use of so-called tactical nuclear weapons, as Henry Kissinger indicated in his controversial speech of 23 April 1973,[7] when he stated, 'There are still unresolved issues in our doctrine, for example, on the crucial question of the role of tactical nuclear weapons.'

(3) Continuation of the American Role as Protector

There is some American dissatisfaction with playing the role of protector, as defined a quarter of a century ago in very different conditions. There is also some European dissatisfaction at being protected in this manner; the dependence of most of a continent on the vagaries of American foreign involvements and internal politics

---

[6] In West Germany during the past decade the number of applicants for recognition as conscientious objectors increased approximately fourfold, to a level of about 5 per cent of the induction. See Wehrstruktur-Kommission der Bundesregierung, *Die Wehrstruktur in der Bundesrepublik Deutschland* (Bonn, 1972/3), pp. 142–4.

[7] Reprinted in *Survival*, July/August 1973, pp. 188–192.

has increasingly caused concern – especially since the whole American–West European relationship has become more and more vulnerable to economic rivalries. While these pressures should not be exaggerated, various factors have combined to produce what Henry Kissinger termed, in the same speech, 'new realities that require new approaches'.

(4) *Problems in American Conventional Force Levels in Europe*

Although the United States has to date maintained substantial conventional forces in Europe, there is some evident Congressional reluctance to continue this situation indefinitely or unconditionally. The reduction of American General Purpose Forces in the Fiscal Year 1973 budget to a level which, allowing for inflation, is 35 per cent short of the 1965 level (the last year before direct involvement in Vietnam) is an indication that there may be a change in the whole American attitude to the strategic doctrine of flexible response.[8] If there is any substantial force withdrawal from Europe, whether unilateral or agreed, the American forces cannot simply be replaced by equivalent European forces, with no other changes, because of the well-known symbolic role of the American troops. There would need to be, at the very least, a substantial restructuring of forces in Europe.

(5) *Problems of European Conventional Force Levels*

One of the numerous paradoxes of the present situation is that within the European countries of NATO a reluctance to rely on the use of nuclear weapons has been growing at the same time as a reluctance to keep large standing conventional forces. United States Defence Secretary Laird, in his last major statement before leaving the Pentagon, gave vent to what are evidently strong American pressures for a greater contribution by West European states to their own defence. More specifically, and on a much more limited issue, the Defence Planning Committee of NATO has complained on 13 March 1973 about the adequacy of Danish defence plans for the next four years.

(6) *Lack of Immediacy of Defence Issues*

An underlying cause of many current defence problems is the awkward fact that in most

[8] See Alvin Paul Drischler, 'General Purpose Forces in the Nixon Budgets', *Survival*, May–June 1973, pp. 119–123.

countries of Western Europe (including the neutrals) the problem of defence is simultaneously both very difficult (suggesting to professional soldiers the need for very large forces with the most advanced equipment) and politically not very immediate. This lack of political immediacy is no mere illusion: Europe is singularly free of international territorial claims, frontier disputes, etc., and the diplomatic initiatives of recent years (*Ostpolitik*, the American–Soviet *détente*, the European Security Conference, etc.) are evidence of a general commitment to stability in Europe. But all this has not made the problem of defence significantly easier: a fact of which the large number of Soviet forces presently maintained in Eastern Europe is a reminder. A situation like this, both exceptionally difficult and not very urgent, is likely to be the subject of compromises, quite possibly unsatisfactory in nature.

The ambiguous character of the possible Soviet threat to Western Europe is evident in the very issue of Soviet and Warsaw Pact forces, so frequently cited as evidence of the unambiguous nature of the threat. The size of these forces may well be influenced by the Soviet Union's obsessive anxiety to keep things in order in its part of Europe; after all, Communism has been in a highly fissiparous state in recent years, and periods of international *détente* have in the past been, in Soviet eyes, periods of danger for their interests in Eastern Europe. A link is clearly now developing between *détente* with adversaries and repression within the bloc, and only a Clausewitzian obsession with numbers can justify an automatic assumption that high Soviet troop levels in Eastern Europe necessarily mean danger for Western Europe. It is perhaps equally reasonable to take the view that the Soviet Union's interests remain fundamentally defensive, and that the area in Europe where the large scale use of conventional force is most likely remains what it became in the 1950s and 1960s: within Eastern Europe, rather than on the NATO Central Front. It is there that strategic arrangements remain most vulnerable to political crises, and it may be there, rather than further West, that Europe's main earthquake fault line runs, though it is neither in NATO's nor in Moscow's interest to say so.

The frequent response of soldiers to the view that defence issues have lost their immediacy is of course that that is only thanks to nuclear deterrence and the exceptionally high levels of armaments generally in Central Europe that the peace has been kept. Even if this statement were wholly correct, it would not necessarily constitute a conclusive argument for maintaining those high levels indefinitely; and in any case there are other reasons why Europe has been relatively more stable than other parts of the world. European countries have learned some hard lessons about the dangers of international adventurism in two world wars and in numerous colonial conflicts, and for these historical reasons, not to mention the high degree of legitimation of European frontiers and (with some exceptions) political systems, war does not seem particularly necessary or attractive to most European countries. It was such factors which made the whole stability-oriented strategy of containment plausible in Europe, whereas the same strategy was disastrous in South-East Asia.

(7) Arms Talks

Negotiations for the reduction of forces and armaments in Europe may conceivably result in significant force changes, possibly in the old Rapacki Plan area. Up to now, much comment on these talks, including some statements by President Nixon (e.g., in his Foreign Policy Report to Congress on 3 May 1973), has concentrated on the issue of quantitative reductions. Important as this is, there is a need to concentrate on the related question of a restructuring of forces and on qualitative changes. These latter might be subjects of agreement in themselves, or be the necessary concomitants of an agreement on quantitative reductions.

Relevance of the Neutrals

In general, as the above-listed problems suggest, there has been something of a qualitative change in the context in which Western European defence operates. One could roughly characterize this change by saying that in certain respects (and in certain respects only) the problem of Western European defence has come to resemble the problems of the defence of the neutral European states. Some of the global developments which have occurred since the time when NATO was founded underline the point:

(a) The colonial powers of Western Europe have largely abandoned their ill-gotten gains. Portugal remains an obvious exception, and Britain continues of course to have a situation colonial in origin in Northern Ireland. In general, however, the problem of external defence is increasingly concerned with the defence of the national territory or the general area (Western Europe) against foreign attack, and the defence of freedom of the seas, international trade, etc., rather than with involvement in distant alliances and overseas colonial operations.

(b) Western Europe is achieving economic unification of a sort, but there is far less unification in the fields of foreign and defence policy. There is the possibility of Western Europe being simultaneously a major trading power and a weak military power. Certainly it may share a traditional characteristic of European neutrals – a reluctance to engage or participate in foreign military interventions in support of its perceived interests.

(c) At the same time as the military resources of the Soviet Union, especially in the nuclear field, have increased, the nexus of rivalries, uncertainties and fears covered by the term 'cold war' has abated. While the Western aim throughout has remained essentially one of deterrence, the problem has become one of how to meet an unlikely but extreme emergency, rather than how to meet a measurable, continuous and relatively easily identified threat. Neutrals are familiar with this situation.

(d) For a number of reasons Central Europe has ceased to be quite so much of a unique focus of interest for the United States or Soviet governments and armed forces as it was twenty, or perhaps even ten, years ago. And at least some European states, East and West, have been concerned to achieve a degree of disengagement from the external involvements of their super-power allies. Europe is not now quite so unavoidably the hostage for American good behaviour it was fifteen years ago, when the Soviet Union lacked a capacity to inflict damage on the United States.

(e) The uncertainty of external responses if one is attacked – so familiar an imponderable to defence planners in neutral states – is not wholly absent in Western European aligned states either.

NATO Europe is certainly not neutral or non-aligned in the sense that Switzerland or Yugoslavia is, and its history, geo-strategic position and enormous economic power, mean that, even if it should so wish, it cannot seriously hope to enjoy a situation of natural strategic security comparable to that of some of the more fortunate neutrals, such as Sweden. There may still be some danger of European powers being tempted to intervene in foreign countries to secure the resources on which Europe is so dependent. But Western Europe's defence problems do have some resemblance to those of neutral or non-aligned states, from whom there might be a few things to be learned – if not in the actual conduct of war, then at least in the matter of attitudes to, and the organization of, defence.

Curiously enough, at the very time when it is possible that there are things to be learned from the neutrals, there has been a tendency on the part of many Western defence experts to criticize certain neutrals, for example Sweden, for allegedly kow-towing to the Soviet Union. This allegation has not been supported by any serious evidence. The case of Finland is referred to even more often, the spectre of 'Finlandization' being frequently held up as a warning that a militarily weak Western Europe might become subject to intense Soviet pressure. In this context it needs to be said that the Finnish conduct of relations with the Soviet Union since World War II, while it has undeniably involved compromises, has been very impressive. It is not hard to argue that, in Finland's unique circumstances, it has been a far wiser policy than the less accommodating – and also perhaps less neutral – policy pursued in the inter-war years. While it may not be a model for others to follow, it does not deserve to become the subject of continual deprecation. A better word than 'Finlandization' needs to be found to describe a situation where on certain specific issues a state or a group of states feels obliged to defer to a more powerful neighbour, even in the absence of military action by the latter.

Some Possible Alternatives

It would be foolish to suggest that there are any simple solutions, whether drawn from the neutrals or from anywhere else, to the problems of Western European defence. If experience is any guide, it might well be possible to learn to live with logically insoluble problems of nuclear strategy and politically insoluble problems of conventional force levels. NATO's current structure and doctrine have been carefully worked out over a long period and are the results of a great deal of hard bargaining, and they will not be changed lightly – especially as there is a good deal of understandable reluctance in NATO Europe to think about defence problems at all. A minor, or possibly major, tinkering with NATO forces seems the most likely – though not necessarily the soundest – course in the immediate future. However, the kind of factors cited in the preceding section do suggest that Western European forces are not very likely to survive the 1980s (and perhaps not the 1970s) without major changes in structure.

Yet to propose alternatives is not easy. The very numerous and varied pressures for a reduction in defence budgets and defence efforts in recent years have had one thing in common: they have not been accompanied by proposals for alternatives to existing military arrangements. Of the approaches to the problem of defence which may be worthy of investigation at the present juncture, three stand out, involving greater reliance respectively on:

Technology as a substitute for manpower.

Militia-type forces.

Civil resistance and other non-military forms of action in the event of occupation or other threat.

These three should not necessarily be seen as mutually exclusive alternatives, or as complete substitutes for all existing forces. Relatively little, for example, is said here about the problem of air and naval action. While it is often necessary to think, write and debate in terms of paradigms, a good deal of the discussion about defence may have been confused rather than clarified by the presentation of over-simplified 'models'. The distinctions between the various approaches to defence are of course fairly sharp – at least in theory – and in fact there are often serious problems of compatibility between different approaches, but there should at the very least be no *a priori* assumption that one option excludes the others. The three approaches have been suggested because in each case one can claim that they offer some form of deterrence or defence suited to what are taken to be the basically defensive purposes of West European states.

One important criterion to bear in mind in evaluating defence options in Europe today is precisely that military forces should play some part in communicating a generally defensive posture. Helmut Schmidt has referred to 'the inestimable political advantage' of a strategy which is 'minimally provocative', and has suggested that: 'The optimum goal of German defence and strategy would ... be the creation of an armaments structure clearly unsuited for the offensive role, yet adequate beyond the shadow of a doubt to defend German territory.'[9] There is no simple means of achieving this optimum goal. Certainly the choice of weapons alone cannot effectively do it, since a powerful defensive array can all too easily provide a screen which guarantees for a state immunity from outside reactions to its own aggressive moves. If manifest defensiveness is to be communicated at all, it has to be done by a combination of internal factors, foreign policy moves, force structures and weapons.

Although manifest defensiveness is taken as one important criterion, so also is the possibly conflicting one of deterrence. It is assumed that deterrence is the primary aim of any policy and that there is likely to be a gravitation towards options which, whether or not they provide anything by way of defence against an attack once it is under way, do offer the possibility of deterring attack in the first place. The primacy of the aim of deterrence, however reluctant governments are to face its possible consequences, has been alluded to by Henry Kissinger: 'What our allies understand by nuclear support is less clear. They want the *appearance* of nuclear support so that the Soviets never challenge their vital interests. Whether they are actually prepared to face the consequences of nuclear war is ambiguous.'[10]

If Kissinger was right in attributing ambiguity to West Europeans so far as nuclear deterrence is concerned, then there is an increased case for looking at alternatives, not only as total peacetime replacements for existing systems but also as emergency options which might be implemented in a time of crisis or war. The alternatives suggested may not necessarily be better in all respects and for everyone than the existing policies pursued by NATO; but they might seem more attractive in certain crises. The consideration of alternatives is not necessarily an act of bland optimism – it can equally be a sign of realism or pessimism.

Technology

The desire for technical solutions is a strong one, and a great variety of proposals containing a high element of reliance on technology have been proposed for NATO in recent years. They have included:

A return to increased emphasis on tactical nuclear weapons and/or immediate and semi-automatic strategic nuclear retaliation. (One hesitates to call this 'massive retaliation' because the Dulles concept, announced in January 1954, was somewhat more flexible and related to Asia as much as to Europe.)

The development of a European or Anglo-French strategic nuclear force to take primary responsibility for the defence of NATO Europe.

Static defence based on the construction of extensive minefields, possibly with nuclear charges, precision-guided munitions, anti-tank weapons, etc.

There seems to be a general tendency in the United States today to substitute technology for manpower. In part this is because of the change-over to an all-volunteer army, but it goes back further and can be seen in many of the campaigns of strategic bombing – as questionable militarily as they have been morally. The unlamented Multilateral Force was rightly seen by Henry Kissinger as a warning 'not to try to solve political problems with technical expedients'.[11] But when difficult problems press, many of them military as much as political, the temptation to solve them with technical expedients is likely to be a strong one – for European states as well as for the United States. This is not to say that there is in fact a simple correlation between technology and manpower: some technological innovations necessitate the employment within

---

[9] Helmut Schmidt, *Defence or Retaliation* (Edinburgh and London: Oliver and Boyd, 1962), pp. 169 and 198–9.
[10] Henry Kissinger, *The Troubled Partnership* (New York: McGraw-Hill, 1965), p. 162.

[11] Henry Kissinger, *op. cit.*, p. 156.

the armed forces of large numbers of men – and often, what is more, highly qualified men, who are in great demand in the civilian sector of the economy.

Those technological solutions which require an increased dependence on nuclear weapons, whether European or American, are hampered by the fact that a return to nuclear strategies is unlikely in an age when nuclear powers are so vulnerable. They also go against the modest, but possibly growing, pressures for an explicit no-first-strike policy on nuclear weapons. The idea of an Anglo-French nuclear force might conceivably be welcomed by West Germany if it served to bring France back into full and active membership of NATO, but it is not likely to seem a more certain guarantee of West German territory than the American guarantee, however qualified and limited that is.

The question of static defence has received a good deal of attention in recent years, and it fits in well with the current NATO emphasis on forward defence. There are two principal difficulties, however. First, static defence is no solution to the problem of the attack from an unexpected direction, and may not be well suited to the problem of seaborne or airborne assaults. Second, many schemes for static defence involve the use of atomic weapons, such as demolition mines, and a state may be justifiably reluctant to depend on a strategy which gave the rather brittle protection of a choice between using a very drastic means very early or else not using it at all.[12]

Technological solutions on a more modest level are likely to be less controversial and to have wider appeal. If cost-effectiveness and a defensive posture are important criteria, there is likely to be increased emphasis on, for example, anti-tank weapons rather than on tanks,[13] and perhaps on surface-to-air missiles (bearing in mind the experience of their use in North Vietnam

between 1965 and 1973) rather than on fighter or bomber aircraft.[14]

Militia-type Forces

The proposal that militia-type forces should play a significant role in NATO is increasingly heard. In this, as in other matters, Switzerland is something of a paradigm. The Swiss Army, with its universal conscription, relatively short initial training, emphasis on subsequent refresher courses and lack of a large permanent cadre, is the extreme case of a citizen army. To produce a total mobilizable strength of 600,000 out of a population of 6,400,000 is incontestably a remarkable achievement. A Swiss writer has calculated that 'if all Western Europe had the same proportion of armed forces, there would be 360 divisions at its disposal'[15] – a prospect which might frighten even NATO planners.

However, while Switzerland is interesting, it is not the only state to think of in considering solutions to the defence problems faced by Western Europe. When the West German Defence Commission considered the question of militia forces, it appears to have concentrated on the Swiss model and then rejected it on the grounds that it would not guarantee sufficient forces at the decisive point on M-day.[16] This rejection may possibly have been based on too strong an attachment to the notion of having maximum forces instantly available at the frontier to meet an attack out of the blue, and too little attention may have been paid to Swedish – and, particularly, Yugoslav – force structures, with their complex relationship between forces-in-being and mobilizable reserves. Sweden and Yugoslavia, precisely because they are not such pure paradigms, may be better models.

Yugoslavia is particularly interesting because,

[12] For a report suggesting that there has been West German opposition to reported American plans for 'prechambering' holes for atomic mines, see John W. Finney, 'Some NATO Allies Reluctant to Let US Use Atomic Arms', *International Herald Tribune*, Paris, 16 July 1973.

[13] See, for example, Steven L. Canby's article 'NATO Muscle: More Shadow Than Substance', *Foreign Policy*, Fall 1972, p. 49 (reprinted *Survival*, Jan/Feb 1973). See also the eulogy of various new weapons, principally of an anti-tank variety, in Stefan Geisenheyner, 'A Defensive Weapons Mix for Europe: *Pandora, Medusa, Dragon Seed*', *Survival*, September 1971.

[14] The use of surface-to-air missiles in the Middle East war in October 1973 would appear to confirm this line of argument, although whether one regards their use as defensive or otherwise depends, in part at least, on one's politics.

[15] Max Petitpierre, 'Is Swiss Neutrality Still Justified?', quoted in Roderick Ogley (ed.), *The Theory and Practice of Neutrality in the Twentieth Century* (London: Routledge and Kegan Paul, 1970), p. 174.

[16] Wehrstruktur-Kommission der Bundesregierung, *Die Wehrstruktur in der Bundesrepublik Deutschland* (Bonn, 1972/73), pp. 29–30. M-day is defined as the day on which national governments begin to convert their forces from a peacetime posture to one of defence readiness. (*Ibid.*, p. 31 n.)

at a time when it is generally alleged that there is a trend towards professional armies, the Yugoslavs have quite deliberately (it was not done as a mere panic reaction to the occupation of Czechoslovakia) increased the participation of the population as a whole in defence activities. The concept of 'General People's Defence' envisages a combination of frontal and guerrilla operations, in which there are two hierarchically equal and organizationally distinct parts: the Yugoslav People's Army on the one hand, and Territorial Defence on the other. Yugoslav forces of course reflect the country's unique position, but Yugoslavs, while not advocating their defence system indiscriminately, clearly believe it might have relevance for other states, including other European ones.

It is certainly reasonable to argue that purely professional armies are less suitable to countries in exposed situations, such as Yugoslavia, than they are to more geographically secure states. It may make sense for the United States or Britain to have an exclusively volunteer army, because their main interests are overseas, and the likelihood of having to resist a massive invasion of the national territory is slight. The interests of most continental European powers are different. The fact that, for highly understandable reasons, NATO Europe has in the past generally followed and accommodated itself to changing fashions in American strategic doctrine does not mean that it has to accommodate itself to the latest fashions in American force structures as well. The functions of American and European forces are quite simply different.

There is a serious argument that the increasing technological sophistication of weapons systems necessitates the professionalization of armed forces. Clearly this is true to some extent, particularly with regard to air forces – in Sweden's air force, for example, the percentage of regulars in the total strength increased between 1966 and 1970 from 25 per cent to 37 per cent – but it is not necessarily true in every case that technologically advanced weapons require full-time professional operators. Anti-tank missiles, for example, might well constitute an exception.[17]

If militia forces are to be increasingly used,

they may have consequences in strategic doctrine. At its most extreme, this might involve a change-over to the concept of territorial defence as defined below.

Territorial Defence is a system of defence in depth; it is the governmentally-organized defence of a state's own territory, conducted on its own territory. It is aimed at creating a situation in which an invader, even though he may at least for a time gain geographical possession of part or all of the territory, is constantly harassed and attacked from all sides. It is a form of defence strategy which has important organizational implications, being liable to involve substantial reliance on a citizen army, including local units of a militia type. Characteristically, a territorial defence system is based on weapons systems, strategies and methods of military organization which are better suited to their defensive role than to major military actions abroad.

It cannot be claimed that there is a completely indissoluble link between the strategic concept of territorial defence on the one hand, and the organizational system of citizen armies or militias on the other. Israel has a largely citizen army system, but has waged numerous offensive military actions in her twenty-five years' existence, has held on to conquered territory and has shown some capacity to maintain substantial forces along her extended frontiers in times of relative peace as well as in wars. It can even be argued that the citizen army system has been a significant factor impelling Israel into aggressive tactics, on the grounds that the country can only afford short wars before the economy is seriously disrupted by the drain of manpower into the army.

However, the idea of territorial defence is often linked to that of militias or citizen armies, and it does have an important place in the defence policies of numerous countries, including China, North Korea, Rumania, Yugoslavia and Albania. This approach has a certain logic in the nuclear age, since the degree of dispersion of forces involved reduces (though, of course, it by no means eliminates) the vulnerability of massed conventional forces to nuclear weapons. Such a conception of defence is something akin to what Kennan suggested in some brief and controversial passages of his 1957 Reith lectures.[18]

---

[17] The use of such weapons by Egyptian infantrymen in the first week of the 1973 Middle East war is an illustration of a technologically advanced system not requiring especially highly qualified operators.

[18] George F. Kennan, *Russia, The Atom, and the West* (London: Oxford University Press, 1958), pp. 64–66.

There are a number of strong West European objections, and the concept seems to go against the grain of contemporary European thought. Raymond Aron's description of the time when NATO was formed still has some force: 'European leaders, "rushing backward into the future", unearthed the experiences of the preceding [war] and, with their still green memories of occupation and liberation, loudly proclaimed that they wished to be defended and not liberated this time; only ruins or corpses would be liberated '[19] But some of the objections to the idea of territorial defence which might have had merit twenty-five years ago are less persuasive now. NATO was set up at a time when Germany was a defeated and occupied nation for which any defence from an outside threat could only be achieved by outside forces of conventional type or by nuclear deterrence. These circumstances have changed, and, in particular, the two Germanies have become fully-fledged states, fairly stable internally and recognized by foreigners. Although there are, of course, some serious difficulties, there would seem to be a need for more penetrating discussion than hitherto on the possibilities of redefining West Germany's military role. The United States is increasingly committed to the notion that American support is only given to those states which are prepared to help themselves, and reliance on militia forces might be one means of demonstrating self-help.

The concept of territorial defence also runs into the familiar West German objection that 'a strip 100 kilometres west of the D-line already comprises 30 per cent of the West German population and 25 per cent of the West German industrial capacity'[20] – considerations which are seen, rightly or wrongly, as necessitating frontal defence. Certainly anything resembling a territorial defence system would place a very heavy burden on areas and countries in the front line.

Despite such criticisms, which undoubtedly have some force, the concept of defence in depth has considerable value if it is regarded essentially as a form of deterrence – which is certainly how the Yugoslavs see it. Vietnam is an example (admittedly from a different context and continent) of the difficulties which protracted struggle can pose even to the best-equipped army, while the post-war histories of both Yugoslavia and Finland indicate that territorial defence may have some deterrent power. If it is to be rejected because it is highly destructive when implemented, then nuclear defence policies should be rejected on the same grounds.

Of course neither the organizational form of militia forces nor the strategic concept of territorial defence should necessarily be seen as complete and total alternatives to what exists at present in NATO countries. They certainly provide no easy solution to the problem of the defence of Berlin, and the question of their viability in a modern industrialized society (in which people are conveniently grouped into target areas known as towns) is extremely difficult. It may be significant that the European countries which proved most adept at conducting defence in depth in the Second World War – Finland and Yugoslavia – were both relatively undeveloped, not heavily urbanized, and covered with large expanses of forest.

A more modest possibility for the use of militia forces in a NATO context has been suggested by Kenneth Hunt. One of several models he offers for consideration is a three-layer structure for the conduct of defence in depth, consisting of:

a. Light formations or units in defence across almost the whole front, to be largely regular and partly militia.
b. Behind, and in key areas, the main weight of the defence in the form of heavy counter-attack formations of the existing type.
c. Behind these, to some depth, cadre formations designed to receive local and other reservists, and some of the reinforcing units and formations.[21]

Any proposals for militia forces, however modest, raise a political problem. As Julian Symons said in another context, 'an appeal to enrol for the purpose of dealing with some future, hypothetical danger is never one calculated to arouse enthusiasm . . .'.[22] To create and

[19] Raymond Aron, *The Great Debate: Theories of Nuclear Strategy* (New York: Doubleday, 1965), p. 22.
[20] Uwe Nerlich, 'Alternative Strategic and Tactical Doctrines in the Central European Theater', in *European Security and the Nixon Doctrine*, report of a conference in April 1972 at the Fletcher School of Law and Diplomacy, Medford, Massachusetts, p. 90.

[21] Kenneth Hunt, *The Alliance and Europe: Part II: Defence With Fewer Men*, Adelphi Paper No. 98 (London: IISS, 1973), p. 37.
[22] Julian Symons, *The General Strike* (London: Cresset Press, 1957), p. 23.

train a militia in peacetime is a difficult operation, and might be particularly so in West Germany, which is short of officers and NCOs anyway.[23] The history of militia-type formations, such as the *Heimatschutztruppe* in West Germany, formed in 1965, do not suggest that there would be immediate and overwhelming public enthusiasm. Plans for militias and/or for defence in depth can easily end up being more impressive on paper than they are in fact – as may well be the case with French schemes for *Défense Opérationelle du Territoire*, established in 1962.[24]

An element of voluntary recruiting might mean that a militia became identified with a particular social class or political viewpoint. There may be more to be said in favour of full-blown citizen armies on the Swiss, Swedish and, to a lesser extent, Yugoslav models, with their emphasis on universal compulsory conscription. Like taxation (of which in fact it is a form), universal conscription may sometimes be more just and egalitarian than some more selective or voluntary systems.

On the other hand, a citizen army raised by conscription, although it can have the political virtue of democratizing the use of force by the state, depends upon a degree of national unanimity and willingness to take an active interest in military affairs which is not likely to be found in many Western European states at the present time, and which would seem to many to smack of dull political conformism. A defence system of this kind might abolish the distinction between army and nation only to swamp the army with such civilian attitudes as a dislike of the use of force and an aversion to discipline. If the idea of militia forces were to be pursued at a time when the threat from outside is not self-evident to all, it might be unattractive to many people of military age unless it not only could be convincingly presented as being strictly geared to the functions of defence and deterrence but also appealed to more positive sentiments – possibly nationalism. 'My NATO right or wrong' would perhaps be a less plausible rallying cry than '*defense à tous azimuts*'.

The question of the style, the political assumptions and the mode of organization of such forces is crucial, and the mentors might have to be Marx as much as MacArthur. It should not be presumed without question (it is certainly not presumed in Yugoslavia) that the sole active participants should be of the male sex, that the only possible organizing body is the central government, or that the only potential enemy is the Soviet Union.

There does seem to be the possibility of a trend in Western Europe towards a territorial defence approach. As Erwin Häckel said, 'Although no NATO nation is likely to take any single step which cannot be defended politically as a contribution to alliance efficiency, it is impossible to avoid the overall impression that there is in Europe an emergence or a revival of interest in military manpower systems which, without marking any overt abandonment of collective security, will best serve the primary purpose of "territorial defence" for a single nation.'[25] If there is a trend towards territorial defence, it is an extremely slow and cautious one. The difficulties which a complete changeover would involve both for West Germany in particular and for NATO in general have been widely recognized. The acute problems it would pose for urban areas and highly developed societies have been identified, if not explored, and the fact that guerrilla or semi-guerrilla methods of warfare are peculiarly prone to lead to reprisals against the civilian population has not escaped attention. None of these difficulties is a conclusive objection if territorial defence is seen as essentially a form of deterrence: but they do suggest that other options may also be worth investigation.

Civil Resistance
This is the most radical and controversial of the three alternatives considered in this Paper. It is possible that all, or some, types of threat might best be met by essentially political or economic forms of resistance – not by the use of organized violence. There has certainly been a tendency in much strategic writing to underestimate the means of pressure which states or groups apparently dominated from outside can on

---

[23] This is of course not a conclusive objection. A full-blooded militia or citizen army system has largely part-time officers and NCOs, who might be easier to recruit, and higher in quality, than full-time ones.

[24] The *DOT* was not set up as a fixed body of specific size, but rather as an elaborate system of command and co-ordination drawing on a wide variety of forces.

[25] Erwin Häckel, *Military Manpower and Political Purpose*, Adelphi Paper No. 72 (London: IISS, 1970), pp. 30–31.

occasion exert for the reassertion of some degree of independence. One might for example, with the benefit of hindsight, differ from Henry Kissinger's judgment of 1955 that 'A split between the USSR and its satellites, and even more a split with China, can come about only through outside pressure.'[26]

Of course the range of pressures which a people or a state can exert against foreign domination is extremely wide, often includes military elements, and varies enormously with the political, geographical and strategic context. Here the discussion will be largely, though not exclusively, confined to how such pressures might be opposed by techniques of civil resistance.

There are many reasons for believing that there might be some function for civil resistance, at least in facing certain types of opponent or certain types of threat. The highly urbanized, industrialized and densely populated character of much of Western Europe would make any large-scale military conflict extremely destructive, even if nuclear weapons were not used,[27] and the political traditions and cultures of these countries, and their means of communication, might make various forms of common political action possible.

Civil resistance is a form of political struggle relying on non-violent methods of action. The reasons for the avoidance of violence can be various, deriving from ethics, habit, law or prudence. It can be used as an alternative to, or in various kinds of conjunction with, more violent forms of pressure or struggle.

One of the reasons why the subject is so controversial is that, to many people, it is associated with the ideas of unilateral disarmament, pacifism, and defeatism. This association of ideas may not be a completely necessary one: it is perfectly reasonable to argue that states, like many organizations, not to mention individuals, can pursue conflicts by different means, according to the situation.

The difficulty in this kind of argument, of course, is that when a state's defence policy is based, if not on bluff, then at least on the reiteration of extreme threats, then the assertion of a 'reasonable' alternative is liable to be seen as rocking the boat. But the fundamental question about civil resistance is not whether there might be some function for it if it were considered to have some effectiveness, but rather whether it has that effectiveness in the first place.

Raymond Aron has rejected the whole idea on the grounds that 'it presumes that the age of massacres and exterminations is definitely over, and that a nation which puts down its arms will be neither deported nor reduced to slavery nor purely and simply exterminated'.[28] The main way in which it is possible even to begin to resolve the question of the effectiveness of civil resistance is by detailed examination of historical cases.[29] However, a study of many cases of civil resistance (in European national struggles of the late nineteenth century, as in Hungary and Finland; in anti-colonial movements, as in India and Ghana; in resistance to foreign military occupation, as in Norway or Denmark in World War II; and in resistance to internal military coups, as in Germany in 1920 or in Algiers in 1961) suggests that Aron's comments on the very important issue of massacres should not be taken as constituting a conclusive or universal refutation. In some circumstances at least (including cases in the British and French empires) massacres can be attributed as much to the weakness of the offending power as to the lack of violence of any resistance, while the tendency for massacres to occur in the context of wars or in their immediate aftermath is notorious.

A study of cases of civil resistance also suggests that the relationship between violence and non-violent forms of action is extremely complex. Some violence and repression was always used against civil resisters, although it is arguable that the non-violent character of the resistance had an overall tendency to inhibit, but not totally

---

[26] Henry A. Kissinger, 'Military Policy and the Defence of the Grey Areas', *Foreign Affairs*, April 1955.

[27] The lack of attention in the strategic literature to these factors is pointed out in an interesting and highly critical study of the whole American theory of limited war, Nordal Åkerman, *On the Doctrine of Limited War* (Lund: Berlingska Boktryckeriet, 1972), p. 243.

[28] Raymond Aron, *Paix et Guerre Entre Les Nations*, 4th ed. (Paris: Calmann-Lévy, 1966), p. 617.

[29] By far the most comprehensive study of the whole field of non-violent action, dealing with its past use in a wide variety of contexts including resistance to foreign occupations, is Dr Gene Sharp's encyclopaedic work *The Politics of Nonviolent Action* (Boston: Porter Sargent, 1973), prepared under the auspices of the Center for International Affairs, Harvard University.

28

prevent, this.[30] However, to describe the contending parties as being 'violent' on the one side, and 'non-violent' on the other, might in some of these cases be too simple, for there were at times complex inter-connections between civil resistance and the use or threat of violence. International wars may have created the conditions for the results achieved by the Hungarians in 1867, by the Finns in 1905 and 1917, and by the people of El Salvador and Guatemala in 1944; on the other hand, it is at least arguable that World War II served only to delay the advent of Indian independence.[31] The Indian case, however, raises a quite separate question related to the connections between civil resistance and violence: the extent to which the British may have been influenced not merely by the known costs of the various non-violent campaigns, but also by the real threat that, if concessions were not made, rioting and terrorism might result. Although such a factor was probably unimportant in many of the cases considered, and although at times the use of such weapons as terrorism may reinforce the unity and resolve of an opponent, it is disturbing that so much literature in this field has avoided these questions which are both politically complex and morally ambiguous.

To recognize the importance of factors such as these, and the intricate modalities of the relationship between civil resistance and violence, is not to deny the value of civil resistance – but it is to suggest that this technique needs to be assessed in a less simplistic manner than hitherto, both by those who accept, and those who are doubtful of, its relevance to international conflict. The question of the context for civil resistance, and the manner in which it operates, needs more systematic treatment than it has been accorded in most of the literature. The influence of Gandhi, who stressed will-power above all else, and whose statements urging all-round non-violence to the Swiss, Czechs, Jews and everyone, were dogmatic and indiscriminate in character, is perhaps partly responsible for the general failure to devote attention to the more mundane economic, political, military and ideological context of civil resistance.

It is conceivable that some developments in Europe have increased the possibilities of pursuing struggles by non-military means. The fact that there is now general international acceptance of states and frontiers would provide any resistance against a new military challenge with a sense of international as well as national legitimacy – an important factor in many cases of resistance, whether guerrilla or civil. Improved communications could increase the chances of gaining foreign support – whether political, economic, or military. It is sometimes argued that an increasingly complex pattern of mutual economic relationships, for example in co-production agreements, may extend the potential for reprisals and the possibilities of conducting various forms of economic struggle. However, such forms of conflict are perhaps more likely to hurt small European states, highly dependent on trade, then they are large super-powers, for which the proportion of foreign trade in the Gross National Product is lower. What is perhaps more plausible is that increased economic integration between Eastern and Western Europe will reduce mutual antagonisms in the first place – but this may only be more plausible for the somewhat slender reason that Soviet and East European leaders seem (despite everything Lenin said about imperialism) to believe it.

Civil resistance should not necessarily be regarded as taking the form of a short, intense campaign: it can also be a process as much as a policy. It can assume a much less well-defined shape as a long-drawn-out series of encounters: clashes of interest or of culture, the preservation of certain social norms, concealed inefficiency and non-compliance, or the search for allies within the opponent's camp. This may bear some relation to the process described by Lenin when trying to elucidate the problems of imposing a new political order in Russia in his report to the March 1922 congress of the Russian Communist Party. Referring to 'what we were told in our history lessons when we were children', he said: 'Sometimes one nation conquers another, the nation that conquers is the conqueror and the nation that is vanquished is the conquered nation. This is simple and intelligible to all. But what happens to the culture of these nations? Here things are not so simple. If the conquering

---

[30] A preliminary discussion of this controversial and difficult question is in my article on 'Civilian Defense and the Inhibition of Violence', *Philosophy East and West*, Vol. XIX, no. 2, April 1969.
[31] A point made by Alastair Buchan in *War in Modern Society* (London: Fontana Books, 1968), pp. 68–69.

29

nation is more cultured than the vanquished nation, the former imposes its culture on the latter; but if the opposite is the case, the vanquished nation imposes its culture on the conqueror.'[32]

Of course, there are many cases of cultural defeat as well as of cultural survival, and Lenin made his statement in order to urge the 4,700 Communists in responsible positions in Moscow not to come 'under the influence of an alien culture'. It would be sanguine to the point of idiocy to assert that in all situations a developed culture is assured of immortality. Even if this were true it would not on its own be seen as a necessarily adequate ground for abandoning military defence. But if cultural survival came to be seen as more important than, say, the defence of specific frontiers or governments, and if a convincing distinction could in fact be drawn along these lines, then the case for defence based on some form of civil resistance would be reinforced.

The value of any planned and prepared civil resistance for defence does, of course, need to be assessed with the issue of deterrence in mind. Does a widespread campaign of non-co-operation, attempts at undermining the morale of invading forces, etc., have any potential for dissuading a would-be attacker? It does seem possible. The struggle in the Ruhr area of Germany in 1923 against Franco-Belgian occupation was in one sense a failure, and the Germans ultimately had to declare unconditional surrender. It was an unpleasant exercise in the mutual denial of goods and services, but it may (for better or for worse) have discouraged the French from getting involved in any further punitive ventures in Germany. Equally, the Czechoslovak resistance in 1968, completely ineffective as it ultimately was in preserving the reforms of the Prague Spring, may conceivably have had some deterrent power. The difficulties and the odium that attached to an invasion which was so plainly opposed by Czechoslovaks may have made the Soviet leaders more cautious in the next major crisis in the Soviet empire – the troubles in the Baltic ports of Poland in the winter of 1970–71.

Soviet credits rather than troops were sent. As Adam Bromke wrote, 'the Soviet Union . . . acted with unusual restraint during the December 1970 crisis, carefully avoiding any impression of overt interference in Polish affairs'.[33] Of course there may also have been a deterrent element in the possibility that the Poles might have reacted more violently than the Czechoslovaks to any direct intervention by Soviet armed forces, but one deterrent element does not necessarily cancel out the other. Liddell Hart suggested that the fear of 'their troops mixing with the people of the West' was one of the reasons for Soviet reluctance to advance further into Western Europe after 1945,[34] and the difficulties experienced by the Soviet Union within its empire since 1965 may well have made it extremely cautious about expanding its hegemony further.[35]

It is significant that both the resistance in the Ruhr in 1923 and that in Czechoslovakia in 1968 – perhaps the two most striking cases to date of immediate and general civil resistance against foreign occupation – were in highly industrialized areas of Central Europe. In both cases there was a good deal of awareness that violent conflict would be extremely destructive of the whole industrial base on which society depended. In both cases special relationships with the principal invading power, coupled with an awareness of the difficulties of guerrilla resistance in urban and industrial surroundings, made military action inadvisable. In both cases, also, the invading forces were from more than one country, and had a clearly defined purpose – in the case of the Ruhr economic, and in that of Czechoslovakia political. Both invasions were attempts to secure co-operation, and not just territory as such; thus the refusal of co-operation was an obvious and seemingly relevant type of response.

---

[32] Political Report of the Central Committee at the Eleventh Congress of the Russian Communist Party (Bolsheviks), 27 March 1922, in V. I. Lenin, *Collected Works* (Moscow: Progress Publishers, 1966), Vol. 33, p. 288.

[33] Adam Bromke, 'Poland Under Gierek: A New Political Style', *Problems of Communism*, September–October 1972, p. 2. See also a report from Moscow in similar vein which appeared in *The Times*, 22 December 1970.

[34] B. H. Liddell Hart in Roberts (ed.), *Civilian Resistance as a National Defence* (Harmondsworth: Penguin Books, 1969), p. 243.

[35] On this see Milovan Djilas, *Conversations with Stalin* (London: Hart-Davis, 1962), p. 165. The same point is made at greater length in Sir Bernard Burrows and Christopher Irwin, *The Security of Western Europe: Towards a Common Defence Policy* (London: Charles Knight, 1972), pp. 58–59.

Clearly civil resistance may not be able to do everything that military defence may be able to do, and, if it is to be regarded as an alternative, it is one which would be better suited to certain types of situation than others. It might, furthermore, have significant internal political implications. Nevertheless it could have some role: conceivably in West Berlin, where the problems of military defence are notorious and where at some points in the past twenty-five years (and especially in the period around 1948) the political resolve of West Berliners was itself an important factor in the equation; perhaps in a neutral state such as Austria, whose military defence has extremely modest aims; perhaps in the event of some limited projects of military disengagement being implemented in central Europe; or conceivably in a crisis where the alternatives to civil resistance seemed even more disastrous. Perhaps most important of all, civil resistance might have relevance in a situation where there were limited or ambiguous threats from some quarters, or where there was a desire to undertake action which would not undermine the basic relationship with a power which was only in a limited sense an adversary. For some European powers it might be a relevant form of 'defence against help' in a situation where it was an ally, rather than an adversary, who was thought likely to attack or interfere.[36] Civil resistance might be a first strike, if the pun can be forgiven, or a last resort.

It must be confessed that usually in the past civil resistance has been used without preparation in extreme situations and, if past form is anything to go by, it might be most likely to be used again only in an *ad hoc* manner. It would probably however have a better chance of success if there were at least some advance preparations; and there could be some deterrent effect therein.

But the problem of advance preparations for civil resistance is in some respects even more complex than that of organizing a citizen army. It is also politically sensitive. The questions of who, if anyone, should organize such preparations, against whom, and in what form, do not admit of simple or uniform answers. The obvious first necessity is some general awareness of the mere existence of civil resistance as one possible course of action. Like other possible alternatives to existing forces it is not a substitute for thought.

---

[36] For an exploration of the idea of defence against importunate 'friendly' interventions see Nils Ørvik, 'Defence Against Help – A Strategy for Small States?', *Survival*, September–October 1973.

Committee Discussions on the Future of Military Force in Modern Societies: Report to the Conference

THEO SOMMER

When Marshal MacMahon once visited France's famous Military Academy of St Cyr, a negro cadet was introduced to him.

'Ah, vous êtes le nègre', he remarked.

'Oui, mon maréchal', replied the cadet.

'Eh bien', said MacMahon, 'continuez comme ça!'

I was reminded of this story as I tried to compress the gist of the discussions in Stream B into this necessarily scant report. *Continuez comme ça!* – it seemed to me that this was the burden of the message formulated in both Committee IV and Committee V; on the basis of three excellent papers, I should like to add, and during the course of six most lively and rewarding sessions.

Now I don't want to be misunderstood. *Continuez comme ça* does not mean leaving everything as it used to be. There was practically universal recognition that change, that reform was inevitable. But I think it is fair to say that the majority of participants could not conceive of any basic alternative to existing forces which would be militarily viable, financially tolerable and socially acceptable. *Continuez comme ça*, then, meant two things. On the one hand it implied sticking to the kind of forces we have grown accustomed to. On the other hand, however, it implied improving these forces as far as we can – although in a manner which supplements present force postures rather than replaces them.

The first paper (see pp. 11–16) laid before Stream B dealt with the problems of military manpower. Mr Harries-Jenkins, its author, thought that this problem would and should be solved by a transformation of conscript armies into all-volunteer forces; the trend in this direction seemed to him to be inevitable, although he conceded that the outlook for recruiting was perhaps rather grim, and the public image of volunteer forces not altogether satisfactory.

The surprising thing was that this assessment was not at all widely shared. Serious doubt was expressed as to whether the volunteer bandwagon was really rolling; in fact, there was much extolling of the virtues of conscription. I was left with the impression that there is by no means an iron-clad predetermined, ineluctable movement in that direction. There was some debate as to the real meaning of recent recruitment figures in the United States, and in Britain, but it seemed to me they were regarded as discouraging rather than encouraging figures. For many speakers the Volunteer Army was saddled with so many problems that, in comparison, conscript armies appeared without doubt as the lesser evil. I should like to list at least some of the problems mentioned.

Problem No. 1 results from the fact that in times of high employment volunteer armies must compete with other public services, and with private enterprise for the sort of people they need. This presupposes comparable pay and educational incentives of an order of magnitude that would rip all defence budgets apart.

Problem No. 2. If you decide to stay within current and foreseeable defence budgets, all-volunteer forces can be equipped and maintained only if they are severely reduced in size and number. This would presuppose a drastic downward revision of NATO's present force requirements. In the case of the Federal Republic, for instance, a volunteer force could hardly be considered a realistic proposition unless, and until, SHAPE agreed that 300,000 West German soldiers – rather than the 460,000 we have at present – would be sufficient. It is obvious that such a scaling-down process can at best result from successful – though no doubt protracted –

MBFR negotiations. It would be quite foolhardy to anticipate the positive outcome of such a process at a time when there is not a shred of reliable evidence that MBFR will in fact lead anywhere.

Committees IV and V did of course investigate possibilities of overcoming these two problems.

Thus, they considered a revamping of the military image by turning armed forces more and more into constabulary units or fire brigades, by organizing them, for example, into a comprehensive disaster relief or search-and-rescue effort so as to make them more attractive for young men. It was pointed out, however, that there must be limits to this 'socialization' of armed forces; and these limits must be quite narrowly drawn to prevent the combat effectiveness of troops being impaired beyond recovery – at least in those countries where defence of territory continues to be the ultimate criterion against which the effectiveness of troops must be judged.

A further possibility to be considered was segmentation, i.e., allotting more jobs now held by soldiers to civilians. The obvious counter-argument was, of course, that there is a great deal of segmentation already – in West Germany, for example, 170,000 civilians provide the vital underpinning for 460,000 men in uniform – and that further civilianization would certainly increase personnel costs, for the simple reason that a conscript with a desk job, or who works at a specialized task, is indisputably less expensive than a civilian specialist hired at market rates.

It is hard to see what savings would accrue from pushing civilianization or segmentation any further. For civilianization would undoubtedly increase personnel problems within the armed forces if it just led to an influx of civilians blocking soldiers' careers.

Another possibility of overcoming the considerable problems posed by a shift to volunteer forces – a much more stringent division of labour amongst NATO countries, eliminating the need for each alliance member to maintain all three services – was also discussed, but it was realized that such rationalization was still a long way off, where it mattered most – in Western Europe; and that approach could be brought to fruition only by a very gradual habit-forming process that would take rather too long to have any bearing on the immediate situation.

One proposal for remedial action envisaged a kind of 'rent-a-division scheme', modelled probably on the *Hertz* car operation. If we have guest-workers from many countries, so the argument went, why be bashful about having guest-divisions from NATO's Southern European countries? This proposal, interesting though it sounded, was not taken up, I'm sorry to say. There was equally a considerable reluctance to follow a suggestion that the armed forces could be made much more attractive if we recruited or called-up more women into military service.

In the end we all seemed quite happy to return to the idea of conscript armies – at least for continental Europe. We recognized, of course, the difficulties connected with conscription, especially the inequity which results from all eligible young men not being actually drafted. In this context we considered briefly and inconclusively the prospects for a system of universal national service which would provide socially useful jobs for those not actually called up. But these difficulties appeared preferable to the problems that would be created by all-volunteer forces – quite apart from the fact that in some countries there is a deeply ingrained historical and ideological aversion towards purely professional armies with their tendency to lead an élitist life in a secluded 'state-within-the-state'. For even in all-volunteer forces you need a constant turnover because you have to keep your forces young; and volunteer armies do not produce reservists in sufficient numbers to permit meaningful expansion of forces in the event of crisis or war.

If there was any consensus at the end of our deliberations it was probably on the three following points:

(1) Countries with a conscription system would be well advised to hang on to it for a variety of reasons.

(2) It would be advisable to make a greater distinction between forces in being and reserve forces; at least in NATO Europe a *strategy of mobilization* might to some extent replace the present *strategy of presence* (which is actually a strategy tailored chiefly to the requirements of countries which – like the United States and Britain – keep expeditionary forces stationed abroad). In this context, *cadrification* – if there is such a word in the

33
102

English language – of an increasing number of units, which would be at skeleton strength, to be filled out by mobilization when needed, seemed to hold out considerable promise for some of the participants.

(3) There is no better way of strengthening our military establishment than by making military service more attractive by teaching the soldier skills which can be used once he returns to civilian life – ideally skills which would not have been acquired if he had never donned uniform.

The question how this could actually be done in practice was the central theme of General von Baudissin's paper 'Officer Education and the Officer's Career' (pp. 36–45). It sparked off a lively discussion on the professional requirements for officers, in fact about what it means to be an officer in today's complex world. General Baudissin submitted a detailed plan in which longer-serving officers would complete a university course related to their field of expertise and obtain a qualification for employment both recognized and usable beyond the barrack walls. He argued that a training course strictly limited to the study of military theory was no longer sufficient; it should be replaced by a broad university education which took up roughly four years out of twelve years's service.

Discussion at first focused on the basic concept underlying General Baudissin's approach: that an officer's training, career profile and general outlook on life should be as near as possible to that of his civilian contemporaries. Many people shared this view. There were others, however, who felt that Baudissin really wanted officers all to be philosopher kings and that this was a dangerous tendency to be resisted by every means. They were particularly worried about the combat effectiveness of junior officers; if these were all to be turned into intellectuals with their fighting instinct bred out of them then they would be useless on the battlefield; after all, soldiers were 'licensed assassins' and their primary mission was to kill. Rommel, as one participant suggested, won his battles without the benefit of a university education. This line of argument boiled down to the scathing remark that making the officer's career indistinguishable from the civilian pattern was like castrating a man and then wondering why he speaks with a high voice.

General Baudissin returned to the charge with redoubled vigour. Rommel, he argued, would find today great difficulties in leading men, for two reasons: he had never been able to understand that others were afraid, because he himself was such a courageous man; and he had never understood the political context of military operations until it was too late. General Baudissin reminded everyone of the fact that only 13 per cent of all officers actually serve in combat roles. He insisted, furthermore, that it was quite impossible to simulate battlefield conditions convincingly in peacetime; the 'toughie' trained purely for combat might turn out to be a coward under fire while the Ph.D.-officer might emerge as a hero. One just can't predict who will be the better leader in wartime.

It seemed to me that Baudissin's philosophy in the end carried the day. There was general agreement that education within the armed forces must keep pace with the increased education of society at large; you cannot have an uneducated officers' corps in a population of college graduates. The focus of our discussions then shifted to two more specific questions:

(1) When should an officer receive his university education: should it be earlier or later in his career? There were different opinions about this: and naturally so, for obviously the young officer is both the best platoon leader and the best student. Many were in favour of according chronological priority to university education; but a strong case was also made for a segmented education, with different training being offered in courses phased over the whole length of service; mid-career education should not be neglected. But no one really thought that they had an answer.

(2) The other question concerned the *locus* of officers' university education. Here, there was a clear uneasiness about strictly military universities. After all, so the prevailing argument ran, if the young officers would be susceptible to contagion to the point where they could not survive frank debate with other students, they were not worth having in a modern army in the first place.

If General Baudissin's paper explored one way of improving existing forces, Adam Roberts' dealt with 'Alternatives to Existing Forces' (pp. 17–31). Three possible alternatives were suggested: technology, militia-type forces and civil resistance techniques. Each of these solutions was looked at in more or less detail, but in the end there was almost universal consensus that none of them really provided a viable alternative, although each or all of them could usefully supplement the existing defence set-up.

On *technology* it was pointed out that improvements were certainly worthwhile making but that there were natural limits beyond which they could not be pressed to any useful purpose. Technological development should be directed towards better, eg., precision-guided, anti-tank and anti-aircraft weapons. But any advantage gained here would remain temporary, as the other side was soon bound to catch up. In any case, technology could not be expected to solve our manpower problems.

Militia forces, in turn, looked attractive to a number of participants, but there were also serious doubts voiced here about the whole concept. Psychological doubts arose from the fact that in Central Europe there was no historical base for militia forces – with the exception of Switzerland, of course. Strategic doubts arose from the question whether one could really expect militia forces to match the regular forces of the other side and bear the brunt of armoured attack; it was stated that we simply don't have the technology for militia forces – *TOW* and *HOT* being much too expensive, and cheap stand-off weapons still a long way off. These strategic doubts were increased by the further consideration that leaving front-line defence to militia units would upset the basic NATO tenet that in Central Europe an aggressor must from the very outset engage the forces of as many allies as possible. If militia simply meant 'The Germans to the front' this would dangerously impair the West's defence and deterrence postures. Doubts about finance and manpower further dampened down enthusiasm for militia-type alternatives. Well-equipped militia forces would be extremely expensive; and it would be hard to find the NCOs and officers to train them.

One British RAF officer expressed misgivings of a different sort. He said, perhaps tongue-in-cheek, that he was doubtful about the wisdom of issuing anti-aircraft weapons to some of his Scottish friends who keep protesting about his low flying.

However, there was a suggestion that experiments might be made with small militia units simply to see whether the idea was feasible, and the role of this type of force to be slowly increased within the existing framework of conscript/cadre armies.

Finally, *civil resistance*. This, it was said, might recommend itself to countries like Yugoslavia, but would hardly work in the urbanized regions of Western Europe, especially as an occupying power could easily cut water, gas and electricity supplies off from populations absolutely dependent on them. Historical precedents – the Ruhr in 1923, Czechoslovakia in 1968 – were highly discouraging; in both cases the occupying power was strong and ruthless enough to force the resisting populations first into submission and then into co-operation. Civil resistance, it was said, requires either heroes or fanatics – and you can't count on a great many of either type.

So the general conclusion was that none of the possibilities raised by Mr Roberts provided real alternatives to existing forces. At best they could be considered as supplementary measures. For the rest, however, it was more important to improve present forces along lines of structural reform already apparent than to look for seemingly revolutionary, but rather theoretical models. This, at least, seemed to be the predominant impression: you can't really change a great deal; alternatives are either unavailable or unworkable. This leads me back to Marshal MacMahon's admonition: *Continuez*, although I hasten to add that carrying on – soldiering on, as it were – cannot possibly signify staleness and stagnation but can only mean a determined effort at piecemeal reform. If I may try my French once more: '*plus c'est la même chose, plus ça change*' – the more things seem to remain the same, the more they change.

I have tried to encapsulate the long, lively and intelligent discussions of Stream B in a brief report. If I seem to have done so with malice towards all and justice to none, I offer my sincere apologies.

Officer Education and the Officer's Career

LIEUTENANT-GENERAL WOLF GRAF VON BAUDISSIN

Foreword

This paper is based essentially on West German experience and concepts. However, in most industrialized societies the armed forces face the same basic functional, psychological and political problems (one should not be deceived about this by occasional genuine differences in organization, emphasis and possible solutions), and not even the rigidity of the Socialist systems and their armed forces seems able to dam up these sources of friction permanently. I hope, therefore, that national experience is not quite without use as a basis for discussion. That said, however, it is obvious that there are differences in the solutions advisable at given times for other armed forces, for history, outlook, geographical position (to mention only some factors) influence the structure of the armed forces, and with it the system of officer training. The general educational system of the country in question naturally also plays a decisive part, and specialist military training must be seen as part of this; to wish it to be autonomous would be uneconomic and inefficient, and seems to me to be a particular form of militarism.

The planning of effective education and careers for officers should be based on what is professionally required of them in a given sphere, i.e., in the social and security situation to be expected. Upon this depend the answers to certain important questions – for example, how far the officer should be a specialist or 'generalist'; whether a purely practical education is sufficient, or whether appropriate theoretical grounding is required; whether the officer's career should as a rule be for life, or whether the rational use of resources does not demand different solutions; and whether his education and career should be made as 'civil' or as 'military' as possible.

The Social Context and its Effects

Social Factors

Pluralism in society has abolished the general validity of certain values. There is consequently no generally recognized authority or single exterior and extrinsic motivation. The great mass of individuals have to be addressed on their own wavelength if they are to become committed.

The state has lost its metaphysical character, and the nation as the highest value is called in question. Both these factors – like religious, ethical or class beliefs – operate only with strong reservations, and only in particular cases do they supply a motive for service; consensus in matters of security policy can at best be expected now only in moments of danger. In view of the mentality and vulnerability of society, the regulation of conflicts without use of force seems to most people to be the only possible policy, and this basic feeling contrasts with the received view of the military as 'in the killing business', with its enormous costs. Thus it is that questions of security policy are increasingly losing their position of overriding importance in political discussion. In the eyes of considerable sections of society the armed forces are becoming less a 'necessary evil' than a superfluous one.

The value given to the military, and the conventional status of soldiers as a professional group, including officers, are determined against this background – making it increasingly difficult to form an objective picture of either the political necessity or the military effectiveness of the armed forces. This is due not least to the fact that obsolete notions of security policy and military strategy, hierarchy, authority, leadership, discipline, command and obedience still play a part in the thinking of the majority. Often the armed forces are unjustly judged precisely by their main supporters, who apply the standards of the past to the soldiers of today.

A growing part of the population, however, (in particular the more educated) are alienated from the armed forces for ideological and political reasons, and also for private and professional reasons. Military expenditure and military service are anything but a matter of course. This leads to internal frictions in the everyday working of the services, which can be overcome only by consistent leadership. Today, giving leadership means constantly motivating people – in the case of the armed forces, giving them a commitment to the security policy mission of the military institution and to the conscientious performance of their own duties.

Support for such motivation is supplied either when military structures harmonize with society as a whole, or when they deliberately diverge from it. Conservative ideology usually counsels the latter course, so as to keep the armed forces and their officer corps so far as possible homogeneous and isolated from social conflicts; such a course, however, leads in the last analysis to a 'ghetto' existence for the military, thus endangering both the internal and external security of society. An atmosphere out of harmony with society as a whole runs counter to the life-style and expectations of the great majority of young people in highly developed societies. Those whom it moves to choose an officer's career are mainly people who differ from the norm and whose technical, as well as political, qualities are as a general rule questionable. Where the atmosphere and image of the profession are determined by the propagandists of reactionary concepts of order and of the 'killing business', the alienation between military and civilians is exacerbated.

An extensive conformity with society has an integrating effect in both directions, and also promotes a 'transparency' that is in the interest of the armed forces. When one is thinking of motivation, it is on this basis that the needs and expectations of the individual can most easily be brought into harmony with military requirements. That is an important step towards proper political and military disposition of the armed forces (of soldiers as a professional group and of individual members of the military) within the state or society, so as to prevent a dualism arising between military and political matters.

In addition to this the advance of technology has so changed war and military methods that a general distinction between what is military and what is civil can only be maintained with difficulty. This is not to dispute that there are quite special military functions and requirements, especially in waging war; military structure and organization are designed accordingly. But, particularly in peacetime, there are a number of military functions (probably even the majority) which, when properly performed, follow a very 'civilian' course – while, conversely, in conditions of catastrophe many civilians have to act in a 'military' manner. When extraordinary moments of danger, strain and disturbance occur in peacetime, supplementary monetary and other compensation must be given, as in civil professional life. The demand for an *esprit de corps* sounds somewhat class-bound and does not correspond to present-day circumstances, for *esprit de corps* is above all an exclusive characteristic and therefore does not fit in with either the social background or the constitutional definition of the armed forces as part of the Executive. It creates a temptation to idealization and self-imposed isolation on the part of the military, makes it more difficult to regulate the inevitable internal conflicts because of false harmonization, and creates obstacles to the external representation of the interests of the profession which is the practice of every group in a modern society.

Of course, soldiers as a professional group – and particularly their leadership, the officers – will and should develop a sense of group identity, a certain style of behaviour, even a code of prohibitions. There are no doubt many actions and imputations that call in question the credibility of the individual as a soldier, and thus are harmful to his function, but this must not mean setting up an order of values standing in conscious opposition to our society and its politics. If the military becomes a sub-culture, a closed community with a distinct social order, then tensions arise that are harmful to the armed forces.

Undoubtedly a distinguishing characteristic of the military is its strong intellectual and psychological bent towards war and other catastrophes. But this is a question of training, which, in the interest of the effectiveness of the armed forces, should counteract any inherent bias towards pessimism (preferring the worst) and cynicism over the peaceful settlement of conflicts, and

37

should impart to officers an understanding of their own function and their integration into society.

Security Factors

The armed forces as a political instrument have taken on a purely prohibitive character: they are meant to demonstrate credibly how slight are the chances of unilateral solutions by force. The measure of achievement in security policy is therefore no longer 'superiority' but 'sufficiency'.

Classical military strategy of the type dating from the time of the French Revolution has been overtaken by technology, for settlement by war of a dispute between industrialized societies has lost its political sense. On the other hand, the individual nation-state is no longer in a position to guarantee its own security in isolation, and is dependent upon a security system in a framework of alliances. Solidarity within the alliance has taken the place of the assertion of the interests of the nation-state.

Security can be decreasingly guaranteed by military means alone. To give society a form that is attractive and competitive, expensive reforms are needed in almost all spheres of life, and yet maintaining existing military potential already gives rise to rapidly mounting costs. Security policy must therefore aim at a division of labour within an alliance and at co-operative arms control between alliances. Within the armed forces themselves there should be the most intensive exploitation of resources, personnel, training and time. This applies also to the formation of career structures for officers and to the system for their education.

The demand for far-reaching rationalization raises the question of whether the armed forces could not take over other social tasks in addition to their existing functions of keeping and restoring the peace. Their scale and technical resources, their leadership structure and capacity for planning and instruction, their availability, flexibility and mobility make it possible to bring in military units in support in special and emergency situations where the regular organs of the state are no longer sufficient. Moreover, assistance in catastrophes (in both a national and international framework) as one of their natural functions is appropriate both to the forces' view of themselves and their general competence and to their position in society. One has in mind here,

for example, multi-national participation in a UN or regional framework in environmental protection, verification of the fulfilment of agreements or emergencies of all kinds. The services may lose something of their character of unreality – of being a game – and gain in attractiveness instead. The attitude of some officers towards co-operative arms control and disarmament would become more relaxed.

At this point many people raise the question of whether such an extension of function does not create a 'civilian' mentality, unfitted for participation in battle (the possibility of which cannot be excluded). Representatives of the 'killing business' approach will certainly register concern here. Against them it should be maintained that any attempt to simulate the psychological stresses of combat is condemned to failure; it only leads to artificiality which often gives the impression of a charade. Motivation for defence, service and battle are quite different problems, and experience shows many an outstanding 'fighting man' was unruly in terms of discipline during his period of service.

In peacetime, training must be restricted to practising functional effectiveness, even under difficult external conditions, and above all to developing the motivation for the conscientious performance of duty. In combat itself a specific psychological situation holds groups and units together – the will to effective action offering the highest chance of survival, and the need for respect by others, and for self-respect, ruling out leaving the group in the lurch.

If, however, one distinguishes between motives for service and for battle, it cannot be disputed that extension of the range of military tasks itself brings with it an important shift of orientation and offers a protection against crises of identity. The classical understanding of the military function, related simply to war, is necessarily exposed to such crises during a period of political relaxation. A broader working basis, on the other hand, impedes the ideological and professional tendency to see war as innocuous, the seeds of which are sown in peacetime, and removes the grounds for superfluous forms of 'heroic leadership'. In addition to their deterrent role, which is hard to understand and scarcely measurable in its actual effectiveness, the armed forces take on functions that satisfy direct, visible social needs. The fact that these functions also imply non-violent protective tasks should have its effect on their mutual relationship with society.

Professional Requirements
General Functional Effectiveness
Officer functions can be roughly classified (see Appendix 1), though the boundaries between these categories are, of course, often somewhat arbitrary in detail, and the transitions are fluid.

1. *The officer at regimental duty* works directly in the deployment of men and material or as an instructor; he will therefore be a unit or platoon commander, pilot, frogman or the like; or he may be on the field staffs - for example, in Intelligence, Logistics, etc. The functions of this category are comparable with those of junior management in the business field: e.g., company engineers, heads of sales or production scheduling departments, etc.
2. *The officer on the staff* works in the higher grades, offices and specialist commissions, or he may be the commander of a battalion, brigade or division. This category is fully comparable with middle-level management in business or in government departments: e.g., directors of companies and their immediate advisers, or heads of police, railways, postal communications, etc.
3. *The officer in posts bordering on politics.* This group includes the holders of posts in the ministry and in the highest national and NATO staffs and the commanders of large formations. This category has similarities in function and method of operation with top management in business and also with the most senior administrators in government departments.

Many posts, like their corresponding functions in public life, administration and business, require from officers a certain minimum of human and political qualities, which increase with responsibility; those who turn out to be pronounced failures in these areas can have particularly unfortunate effects.

In the selection, education and employment of officers it should always be borne in mind that the military 'sub-system' tends to acquire a momentum of its own that runs counter to the political aspect of its executive function. The extent and complexity of security problems make civil control from above difficult, but so too do the military *apparat* and its attendant complex of armaments. The primacy of politics can only be enforced if it is recognized unreservedly by the majority of officers, or at any rate by those exercising the relevant functions. But, over and above this, it is of decisive importance for the credibility of the state and the social order, and also for the effectiveness of the troops, that - even in exceptional circumstances, such as the application of force under orders - officers should continue to feel bound by the laws and general assumptions of humanity.

So far as professional requirements for officers are concerned, preparations for emergency situations, in which there may be panic and chaos, demand a considerable measure of flexibility, ability to improvise and also physical effectiveness. Even practising for an emergency in training simulates a field of action characterized by greater dynamism than a static job; for this reason alone the fear of 'overeducation', expressed by some people, is far removed from reality. Over and above this, political, social and technical developments cause a general movement from the purely practical into a mixed area of theory and practice. The complexity of problems, procedures and equipment requires an attitude towards science and technology long regarded as 'unmilitary'. The factors of physical strength and of mere numbers of officers have declined considerably in importance, and broad general knowledge with only limited acquaintance with any particular subject has given way to a necessary specialization. The functions of subordinates are now of such complexity that they can no longer be carried out by superiors, who can normally only judge their subordinates by results and co-ordinate the various elements. The concept of the 'generalist' has changed accordingly.

Interchangeability
The concept of the 'career officer' covers people responsible for a large number of very varied functions, and for the most part they have little in common with their predecessors in earlier times. The man who can still be most readily compared with this 'archetype' is the specialist in tactics within a simple weapons system - but if one were to model the image of the armed forces on him, it would be like modelling the image of the railways on the engine driver. All activities, however,

more or less resemble equivalent functions in the civil sphere, and to a large extent correspond both in training and practice. Exchanges are thus possible, indeed necessary. Moreover, the practice of a single profession for a lifetime is increasingly rarely sought by applicants or demanded by employers, so that in future people will have to count on two or more changes of profession. If one thinks about it, one sees that today most officers already change their profession with the transition from regimental to staff duty – at any rate, the commander of a pioneer company, for example, would remain closer to his previous profession by changing over to a corresponding civil activity than by taking up a staff appointment outside his former type of posting.

The determinants of career structures and the courses of training hitherto in force do not, of course, take sufficient account of such changes, necessary though they may be for financial or other reasons peculiar to the individual. The fundamental concept of the general duty officer either makes no preparation for his later functions and their special requirements or does so only imperfectly and with little method. If, however, specialization leads to vertical lines of employment and horizontal fields of responsibility, changes of 'profession' can be carried out in both directions without any discontinuity arising; the earlier training is extended organically and previous experience is worked in.

Such changes should not, as in the past, be decided solely by the needs of the armed forces but should also take into account the personal preferences and the potentialities for further education of those affected, as well as their special qualities. In the general congruence of military and civil occupations, military courses of education will take in the requirements of civil professions, mostly without special supplementation and, in the case of those transferring from civil professions, will build on the knowledge and experience they bring with them. The armed forces are as much interested in such exchanges for their own financial reasons as are civil employers, and the benefit for both the individual and for society is clear. If one continues to attach importance to the 'uniformity' of officer careers, it should be pointed out that quality is to be found not in the contents of the syllabus but in the academic level of education. Reasons for the desirability of uniformity in this sense are not only its help in meeting technical requirements but also its contribution to ensuring the necessary attractiveness of a career as an officer, and to equality of opportunity and social homogeneity, which are also sources of prestige.

Types of Activity
Management
To direct no longer means to occupy and preserve hierarchies of offices, but to create goal-directed hierarchies corresponding to areas of responsibility, and so to establish priorities. This requires management to adopt pre-set objectives according to the current area of responsibility and to monitor the extent of success. This can only work properly if the basic principles of co-operation and participation are observed. There must be the maximum of delegation and information combined with the minimum of invasion and by-passing of areas of responsibility. Direction is concerned, therefore, not so much with command as with co-ordinating co-operation, as in a business concern.

Leadership
The lack of any common external and extrinsic motivation, mentioned above, gives a special importance to the small group, the functional team at regimental level, such as the tank crew, or staff level. Here soldiers of all ranks can experience social ties and stability, find emotional security and develop common binding principles. The man who is to lead must therefore be able to recognize and guide the processes of group dynamics; the study of sociology, psychology and the science of labour provide the appropriate theoretical basis here.

Fighting and Tactics
Only some 13 per cent of officers can be defined directly as potential combatants; all other officers have to perform functions which are related only indirectly to the possible combat mission of the armed forces. For them 'combat' arises only in the sense of self-defence – i.e., in an exceptional situation in which their primary function is greatly restricted or cannot be carried out at all. To seek to centre the image of the armed forces solely on the 'fighting man' would run counter to

1. the spirit of deterrence, rightly understood, and with it the security policy function of the armed forces;

2. the fact that today it is more difficult, from an economic point of view, to maintain weapons systems in readiness, than to use them;
3. the fact that the position of 'fighting man' is only a staging post *or* ancillary function for all officers.

Technology (application)
As far as the technical field is concerned, about 20 per cent of officers serve as technical specialists, though there is, of course, no leadership and combat activity which does not also require the mastery and application of some technical skills. A certain basic technical knowledge is therefore indispensable, but this has nothing to do with specialist functions that involve university-level study because of their necessary theoretical content.

Specialist and Generalist
An officer's career initially involves only specialized employment and courses of training in specialized functions; hence the officer is primarily a specialist, but he can and should expand his operational and professional basis by extending his knowledge to other specialist fields. Only a relatively small number are qualified for 'general' employment. During the period of regimental duty it is more or less up to the individual to acquire certain general basic principles through private study. On the other hand, the officer serving with the staff, by experience in various tasks and by training for top management (economic and budgetary affairs, political science, systems analysis, etc.), is given the possibility of rising to employment in the area bordering on the political decision-making process.

The *specialist* is the man who has mastered a complex professional field in theory and in practice. Theoretical mastery presupposes intensive training and, for most officer functions, a university course in the field concerned or an allied one; as a rule one can speak of practical mastery only after several (two to five) years of uninterrupted activity. The shuffling of officers that has been widely practised perceptibly disturbs this course of development, and here, too, the drive towards rationalization suggests an overhaul of personnel planning. A pre-technical,

dillettante professional knowledge is not sufficient.

A *generalist* therefore, does not mean some kind of officer who is not an expert in any professional field. A generalist must rather, as an expert in at least one field and with some knowledge of others, be able competently to relate the findings and knowledge of his own expert field to the problems of others. This is in any case necessary if a number of specialists and complex sub-systems are to be co-ordinated and their leaders motivated both to co-operate with other officers of the same rank and to see the tasks in their own area of responsibility in the larger military and political context.

The Training System
The training and careers of officers differ fundamentally according to their previous education or length of engagement. Appendix 2 shows a rough scheme which attempts to satisfy the criteria and requirements that have been described. In essence it follows the ideas that are to be put into practice in the West German Federal forces; training concepts differ considerably between countries, however, as can be seen from the diagrams on pp. 184–186 of the 1971 Report of the Educational Commission to Federal Defence Minister.[1]

The proposed course of education for career officers (and limited-service officers) presupposes that a purely military-theoretical training no longer suffices and must therefore be replaced by scientific university study in selected expert fields. Most such fields mentioned in Appendix 1 require special study in any case, but it is also an advantage for specialists in tactics or Intelligence to have completed a course in one of the subjects bordering on their own. Military leadership also requires scientific bases and methods, while various branches of mathematics and information science supply an objective basis for tactical decisions, making possible systematic organization of information used in the decision-making process. For these reasons technical specialists are offered courses not only in science and technology but also in the social sciences and organizational science, with courses in teaching

[1] *Neuordnung der Ausbildung und Bildung in der Bundeswehr: Gutachten der Bildungskommission an den Bundesminister der Verteidigung* (Bonn: 18 May 1971).

methods, psychology, etc., for other specialist areas.

Study is concentrated in a single period at the beginning of the officer's career, to take advantage of the period of greatest capacity and will to learn, and so that the benefits of successful training take effect over the whole period of service. Like officials and public servants, officers who make a career without any scientific dimension almost inevitably acquire a certain intellectual complacency or even an aversion to creative and scientific solutions to problems. The specific course of studies is so arranged as to leave open the option of later 'job-changing' either within the forces or into civil life. An education and social science orientation is common to all the courses of study, so that they open up an insight into political and social interrelationships and thus confront specialists with the context in and for which they have to co-operate and co-ordinate. It is here that the bases are laid of the common self-image of the professional group. In the ideal case this study should be carried out in the ordinary institutions of higher education, but when this is not possible – as at present in the Federal Republic – the special academies should maintain close connections and co-operation with the universities.

The criticism is occasionally made that a study course always involves learning more than is directly applicable to the job immediately following it. This fact, however, does not mean there is 'overeducation'; on the contrary, an academic training promotes a broad capacity to deal with problems of the future. The consequence that training also contributes to the quality of life of the individual is as advantageous to recruiting as it is to the required motivation for service. One comes across this fear of 'overeducation' in a large number of professions. Simply from the point of view of time, periods of training are increasing considerably, under the slogan of 'lifelong learning'. A deliberate rationalization is needed here. In practice training systems of the kind contemplated here are felt to be 'overeducation' most of all by those who see an officer's profession as a purely practical one. They are inclined to exaggerate uncritically the value of practical experience and mere factual knowledge, and even to see critical, analytical thought as a diminution of vitality of decision – this is a malignant survival of certain pre-technical, late feudal attitudes.

To the study period and the training strictly related to regimental duty are added seven years of uninterrupted practical experience; first in subordinate, then in responsible positions. After a total of twelve years of service a number of officers leave the forces, their higher educational qualifications and practical experience giving them good opportunities for a career in civil life. The others remain in the forces as career officers, and are prepared both generally and specifically for their functions on the staff. The same thing happens again later on with regard to the military top management posts.

Officers with a period of service that allows no time for a study course obtain the practical knowledge they need to carry out their functions on military courses. Like senior NCOs, they are to be employed in special activities for which there is either no study course or which can be managed, under guidance, without such study.

Conclusions

The officer's profession has lost its social and professional homogeneity. The soldiers in modern armed forces, and with them the officers, form one of the major professional groups in society.

The academic level should be uniform only in the interest of:

1. professional and social requirements;
2. the attractiveness and self-image of the profession;
3. equality of opportunity within the profession;
4. interchangeability in both the narrower and the broader framework.

A characteristic of this professional group is that by comparison with other groups it includes an unusually large number and variety of expert groupings. These must – and this is a general characteristic of military life – co-operate with each other in a self-contained way in conditions of great mobility and flexibility within the framework of the military role.

Definitions of what is 'military' and what is 'civilian' have lost their sharpness and applicability as a result of technical development; thus there are 'nine-to-five' jobs in the forces just as there are 'round-the-clock' operations in civil organizations. It is of central importance for motivation that, in the forces also, only what is actually needed for functional effectiveness should be required and enforced. More important in this context, however, is the fact that the general development of all military decision and action can only superficially be determined in a purely 'military' way, for everywhere a considerable part is played by personal preconceptions of a social and political nature. Most officers have to take account of 'civilian' factors in making decisions, and in any case their service actions and omissions have direct or indirect consequences for the public, for society and politics.

In order to engender awareness of these connections and to prepare for operational requirements at many levels, academic training is needed in subjects which may appear more 'civil' than 'military' and which at first sight have little or nothing to do with the daily professional life of an officer.

Like all soldiers, officers must, in addition to their specialized functions, be trained in self-defence or its organization. As a general rule their special functions also involve a certain basic understanding of how to lead men: in almost all cases subordinate specialists have to be motivated to co-operate conscientiously.

There is no special career for 'generalists', since to ask for people of a 'universal education' in the nineteenth-century sense, would be illusory today. To attempt all specialist fields would indeed support claims to recognition, but would lead to a dilettantism which is disastrous in all functions, and especially for the generalist. The officers who are suitable for top management functions are those who have proved themselves as specialists in several expert fields and have received special training for such functions.

The careers and training of officers have become fluid. Behind this process of constant change lie both technical requirements and the demands of society and of security policy. Any new scheme for a training system has therefore to be kept flexible and should be deliberately geared to change. The maintenance of academic standards in training is a necessary part; only this provides the knowledge of method that enables the officer to master the changing demands upon him in a rational way. In addition, alternative and complementary courses of training should enable changes of profession to be made within the armed forces, as well as between military and civilian careers. This is particularly important for fairness when cutting down the surplus of field officers.

Longer-serving officers should complete a university course related to their field of expertise and providing a qualification recognized outside the armed forces. The forces thus obtain a well-founded prospect of acquiring officers of high competence, flexibility, adaptability and job satisfaction. At the same time the training and formation of officers is linked to the general educational system, and in this way service as an officer becomes attractive for the qualified members of the rising generation.

The requirement, therefore, is for a training corresponding to the technical requirements of a dynamic world; a meaningful and hence satisfying function; a flexible career which takes account of personal expectations; and the degree of co-determination in vocational, social and political matters that is customary in society at large. These are the preconditions for effective functioning by the armed forces in changing political conditions, for the understanding by the military of their own role as a safeguard against emergencies, and for the integration of soldiers as a professional group and as individuals into a pluralist society.

For the armed forces this concept is concerned in the first instance with fulfilling military requirements. Of course one must not think here only in terms of today's professional requirements, for training and career structure works itself out only over twenty years, and one can only guess at the requirements that will prevail then. But it is certain that in order to carry them out officers will be needed who have a command of rational methods of thinking and working, who think in terms of models and alternatives, are in continuous touch with other relevant fields and show a high ability to learn.

Various effects can be expected from the appropriate fulfilment of military requirements. With rising effectiveness in the performance of duties the atmosphere within the armed forces will improve, and with rational service planning many disciplinary difficulties will disappear. It is, however, of decisive importance that well-prepared officers should find satisfaction in their profession and, with it, a well-founded motivation towards defence and service. The improved atmosphere will also radiate outwards, making the profession attractive and securing social recognition for it through both the quality of its élite and its achievements.

43

APPENDIX I. PROFESSIONAL QUALIFICATIONS TO BE REQUIRED OF OFFICERS

		1. Regimental Officer		2. Staff Officer		3. Officer In Posts Bordering On Politics
A. Specialist		Knowledge of one or more of: *Leadership:* administration (i.e. planning/ organization/ management) *and/or* sociology, labour studies, psychology, etc. *Special Subjects:* e.g., medicine, chemistry, law, history, etc. *Education/Teaching* (also, in exceptional cases, research) with emphasis on teaching methods and educational science *and/or* content of all above fields, plus civics and knowledge of potential opponents and sources of danger.		Knowledge of one or more of the subjects in 1A, including university-level study in at least one.	*and*	Maximum knowledge and practical experience of aids to decision-making, so as to provide the best possible management of complex, large-scale systems.
				A certain minimum knowledge of aids to decision-making, as a result of continuous training in systems analysis, decision theory, operations research, electronic data processing, etc.		A certain minimum knowledge of political science, including economics.
B. Generalist		A certain minimum knowledge of subjects adjacent to the officer's specialist field(s).	*and*	Knowledge of one or more of the subjects in 1A, including university-level study in at least one.	*and*	Knowledge of one or more of the subjects in 1A, including university-level study in at least one.
		A certain minimum of general education (University entrance standard).		A certain minimum knowledge of all fields in 1A.		A certain minimum knowledge of all fields in 1A.
				A maximum of general, and especially political, education.	*and*	A maximum of general, and especially political, education.
					and	international experience (i.e., practical collaboration with officers/officials of other countries).

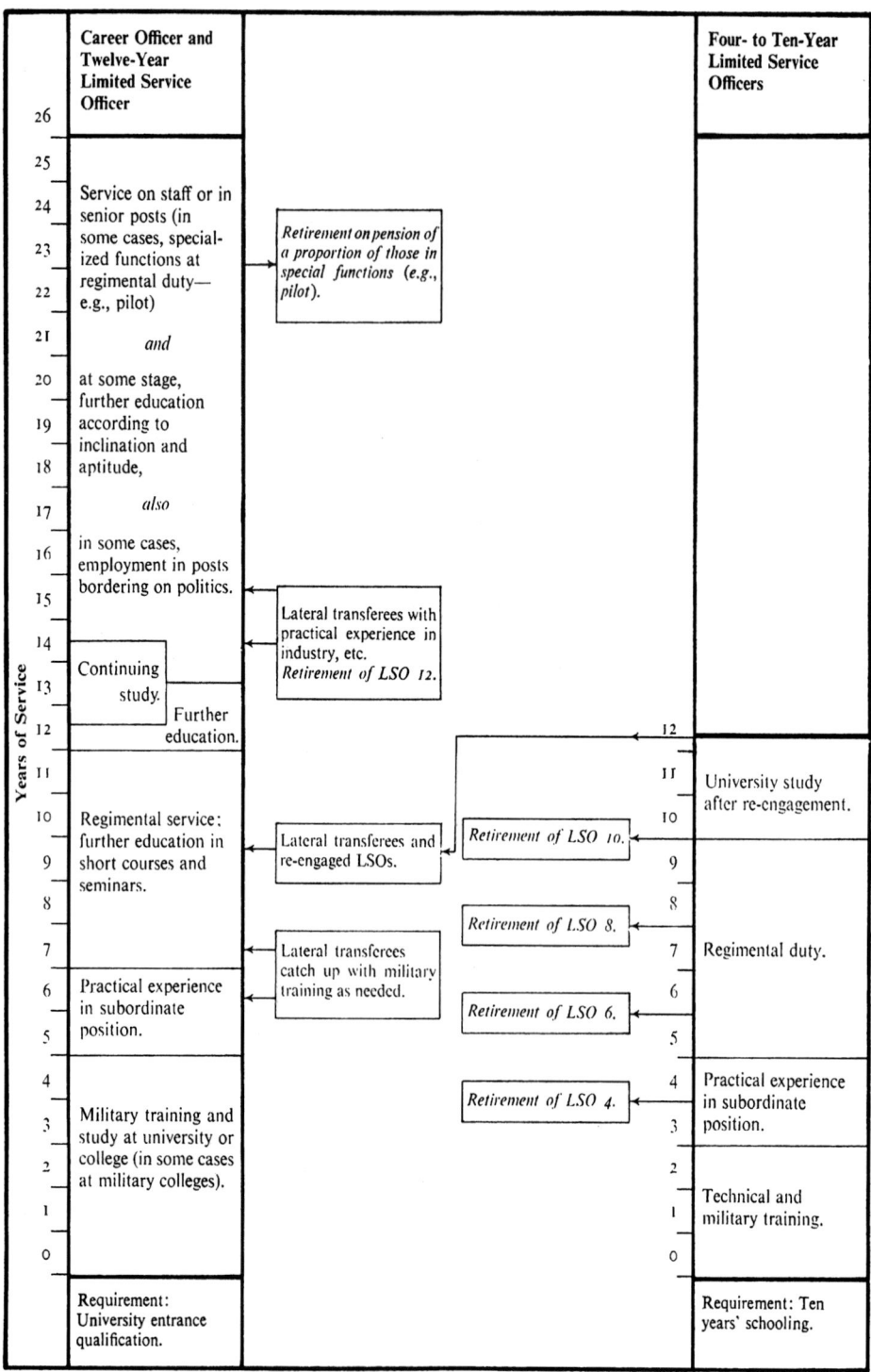

ADELPHI PAPERS

NUMBER ONE HUNDRED AND FIFTY-THREE

Congressional Power:
Implications for American Security Policy

by Richard Haass

THE INTERNATIONAL INSTITUTE FOR STRATEGIC STUDIES
23 TAVISTOCK STREET LONDON WC2E 7NQ

ADELPHI PAPER NO.153

Richard Haass, formerly Special Assistant for Foreign Relations to a
United States Senator, was a Research Associate at the IISS 1977–79.

First published Summer 1979

ISBN 0 86079 024 X
ISSN 0567-932X

© The International Institute for Strategic Studies 1979

All rights reserved. No part of this publication may be reproduced,
stored in a retrieval system, or transmitted in any form or by any
means, electronic, mechanical, photo-copying, recording or
otherwise, without the prior permission of the International Institute
for Strategic Studies.

*The International Institute for Strategic Studies was founded in 1958 as a centre for
the provision of information on and research into the problems of international security,
defence and arms control in the nuclear age. It is international in its Council and staff,
and its membership is drawn from over fifty countries. It is independent of governments
and is not the advocate of any particular interest.*

*The Institute is concerned with strategic questions – not just with the military aspects
of security but with the social and economic sources and political and moral
implications of the use and existence of armed force: in other words, with the basic
problems of peace.*

*The Institute's publications are intended for a much wider audience than its own
membership and are available to the general public on subscription or singly.*

Printed in England by McCorquodale (Newton) Ltd., Newton-le-Willows, Lancashire.

CONTENTS

Congressional Power:
Implications for American Security Policy

INTRODUCTION

States arrive at their foreign and defence policies by means as numerous as they are complex. The processes are both creative and reactive, and reflect an attempt by governments to assess rationally the available options. Yet, as a large body of literature has revealed, policies also reflect the interplay of bureaucratic, oranizational, and personal forces. The image, for example, of a single entity, 'the United States', both determining and carrying out policy is but a caricature of a far more complicated reality involving individuals, agencies and departments.

Policy-making in the United States, however, is further complicated by the participation of Congress. Issues ranging from strategic arms, budgeting, intelligence operations and arms sales to uranium exports, terms of trade and treaties are affected directly by the workings of the Senate and the House of Representatives, their 535 members, hundreds of committees and sub-committees and thousands of staff assistants. Indeed, it is no more possible to understand the making of American security policy without assessing the role of Congress than it is to understand the working of the international system without assessing the role of the United States. Congress cannot be seen as an adjunct to the policy-making process; rather, it must be viewed as an integral part.

To claim, as some do, that there is nothing inherently new in this situation is to be only partially correct. It is true that the Congressional role has its roots in the American Constitution, and that every President since George Washington has had to struggle with an often unruly legislature. Lincoln's successor, Andrew Johnson,

only narrowly escaped removal from office by Congress, while Woodrow Wilson saw his presidency destroyed by the Senate's refusal to ratify the Versailles Treaty and permit American participation in the League of Nations in the wake of World War I. Equally dramatic but more recent examples of confrontation between executive and legislature include the termination of American involvement in Indo-China and the entire set of issues that fall under the heading 'Watergate'. Yet what is qualitatively different today is not simply Congressional willingness to challenge the executive across a broad spectrum of issues, but also its expanded legal, structural and political capacity to do so. No ally or adversary, interest or institution, will remain unaffected.

This changed role has not gone unnoticed. 'Congressional involvement will mark the largest single difference between American foreign policy-making in the last quarter of this century and that of the preceding decades,' predicted one recent study,[1] while a leading columnist has described the present relationship between President and Congress as a 'fundamental or even institutional crisis'.[2] Nor has this change in role gone uncriticized. A school of 'congressional revisionism' has emerged, less concerned with the discredited 'imperial presidency' of the past than the alleged 'imperilled presidency' of the present.

That a debate has begun is clear. But too often the question is raised of whether increased Congressional involvement in the determination of American security policy is good or bad, and too often the response reflects the concerns of the particular matter at hand. Thus, some advocates

119

1

of Congressional involvement in the making of strategic arms policy question the role of Congress in the dispute between Greece and Turkey over Cyprus, and critics of Congressional influence on Middle East policy may applaud its impact on human rights or nuclear proliferation. 'Congressional influence is good when I agree and bad when I don't' has become an all too familiar refrain.

The purpose of this paper is not to add another voice to the chorus already debating the desirability of the influence of a powerful Congress on American security policy. Desirable or not, such an influence is, and will continue to be, a reality for the forseeable future. Instead, the purpose here is essentially twofold: to explain how Congress exercises its influence, and to assess its implications for American security policy. More specifically, the evolution of the role of Congress will be traced from its inception, through its recovery of traditional powers, to the legislation of new and additional ones. The changing shape and machinery of the institution will also be examined. In all cases, the central concern is scope and impact: to what extent, and in what way, will Congress affect the foreign and defence policies of the United States in the years ahead?

I. FROM PHILADELPHIA TO WATERGATE

It was 'in Order to form a more perfect Union' that delegates to the Continental Congress interpreted their mandate in Philadelphia in the summer of 1787. As the phrase implies, a union already existed. But the Articles of Confederation had shown themselves to be inadequate, granting insufficient authority to the national government in general and to the executive in particular. At the same time, the decade of life under a weak and inefficient form of rule had not erased the memory of, and opposition to, tyranny, then commonly seen as the inevitable result of powerful, centralized government. The thought is clearly expressed by Madison in *Federalist 47*: 'The accumulation of all powers, legislative, executive, and judiciary, in the same hands, whether of one, a few, or many, and whether hereditary, self-appointed, or elective, may justly be pronounced the very definition of tyranny.'[3]

The new constitution was thus an ingenious attempt to reconcile the twin aims of establishing central authority without endangering liberty. Of the two concerns, the latter took precedence; in Justice Brandeis's memorable commentary, the purpose of the Constitution's framers was 'not to promote efficiency but to preclude the exercise of arbitrary power'. Towards this end, the document distributed powers along three different axes: between the individual and the government; between state and federal government; and, within the federal government, among the legislature, the executive and the judiciary.

The structure which emerged did not always appear perfect to observers. Writing after the American Civil War, Walter Bagehot criticized the Constitution for promoting stalemate: 'The President wants one course, and has the power to prevent any other; the Congress wants another course, and has the power to prevent any other. The splitting of sovereignty into many parts amounts to there being no sovereign.'[4] A similar thought was expressed by a fellow Englishman, James Bryce, who, while generally well-disposed toward the American system, remarked that the framers had 'underrated the inconveniences which arise from the distinction of the two chief organs of government'.[5] For de Tocqueville, the problem resulted less from the idiosyncracies of the American system than from the nature of democracy itself: 'Foreign politics demand scarcely any of those qualities which are peculiar to a democracy; they require, on the contrary, the perfect use of all those in which it is deficient.'[6]

Criticisms such as these have been voiced by native and foreigner alike throughout the two centuries of the United States. Central to them are the problems caused by the nature of the relationship between executive and legislature, or President and Congress. Some of the difficulties for foreign observers may stem from a misunderstanding of the American political system. Unlike the parliamentary systems common throughout Western Europe, in which executive is tied organically to legislature, party discipline is traditionally high and voters provide ruling mandates for varying degrees of time, the system in the United States divides legislature from executive both electorally and politically, is

2

characterized by weak parties commanding little loyalty and has no equivalent mechanism for the expression of a single mandate. Like the Constitution, the political process in the United States distributes and balances power rather than consolidating and focusing it. Moreover, this tendency has been strengthened in recent years. Not only has the appeal of political parties at all levels declined, but American politics are determined increasingly by single-issue or special-interest 'citizen action groups' or 'political action committees' working aggressively on behalf of concerns that are narrow rather than either comprehensive or coherent.

This pattern is especially noticeable in the realm of foreign affairs. The Constitution mentions no foreign affairs or national security power; instead, it assigns several lesser powers to either the Congress or the President, or both. Congress (the subject of Article I) is accorded the greatest number of explicit powers: to provide for the common defence; to regulate commerce with foreign nations; to define and punish piracies and felonies committed on the high seas and offences against the law of nations; to declare war, grant letters of marque and reprisal and make rules concerning captures on land and water; to raise and support armies; to provide and maintain a navy; to make rules for the regulation and government of land and naval forces; to set tariffs; and to control immigration. In addition, Congress was given the general power to tax and make appropriations, as well as the right to 'make all Laws which shall be necessary and proper for carrying into execution the foregoing powers, and all other powers vested by this Constitution in the Government of the United States, or in any Department or Officer thereof'. By contrast, the powers allotted to the executive are few. The only specific 'national security' powers given to the President alone is that he 'shall be Commander in Chief of the Army and Navy' and that 'he shall receive Ambassadors and other public ministers'. There are also those powers of treaty-making and official appointments explicitly designated to be shared by the executive and the Senate. Otherwise, the President must rely on the general 'executive power' vested in the office by Section I of Article II.

What is initially striking about this constitutional apportionment of powers is its brevity and lack of detail, particularly in regard to the executive branch. Indeed, some basic components of foreign policy – the granting of recognition, the making of international agreements other than treaties, the declaration of neutrality or the termination of war – are not mentioned at all. Brevity in the Constitution is not necessarily a weakness; as Woodrow Wilson observed nearly a century ago, 'Our constitution has proved lasting because of its simplicity.'[7] All the same, this flexibility has been purchased at the high price of confusion and considerable inter-institutional conflict.

This is the case particularly because of the other dominant characteristic of the constitutional allocation of national security powers: the lack of any clear demarcation between those powers given to the executive and those given to the legislature. As Richard Neustadt pointed out in his well-known study of the presidency, 'the Constitutional Convention of 1787 is supposed to have created a government of "separated powers". It did nothing of the sort. Rather, it created a government of separated institutions *sharing* powers.'[8] That this was intentional is clear. 'Ambition must be made to counteract ambition,' wrote Madison in *Federalist 51*. The aim was Newtonian, to contrive the interior structure of the government so that 'its several constituent parts may, by their mutual relations, be the means of keeping each other in their proper places'.[9]

For the most part, uncertainties created by this sharing of powers rather than their separation have not been addressed by the third branch of the federal government. Although in a 1962 decision the Supreme Court stated, 'It is an error to suppose that every case or controversy which touches foreign relations lies beyond judicial cognizance,'[10] the dominant and prevailing view, as expressed by Justice Jackson in 1948, has been that 'the very nature of executive decisions as to foreign policy is political, not judicial.'[11] Moreover, two landmark rulings by the Court have reinforced this tradition of judicial abstinence. Chief Justice Marshall established the principle for loose rather than strict or explicit interpretation of the Constitution. 'Let the end be legitimate, let it be within the scope of the constitution, and all means which are appropriate, which are plainly adapted to that end, which are not prohibited, but consist with the letter and spirit of the constitution, are constitutional.'[12]

Over a century later the Supreme Court further reduced the constitutional basis for determining the distribution of foreign-affairs powers. Writing in 1936, Justice Sutherland concluded:

the investment of the Federal government with the powers of external sovereignty did not depend upon the affirmative grants of the Constitution. The powers to declare and wage war, to conclude peace, to make treaties, to maintain diplomatic relations with other sovereignties, if they had never been mentioned in the Constitution, would have (been) vested in the Federal government as necessary concomitants of nationality.[13]

These two rulings made available to the federal government any reasonable power not specifically denied to it; particularly in the foreign-affairs realm, neither the President nor Congress would be limited to those powers explicitly enumerated and distributed by the Constitution. The result, to quote Edwin Corwin, is that the Constitution 'is an invitation to struggle for the privilege of directing American foreign policy'.[14]

Thus, neither Constitution nor court provides a solution to the inherent friction between the other two branches. Rather, as Louis Henkin has argued, 'What has shaped the system primarily has been the character and nature of foreign relations.'[15] This is a persuasive thought and one echoed by other observers. Yet the key is not to be found in the nature of foreign or security affairs alone, but also in the nature of the two institutions themselves. The presidency has certain innate advantages. Although subject to bureaucratic limitations, the President can act alone, often with a speed and a secrecy that promote initiative. Congress, however, is slowed and tied by its own size and procedures; more often than not, it has been the reactive institution of the two.

The ability of the President to represent the country abroad, to control the negotiating process and to command the armed forces also worked to establish the historical pattern of presidential action and congressional reaction. Where the two branches agreed, there was by definition little problem; in instances of disagreement, Congress was often too divided or too slow to contain the executive. Congress tended to be most influential, however, in periods of basic policy disagreement and when the Constitution

provided it with explicit power either to frustrate the executive or to enact its own will, as took place on the occasion of the Senate's use of the treaty power to break President Wilson. Such situations, however, were the exception; the rule was executive dominance.

The degree of this dominance was kept within relatively narrow limits until World War II and its aftermath. The growth of the 'imperial presidency' reflected the traditional wartime advantages of the executive as well as some new factors. Nuclear weapons had changed the nature of war and made obsolete, in certain conditions, the slow and deliberate mechanism for declaring war enshrined in the Constitution.[16] In addition, the imperial presidency was in part the result of an imperial policy. Arthur Schlesinger argued:

It was hard to reconcile the separation of powers with a foreign policy animated by an indignant ideology and marked by a readiness to intervene speedily and unilaterally in the affairs of other states, nor with an executive branch that saw everywhere on earth interests and threats demanding immediate, and often secret, American commitment and action.[17]

But the imperial presidency was not simply the inevitable result of presidential advantage, a world of nuclear weapons or a particular policy. Equally, it was the result of congressional acquiescence. The presidency became imperial in large part because Congress, failing to fulfil its own constitutional and political responsibilities, allowed it to become so. As former Senator Fulbright remarked, 'It was not a lack of power which prevented the Congress from ending the war in Indo-China but a lack of will.'[18] The explanation, however, has another facet. The Congress after World War II was chastened by the behaviour of Congress before the war; the desire not to repeat the error of isolationism broadened into the desire to avoid the 'error' of limiting the presidency. Reinforced by the general consensus over the wisdom of the containment policy, Congress acquiesced in the establishment of a large, executive-branch national security apparatus and the conduct of major covert activities, and to requests for a broad delegation of authority in a series of 'blank cheque' resolutions including Formosa (1955), Cuba (1962) and the Gulf of Tonkin (1964).[19]

Beginning in the mid-1960s, congressional reaction to this clear imbalance of power between

4

the two branches entrusted with the nation's security gathered considerable momentum. In retrospect, a number of discrete actions or events appear as signposts along this road of institutional recovery. In many of the initial instances the significance lies less in what Congress actually achieved than in the fact that it sought to achieve ends greatly different from those of the executive. Challenges to presidential policy were made by a growing number of Congressmen, and on certain occasions alternative policies were put forth with some success.

The war in Indo-China, the issue which represented to many the essence of the 'imperial presidency', also became the instrument through which Congress most seriously challenged presidential prerogative. Beginning only a few years after the expression of overwhelming support for the Gulf of Tonkin Resolution, and continuing through 1975, congressional opposition to both the expansion and the continuation of American military involvement in South-east Asia had a major impact on the policies of all the countries involved. Televised hearings of the Senate Foreign Relations Committee raised widespread public doubts about the wisdom of the Administration's official policy.

The invasion of Cambodia on 30 April 1970 sparked a new round of congressional involvement, after the programme of 'Vietnamization' and the curtailment of conscription had defused much of the opposition to the war. Although the attempt by Senators Cooper and Church to end funding for all American military activities in Cambodia failed, the effort limited the length and scale of the military initiative and forced the Administration to reassess its political support at home. Nearly five years later, congressional divergence from executive policy culminated in its refusal to provide requested assistance to South Vietnam in the final months of the Saigon regime's existence.[20]

For all its importance, however, the involvement of the United States in Indo-China was not the only issue that attracted congressional interest and provoked alternatives to executive policy. Beginning in 1966, a coalition of Senators led by Majority Leader Mike Mansfield pressed for unilateral reductions in the American troop presence in Europe.[21] Senator Mansfield, by January 1967, had amassed forty-one other Senators on behalf of his cause. This, however,

turned out to be the high-water mark of his initiative. Initially support waned because of the Soviet-Warsaw Pact invasion of Czechoslovakia in August 1968 and progress in the negotiation of 'offset' arrangements between the United States and her European allies for redistributing the financial burden of maintaining American troops in Europe; in later years political support further declined owing to the Mutual and Balanced Force Reductions (MBFR) negotiations and the impact of withdrawal from Asia. But although these efforts never succeeded in the Senate, and received relatively little support in the House of Representatives, they helped to bring about both the 'offset' arrangements and the MBFR talks, besides adding a new element of uncertainty about the future of the United States' commitment to the Atlantic Alliance.

A third area of congressional initiative ('on what, next to Vietnam, had become the most divisive question in contemporary national security')[22] concerned the anti-ballistic missile (ABM) proposals of the Johnson and Nixon Administrations: 'ABM had become a symbol, a test of many values – national priorities, attitudes towards arms limitation, the balance of power between Congress and the executive.'[23] While votes to delete funding failed narrowly, the resistance in the Senate did contribute to a reorientation of the system away from a thin, national city defence towards a more modest and more readily justifiable attempt to protect elements of the fixed, land-based *Minuteman* intercontinental ballistic missile (ICBM) force. Again, though, the significance of the congressional effort transcended the immediate issue: once more, the executive had been challenged strongly on a matter of national security and forced to reconsider its intentions. Moreover, the ABM debate had the added effect of creating widespread demand throughout Congress for the expansion of regular sources of specialized, technical expertise and information available to the Congress and independent of the executive.

A number of other issues appeared in the 1970s which both reflected the new congressional involvement in national security matters and encouraged its growth. A 1972 amendment, sponsored by Senator Henry Jackson, to a resolution supporting the SALT I Interim Agreement urged the President to seek a future treaty that 'would not limit the United States to levels of inter-continental strategic forces inferior to the limits provided for the Soviet Union'.[24] Importation of chrome from Rhodesia was permitted by the 'Byrd Amendment' despite the UN sanctions and the impact of their violation on United States policy towards Africa. Both most-favoured nation (MFN) status and large, government-subsidized credits were denied the USSR, which affected both Soviet emigration policy and the state of detente between the two super-powers. For more than three-and-a-half years policy towards Turkey and Turkey's role in the Atlantic Alliance were altered by the arms embargo imposed by Congress. Department of Defense plans for developing air and naval facilities on the Indian Ocean island of Diego Garcia were subjected to unparalleled scrutiny and, ultimately, both delayed and reduced in scope. Most dramatically, in late 1975 the Senate terminated all covert and overt American operations in Angola, while in 1978 the Panama Canal Treaties were ratified only after long debate and amendment. Whether or not one agrees with the wisdom of these and other congressional initiatives, their impact on the foreign and defence policies of the United States of the past decade can hardly be exaggerated.

Motivating these and other challenges to presidential control of foreign and defence policy was more than an abstract desire to affect security issues or to correct a perceived institutional imbalance. The key to the initial reaction was Vietnam. 'Vietnam discredited executive control of foreign relations as profoundly as Versailles and mandatory neutrality has discredited congressional control.'[25] But Vietnam did more than simply discredit the imperial presidency; it undermined the consensus that had for a generation supported the tenets of containment and what in effect had evolved into an imperial policy. The era of so-called bi-partisan foreign policy, symbolized by the close post-World War II co-operation between the Republican Senator Arthur Vandenburg and the Democratic Administration of Harry Truman, had been as well an era of bi-institutional foreign and defence policy built on the solid foundation of a widely shared approach to the world.[26]

Without a guiding or fundamental principle, the specific merits and politics of every potential interest, commitment or response connected with security policy was open to challenge.

It was not simply the substance of policy that had become vulnerable to attack from Congress; in addition, the principle of executive primacy was challenged. Two reasons stand out. First, the mismanagement of the war in Indo-China and the lack of success worked to weaken the myth of executive expertise that had been nurtured for a generation. In the wake of the Bay of Pigs *débâcle* and Vietnam, increasing numbers of Congressmen no longer equated executive access to greater information with executive exercise of superior judgment. Moreover, the ABM issue had taught Congress that it too could tap a large body of expertise and thus compete with the executive on equal or near-equal terms.

Second, perceived and proven abuses of power by the executive alienated many in Congress, again undermining the credibility of, and trust in, the presidency. The incomplete and allegedly distorted release of information at the time of the 1964 invasion of the Dominican Republic and the Gulf of Tonkin Resolution had a major impact, as did the revelations of illegal activities on the part of the Central Intelligence Agency (CIA) and the Federal Bureau of Investigation (FBI). Most important, the pattern of abuse of power and office associated with the Watergate affair convinced a majority in Congress that major reform was both necessary and overdue.

The resulting reassertion of congressional involvement in the many dimensions of American security policy can only be understood in the foregoing context of the break-down of policy consensus, the erosion of the notion of executive competence, the shock of widespread illegal activities, and the impetus each of these developments gave to the growth of congressional ability independently to create and criticize policy. At the same time, the reassertion must also be viewed in the broader context of constitutional flexibility and the historical pattern of shifting balances between executive and legislature. How far the pendulum has now shifted, and with what effect, is the subject of what follows.

6

II. THE CHANGING SHAPE OF CONGRESS

The terms 'Congress' and 'President', or 'legislature' and 'executive', can often be misleading. As David Truman has written:

the political process rarely, if ever, involves a conflict between the legislature and the executive viewed as two monolithic and unified institutions. The actual competing structures on each side are made up of elements in the legislature and in the executive, reflecting and supported by organized and unorganized interests.[27]

In reality, the picture is further complicated by the influence of coalitions consisting of like-minded individuals and groups from both institutions, who are arrayed against similar coalitions, also based in both institutions, pursuing an alternative policy. This willingness of Congressmen to align themselves with other members or outsiders underscores a central point: to understand the collective impact of Congress one must understand that its influence is often exerted by one of its many parts.

One can examine Congress through many lenses: parties, the two chambers, committees, sub-committees, joint and conference committees, leadership, staff assistants, outside agencies, issue coalitions and individual members. Such disaggregation *per se* is not new; Congress has never been a simple or single institution. What is new, however, and what is basic to any appreciation of the workings and impact of Congress, is the far greater degree of decentralization that has evolved over recent years. This is in part a result of structural reform designed specifically to democratize the institution; at the same time, it is a product of the explosion of personnel and information sources available to individual members. In both cases, what has been altered is not simply the processes within Congress but also the products which emerge.

The most powerful administrative units within Congress have traditionally been the committees. Both the Senate and the House of Representatives are divided into more than twenty committees apiece, to which members are assigned by their respective parties in numbers reflecting the overall balance between the parties in Congress. In all cases chairmen are members of the majority (presently Democratic) party. Each committee has responsibility for a broad area:

foreign relations, armed services, energy and so on, and consideration of legislation and other matters by the full membership of each chamber only comes after the relevant committee or committees have had the opportunity to hold hearings and rewrite the legislation. Until recently, committee recommendations would rarely be over-ruled by the full membership; indeed, Woodrow Wilson once described the United States as a 'government by the standing committees of Congress'.[28]

Today, the situation is quite changed, particularly in area of foreign and defence policy. Neither the Senate nor the House has a single 'National Security Affairs Committee'. The principal Senate and House committees in this area – the Foreign Relations and Foreign Affairs Committees respectively – are quite limited in their purview. Their primary legislative responsibilities – the annual foreign military and economic assistance packages – are shared with the appropriations committees, and in many cases are amended heavily by the full membership when the legislation 'reaches the floor'. Moreover, neither committee has a monopoly on the consideration of most national security matters. Issues in this area are, by one account, dealt with by sixteen Senate and nineteen House committees and an even larger number of sub-committees.[29] What results are two types of jurisdictional tangle: not only are foreign and defence policy issues considered by a large number of separate committees, but often the same matter is considered by two or more committees.

The chief consequence of this structural disunity is to divide the congressional perspective, making the creation of integrated and coherent legislation and policy almost impossible. Compromise becomes the paramount concern: 'Legislative conflicts in Congress are resolved more often than not by political pressure, not by any rational presentation of the issues.'[30] The tendency is both to isolate and to emphasize the dimension of an issue that comes under the committee's authority; as a result, one dimension of relations between the United States and a foreign country can sour the larger relationship and injure more important interests. In addition, little thought is given to trade-offs – that is, to how the emphasis on one issue might directly affect others, or how bargaining and compromise over one goal may help to achieve another. That the policies emerging from such a system are at times in conflict with the requirements of a sensitive and comprehensive foreign policy should come as little surprise.

The capacity of Congress to produce coherent policy has been further eroded by other trends within the institution. Formal authorities, whether party leaders or committee chairmen, have been successfully challenged and weakened. With neither position nor seniority a guarantee of influence, power has flowed mostly to individual members, *ad hoc* groups and coalitions. There is no central authority capable of co-ordinating the initiatives of these diverse sources. At the same time, the high rate of turnover – more than half the current membership entered Congress this decade – has not only had the effect of removing many powerful members from Congress, but has also brought into office a large number of representatives unwilling to accept the old order within the institution and often unfamiliar with the traditions of American foreign and defence policies. The Congress may be more democratic and decentralized, but it is also less manageable and predictable.

Closely connected with this redistribution of power within Congress has been a growth and redistribution of resources. The expansion of congressional capacity and access to information has been nothing less than spectacular. Three areas stand out: the increase in the staff assistance available to all members, either on their personal staffs or through committees on which they serve; the enlargement of existing 'support agencies' as well as the creation of new ones; and the greater capacity of Congress to benefit from the information and expertise of the executive branch.

The increase in staff has been a gradual but accelerating development since the end of World War II. In addition to the provision every member receives for personal staff to serve in Washington and one or more offices in his home state or district, the Legislative Reorganization Act of 1947 authorized each committee to hire four professional and six clerical aides as well as a number of temporary assistants. This Act set the pattern for the next thirty years. By 1947 congressional committee staffs totalled nearly 500 people, and personal staffs 2,000. Twenty

years later, in 1967, committee staffs had risen in number to over 1,200, and personal staffs had tripled to some 5,800 people. Today, after additional reforms, committees employ more than 3,000 aides – over six times the post-war figure – and personal staffs number over 10,000 employees. By 1976 the average staff of each of the 100 Senators was thirty-one; some included more than seventy. Allowances for staff and office operations for Senators from the larger states had climbed over $1 million per year.[31]

This sharp increase in the availability of staff has transformed the role of the individual member. With the average Senator serving on ten or more committees and sub-committees, casting thousands of votes every year, serving constituents and working for re-election, it is the staff assistants who do most of the actual work. This includes drafting legislation and amendments, preparing background material for hearings, writing speeches and offering advice. 'Senators ... are functioning more and more like the president or chief presiding officer of a corporation, giving direction to policy and giving staff the responsibility for details.'[32]

Members of Congress also have a wide range of congressional support agencies to tap for information, analysis and guidance. The oldest of these is the Congressional Research Service (CRS), established as the Legislative Reference Service under the rubric of the Library of Congress in 1914. With its change of name in 1970 came a redirection of purpose. The CRS was ordered to become a 'policy and research arm of the Congress' rather than simply providing more narrow services related to legislation. Today the approximately 700 employees of the non-partisan CRS answer nearly 200,000 requests annually from members, committees and staffs, and provide a growing number of issue and legislative briefs, background reports and analyses.[33] Similar in function, but both smaller and more restricted is the Office of Technology Assessment (OTA). Established in 1972, the OTA was created to provide Congress with an independent source of scientific and technical expertise.[34]

Like both the CRS and the OTA the General Accounting Office or GAO is another source of information and analysis for the Congress. Where it differs, however, is in its additional role of 'watchdog'. In the original 1921 legislation, as well as in the subsequent reforms brought about

8

in 1970 and 1974, the GAO is given the unique mandate to oversee and audit federal government programmes and operations. The term 'audit' is used broadly. It consists of surveys, detailed reviews and reporting, and covers such matters as federal compliance with laws and regulations passed by Congress, the efficiency and economy of operations and the quality of results. The scope of the GAO is wide. In 1975 nearly one half its staff, or 2,000 people, were located outside Washington and conducted more than 2,000 surveys and reviews of government programmes in the United States and seventy-eight foreign countries.[35]

Created by the Congressional Budget and Impoundment Control Act of 1974, the Congressional Budget Office (CBO) is the most recent of the four support agencies. It is also the most closely connected with the day-to-day operations of the Congress, as the CBO is allied with the two new House and Senate Budget Committees. Together, they perform two important functions. On one hand, they provide Congress with an overall budgetary perspective, totalling receipts and expenditures, thereby introducing a measure of fiscal discipline into what had often been an uncontrolled process of considering separate measures with little regard for their composite impact. At the same time the CBO can present analyses of policy options in terms of budgetary implications; for example, their papers on the United States Navy or strategic arms have indicated the kinds of forces the country can choose, the arguments on behalf of each and what each option or mix would cost. But the CBO and the two committees do have their limitations. They can only present analyses of options; they cannot favour one system or alternative. More important, their power is the power of persuasion. They cannot force Congress to adopt or adhere to their spending resolutions; nor can they directly overrule a committee or individual who promotes an initiative in conflict with budgetary guidelines. This latter weakness became obvious during the initial years of the new congressional budget system: while the committees can plead a 'disinterested' case along fiscal lines, it can easily be defeated by coalitions designed to promote a particular issue.[36]

The combined resources of the support agencies and both personal and committee staff have gone a long way towards eliminating the 'infor-mation gap' that many members of Congress felt was basic to executive supremacy in foreign affairs. Thus, the fact that Congress has also turned to the executive itself to help fill this gap is not without its irony. The mechanisms are both formal and informal, authorized and otherwise. Briefings of Congressmen and their staffs are commonplace, and the CIA has been transformed into a fifth support agency by many in Congress. Congressional policy oversight provides members with the right to question executive officials, and the hearing process, with its mixture of testimony and questions, has become an intrinsic part of the policy-making process.

This is not to say that there are no limits to congressional access to executive information. The Supreme Court has lent support to the concept of 'executive privilege' and the right of the President to withhold certain information from the Congress, particularly in the realm of military and diplomatic affairs.[37] In addition, certain key officials, including the Assistant to the President for National Security Affairs, cannot be compelled to testify before Congress. In general, though, the trend has favoured increased co-operation in maintaining the flow of information, and the Freedom of Information Act in particular has been responsible for increasing congressional (and, more generally, public) access to the documents of the executive branch.[38]

Congress has also turned to legislation to ensure access to certain kinds of information and analysis available to the executive branch. A large number of executive initiatives – arms transfers, nuclear exports, assistance programmes – must be accompanied by reports detailing their justification and impact on local stability, nuclear proliferation and human rights respectively. The best-known of these executive reporting requirements, however, are the Arms Control Impact Statements, mandated in 1975. Congress ordered the executive branch to prepare annual statements discussing the arms-control implications of proposed defence programmes being sent to Congress for authorization and appropriation. Not only were these statements intended to assist Congress in its consideration of defence requests, but they were instituted as well to force the Administration to consider the arms-control implications of new weapon systems at a sufficiently early stage in their development for either their programmes or American policy to be

9

adjusted if necessary. In addition, it was hoped that the statements would enhance the role of the Arms Control and Disarmament Agency (ACDA) within the executive branch. In practice, the exercise has had but a modest effect. Nevertheless, over the years the statements have grown in both number and quality, and have proved useful both as a means of transmitting information to Congress and as a procedure for raising the salience of arms-control concerns within the executive.[39]

Sources of information, analysis and advice outside those mentioned above also exist. A large number of research organizations, universities, constituents, lobbyists and media are actively attempting to influence Congressmen. Indeed, the difficulty now appears to be less a shortage than a glut of information. As Congressman Les Aspin has remarked, 'Most congressional offices are deluged with more information than they can possibly absorb.'[40] The impact of this fundamental change in the availability of both assistance and information is basic to the understanding of the influence of Congress. In part, it has brought about a classic demonstration of Parkinson's Law. Congressional activities have increased parallel to the enlargement of congressional capacities. The number of bills and amendments considered, the number and length of hearings and reports and the degree of oversight of executive operations – all have increased sharply over the past decade. In the process, Congress has not only placed greater demands on the resources of the executive branch, but it has also overloaded its own members.[41]

The 'inputs' to Congress have multiplied many times over, but the institution still consists of 535 members. The congressional bureaucracy has made itself essential at the cost of demanding too much of the members it allegedly serves. Whatever the initial justification for augmenting support capabilities, continued expansion will at best be of marginal use and will more probably be a liability.

The growth of resources has also had the effect of enhancing the role of the individual member, however overloaded he may be as a result. In the past the severely limited resources available to Congress as a whole were reserved largely for the senior members, usually committee chairman and party leaders. Today new provisions for personal staff and guaranteed minority shares in committee staffs, along with the equally available support agencies, have assured individual members of resources adequate for the preparation of initiatives and serious challenges to executive policy. Every member has become a potential source of independent policy.

Other reforms have also contributed to decentralization. Senators are now limited to a maximum of eleven committee and subcommittee assignments apiece (down from an average of eighteen), and no one may chair more than three committees or sub-committees. As a result, power continues to be distributed more widely. Although the number of committees has been reduced slightly, referrals to more than one committee have become more common, and the allocation of authority for considering national security issues less precisely focused. Seniority as the sole criterion for appointment has been successfully challenged, and chairmen have been removed.[42] Again, the institution has traded centralization for democracy. To the extent that the whole can be judged as the sum of its parts, Congress is more active than ever before; in reality, though, the parts are increasingly autonomous, and there is little or no means of ensuring their integration or moderation.

III. THE RECOVERY OF TRADITIONAL POWERS

One of the principal means by which the Congress has reasserted its influence over foreign policy has been through the use of its inherent but often dormant powers. To a large extent, this reassertion has centred on the Senate, given its unique constitutional responsibilities for the making of treaties and the approval of certain executive officials. In other areas, however, the recovery of traditional powers has involved both chambers, often resulting more from inferred or inherent powers, both legal and political, than from explicit constitutional decrees. Indeed, in its use of these powers the 'new' Congress most resembles many or its influential predecessors.

10

The Constitution is characteristically terse in its coverage of the treaty power: The President 'shall have power, by and with the Advice and Consent of the Senate, to make Treaties, provided two thirds of the Senators present concur.' The power to make treaties, unlike most others, is thus a shared power, forming, in Hamilton's words, 'a distinct department ... to belong, properly, neither to the legislature nor to the executive'.[43] Moreover, the power is shared not between President and Congress, but only between President and Senate. Again the *Federalists,* in this case Jay, provide a rationale. Describing senators as 'men ... the most distinguished by their abilities and virtue', he claimed 'it was wise ... to provide not only that the power of making treaties should be committed to able and honest men, but also that they should continue in place a sufficient time to become perfectly acquainted with our national concerns'.[44]

Yet although in theory the treaty power is to be shared beween executive and Senate, most of the responsibility has devolved on the former. The executive is far better placed and constituted to conduct negotiations with foreign states. After some initial experimentation with a major role for Congress in the negotiating phase, both executive and Senate were willing to accept a division of labour in which the former negotiated and the latter passed final judgment. The constitutional provision for senatorial advice and consent evolved, with the function of advice decreasing and that of granting (or withholding) consent rising.

Consequently, to the dismay of more than one President, the doctrine of automatic or 'obligatory consent' grew obsolete as the Senate effectively exchanged its right to assist in the making of a treaty for the right to reject what had been negotiated. Writing at the turn of the century, the powerful senator Henry Cabot Lodge expressed this notion clearly. 'The treaty, so called, is therefore still inchoate, a mere project for a treaty, until the consent of the Senate has been given to it.'[45] As a result, the Constitution's 'Advice and Consent' charge came to refer to the 'Senate's action on a treaty which had been submitted to it by the President after negotiations are completed but before ratification'.[46]

But whatever the legal right of the Senate to refuse consent, in political terms its refusal would necessarily have a major impact on relations with the foreign state or states involved. As Louis Henkin has noted, 'By the time ... the Senate considers a treaty, negotiations have been held, understandings reached, and commitments made (political if not legal), and Congress [sic] is far from free to exercise its independent political judgment.'[47] In recent years, however, the Senate has demonstrated a greater willingness to exercise 'its independent political judgment' regardless of the risks involved. Moreover, it has also begun to reverse the historical shift in its role towards 'consent'; as was perhaps intended by the framers of the Constitution, the Senate is once more offering specific advice on treaty negotiations themselves.

Congressional involvement in the advice or treaty-making phase has taken several forms. The most common is by resolution, which can either 'liberate' the executive by urging a particular course of action, as was done before the Partial Test Ban, the Non-Proliferation and the SALT I negotiations, or constrain, an expedient adopted by Congress before the Panama Canal and SALT II negotiations.[48] Although expressions of the latter type are not legally binding, they do warn the President of the unwillingness of Congress to accept terms inconsistent with its wishes. The SALT II negotiations have also been the occasion of other congressional attempts to influence the executive. Fourteen Representatives and twenty-five Senators were appointed 'advisers' to the American delegation, while formal and informal communications between the branches, particularly in the early months of the Carter Administration, affected the Administration's proposals as much as they informed Congress of the Administration's intentions.[49]

A more public and dramatic sign of the Senate's using its constitutional powers is reflected in its increased willingness to consider alternatives to either outright approval or non-approval of proposed treaties. Three classes of option are available to the Senate as it considers the resolution of ratification: the addition of 'understandings' or 'interpretations', which clarify certain provisions without changing their legal effect; the addition of 'reservations', which act to limit rather than simply clarify, the legal effects of the treaty, and which can provoke the foreign state or states to make reservations of their own – or even to repudiate the proposed treaty; and, most serious, the amendment of the terms of the treaty itself, which automatically requires renegotiation with the foreign party.[50] The impact of amendment is obvious; in the case of understandings and reservations, however, the distinction between them is unclear, and it falls to the other state or states involved to decide how to react to them.

All three options have been used; understandings are the most common and least controversial, and actual amendments the least common but potentially the most controversial. Reservations, however, are another matter. The passage in March 1978 of the First (or 'Permanent Neutrality') Panama Canal Treaty, with a reservation giving the United States the right 'to take such steps as [she] deems necessary ... including the use of military force in Panama, to reopen the Canal or restore [her] operations', brought forth angry denunciations from the Government of Panama. The entire relationship was salvaged only when the second (or 'Basic Treaty') was approved, with a reservation that nothing in the treaties should be interpreted 'as a right of [United States] intervention in the internal affairs of the Republic of Panama'. Over a decade of careful negotiations, the position of the United States in Latin America and the fate of the Canal itself were thus jeopardized by a single reservation in the Senate.[51]

The differences between the three Senate options to alter a proposed treaty can best be illustrated by using as an example the SALT II Treaty. The insertion of a clause stipulating that no restriction in the Protocol shall continue in force after its expiration (but still during the life of the Treaty) unless formally renegotiated constitutes an understanding and requires no response from the Soviet Union. The addition of a clause stating that nothing in the treaty precludes the introduction by United States of a particular basing system for new land-based ICBM, however, constitutes a reservation, perhaps requiring formal Soviet acquiescence. By contrast, the terms of the agreement would be altered by an amendment – for example, a demand that the four prototype B-1 bombers be eliminated from American totals, or that the *Backfire* bomber be included in Soviet force totals – and would require Soviet willingness to reopen the negotiations of the treaty.

These courses of action hold important attractions for critics or opponents of proposed treaties.

While a final resolution of ratification for treaties requires that two-thirds of the Senators present approve for passage, the changes described above require approval by only a simple majority, although then any changes are subject, along with the rest of the treaty, to the two-thirds vote at the end of the process. This places initial supporters in the uncomfortable position of voting either for the changed treaty or against what they originally sought, while providing initial opponents with the opportunity to vote in favour of an 'improved' treaty, thereby avoiding to some extent the appearance of, and responsibility for, being in opposition. The former was the dilemma of the followers of Woodrow Wilson, who felt forced to vote against the Versailles Treaty and its many reservations; the latter could describe the choices to be made if an amended SALT II Treaty is brought to a final vote.

An additional means by which Congress has sought to recapture its treaty power, and a natural corollary to the others, is the limitation of the executive's ability to terminate a treaty without receiving the approval of a majority of Congress, if not two-thirds of the Senate. The question surfaced recently (in December 1978) with President Carter's announcement of his intention to give notice to the Republic of China (Taiwan), on 1 January 1979, to terminate the Mutual Defense Treaty a year later, the delay reflecting the terms of Article X of the treaty. In defence of this action, the State Deparment's legal adviser argued:

The President's constitutional power to give notice of termination provided for by the terms of a treaty derives from the President's authority and responsibility as chief executive to conduct the nation's foreign affairs and execute the laws ... The Senate's role in giving advice and consent to the making of a treaty is fulfilled when the treaty is made; thereafter execution and performance of its terms, including terms relating to its duration or termination, are delegated by the Constitution to the nation's chief executive.[52]

This position has been challenged by a number of senators, who have argued that since the Constitution makes no reference of the power of termination, but only sets forth a procedure for sharing the power to make treaties between executive and Senate, then it must be inferred that the power to break treaties must also be shared.

12

Precedent is inconclusive; as a recent study has noted, 'In practice no settled rule or procedure has been followed in the termination of treaties.'[53] Although the legal question can only be settled by the courts, in terms of policy the power of unilateral termination of treaties by either branch appears potentially undesirable in a context in which the sanctity of the commitments and treaty guarantees of the United States is critical to her performance as a global power.

This greater willingness on the part of the Senate to exercise its treaty power has in part been offset, however, by another development. The role of the treaty as the accepted form of international compact between the United States and foreign countries has been steadily declining. Various types of 'international agreements other than treaties' (IAOTT) – in many cases, treaties in every way but name – have become increasingly common. This development has permitted the executive to enter into arrangements, and in some cases undertake commitments, either without the Senate's approval or with only a simple majority in both Houses. Moreover, until recently many of these IAOTT, commonly known as 'executive agreements', were reached and maintained even without the Senate's knowledge.

There is no constitutional distinction between treaties and executive agreements, the latter being, in the words of one historian, 'one of the mysteries of the constitutional order'.[54] Nor is there any accepted distinction between their legal standing, although the Supreme Court has ruled that the treaty need not be used for all international agreements.[55] Distinctions can be drawn, however, between different types of executive agreements. 'Congressional—Executive Agreements' are made by the executive, either under the authority of already existing legislation or subject to congressional approval or legislation, while 'Treaty–Executive agreements' can be made pursuant to an existing and hence senatorially approved treaty. There are also 'Presidential–Executive agreements', based solely upon the general executive authority allegedly accorded the President by the Constitution. It is this last type that has often been the subject of controversy, although the first two have also been questioned on occasions when it was claimed that the President had exceeded his authority.[56]

The use of the executive agreement can be traced back to the 1817 Rush–Bagot Agreement between the United States and Britain governing the level of military force on the Great Lakes. Partially pursuant to authorising legislation passed two years earlier, the agreement was presented to the Senate in 1818, when the decision was made to endorse it but not as a treaty. Use of the executive agreement grew slowly throughout the nineteenth century. It was expanded significantly by McKinley, who used it to conclude the Spanish–American War and to proclaim the Open Door Policy, and by Theodore Roosevelt, who took the significant step of using it after the Senate had refused to ratify a treaty placing certain customs houses under the control of the United States. It was after World War II, however, during the 'imperial presidency', that the use of the executive agreement became widespread.

The Senate Foreign Relations Sub-committee on United States Security Agreements and Commitments Abroad, established in the late 1960s under Senator Symington – who, by his position on the Committees on Foreign Relations, Armed Services and Atomic Energy, probably had more access to classified information than any other member of Congress – was shocked to discover not only a large number of secret agreements with foreign countries, but also several that were tantamount to security commitments.[57] Indeed, by 1969 the United States recognized her adherence to 909 treaties and 3,973 executive agreements, and during the first Nixon Administration a further 1,087 executive agreements were concluded, as opposed to only eight treaties;[58] what these statistics do not show is the increasing use of the former for the more significant arrangements. As the Senate Foreign Relations Committee wrote in 1969, 'We have come close to reversing the traditional distinction between the treaty as the instrument of major commitment and the Executive Agreement as the instrument of a minor one'.[59]

Although there was a reaction against the executive agreement in the immediate aftermath of the Second World War owing to fears that human rights undertakings abroad would affect the domestic laws of the United States,[60] the bulk of the resistance began some twenty years later. In June 1969 the Senate passed overwhelmingly the National Commitments Resolution, defining what constituted a 'national commitment' from the Senate's perspective.[61] Although the resolution was non-binding, it served as a signal both to the executive and to foreign countries that a commitment by the United States to provide armed forces or other resources on behalf of another country could only come about as the result of a positive action, in the form of a treaty, a statute or a concurrent resolution, involving both branches of government. Thus, it placed in jeopardy those pledges given unilaterally to foreign states by the President. Some three years later, in August 1972, Congress passed the 'Case Act', requiring the Secretary of State to transmit the text of any international agreement other than a treaty to which the United States is a party not later than sixty days after it has come into force.[62] If the President so decides, the text can be transmitted under an injunction of secrecy to the two Foreign Affairs committees. For many in Congress, however, the 'Case Act' did not go far enough. While it ensured that no agreement would remain secret from Congress for more than sixty days, it failed to guarantee Congress either a voice in the making of the agreement or an opportunity to act upon it once it was negotiated. Moreover, the executive alone could decide whether a particular agreement would be submitted to the Senate as a treaty requiring two-thirds approval or merely transmitted to Congress for its information.[63] Since that time numerous efforts to legislate mechanisms for congressional approval of executive agreements, as well as congressional involvement in the choice of forms some compacts assume, have been defeated. Although Congress retains the power indirectly to affect implementation of certain executive agreements by denying appropriations, it has avoided a more direct role.[64]

One compromise between executive unilateralism and the Senate treaty role is provided by the joint resolution process, in which negotiated agreements are approved by a simple majority of each chamber and signed into law by the President. The instrument is an attractive one: it permits both chambers of Congress a voice in the agreement procedure, but eliminates the severe constraint of the approval of two-thirds of the Senate that is basic to the treaty. Indeed, one constitutional expert has claimed, 'It is now widely accepted that the Congressional – Executive Agreement is a complete alternative to a treaty: the President can seek approval of any agreement by joint resolution of both Houses of Congress instead of two-thirds of the Senate only'.[65]

This overstates the situation, however, as shown by the Senate's ability to ground the trial balloon floated by the Carter Administration to submit the SALT II Agreement as an executive agreement requiring a joint resolution rather than as a treaty requiring the approval of two-thirds of the Senate.[66] In other cases, though, the joint resolution has been used successfully. It was the instrument of congressional approval of the 1975 'Sinai' Middle East Agreements, as well as the 1972 SALT I Interim Agreement. In the latter case the joint resolution conformed to existing law, which prohibited the President from agreeing 'to disarm or to reduce or to limit the Armed Forces or armaments of the United States, except pursuant to the treaty-making power of the President under the Constitution or unless authorized by further affirmative legislation by the Congress of the United States'.[67]

Clearly, what has evolved is an atmosphere less tolerant of unilateral executive power to enter into agreements with foreign countries. Whatever the form of arrangement, Congress has tended to demand a greater say in the negotiations and has reserved the right of approval. Not surprisingly, this has had an impact both on the process of negotiations and on the ability of the United States to enter into binding compacts with foreign countries. At least two benefits are readily apparent. First, as Alton Frye has argued, 'Congress represents the most potent and credible constraint which the executive can cite in its dealings with foreign powers.'[68] Certainly, congressional pressure can enhance the bargaining strength of any American representative. Second, congressional support for commitments can help to lessen doubt in the minds of allies and adversaries alike that the President may lack domestic support and, consequently, the ability to follow through on what he has promised.

Yet these and other consequences of a Congress more active in the process of making treaties and other agreements have certain less desirable implications. While the threat of congressional sanction may induce another party to compromise, the reality of sanction may do just the opposite. Thus, whereas congressional power to deny MFN status and credits to the Soviet Union appeared to prompt an increase in the emigration of Soviet Jews during the 1973 and

14

1974 trade negotiations, the writing into the proposed agreement of 'human rights' condititions caused the USSR to repudiate the entire arrangement. More generally, actual or potential congressional constraints on the policy of the United States can limit the flexibility of negotiators and make compromise more difficult. To bargain in a context where a number of incentives may be or have been denied, and where a number of points are 'non-negotiable', is often to burden the process with more than it can carry. At the same time, although congressional support of undertakings can help to reduce uncertainties, the unwillingness of Congress to approve commitments, as well as its power to alter or terminate them, inject new elements of doubt into perceptions of the ability of the United States to play a leading and lasting role on behalf of its allies and interests.

The treaty power, although the most important of the traditional powers, is not the only one. The President 'shall nominate, and by and with the Advice and Consent of the Senate, shall appoint Ambassadors, other public Ministers and Consuls, Judges of the Supreme Court, and all other officers of the United States'. While nominally similar to the treaty power, in that it is shared between executive and Senate, the power to nominate and appoint ambassadors and other major officials (including the Cabinet) is distinct from the treaty power in two important ways, which emerge from a careful reading of the Constitution. Only a simple majority, rather than a majority of two-thirds, is required of the Senate. In addition, whereas the treaty power is an undivided one – that is, both branches are involved in the making of treaties – the nomination and appointment power is divided. The President alone has the power to nominate; the Senate is only called upon to advise on and consent to appointment.

Although in practice this shared power has been diluted by the increase in the size and influence of the executive branch and the White House staff, many of whom (including the Assistant to the President for National Security Affairs) need not be confirmed in their post and remain outside the purview of congressional scrutiny, in practice it has mostly worked as intended. There are sporadic examples of individuals being refused confirmation, including two of President Nixon's Supreme Court nominees, although usually prior consultation allows for the withdrawal of those nominees likely to be rejected, as occurred with President Carter's first choice to head the CIA, Theodore Sorenson. Two aspects of the process are of indirect importance for security matters, though. The procedure provides the senate with a good opportunity to examine the qualifications of individuals about to assume great responsibility, and the nomination hearing can be the occasion of a full airing of major issues. In addition, the vote to conform can be used as a signal or vote of confidence regarding relevant policies. For example, the Senate's confirmation of Paul Warnke as Director of ACDA and Ambassador to the SALT negotiations by a simple and not a two-thirds majority, while legally adequate, indicated its capacity to reject any proposed strategic-arms treaty not to its liking – a signal which was read clearly by the then newly-elected President, by his representative and by the Soviet Union.

IV. LEGISLATING SECURITY

Some fifteen years ago an observer of the American system noted 'the increasing tendency to monitor, to establish political parameters of tolerance and expectation, rather than to use power to intervene deeply in shaping the substance of policies, is perhaps the most striking development in congressional behaviour'.[69] Although Congress had begun to challenge the Kennedy Administration on the substance of its annual foreign assistance programmes, the observation was largely accurate in the context of most of the foreign and defence policy issues of the day. In recent years, however, Congress has turned towards legislation to provide more explicit powers (not specifically denied to it under the Constitution) in six critical areas of foreign and defence policy. This has brought about not only greater control of defence and foreign assistance programmes, but also increased congressional authority in the areas of war powers, arms transfers, nuclear proliferation concerns and intelligence activities. The general intent has been

15

to legislate and clarify powers that were often unspecified and unclear in the past and tended to devolve upon the presidency. More specifically, legislation has been used to ensure that the executive provides Congress with adequate information both to permit the execution of its full range of functions and to ensure a more influential congressional role, and a more restricted executive role, in the shaping of policies. To what extent these aims have been fulfilled, and with what effect on American security policy, is the subject of this chapter.

Defence

The Constitution makes no provision for a clear division of labour in the design of the shape and size of the armed forces of the United States. Nevertheless, since the creation of the Bureau of the Budget in 1921 (from 1974 known as the Office of Management and the Budget, or OMB), in the defence budgeting area the initiative has shifted to the executive. As one recent study has stated, 'Congressional participation mainly takes the form of acting on proposals or choosing between alternatives presented by the executive branch.'[70] Several factors account for this development. First, there are the President's role of Commander-in-Chief, the large executive bureaucracy and the close ties between the executive branch and the uniformed services. Second, Congress has lacked the staff and expertise to compete in this highly complex and important area, and could offer no alternative to the systems analysis capability developed in the early 1960s by the Department of Defense. However, there are also political and even pyschological reasons. As Samuel Huntington observed;

> throughout the dozen years after World War II, except when confronted by similar competing programs, Congress never vetoed directly a major strategic program, a force level recommendation, or a major weapons systems proposal by the Administration in power ... During the Cold War Congress was simply not going to assume the responsibility for weapons selection.[71]

Congressman Les Aspin has made a similar point more bluntly: 'Playing it safe usually means buying more.'[72] Moreover, the bias produced by this tendency to err on the side of approving more rather than fewer forces is reflected in the

committees on which members choose to serve: 'Liberals who are interested in national security matters tend to seek assignment to the Foreign Affairs Committees where the cosmic issues are discussed. Conservatives tend toward the Armed Services Committee, where the money is divided up.'[73]

Recently, however, these patterns have changed to some extent. Committee membership is less directly related to ideological disposition; Congress has reduced both overall and specific budgetary requests; and, most important, Congress has gained a significant degree of influence over the defence budgeting process, at times even taking the initiative. These developments have three basic components.

First, Congress has gradually limited the discretion available to the executive in the spending of defence appropriations. Specifically, limits have been set on executive ability to shift congressionally appropriated funds within or between individual accounts, to impound (or refuse to spend) allocated funds, to carry over unspent funds indefinitely, and to make widespread use of large, undesignated contingency funds.[74] As a result, executive determination of actual defence spending is increasingly confined to what Congress has expressly stipulated.

Second, whereas before 1959 defence budget requests were scrutinized only by the Defence Sub-committees of the House and Senate Appropriations Committees, today approximately one-third of all requests, including those covering the procurement of virtually all weapon systems, research and development and military construction, must be approved, or 'authorized', by the two Armed Services Committees.[75] Thus, almost all defence items other than pay must face an annual legislative 'double jeopardy': authorization (a process by which programmes are designated and costs established) and appropriation (by which the actual monies are approved to fulfill the authorization).

Finally, the extra review provided by the authorization process is but part of the larger increase in the capacity of Congress to affect defence budgets. The 1974 Budget Act, besides establishing a much more disciplined procedure for congressional consideration of defence and other requests, also created a rudimentary systems analysis capability, as the CBO staff is

16

capable of producing life-cycle costs of alternative weapon systems and force postures. Increases in staff, both on committees and in personal offices, and increases in the resources of the other support agencies have similarly extended the capacity of Congress both to examine Administration proposals and to put forth some of its own. These legal and structural changes, along with a greater readiness to challenge the executive in the defence area, have transformed the role of Congress in the process of defence budgeting.

The impact of congressional participation in the budget process can be viewed at two levels. At the total (or macro) level the impact is relatively small. For the past decade congressional appropriations have deviated from administration requests only by some 5 per cent on average – and less if certain supplemental requests, financing adjustments and military assistance programmes are removed from the equation.[76] Indeed, the conclusion of a recent CRS study, that 'Congress has largely confined its budget review actions to identifying areas where waste seems likely to be found rather than to major realignments of the proposed defence program,'[77] resembles that of Huntington's, written nearly two decades before. Yet, if one approaches congressional action at a more specific (or micro) level, it is possible to detect a shift in influence. A number of important programmes, including the C-5A and F-111 aircraft, as well as the ABM proposal, have been substantially reduced, while such proposals as the *Cheyenne* helicopter and the MBT-70, or advanced main battle tank programme, have been eliminated. At the same time initiatives – the requirement that major surface vessels be nuclear-powered, reforms of NATO, the inclusion of a large nuclear-powered aircraft carrier – have become more common.[78]

These trends, and the annual legislative cycle, can best be illustrated by examining the FY79 Department of Defense Authorization legislation. The authorization Bill, introduced in January 1978 following its submission by the Carter Administration, requested a total of $35.5 billion for the procurement of major weapons systems, research, development, testing and evaluation (RDT&E), civil defense and other purposes, for the period 1 October 1978 through 30 September 1979. The bill was immediately sent to the two Armed Service committees, which over the next several months held hearings and considered amendments. Each committee then reported a modified version of the Bill to its chamber, where, after further debate and amendment, the House of Representatives passed a $37.9 billion authorization Bill in May and the Senate passed a $36.1 billion Bill in July. Differences between the passed versions were ironed out in a conference committee, the so-called 'third House of Congress,' where representatives from each chamber met and agreed to a common compromise version, or 'conference report.' On the last day of July 1978 a conference report authorizing expenditure of $36.96 billion was issued; not only was this figure nearly $1.5 billion more than the Carter Administration had requested, but the report also sanctioned a large nuclear-powered aircraft carrier specifically rejected by the executive branch, while altering a large number of other programme requests. Indeed, in the RDT&E part of the bill alone, while only reducing the overall $12.47 billion requested by the Administration by $210 million, or less than 2 per cent, Congress changed over a hundred specific requests, eliminated thirty others, and introduced funding in some fifteen areas for which finance had not even been requested by the Defense Department. This conference report was approved in identical form, and without further amendment, by both chambers and sent to President Carter for his signature. The President, however, exercised his power of veto, claiming 'We cannot have both an adequately balanced defense program and the luxury of an unneeded nuclear-powered aircraft carrier.'[79] Several weeks after the 17 August veto, on 7 September, the House failed to produce the necessary two-thirds majority to override the veto; as a result, the Senate did not even try. The authorization legislation then returned to the two Armed Services committees, which amended the conference report by eliminating the funds for the aircraft carrier and inserting some necessary funds to cover shipbuilding claims. Neither committee, however, would consider any other revisions desired by the Defense Department, instead instructing the Administration to include these matters in the regular FY80 authorization bill. Thus, on 4 October, the House passed the changed authorization reported out by the House Armed Services Committee, and three days later the Senate passed a similar Bill, followed by a vote to accept the House version and thereby avoid a second conference committee. The identical Bill was thus sent to the President, who signed the FY79 authorization of $35.2 billion into law.

This example highlights elements of continuity and change in congressional participation in defence budgeting. Initiative remains largely with the executive, reflecting its greater resources and its sophisticated systems analysis capacity in particular. But although Congress continues to be largely reactive, it is also more able and more willing than previously to challenge the executive on more specific programmes. In addition, and perhaps of equal importance, is the increase in general oversight; even where Congress consents to requests, the requests themselves are scrutinized more thoroughly than in the past. The costs and benefits of this increased involvement are difficult to assess: Congress can enhance the quality of American forces through oversight and effective initiative; at the same time its lack of any adequate systems analysis capability, and its particular vulnerability to the domestic political pressures of weapons production, can easily distort its perspective. Budget requests may be increased or decreased, in part or in whole; rarely, however, will they be left alone.

Foreign Assistance

Some similar trends have emerged in the realm of foreign economic and military assistance. Indeed, many appeared in this context some time ago, as shown by the problems the Kennedy Administration encountered in gaining approval for its aid programmes. A large number of members have traditionally opposed assistance on grounds of cost, while the lack of clear benefits from often 'ungrateful' recipients has made the task of obtaining congressional approval more difficult. In addition, the often less technical and, from the perspective of many, less critical nature of the foreign assistance programme has encouraged the participation of many Congressmen and their aides, who are more wary of challenging the armed services or the Defense Department in the defence budgeting process than they are the State Department in the aid process.

Congress has asserted its influence over the assistance process through the establishment of a large number of general and specific conditions.

As is the case with defence items, assistance requests are now subject to specific authorization as well as appropriation; in addition, presidential discretion has been limited, in terms of both the adjustment of specific-country programmes and the use of general-purpose funds. Military assistance has been particularly affected by these reforms, as in the past it provided the President with a major policy instrument often left unregulated by congressional dictates. Moreover, Congress now requires not only that all military assistance requests be accompanied and justified by presidential determination of national security interests, but it has also declared unequivocally that recipients should not confuse the availability of assistance with the extension of a security guarantee or commitment in any sense.[80]

Challenge by Congress to executive aid requests have not been limited to the amount or the focus of funding; increasingly, legislation has become an instrument by which members seek to alter the domestic or foreign policies of recipients. Nowhere is this as evident as in the area of 'human rights'. No economic assistance may be provided for any country 'which engages in a consistent pattern of gross violations of internationally recognized human rights . . . unless such assistance will directly benefit the needy people in such country'. Similarly, security assistance is to be denied unless 'extraordinary circumstances exist' which necessitate the continuation of military aid. In both categories, Congress has established a principle or provided a waiver or 'escape' clause for the executive, but retained the right of final approval itself. Moreover, in addition to these general approaches on behalf of human rights, Congress has also legislated specific-country restrictions either limiting or prohibiting the availability of assistance (usually security) to some ten countries.[81]

Assistance can also be affected by a host of other actions or policies on the part of recipient countries. Amendments prohibit aid to countries nationalizing American property without adequate compensation, to those defaulting on loans for more than one year, to any countries harbouring terrorists, or to states which permit discrimination on the basis of religion, race, national origin or sex against 'United States persons' involved in programmes. Military assistance requirements also prohibit any retransfer of equipment supplied by the United States to

18

third parties without the prior consent of the United States and limit the permissible use of any item of American military assistance.[82]

It was this last condition, the one that restricts use of equipment, which influenced the controversial decision taken by Congress in early 1975 to terminate military assistance, and especially foreign military sales (FMS) credits, to Turkey in the aftermath of her military action in Cyprus. Although these prohibitions have been relaxed, the low ceiling on credits constrained Turkey's ability to buy arms, while the legislation as a whole angered Turkey and affected both her bilateral relationship with the United States and her position in the Atlantic Alliance. Advocates of the prohibition argued that aid limits provided the only leverage likely to effect a change of Turkish policy towards Cyprus; opponents argued the contrary, claiming that penalties were less likely than incentives to induce moderation and compromise. After repeated but unsuccessful efforts to repeal the 'embargo', the Carter Administration finally succeeded in building a majority in both chambers in mid-1978. The repeal was a conditional one: it required not only an initial statement from the President that the resumption of military assistance was in the national interest, but also regular reports to be submitted by the President every sixty days, confirming that Turkey is acting 'in good faith' to promote a solution to the Cyprus dispute.[83] In the absence of such a solution, an attempt to reinstate either a partial or a total embargo against Turkey is both within the powers of Congress and politically feasible.

What is certain is that the entire assistance programme has become highly politicized and a potential source of friction between the United States and foreign countries. The adjustment of aid levels, whether for the purposes of promoting human rights, changing foreign policy positions or even protecting American industries from aid-assisted foreign competitors, can easily harm relations with actual or potential recipients, who may resent such blatant interference in their internal affairs and such public demonstrations of American power. The alternative option, that of channelling assistance through multilateral institutions such as the World Bank, is increasingly unpopular with many Congressmen; not only does it lessen the control of the United States over the use of the assistance itself, but it

weakens her ability (and that of Congress) to use aid for her own ends. But whether the more conditional provision of assistance is likely to enhance the influence of the United States in recipient countries is far from apparent; indeed, what was intended as a means of building strong and friendly states throughout the world could prove counter-productive if manipulated without caution.

War Powers

No single piece of legislation has been as controversial, or as central to the debate concerning the sharing of security powers between executive and Congress, as the War Powers Resolution. One student of congressional foreign-policy influence has hailed it as 'a decisive turning-point in the history of legislative-executive relations' and 'the cornerstone of the changing structure' of American foreign policy-making.[84] Another observer, however, has offered a rather different perspective: 'Having created the myth of presidential usurpation, Congress passed the War Powers Resolution to cure the imaginary disease.'[85]

Coming into law on 7 November 1973, after two-thirds of both the Senate and the House of Representatives voted to override President Nixon's veto, the War Powers Resolution (or, more formally, Act) is an attempt, via legislation, to control the ability of the President unilaterally to introduce American armed forces into situations of imminent or actual hostilities, into the territory, air space or waters of a foreign nation while equipped for combat, or in numbers which 'substantially enlarge' American forces located in a foreign state and equipped for combat in the absence of a formal declaration of war or specific congressional authorization.[86] The Resolution does not apply in such circumstances as a national emergency resulting from an attack upon the United States, her territories and possessions or her armed forces. If the President introduces forces in situations other than such emergencies, he is required to provide congressional leaders, within forty-eight hours and in writing, with his reasons for so doing, the constitutional and legal authority for his action and an estimation of the scope and duration of the involvement. Moreover, before the forces are introduced the President is required to consult with Congress. The involvement of forces can

19

then continue for sixty days, and for another thirty days thereafter, if the President certifies in writing that the safety of the forces so requires, *unless* Congress passes a concurrent resolution at any time during this sixty- or ninety-day period ordering that the forces be removed. Thus, by a simple majority vote in both chambers which cannot be vetoed by the President,[87] Congress has the power to terminate the involvement of armed forces in a situation whenever it so desires, and potentially before either the sixty-day or the additional thirty-day period is completed. Moreover, after the completion of these periods the involvement cannot be continued unless Congress specifically authorizes it by declaration of war, resolution or legislation. Thus, the President has a 'free hand', for a maximum of ninety-two days, to commit American forces abroad to involvement in situations of possible, imminent or actual hostilities; this period of unilateral commitment can be reduced by explicit congressional action and cannot be extended without it.

The Resolution was in many ways the culmination of a debate that had flared periodically during the history of the United States. The Constitution, as ever, was vague, referring only to the 'declaration of war' but not to the possibility of using force in situations short of full-scale war, nor to the then already discernible trend of governments resorting to war in the absence of formal declarations. The view of the framers was that 'no one wanted either to deny the President the power to respond to surprise attack or to give the President general power to initiate hostilities.'[88]

These twin aims posed a dilemma difficult to resolve, and from the outset the war power began to devolve upon the presidency. The armed forces of the United States were ordered into action by early Presidents against pirates and Indians to redress acts committed against property and persons. Lincoln, with both an expanded notion of Locke's doctrine of necessity and self-preservation and a liberal reading of presidential power under the Constitution, responded militarily to the Confederate attack on Fort Sumpter for some three months before congressional approval was obtained. The scope for presidential initiative was further expanded by action taken against Spain toward the end of the nineteenth century, and by the participation of the United States, without congressional approval

or protest, in the seige of Peking and the suppression of the Boxer Rebellion. Although these tendencies were reinforced even further by the experiences of both world wars, it was the wars in Korea and Indochina, owing to their scope and duration, that marked the Rubicon of the executive's power unilaterally to wage war.

Although it can be argued that the executive did not always act unilaterally, and that various resolutions and authorization or appropriation measures constituted a *de facto* sanctioning of presidential policy,[89] a majority of Congressmen reached the conclusion that the balance of war powers between the branches had become seriously imbalanced and was in urgent need of remedy. This was not the first time frustrated members of Congress turned to legislation to solve this problem; in 1912 Senator Bacon unsuccessfully attempted to deny appropriations for forces sent outside the jurisdiction of the United States without congressional consent, except during emergencies when Congress was not in session. By the 1970s the frustration over presidential power in this area had manifested itself in repeated efforts to curtail the involvement of the United States in Indochina, in an attempt to define the notion of 'national commitment' and finally in the War Powers Resolution itself.

To date, the historical record of the War Powers Resolution is a meagre one.[90] Four reports have been issued by the executive pursuant to the legislation relating to the transport of refugees from Danang in April 1975, the evacuation of American nationals from Cambodia and the evacuation of American nationals and other persons from South Vietnam, as well as to the *Mayaguez* incident in May 1975, in which President Ford introduced American forces to recapture the ship and crew from the Cambodian authorities. In none of these cases did Congress use any of the Act's mechanisms to affect the policy of the United States; nor is there any evidence the Ford Administration was affected in any way by the existence of the war powers legislation.

This is not to say that no controversy has existed during the Act's lifetime. Two areas concerning its application have been challenged by certain members of Congress. First, they have alleged that the executive has failed to fulfil the intention of the law in terms of its consultation requirement. Consultation in effect has amounted to little more than simply informing congressional leaders of executive decisions, and the reports have contained little information. The executive for its part has claimed that constraints imposed by time and the need for secrecy, as well as the logistical problem of arranging consultations, has precluded more detailed discussion.[91]

Secondly, a number of individuals have claimed that on three occasions – the evacuation from Lebanon in June and July 1976, the response of the United States to the Korean 'tree-chopping incident' in the DMZ in August 1976 and American participation in Western military actions in Zaire in May 1978 – executive actions were such that the procedures of the War Powers Act should have been triggered.[92] Again, the executive has demurred. In the Korean situation, for example, the State Department claimed the Act did not apply as hostilities did not appear imminent, American responses were similar to actions taken frequently under the Armistice Agreement and the additions to American forces were marginal rather than substantial. Similarly, the State Department argued that the American pilots who flew aircraft carrying foreign troops and equipment into Zaire were neither equipped for combat nor within 100 miles of the hostilities.

But if the seven incidents cited above demonstrate that thus far the war powers legislation has failed to guarantee Congress a more significant role in the introduction of American forces abroad, they have also failed to settle the larger controversy surrounding the Act. Indeed, to the extent that a debate on the war powers legislation has taken place at all, it has centred less on its implementation and impact to date than on its implications for American security policy in the future.

Although the Act has been attacked on constitutional grounds, the strongest criticism has focused on its effects on policy. This school of thought is best expressed in the veto message of President Nixon, which argued that its passage

would seriously undermine this Nation's ability to act decisively and convincingly in times of international crisis. As a result, the confidence of our allies in our ability to assist them could be diminished and the respect of our adversaries for our deterrent posture could decline. A permanent and substantial element of unpredictability would be injected into the world's assessment of American behaviour,

further increasing the likelihood of miscalculation and war.[93]

Ironically, the Resolution was also attacked by Senator Eagleton, one of its former advocates, who claimed that in its final form the Act actually enhanced presidential ability to go to war in contravention of the intent of the Constitution.[94]

Although the record of recent years has drained much of the enthusiasm of its backers, the Act is still seen as an important symbol of congressional influence and as a real constraint on the ability of the President unilaterally to wage unauthorized war. The former staff chief of the Senate Foreign Relations Committee has written that the legislation 'is designed to make it more difficult for Congress to acquiesce in future situations like Vietnam',[95] while Senator Javits, one of its principal sponsors, argues only that the Act 'establishes a procedure by which the Congress can effectively participate and bring to bear the war powers which the Constitution gave us'.[96]

On balance, it is interesting to note that the War Powers Act appears to worry its critics more than it pleases its backers; in reality, though, it is likely to be neither as constraining as its opponents fear nor as important as its framers intended and its advocates hope. This is not to say it will have no effect. Senator Church's perspective – that the Act is irrelevant in crises which are over before Congress can act, and unnecessary in longer involvements, as Congress possesses its authorization and appropriation powers through which to affect American military actions – is technically correct but politically incomplete.[97] Even without necessarily going as far as a former senior official, who wrote that the Act 'is bound to have a chilling effect on the United States' willingness to use force',[98] the war powers legislation will to some extent inhibit the executive from contemplating the use of force in those situations where a rapid, low-cost and low-risk solution does not seem assured. Indeed, in some circumstances one can foresee the President having to weigh the risk of not acting militarily against the risk of acting only to have the operation terminated by Congress. Equally, an approaching time limit might lead the executive prematurely to curtail American involvement or to escalate the level of involvement, so as to complete an engagement before Congress is forced to act.[99] At the same time, adversaries could be encouraged to prolong conflicts in the expectation that Congress will refuse support for continued American commitment, while allies must take into account yet another factor affecting the reliability of the United States. For Congress, the impact of the legislation is mixed: it does little if anything to enhance the direct influence of Congress in crises, but the law forces Congress to take a decision after two, or at most three, months of confrontation. A vote to continue operations signifies the sharing of responsibility with the executive; a vote to terminate signifies the assumption of responsibility by Congress alone. In light of current American resistance to another military involvement, this aspect of the law suggests that the United States will in future be less able to assume open-ended commitments.

Nuclear Proliferation

Since the end of World War II, interest in the spread and use of nuclear weapons has been a constant feature of American foreign policy. As such, it has also been affected by the decisions of Congress. Several relatively distinct phases of congressional concern, however, can be defined.[100] After the end of the war, and the United States' use of two nuclear devices against Japan, the emphasis of both executive and congressional policy in this area was on preventing any other state from gaining access to nuclear weapons. Not all efforts were successful: the Baruch Plan to internationalize control of nuclear weapons was still-born, while reluctance to honour wartime agreements with Britain caused serious difficulties in post-war relations between the two allies. From the congressional perspective, the dominant themes were non-co-operation and secrecy. The Atomic Energy Act of 1946 chose an odd approach to the problem, though, by banning exchanges of information regarding industrial uses of atomic energy but not those involving scientific and technical uses alone. While his approach may have slowed the introduction of certain alternative technologies around the world, it actually enhanced the dissemination of information crucial to later military and industrial applications of atomic energy alike.

In the early 1950s these rather strict limits on actual industrial co-operation were relaxed, most probably to ensure American access to uranium supplies in countries desiring access to American technical information. In any case, a fundamental change in the entire thrust of the nuclear policy of the United States came with the announcement of Eisenhower's 'Atoms for Peace' programme in December 1953, which made little connection between the spread of information and civil technology on one hand and the possible spread of nuclear weapons on the other. This change was authorized by Congress a year later in the Atomic Energy Act of 1954, which ushered in more than a decade of promotion of nuclear projects domestically and nuclear co-operation internationally. Fourteen years later (by which time the nuclear club had expanded to five actual and a host of potential members) the Senate ratified the Non-Proliferation Treaty (NPT). Like American policy, the NPT attempted to square the circle of proliferating nuclear technology and power without proliferating nuclear weaponry.

This optimistic aim dominated American and Congressional interest in non-proliferation matters for the next six years. In 1974, however, everything changed. In April Senator Ribicoff released the 'Rosenbaum' report, one of several to appear that warned of the dangers of nuclear theft and terrorism. The French revealed their intention to enter into major nuclear co-operation arrangements with South Korea and Pakistan, while the Federal Republic of Germany announced even more far-reaching plans for Brazil. Most important, the Indian 'peaceful nuclear explosion' of May signalled to many Congressmen the inadequacy of the current non-proliferation policy of the United States. Not surprisingly, these events, and the conclusions drawn from them, led to a spate of legislative efforts to fashion a new American policy.

Despite the initial resistance of the Ford Administration and the powerful Joint Committee on Atomic Energy, several efforts reached fruition. Although an amendment requiring congressional approval of all nuclear co-operation agreements was rejected, the International Development Association (IDA) Act of 1974 directed the American representative to the IDA to vote against any loan to a country developing any 'nuclear explosive device' unless it was or became a party to the NPT. The FY75 Foreign Assistance Act, passed in December 1974, besides prohibiting the transfer of any funds to Israel or Egypt for nuclear fuel or reactor programmes, also specifically authorized additional American contributions to the International Atomic Energy Agency (IAEA) for the strengthening of its safeguard procedures. Most significantly, the so-called 'Symington Amendment' (effective 30 June 1976) committed the government to cutting off most forms of assistance to any country receiving sensitive nuclear fuel reprocessing or enrichment facilities unless the President declared in writing the national security reasons for proceding with an assistance programme.[101] Nearly three years later the Amendment was implemented for the first time in response to Pakistan's attempts to acquire a uranium enrichment capability.

By the advent of the Carter Administration in early 1977 the atmosphere had changed considerably. In October 1976 the Ford Administration issued a new set of guidelines more responsive to potential problems raised by the transfer of sensitive nuclear technologies.[102] In April 1977 President Carter expanded these in his message accompanying proposed legislation that offered a comprehensive proliferation policy for the United States.[103] Many of the key members of the Joint Committee on Atomic Energy had left Congress by the end of 1976, and non-proliferation advocates took advantage of the Committee's weakened state by transferring authority for nuclear export controls to the foreign affairs committees.[104] In a single year the environment had changed from one of executive and congressional resistance to the introduction of strong non-proliferation measures to one of widespread support.[105]

The passage of the Nuclear Non-Proliferation Act in March 1978 reflected this change. Combining incentives for international co-operation with threats of unilateral American sanctions, the legislation itself is a complicated maze of procedures and conditions governing all forms of nuclear co-operation between the United States and other countries. In addition, the law changed not only American policy but also the role of Congress in overseeing and enforcing that policy.[106]

The law attempts to expand the framework of international agreements and institutions designed to prevent the proliferation of nuclear weapons, while guaranteeing access to the technology relevant for civil uses of nuclear energy. The President is directed to begin negotiations to establish an International Nuclear Fuel Authority, or INFA, which is to provide fuel

and treatment services to its customers, thus, it is hoped, alleviating demands for national reprocessing and breeder projects. Similarly, the legislation declares congressional support for the negotiations concerning the promise of alternative but less proliferation-prone fuel cycles, the expansion of the NPT regime, the strengthening of IAEA safeguards and greater co-operation among potential nuclear supplier states.

The more controversial aspect of the law, however, is the guidelines that have been established to govern both new and existing nuclear relations between the United States and other countries. The guidelines principally affect four areas: new Agreements for Co-operation, (that is, agreements that form the foundation of all bilateral nuclear relationships with the United States); existing Agreements for Co-operation, all of which require renegotiation as a result; the licensing procedure for all individual nuclear exports made pursuant to the basic Agreement for Co-operation; and 'Subsequent Arrangements', or procedures that recipient states must follow (and on which the approval of the United States is contingent) in regard to a wide range of domestic nuclear activities – including contracts, transfer approvals, physical security arrangements, storage of irradiated fuel, etc – if more general nuclear co-operation with the United States is to continue.

The Act stipulates terms for entering into or maintaining any form of a nuclear relationship with the United States. These include: the application of IAEA safeguards; a guarantee that exports supplied by the United States will not be used for explosive devices of any kind; assurances that adequate security precautions against theft and terrorism will be taken; an undertaking that all American non-proliferation criteria pertain not only to the items exported from the United States but also to anything generated by or derived from an American export. These four conditions came into effect immediately (as of 10 March 1978), affecting all exisiting and future co-operation agreements as well as any particular export of fuel, technology or equipment made pursuant to an agreement. In addition, three other conditions – that recipient countries accept 'full-scope safeguards', that they do not reprocess nuclear material without the prior approval of the United States, and that they transfer no items to third parties without

American approval – are not only applied immediately to all new agreements of co-operation, but also after twenty-four months (10 March 1980) to exports or after only eighteen months (10 September 1979) to licence applications made pursuant to co-operation agreements which existed before the new Act came into being. In effect, the legislation provides a two-year breathing space for the renegotiation of agreements which existed before the Act itself. Moreover, should a recipient at any time violate the Act, co-operation must be terminated unless the President determines that 'cessation of such exports would be seriously prejudicial to the achievement of United States non-proliferation objectives or otherwise jeopardize the common defense and security'. Congress, however, retains the final word: even if the President makes such a determination, he can be overruled by a concurrent resolution.

The Act also empowers the National Regulatory Commission (NRC) to make independent judgements on proposed nuclear exports following an assertion by the Secretary of State that a proposed export is not 'inimical' to the interests of the United States. In the absence of NRC approval, the President possesses the power to overrule the Commission and call for the export. Again, though, he in turn can be overruled by Congress if it passes a concurrent resolution of disapproval within sixty days of the presidential order. Similarly, Congress can block by concurrent resolution any general Agreement for Co-operation by the same procedure.

It did not take long for the new law to have an effect. Indeed, even before it was signed, licences for a large shipment of enriched fuel were approved for export to Euratom countries. After the signing a major diplomatic clash between Washington and the European states was averted, at least for two years, by an agreement to begin renegotiating existing arrangements, thus obeying the letter if not the spirit of the new law.[107] Of more immediate consequence was the failure of the NRC, on 20 April 1978, to approve a licence for the export of low-enriched uranium fuel to India's Tarapur plant. Protesting the delay, Indian Prime Minister Desai charged that 'the refusal to supply such requirements (pursuant to the 1963 Agreement for Co-operation) would be a breach of the agreement' between the two countries.[108] A week after the NRC vote, and three days after Desai's protest, President Carter approved the export, arguing that 'denial of this export would seriously undermine our efforts to persuade India to accept full-scope safeguards, and would seriously prejudice the achievement of other United States non-proliferation goals.'[109] While Congress bowed to this logic, and eschewed an override attempt, it also served notice on both the Administration and India that it had not altered its fundamental position and determination to apply the law: 'The executive branch and the Indian Government should base their discussions on the anticipation that, if full-scope safeguards are not achieved, it is highly unlikely that a waiver allowing continued exports would be acceptable.'[110] The day of reckoning had only been postponed, not averted.

Although it will not be possible to assess the full impact of the Nucelar Non-Proliferation Act until after the eighteen- and twenty-four-month deadlines for renegotiation pass, it is still possible to draw some tentative conclusions. Both the direction and the detail of the legislation appear unlikely to achieve their aims. The law introduces a large amount of unilateralism into an endeavour that can only succeed through international support and consensus. The combination of strict American-determined guidelines and terminations works against development of the trust and co-operation essential to the strengthening of non-proliferation mechanisms in an energy-hungry world. At the same time, not only is the ability of the United States to dictate terms in this area limited by the availability of alternative sources of fuel, technology and equipment, but also the very nature of the Act itself could stimulate efforts by recipients both to locate new sources of assistance and to accelerate their own indigenous capabilities. As one non-American observer has written, 'There is a great risk that a strategy of withholding know-how and maintaining dependence could bring about the opposite of what is intended; namely, political disintegration and nuclear self-sufficiency outside the world-wide non-proliferation system.'[111] A number of relationships could be injured, if not sacrificed, on the altar of proliferation without furthering either non-proliferation or larger security interests.

Military Transfers

Beginning with 'Lend-Lease' just months before the entry of the United States into World War II, and growing after the war through the Truman Doctrine, NATO and other security arrangements, the provision of military equipment and associated services has constituted an integral component of American security policy. In recent years, the advent of strategic parity with the Soviet Union and a marked reluctance on the part of the United States to commit her troops abroad has reinforced this pattern of 'indirect' security, achieved at least initially by a mixture of local national forces and a large percentage of American-produced weapons supervised by American advisers.

But while the strategic conception has endured and, if anything, become even more basic to the policy of the United States, the form of its fulfilment has evolved. The Military Assistance Program (MAP), costing as much as $5.7 billion in FY1952, has declined to a level of only several hundred million dollars in recent years; by contrast, the value of military goods and services sold rather than lent or granted has increased tenfold, reaching more than $11 billion in FY77.[112] Economic factors have been paramount in this transition. American economic weakness, coupled with the improved absolute and relative economic strength of allies have undermined congressional support for the continuation of military programmes. The NATO allies, Japan, Australia and New Zealand could afford to purchase weapons by the late 1960s, while credits assisted such states as Israel to do the same. Moreover, the rapid increase in oil prices enabled oil-producing states (Iran and Saudi Arabia in particular) to purchase military goods and services in large quantities after 1973. Arms sales provided jobs for workers, profits for companies and a means of recycling the so-called 'petro-dollars', as well as other dollars resulting from recurring American payments deficits, back into the United States. Thus the new economics could be made to fit the old strategy as military assistance gave way to military exports.

Although initial congressional reaction to the shift from assistance to sales was favourable – indeed, it came about in large part because of congressional pressures – the atmosphere quickly and drastically changed. The sheer size and value of the transfers created misgivings, and many Congressmen were sympathetic to the notion that arms sales provoked instabilities both within and between recipients. Others became concerned

that an increasingly prominent dimension of American security policy remained beyond effective congressional scrutiny or control. Investigations revealed mismanagment and bribery, which increased doubts about whether the large transfers were serving or harming the interests of either the United States or her allies. As is often the case, investigations led to hearings, and hearings to legislation.[113]

The legislation has sought to make the entire arms-transfer process more considered and more difficult. Reforms in the executive procedure for approving sales have been instituted; impact statements must be prepared and annual statements informing Congress of all intended sales for the current fiscal year must be provided by 15 November each year. More controversially, Congress has increased substantially its capacity to enforce arms-transfer restraint. In 1974 legislation was passed requiring the President to report to Congress every sale of articles or services over $25 million, after which Congress had twenty days to pass a concurrent resolution of disapproval to block the sale. Early experience with this procedure led a majority of Congressmen to vote for reform; legislation approved in 1976 reduced the 'trigger' mechanism to any proposed transfer of $25 million or more in defence articles or services, or $7 million or more involving 'major defense equipment', while extending the time in which a concurrent resolution of disapproval could be passed to thirty days. In addition, the executive branch has agreed to provide Congress with a further twenty days of informal notification before the formal thirty-day notice begins.[114]

Despite the more than 100 resolutions of disapproval introduced in the past few years, no single sale has been formally blocked by this new legislative procedure. This is not to say that the procedure has not had an effect on specific proposals. In its initial years Congress forced the Ford Administration to pledge that the sale of C-130 cargo aircraft to Egypt would not be followed immediately by other requests for military transfers to that country; in addition, a proposed sale of *Pershing* missiles to Israel was withdrawn and a sale of *Sidewinder* and *Hawk* missiles to Saudi Arabia reduced in number. More difficult were three proposals over which compromise proved elusive. Congress only withdrew its threat to disapprove a proposed sale of fourteen *Improved HAWK* (surface-to-air) missile batteries to Jordan in mid-1975 when the Administration guaranteed that they would be deployed only in a fixed manner, thereby diminishing their potential contribution to offensive operations against Israel. Similarly, the Carter Administration was forced both to modify its sale of 7 AWACS aircraft to Iran in mid-1977 to allay fears in Congress that sensitive technologies might be compromised, and to provide assurances about basing restrictions and future transfers in order to gain support for its package arms sale to Israel, Saudi Arabia and Egypt in the spring of 1978.[115]

Interestingly, the arms-transfer legislation constrains presidential options less in crises than in normal periods. Both the general procedure for disapproval and congressional ability to use concurrent resolutions to block transfers to third parties can be waived by the President in times of emergency, as was done during the March 1979 Yemen crisis. In normal times, however, and as the several cases cited above demonstrated, Congress's use of its disapproval powers (as well as the many other grounds for terminating transfers similar to those found in assistance legislation) can pose a major threat not only to the proposed transfer but also to the entire relationship between the United States and the intended recipient. As then Senator Dick Clark has noted, 'Congress gets into the act only after a sale has been promised by the Pentagon. At this stage Congress can reject a sale only at the risk of creating a serious diplomatic incident.'[116] Whether provisions of the 1978 legislation which guarantee Congress some influence in the preliminary or 'survey' stage of the arms transfer process will prove sufficient to alleviate this problem is doubtful; secrecy will be hard to maintain, and the acquiescence of a handful of Congressmen at the 'survey' stage may not guarantee widespread acceptance of a proposed sale as much as five years later in the public domain.[117]

In the long run what may be more serious than difficulties created by the form of congressional involvement are the fruits of a policy clearly biased against arms transfers. Much of the putative linkage between military transfers and instability is unproven, and in many circumstances transfers can enhance stability both militarily and politically. In addition, in the absence of actual or forseeable co-operation among arms suppliers over the restriction of their wares, it is doubtful that unilateral restrictions on the part of the United States will do much more than provide opportunities for economic and, more significant, political competitors. Similarly, the restriction of conventional arms transfers can both stimulate indigenous production of conventional weapons and increase the desirability of nuclear weapons as a substitute (or security) weapon of last resort. For potential recipients, the certainty of a more restrictive American arms-transfer policy, together with the uncertainty surrounding any particular sale, can only lead to a reassessment both of their security requirements and of their relationship with the United States.

Intelligence

Congress has also moved to gain greater control over the activities of the several intelligence agencies and bureaux within the United States Government. The impetus for this came from several sources: the investigations by both Senate and House committees of the intelligence agencies during the mid–1970s; the reaction to the discovery of illegal activities; and the growing realization that intelligence operations represented another important dimension of security policy that had largely been exempted from congressional control during the entire post-war era.

Three events stand out along this road to greater congressional participation in intelligence controls. The first has already been mentioned: the dramatic findings of the Church and Pike Committees.[118] Equally important was the so-called 'Hughes – Ryan' Amendment of 1974, which prohibited action other than that related to the collecting of intelligence by the CIA in foreign countries unless the President found the proposed action important for American national security and reported a description of the operation and its scope to the two foreign affairs committees. Thus, the amendment not only ended the era of 'plausible presidential denial', but it also ensured that Congress would be notified of covert operations through regular channels.[119] Congress went a critical step further, however, during the Angolan controversy of late 1975 and early 1976, by prohibiting 'assistance of any kind ... for the purpose, or which would have the effect, of

26

promoting or augmenting, directly or indirectly, the capacity of any nation, group, organization, movement, or individual to conduct military or paramilitary operations in Angola' unless it so authorized.[120] Moreover, Congress would only consider any authorization after receiving a detailed report justifying and describing the proposed operation.

These three powers – investigation, the right to information and the actual constraint of operations – are incorporated into the 1976 and 1977 Senate and House resolutions establishing select committees on intelligence.[121] The mandate of both committees is a broad one: 'to oversee and make continuing studies of the intelligence activities and programs of the United States Government'. More specifically, the committees' purpose is twofold: to ensure that intelligence operations are legal and of a sufficiently high quality to meet the demands of American foreign policy. The two committees are empowered to consider all legislation and related matters, including the authorization of budgetary appropriations, for all the intelligence agencies and bureaux; in early 1978 President Carter ordered the Director of Central Intelligence (DCI) and the heads of other agencies and bureaux to keep the two committees 'fully and currently informed concerning intelligence activities', to provide any information requested and to report whenever necessary as to illegal activities and measures taken to correct them.[122]

Despite this apparent demonstration of co-operation, executive–congressional relations in the realm of intelligence remain uneasy in two principal areas. The first concerns secrecy and the related matter of congressional right of disclosure. Information of a highly sensitive type reaches not only the two intelligence committees, but also the committees on foreign affairs, appropriations and the armed services. The availability of classified information to virtually all Congressmen and a large number of staff-members has increased the risk of unauthorized leaks that could compromise not only the operations themselves but the willingness of other countries to co-operate with the United States in this area. Moreover, the legislation contains a mechanism for unilateral declassification, by which a chamber (but not the committee alone) could, by majority vote, release information against the wishes of the Executive.[123]

A more direct and serious constraint on the ability of the Government to conduct intelligence activities of all types is to be found in the committees' control of the purse. Although both the resolutions and the executive order make clear that notification of operations by the executive to Congress need not precede their implementation, the budgetary power of the committees does give them the ability to prohibit an operation by type or locale through the authorization procedure, either in advance or after it has begun. (The latter was the case with Angola.) Thus, while it would be legal for the executive to initiate an operation before notifying the committees, it would be politically dangerous for it to do so as the committees could restrict funding *post hoc*. In addition, too great an exercise of unilateral initiative by the executive could provoke a large number of pre-emptive restrictions and prohibitions placed on operations. As a result, what has evolved thus far in practice is an executive notification to the committees of covert operations prior to implementation, which provides members with an opportunity to voice opposition beforehand.[124]

Constraints Unconstrained?

Speaking on 25 May 1978, in the wake of the participation of the United States in Western military efforts on behalf of Zaire's central government, President Carter called for a full review of congressional restrictions on foreign economic and military assistance programmes so as 'to preserve presidental capacity to act in the national interest at a time of rapidly changing circumstances'.[125] Some sixteen months before, his predecessor had argued that the President and his emissaries 'must not be handicapped in advance in their relations with foreign governments'.[126] In both instances what was at issue was not simply restrictions on aid, but the more general phenomenon of congressional constraints on the ability of the executive to conduct foreign and defence policy.

While the increased ability of Congress to amend the defence budget is a constraint of another kind, affecting indirectly the relations of the United States with other countries, the other forms of legislated controls – covering assistance, war powers, nuclear exports, arms transfers and intelligence operations – can inhibit presidential discretion and initiative, and therefore foreign policy, more directly. There are, however, important differences between the controls. In the three areas of assistance, transfers and nuclear exports the President in normal conditions can only act if Congress does not prevent the measure, either by refusing to authorize appropriate assistance or by legislative veto, using a concurrent resolution to disapprove an arms transfer or nuclear export. In the areas of war powers and intelligence operations, however, the executive retains full power to undertake action, but then it must notify Congress which can then terminate such action if it so chooses. Although there are exceptions to the above – during emergencies the President enjoys considerable latitude to dispense assistance and arms transfers, while Congress can preclude military or intelligence operations through the authorization and appropriations process – the basic distinctions are still valid.

These distinctions are important, for the concept of constraint is a complex one. In the first three areas the President is confined to negotiating and indicating intent to a foreign country; if Congress then refuses to approve or acts to disapprove his promise, a serious rupture in relations between countries can result, especially (as is often the case) if the congressional action is accompanied by a good deal of publicity and acrimony. A small issue, representing but one dimension of relations, can easily become a test case of the whole. In part this may be alleviated by procedures such as those introduced into the arms-transfer process, but no such parallel opportunity normally presents itself in the other areas: in any case, changing conditions and politics can lead to changing congressional views on a particular action.

Congressional involvement is not without other difficulties as well. Incentives and penalties, or carrots and sticks, must be manipulated carefully and subtly if they are to succeed in effecting desired results; total bans and withdrawals of help are hardly the stuff of which diplomatic compromises are made. Countries spurned by the United States will increasingly be able to locate an alternative source of supply, at home or abroad. Moreover, such penalties tend to affect friends more than adversaries, as the former are more likely to be closely involved with the United States. Last, as was mentioned before, the separate consideration of matters which can directly affect one another often makes for incoherence, with obvious results. War-powers procedures and intelligence controls provide constraints of a different sort. Neither category precludes initial executive action, nor are the effects of either on other states as clear. Yet fear of political or legal investigations, or the threat of congressional termination of some initiative, can inhibit the executive in both thought and deed. Equally, they produce uncertainty among allies and adversaries alike about American willingness and ability to act; the psychology of constraint can in certain circumstances have a powerful effect on decision-making and policy.

This is not to say that legislation in these areas only has the effect of constraining the executive, or that all such constraint is undesirable. Legislation has also increased both executive and congressional scrutiny of policies before the United States commits herself and the flow of information inside and outside the executive branch, to the benefit of many people in and out of government. Moreover, investigations and events have demonstrated all too frequently that a significant number of past executive initiatives would have benefited from congressional oversight and even cancellation. Whether on balance the foreign policy of the United States will benefit from the new legislating of security or not is a question to which the answer will vary with time and perspective.

V. CONCLUSION

Tension, even struggle, between executive and legislature over control of the foreign and defence policies of the United States is intrinsic to the political system. The Constitution consciously created it and history has failed to resolve it. Consequently, tension is less a problem than simply a characteristic of the American political process. Yet in recent years it has been argued that in its zeal to curb the abuses of the past, Congress has created a situation that is damaging to the security of the United States and her allies. Indeed, one need not claim that the present

28

relationship between two institutions is worse than before to recognize that today's balance creates its own set of difficulties.

Not surprisingly, a number of solutions has been suggested which can be grouped along structural, political or attitudinal lines. Structural solutions include options designed to improve existing congressional machinery as well as those intended to improve channels of communication between executive and legislature. The most common theme among the former is the creation of an umbrella committee on national security or interdependence.[127] There could either be separate Senate and House committees or a single, joint committee, or both. Whatever the specific form, a committee reform along these lines would ease the present jurisdictional tangle, thereby enhancing efficiency and, more important, reducing the lack of coherence inherent in a system in which a plethora of highly independent committees work their own will.

Problems do stand in the way of such an enterprise, however. If the new committee is to be legislative – that is, if it is to be able to write and amend legislation as well as hold hearings and make recommendations – the workload would be overwhelming for its members. It would encompass work presently performed by a large number of committees, each of which already threatens to demand too much of its members. Moreover, Congress would be most unlikely to establish such a super-committee. Existing committees show a marked tendency to guard their jurisdictions jealously, and most Congressmen oppose concentrations of power in the hands of a few. Indeed, such an omnibus national security committee would constitute a clear challenge to the trends of decentralization and individualism; for this reason it remains unlikely to receive much support within Congress.

On the other hand, the creation of new committees or a single, joint committee with a non-legislative mandate – along the lines of the Joint Economic Committee or Budget committees – might be a possibility. Such a 'supra-' rather than 'super-' committee, consisting of the congressional leadership and the chairmen and ranking minority members of specified existing committees, could hold hearings on major national security questions as well as providing a focal point for consultation with the executive. In addition, it could assist in co-ordinating separate committee consideration of pending legislation, although standing committees would retain their legislative authority and independence, as would all members. A supra-committee would not solve the problems of congressional compartmentalization or communication with the executive, but it could mitigate them.

Other structural proposals are concerned with the existing tangle of committees and emphasize the need for joint hearings, concurrent or sequential consideration of legislation and, more basically, further realignment of committee jurisdictions.[128] There are also proposals aimed at easing the relations between the two branches. Some are quite modest, urging the upgrading of liaison and congressional relations offices, while others would establish some form of a joint executive–Congress or 'EXCON' body to oversee national security policy. But whether any such far-reaching reform could be squared with the Constitution, much less receive political support, is doubtful.

On balance, the promise of structural solutions to the dilemma of policy-making appears limited. As a result, political (or policy) solutions have been put forward, predicated on the thesis that institutional harmony can only follow, not precede, agreement over policy. Speaking of executive-congressional relations in 1976, the then Deputy Secretary of State concluded, 'What inhibits bipartisan co-operation today is the divisive and chastening experience of Vietnam and Watergate and the lack of public consensus about America's future role in the world.'[129] Thus, if the breakdown of the post-war consensus over American foreign and defence policy was in part responsible for the current institutional crisis, it is often argued that the restoration of consensus would provide a major contribution to its amelioration.

Yet even if this assessment is correct, it holds out little promise. The restoration of consensus is a pipedream. As James Chace has written:

The kind of broad consensus ... obtained during the post-war era and which became a shibboleth of American foreign policy may no longer be possible to resurrect short of war. American interests are too diverse and American power now much less predominant ... Most issues may have to be taken up on a case-by-case basis, and the President will have to look for support for his foreign policies much as he might seek to do for his domestic programs.[130]

Recent evidence supports this theme. Henry Kissinger's 'world order' efforts lost domestic support, while President Carter's attempt to build a new consensus, in which human rights played a major part, proved unrealistic and inadequate. Indeed, only success seems to rally widespread support for foreign policy in and out of Congress and then only temporarily.

Some of the more realistic writing on the resolution of executive–congressional difficulties rejects the panaceas of structural overhaul or a revival of consensus, calling instead for a mutual reassessment of the quality of the relationship between the branches:

> The problem facing both Congress and the Executive branch is not so much the necessity to rebuild a new foreign policy consensus as it is the need to achieve a working relationship between the two branches that will enhance the United States' capability to conduct a democratic and effective foreign policy ... Many of the problems affecting legislative – executive relations are attitudinal rather than structural, and no amount of structural innovations will solve them.[131]

Basic to this approach is the need to improve consultation, described by one executive official as the 'sacred principle of congressional relations',[132] a claim likely to be accepted by a majority of Congressmen as long as consultation is understood to mean active participation of Congress in policy-making rather than simply its being informed of executive decisions and initiatives. But in a body of 535 members with whom does one consult? The absence of any clear pattern of authority in Congress diminishes the appeal of this solution. In addition, consultation can involve the forfeiting of secrecy, speed and surprise – all valuable diplomatic assets. Consultation also requires a large element of trust and good faith on both sides if it is not simply to be used by each branch to undermine the objectives of the other. Indeed, the very same factors – congressional decentralization and policy divergence – which militate against both the structural and the policy 'solutions' also limit the promise of improving the working relationship between the two institutions. What is more, the entire political process is a bargaining exercise; to the extent that the President requires the support of Congress, the system rewards those who withhold their support. In a world where the squeaky wheel gets the grease, a compliant and co-operative Congress is more likely to be taken for granted than taken into counsel.

One is tempted to concur with Eugene Rostow: 'The problem of harmonizing presidential and congressional authority in the field of foreign affairs is not institutional or constitutional, but human and political. It cannot be solved by constitutional amendments, by statutes, or by more institutionalized procedures of consultation.'[133] But neither is the problem solely 'human and political', for no combination of persons or tactics is likely to bring about a sound partnership. More than anything else, the existence of tension between the two branches reflects a lack of consensus over not policy but power. What is the proper balance between the executive and Congress, and what is the proper role of the latter?

Two opposing concepts exist. There are those who advocate a strong and powerful Congress involved in the details of policy-making. Anything less, it is maintained, will give the executive too much discretion and too much scope to conduct a policy inconsistent either with public opinion or with the Constitution and the law. A number of proposals has been advanced to enhance congressional influence, including a greater capacity for independent defence budgeting; more severe limits on the presidency during crises; positive approval by Congress to sanction (rather than disapproval to prevent) arms transfers and nuclear exports; increased congressional control over the National Security Council system, along with access to its papers and those of the intelligence community; and, in general, a greater role in influencing presidential initiatives before they are launched.[134]

The alternative view of the proper role for Congress offers a very different conception. As expressed by Secretary of State Kissinger:

> The Congress can set broad guidelines and decide basic policies. But the Congress does not have the organization, the information, or the responsibility for deciding the tactical questions that arise daily in the conduct of our foreign relations or for executing a coherent, consistent, comprehensive policy. The President has this responsibility and must be

30

permitted to exercise it on behalf of the entire Nation.[135]

More specifically, it is often maintained that Congress should confine itself to two roles. The first of these emphasizes oversight: 'In foreign affairs, Congress probably serves best as discussant, critic, sharp-eyed investigator and watchdog rather than as policy initiator and formulator.'[136] In doing so publicly and effectively, Congress would be performing another valuable service. As Woodrow Wilson wrote, 'Even more important than legislation is the instruction and guidance in political affairs which the people might receive from a body which kept all national concerns suffused in a broad daylight of discussion.'[137]

Congress has the additional responsibility of establishing limits or parameters for policy: 'Congress are the rear wheels, indispensable and usually obliged to follow, but not without substantial braking power.'[138] This conception receives support from former Senator Fulbright: 'This [congressional] role is to participate in shaping broad policies . . . the executive should be left free, within broadly defined limits of scope and direction, to carry out the program and to adapt it to the constantly changing conditions with which we are confronted throughout the world.'[139]

The problem, of course, is where to draw the line. How does one ensure adequate congressional involvement without unduly confining the executive? As the preceding discussion indicates, there is little agreement about this at present, nor is there likely to be in the future. As John Lehman has pessimistically but realistically noted, 'There are, in short, no frameworks, no cookbooks, no valid models, and no 'golden ages' of administrations past to which we might refer in judging a "proper" distribution of powers or even "constitutional" relationship between branches.'[140]

Implications of Uncertainty

What is possible, however, is to review the changes of recent years and assess their overall implications for the conduct and substance of American security policy. Political and institutional patterns, including the weakening of parties and leaders, the rapid turnover of elected representatives, the increase in access to information and staff resources and the wide distribution of relevant powers, have served to reduce the role of traditional authorities while enhancing the potential of the individual member. With the recovery of former powers and the legislating of new ones, more Congressmen than ever before have acquired more influence in foreign and defence matters. Treaties are now more difficult both to make and to break, and executive requests for budgetary approval of defence programmes and foreign assistance efforts are regularly subjected not only to severe scrutiny but also to widespread additions, reductions or rejections. Similarly, the scope for unilateral presidential discretion, be it to commit troops to hostilities, to undertake intelligence operations or to export arms or nuclear materials, has been circumscribed, both directly by actual legislative vetoes and indirectly by the threat of them.

This array of congressional power and influence is not without its benefits for American security. Congress is vital as a link between the American people and their Government, bringing popular feelings and opinions to the notice of the often isolated ranks of policy-makers in Washington, while at the same time serving as a medium through which policies can be introduced and explained. In a democracy, where lack of public support for a policy can prove fatal to its prospects, the importance of such a function is manifest. Congress can also serve as policy initiator. The Arms Control Impact Statement (ACIS) process, and numerous other reforms of executive assistance programmes are the direct results of congressional efforts. Hearings can provide a forum for new ideas, and resolutions are often trial balloons by which policy departures can be tested before the Government finds itself committed.

Congress also provides the United States with an 'alternative voice'. It can act as an early-warning system, communicating potential changes in the policy of the United States, as the Mansfield troop-withdrawal efforts did for American allies in Europe. During negotiations congressional pressure can enhance the bargaining strength of the United States, as foreign representatives know that an Administration cannot compromise beyond a certain point and still retain domestic support for an agreement. Congressmen can also retain ties and maintain communications with a country, even when official policy advocates a cooling in relations, thereby providing a foundation on which future relations can be based. Perhaps most important, Congress retains the ability to correct the abuses of power and errors of policy sometimes committed by the executive.

Yet an influential Congress does present difficulties. In part this is because Congress remains a highly political institution. Members are vulnerable to the vagaries of the political process, with Senators requiring re-election every six years and Representatives every two. The rapid rate of turnover throughout the past decade indicates just how much uncertainty this process provokes. The perspective of members must often be short-term and attuned to what is popular in the home district or state. Congressmen thus tend to respond less to the national interest *per se* than to their constituency's perception of the national interest. Not surprisingly, most members are highly vulnerable to the political power of active and influential special-interest groups – a disposition which increases the inclination to approach national security issues in terms of votes and voter receptivity. Given the continued weakening of parties at the national level, the limited prospects of reducing the impact of special-interest groups through the introduction of campaign financing reforms and the general decline in voter participation, it is difficult to imagine the curtailment of trends favouring the influence of special interests (whether economic, ethnic or otherwise) and the fragmentation of American politics. Since by definition special interests are special rather than national or common, it appears that the politicization and domestication of issues of state can only work to the detriment of American security concerns.

But problems reflect structural as well as political factors, and equally troubling is congressional difficulty in producing policy, either integrated or coherent. The formal and informal structures of Houses, parties, committees and increasingly powerful individuals all but preclude a co-ordinated approach to policy-making. There is no place in the institution where policies are aggregated and synthesized; rather, each strand tends to be pursued in isolation, and little consideration is given to how different policies affect, or are affected by, other elements of national security. The very same attribute of Congress which was described above as a virtue, that of being an alternative voice, can also be a liability. Congress can call into question

American guarantees and credibility, and it can both confuse allies and encourage adversaries by departures from executive polices.

It is not, of course, simply the congressional perspective that causes concern but also Congress's increasing ability to translate its wishes into policy, either directly or by affecting executive action. Although in most cases Congress cannot prevent presidential initiative, it can thwart the ability of the Government to fulfil pledges and continue actions. Executive awareness of this latent congressional power can have the additional effect of inhibiting presidential initiative in the first instance. Moreover, incentives for foreign countries to compromise on some decision, or the ability of the United States to affect such decisions, can be removed by explicit measures that 'strike both the carrot and the stick from the Administration's hands'[141] and thereby bind the President to a particular course of action. The same tendency towards explicitness has had another result. Congressional foreign policy often lacks subtlety. The denied arms transfer, nuclear export, assistance programme or intervention can elevate any proposal or issue to a test of American reliability and friendship. As a former official has put it. 'The question is whether it is in the national interest to strike with the axe or seek remedy with the scalpel'.[142]

The net impact of an active Congress can be addressed in other contexts as well. For America's allies, an involved and influential Congress promises to complicate at least the process of negotiation and probably the entire range of relations more generally. Perhaps more important, a foreign and defence policy for a United States heavily influenced by Congress will be even more unpredictable than already is the case. Depending on the issues in question, agreements may be more difficult to make, maintain or dissolve. At any time Congress can attempt to introduce new elements or requirements into a relationship, as it has done with Turkey over Cyprus and with NATO over procurement, or as it could do in the future with Israel concerning her policies towards the occupied territories. Equally serious might be the impact of Congress during the longer term of the coming decades. In light of the high rate of turnover, the lack of familiarity of many members with foreign perspectives, and the vulnerability of Congressmen to domestic political pressures, Congress will be less inclined to treat the principles and structures of American foreign policy as given or sacrosanct; indeed, it would be surprising if any of the major post-World War II arrangements remained exempt from periodic congressional demands for a redistribution of alliance costs and responsibilities. Although such uncertainty is inherent in all relationships, and especially in those between unequals, allied doubts about congressional attitudes, well-founded or otherwise, could accelerate a reappraisal of security options by many states – a reappraisal with ramifications more agonizing for the structures of Western security and world order than those entertained at various times by the United States.

Interestingly, the problems posed for allies by a major congressional voice in policy-making are not dissimilar from those which adversaries must consider. Again, the process of negotiation will be a frustrating one, as the executive will rarely have a hand sufficiently free to commit the government to either a particular matter or to an agreement as a whole. Similarly, Congress can introduce added conditions to the relationship at any time, much as was done during the trade negotiations with the Soviet Union concerning her emigration policy. Once more, a high degree of uncertainty is introduced into diplomacy. Depending on the situation, this can be interpreted as a source of deterrence or temptation, strength or weakness, although on balance it is difficult to see how such uncertainty about the responses of the United States would discourage opportunistic probes by adversaries willing and able to test American strength and determination.

The heightening of the unpredictability of American responses inevitably raises the fundamental question of the compatability of such congressional involvement with the requirements of a policy designed to modify and moderate the behaviour of adversaries. If such a policy is to be successful, both rewards and punishments must be available to the Executive and under tight control; availability and precision alike can easily be undermined by independent expressions of congressional will. Indeed, it is impossible to avoid wondering (and worrying) about the compatability of the new Congress, with its decentralization of authority, its vulnerability to special interests and its tendency to legislate

severe but separate norms, with the demands of a world-order policy that could satisfy allies and contain adversaries. Such a policy requires a careful integration of means and ends, a clear sense of priorities and a mixture of flexibility and predictability. Again, such policies are not the ones most likely to emerge from today's Congress.

This said, the influence of Congress is not likely to be the same in all circumstances. Congressional influence will tend to be greatest when the domestic political dimensions of a security-related issue become a major concern of the individual legislator. This pattern manifests itself in several areas, most commonly (but not exclusively) in certain 'ethnic' foreign policy matters. Thus, American foreign policy towards such diverse regions as the Middle East, the Aegean and Africa is constrained in varying degrees by the influence of highly active organizations and individuals in the United States who have a particular interest in one country or area of the world. Domestic economic forces also assert a significant impact on certain policies. Labour unions, once advocates of free trade, have increasingly become a source of protectionist pressures, as have 'single-industry' communities whose livelihood is threatened by particular imports. Firms dependent upon foreign orders work against export controls, thereby affecting the ability of the United States to monitor the flow of goods, technology and credits to adversaries or competitors. Somewhat less directly, oil companies and the varied protagonists of the American energy debate have had a major impact on the energy policy of the United States, with all its implications for American security. There is as well a clear disposition to avoid the commitment of American troops in situations of any significant scope or duration. While advocates of these and other interests seek to influence the executive branch directly, they are often more successful at influencing the more vulnerable member of Congress who can ill afford to alienate powerful political forces in his home district and who rarely has to balance competing demands.

Congress will also be at its most influential when it has adequate time and clear means to work its will. It is most powerful in its consideration of money matters and either continuing or completed presidential actions. More specifically, this points to a major and enduring role for Congress in authorizing and appropriating funds for defence and foreign assistance, and in reviewing and modifying pending or existing agreements with foreign countries. By contrast, Congress lacks the means either to manage crises or to prevent most presidential initiatives. In addition, Congressmen tend to be less active in cases where domestic political pressures are relatively limited, or where the ability to exploit some foreign or defence issue for domestic political benefit is small.

Many of the new powers of the Congress are however, potential rather than actual ones, and Congress retains the option of exercising them or ignoring them. To the degree that certain congressional mechanisms for restraining the Executive remain latent, they will probably atrophy over time; certainly, the psychological and political dimensions of restraint on Executive decision-making will diminish. If, for example, the 'recall' mechanism of the War Powers Act is not used for a generation, it is difficult to imagine some future Administration fearing its potential to the extent that one must do so today. Similarly, the impact of other restraints will decline if intelligence operations go unchallenged or presidential waivers on various exports become commonplace.

This political reality suggests the other major variable in any assessment of the durability and degree of congressional influence: presidential power. A strong President supported by an effective and united Administration can still shape the political environment of the United States to a considerable extent. As the Carter Administration demonstrated at the Camp David Middle East summit, as well as with its recognition of the People's Republic of China and the dispatch of arms to the Republic of Yemen, initiative in the American system continues to reside in the executive branch,

But all too often this same Administration has forfeited initiative, whether through confusion, error or indicisiveness. A number of tendencies – the public expression of unrealistic and incompatable aims, the frequent changes of policy, the difficulty of communicating priorities, the pattern of speaking with several voices – have had the combined effect of eroding the perception of presidential control and direction fundamental to successful leadership. Although the post-Vietnam and post-Watergate Congress would have proved difficult for any executive to handle, the Carter Administration has exacerbated relations by appearing uncertain and divided in purpose.

What can be learned from the above is that political power in the United States is something to be struggled for. At the same time, it would be incorrect to see the amount of power as a constant. Absolute and relative shares can be increased by the office or institution which wields it most effectively. Thus, although the reforms of recent years have strengthened Congress at the expense of the presidency, they have not settled in any permanent way the continuing struggle over the distribution of foreign and defence powers in the American Government. For the forseeable future, however, this struggle will be waged by branches more equal than at any time since the end of World War II.

NOTES

The following abbreviations are used in this section:

USGPO: United States Government Printing Office
CFR: Committee on Foreign Relations
CIR: Committee on International Relations
USS: United States Senate
USHR; United States House of Representatives
CRS: Congressional Research Service

[1] Graham Allison and Peter Szanton, *Remaking Foreign Policy: The Organizational Connection* (New York: Basic Books, 1976), p. 99.
[2] James Reston, 'Is Anybody in Charge?', *International Herald Tribune*, 15–16 April 1978.
[3] James Madison, *The Federalist Papers*, No. 47, p. 301. (*The Federalist Papers* are a collection of letters written during 1787 and 1788 by Madison, Alexander Hamilton and John Jay in order to solicit public support for the then pending Constitution. Over the years the *Papers* have evolved into a major, if not the major, source of interpretation of the Constitution and its framers' intentions. All excerpts used here are from the Mentor Book edition, published by the New American Library in 1961.)
[4] Walter Bagehot, *The English Constitution*, p. 219. (The edition cited here is the 1963 edition published by Fontana/Collins London, rather than the original 1867 version.)
[5] James Bryce, *The American Commonwealth* (New York: Macmillan, 1910), p. 228.

34

[6] Alexis De Tocqueville, *Democracy in America* (Cambridge, Mass: Sever and Francis, 1862; translated by Harry Reeves and edited by Francis Bowen), p. 299.

[7] Woodrow Wilson, *Congressional Government* (New York: Meridian Books, 1956), p. 29. (The work was first published in 1885.)

[8] Richard E. Neustadt, *Presidential Power* (New York: Wiley, 1960), p. 33. Also note the discussion of the 'separation doctrine' in the appendix of Louis Fisher, *President and Congress* (New York: Free Press, 1972).

[9] James Madison, *The Federalist Papers*, No. 51, *op. cit.*, pp. 322, 320.

[10] *Baker v. Carr*, 369 U.S. 186, 211 (1962).

[11] *C&S Airlines v. Waterman Corp.*, 333 U.S. 103, 111 (1948).

[12] *McCulloch v. Maryland*, 4 Wheat 316, 4 L ED 605 (1819).

[13] *United States v. Curtiss-Wright Export Corp.*, 299 U.S. 304–33 (1936). Although Justice Sutherland made a strong case for the federal government's claim to foreign affairs powers, he was on much less firm ground when he argued that such powers in turn should accrue to the executive. For a harsh criticism of the decision, and more generally of the notion of executive primacy, see Raoul Berger, 'The Presidential Monopoly of Foreign Relations', *Michigan Law Review*, 71(1), 1972.

[14] Edwin Corwin, *The President: Office, and Powers* (New York: New York University Press, 1940), p. 200.

[15] Louis Henkin, '"A More Effective System" for Foreign Relations: The Constitutional Framework', in *Commission on the Organization of the Government for the Conduct of Foreign Policy: Appendices*, Vol. 5 (hereafter cited as Murphy Commission 5), Washington: USGPO, 1975) p. 10.

[16] See Samuel P. Huntington, *The Common Defense* (New York: Columbia University Press, 1961), especially pp. 124–7.

[17] Arthur M. Schlesinger, Jr, *The Imperial Presidency* (Boston: Houghton Mifflin, 1973), p. 169.

[18] J. W. Fulbright, 'Congress and Foreign Policy', in Murphy Commission 5, *op. cit.*, p. 59.

[19] Texts of these resolutions, as well as all legislation in the domain of foreign and defence affairs, can be found in the multi-volume *Legislation on Foreign Relations through 1977* (Washington: USGPO, 1978), compiled jointly by two foreign affairs committees and updated regularly.

[20] There are literally hundreds of hearings and studies dealing with Vietnam that have been published by Congress. For summaries of the congressional role during this period, see Schlesinger, *op. cit.*, especially ch. 7; and John H. Lehman, *The Executive, Congress, and Foreign Policy: Studies of the Nixon Administration* (New York: Praeger, 1974), ch 3 and 7; *Congress and the Termination of the Vietnam War*, prepared for the CFR, USS by the CRS (Washington: USGPO, 1973).

[21] See Phil Williams and Scott D. Sagan, 'Congressional Demands for American Troop Withdrawals from Western Europe: The Past as Prologue', in *RUSI Journal*, September 1977; also note Gregory F. Treverton, *The 'Dollar Drain' and American Forces in Germany* (Athens, Ohio: Ohio University Press, 1978).

[22] Alton Frye, *A Responsible Congress: The Politics of National Security* (New York: McGraw Hill, 1975), p. 33.

[23] *Ibid.*, p. 31.

[24] See Alan Platt, *The U.S. Senate and Strategic Arms Policy, 1969–1977* (Boulder Colorado: Westview Press, 1978).

[25] Schlesinger, *op. cit.*, pp. 282–3.

[26] For a fascinating overview of the post-war era and executive–congressional relations, see *Congress, Information, and Foreign Affairs*, prepared for the CFR, USS by the CRS (Harry L. Wrenn) (Washington: USGPO, 1978).

[27] David Truman, *The Governmental Process* (New York: Knopf, 1951), p. 433.

[28] Wilson, *op. cit.*, ch. I, p. 55–6.

[29] *Congress and Foreign Policy*, Report of the Special Subcommittee on Investigations of the CIR, HR (Washington: USGPO, 1977), p. 20.

[30] Les Aspin, 'The Defense Budget and Foreign Policy: The Role of Congress', in *Daedalus*, Summer 1975, p. 164.

[31] See Harrison W. Fox, Jr, and Susan Webb Hammond, *Congressional Staffs: The Invisible Force in American Lawmaking* (New York: Free Press, 1977); see also Michael J. Malbin, 'Congressional Committee Staffs: Who's in Charge Here?' and Michael A. Scully, 'Reflections of a Senate Aide', both of them in *The Public Interest*, No. 47, Spring 1977.

[32] Fox and Hammond, *op. cit.*, p. 143.

[33] See James D. Carroll, 'Policy Analysis for Congress: A Review of the Congressional Research Service', in *Congressional Support Agencies*, A Compilation of Papers prepared for the Commission on the Operation of the Senate (Washington: USGPO, 1976).

[34] See E. B. Skolnikoff, ' The Office of Technology Assessment', in *ibid.*; also Barry M. Casper, 'The Rhetoric and Reality of Congressional Technology Assessment', in *The Bulletin of the Atomic scientists*, Vol. 34, No. 2, 1978.

[35] See Joseph Pois, 'The General Accounting Office as a Congressional Resource', in *Congressional Support Activities, op. cit.*

[36] For discussions of the congressional budget procedure and the performance to date of the new structures, see William M. Capron, 'The Congressional Budget Office', in *ibid,*; Richard Burt, *Defence Budgeting: The British and American Cases*, Adelphi Paper 112 (London: IISS, 1974/5), pp. 18–22; Allen Schick, *The First Years of the Congressional Budget Process* (Washington: CRS, LOC, 1976); *Budgeting in the United States Senate*, A Compilation of Papers prepared for the Commission on the Operation of the Senate (Washington: USGPO, 1977).

[37] This concept was recently reiterated in the key Watergate ruling, United States v. Richard M. Nixon, 418 U.S. 683–716 (1974).

[38] The Freedom of Information Act, passed in 1966 and significantly amended in 1974, provides the basic authority and procedure for the public to petition the executive branch for unreleased documents and records in its possession. The law as amended places the burden of secrecy on the executive; thus, the individual's 'need to know' has given way to the 'right to know', although the right is still restricted in certain areas. A full description of the Act can be found in *Freedom of Information Act and Amendments of 1974 (P.L. 93–502)*, a Joint Committee Print of the HR Committee on Government Operations and the Senate Committee on the Judiciary (Washington: USGPO, 1975).

[39] See *Analysis of Arms Control Impact Statements Submitted in Connection with the Fiscal Year 1978 Budget*

Request, prepared for the CFR, USS and the CIR, USHR by the CRS (Washington: USGPO, 1977); *Fiscal Year 1979 Arms Control Impact Statements* (Washington: USGPO, 1978); *Evaluation of Fiscal Year 1979 Arms Control Impact Statements: Toward More Informed Congressional Participation in National Security Policymaking,* Report prepared for the Subcommittee on International Security and Scientific Affairs of the CIR, USHR by the CRS (Washington: USGPO, 1979); *Statements that Analyze Effects of Proposed Programs on Arms Control Need Improvement* (Washington: GAO, 1977); *Improved Procedures Needed for Identifying Programs Requiring Arms Control Impact Statements* (Washington: GAO, 1978).

[40] Aspin, *op. cit.,* p. 164.

[41] For a fascinating glimpse of a typical week in the life of an American Senator, see James L. Buckley, *If Men were Angels: A View from the Senate* (New York: Putnam, 1975), ch. 6.

[42] A summary of proposed and realized reforms can be found in *Policymaking Role of Leadership in the Senate,* A Compilation of Papers prepared for the Commission on the Operation of the Senate (Washington: USGPO, 1976): *Toward a Modern Senate,* Final Report of the Commission on the Operation of the Senate (Washington: USGPO, 1976); *Committee System Reorganization Amendments of 1977,* Hearings before the Committee on Rules and Administration, US Senate, on S. Res. 4 (Washington: USGPO, 1977); and the various reports of the Temporary Select Committee to Study the Senate Committee System, published in 1976 and 1977.

[43] Alexander Hamilton, *The Federalist Papers,* No. 75, pp. 450–1.

[44] John Jay, *The Federalist Papers,* No. 64, pp. 391–2.

[45] Quoted in *The Role of the Senate in Treaty Ratification,* A Staff Memorandum to the CFR, USS (Washington: USGPO, 1977), p. 45.

[46] Ellen C. Collier, 'The Meaning of "Advice and Consent of the Senate" in the Treaty-Making Process', in *ibid.,* pp. 25–6.

[47] Henkin, *op. cit.* (n. 15. above), p. 15.

[48] In the area of trade Congress has also traditionally 'liberated' the President by granting him prior authority to reduce duties within certain limits. See Fisher, *op. cit.* (n. 8 above) pp. 146–55.

[49] Platt, *op. cit.* (n. 24 above); see also Stephen J. Flanagan, 'Congress, the White House and Salt', in *The Bulletin of the Atomic Scientists,* November 1978.

[50] *Op. cit.* (n. 45 above), pp. 45–6.

[51] See *Senate Debate on the Panama Canal Treaties: A Compendium of Major Statements, Documents, Recorded Votes and Relevant Events,* prepared for the CFR, USS by the CRS (Washington: USGPO, 1979; see also I.M. Destler, 'Treaty Troubles: Versailles in Reverse', in *Foreign Policy,* No. 33, Winter 1978/9.

[52] Memorandum for the Secretary of State of 15 December 1978 from the Legal Adviser, Herbert J. Hansell, and released by the Office of Congressional Relations, Department of State, in January 1979, under the title 'Presidential Authority to Terminate Treaties'. See especially pp. 6–8.

[53] Vita Bite, 'Precedents for U.S. Abrogation of Treaties', in *The Role of the Senate in Treaty Ratification,*

op. cit. (n. 45 above), For a full account of this issue, see *Treaty Termination,* Hearings before the CFR, USS (Washington: USGPO, 1979).

[54] Schlesinger, *op. cit.* (n. 17 above), p. 85.

[55] In *United States v. Belmont,* 301 U.S. 324–37 (1937), the Supreme Court stated, 'an international compact ... is not always a treaty which requires the participation of the Senate.'

[56] For discussions of the types of executive agreements and their evolution, see *Transmittal of Executive Agreements to Congress* Hearings before the CFR, USS, on S. 596 (Washington: USGPO, 1971); David M. Sale, *Executive Agreements: A Survey of Legal and Political Controversies Concerning their Use in United States Practice* (Washington: CRS, 1975); and *Congressional Review of International Agreements,* Hearings before the Subcommittee on International Security and Scientific Affairs of the CIR, USHR (Washington: USGPO, 1976).

[57] The findings of the Symington Subcommittee were published in 1971 in two large volumes entitled *United States Security Agreements and Commitments Abroad.*

[58] Besides those sources mentioned in n. 56 above, see Loch Johnson and James M. McCormick, 'Foreign Policy by Executive Fiat', in *Foreign Policy,* No. 28, Fall 1977; John F. Murphy, 'Treaties and International Agreements other than Treaties', in Murphy Commission 5, *op. cit.* (n. 15 above), pp. 99–115.

[59] *National Commitments,* Report of the CFR, USS (Washington: USGPO, 1969), p. 28.

[60] This refers to the 'Bricker Amendment', which was in fact a series of initiatives proposed by Senator Bricker during the 1950s attempting to ensure that no treaty or IAOTT would have domestic standing in the absence of specific internal legislation.

[61] See Ellen C. Collier, *The National Commitments Resolution of 1969: Background and Issues* (Washington: LRS, 1970).

[62] The text of the Case Act, or P.L. 92–403, can be found in *Legislation on Foreign Relations Through 1977, op. cit.* (n. 19 above), p. 496.

[63] A description of the State Department's 'Circular 175' procedure can be found in *International Agreements: An Analysis of Executive Regulations and Practices,* prepared for the use of the CFR, USS by R. Roger Majak of the CRS (Washington: USGPO, 1977). The procedure is the means by which the executive branch determines what form an international agreement takes and what role, if any, the Senate and/or Congress plays.

[64] Consideration of a more active congressional role in the process can be found in *Treaty Powers Resolution,* Hearings before the CFR, USS on S. Res. 486 (Washington: USGPO, 1976). The most recent debate, during which such a role was rejected by the Senate, is printed in the *Congressional Record* of 28 June 1978, pp. S.9994–10013.

[65] Louis Henkin, *Foreign Affairs and the Constitution* (New York: Norton, 1972), p 175.

[66] See works cited in n. 49 above; also see the discussion in Robert G. Bell, *Implications of Extending the SALT I Interim Agreement* (Washington: CRS, 1977).

[67] This stipulation is in Sec. 33 of the Arms Control and Disarmament Act, as amended, and can be found in *Legislation on Foreign Relations Through 1977, op. cit.* (n. 19 above), p. 426. Also see the discussion in Bell, *ibid.,*

36

especially pp. 17–25.

[68] Frye, *op. cit.* (n. 22 above), p. 153.

[69] Holbert N. Carroll, 'The Congress and National Security Policy', in David B. Truman (ed.), *The Congress and America's Future* (Englewood Cliffs, New Jersey: Prentice-Hall, 1965), p. 151.

[70] *Congressional Decision Making for National Security*, A Statement by the Research and Policy Committee of the Committee for Economic Development (New York: Committee for Economic Development, 1974), p. 20.

[71] Huntington, *op. cit.* (n. 16 above), pp. 133–4. Compare Huntington's view with Edward A. Kolodziej, *The Uncommon Defense and Congress, 1945–1963* (Athens, Ohio: Ohio State University Press, 1966).

[72] Aspin, *op. cit.* (n. 30 above), p. 157.

[73] *Ibid.*, p. 160.

[74] See Louis Fisher, *Presidential Spending Power* (Princeton: Princeton University Press, 1975).

[75] See Nancy J. Bearg and Edwin A. Deagle, Jr, 'Congress and the Defense Budget', in John Endicott and Roy W. Stafford, Jr (eds), *American Defense Policy*, 4th ed (Baltimore: Johns Hopkins University Press, 1977); Edward J. Laurance, 'The Changing Role of Congress in Defense Policy-Making', in *Journal of Conflict Resolution*, vol. 20, No. 2, 1976.

[76] *Ibid.*

[77] Richard P. Cronin, *An Analysis of Congressional Reductions in the Defense Budget: Fiscal Years 1971–1976* (Washington: CRS, 1976), p. 19.

[78] Besides the sources listed in notes 75 and 77 above, see Jonathan E. Medalia, 'Congress and the Political Guidance of Weapons Procurement', in *Naval War College Review*, vol. 28, No. 2, Fall 1975; Richard H. Ichord, 'Micromanagement: The Congressional Perspective', in *Armed Forces Journal International*, October 1977; and Thomas A. Dine, 'Military R & D: Congress's Next Area of Military Penetration', in *Bulletin of the Atomic Scientists*, vol. 34, No. 2, 1978.

[79] The text of President Carter's veto message can be found in *Weekly Compilation of Presidential Documents*, vol. 14, No. 33, 1978, pp. 1447–9. More generally, the route of the FY79 legislation can be traced through reading issues of either *Aviation Week and Space Technology* or the *New York Times* for the relevant period. In addition, the two Armed Services committees published a host of hearings and reports, while full floor debates are in the *Congressional Record*.

[80] A summary of existing controls on the provision of military assistance can be found in *United States Arms Transfer and Security Assistance Programs*, prepared for the Subcommittee on Europe and the Middle East of the CIR, USHR, by the CRS (Washington: USGPO, 1978).

[81] See David Weissbrodt, 'Human Rights Legislation and United States Foreign Policy', in *Georgia Journal of International and Comparative Law*, vol. 7, No. 231, 1977. In addition, in accordance with Section 502(B) of the Foreign Assistance Act, as amended, the State Department must prepare reports on human rights conditions in every proposed recipient country. These are normally published by the foreign affairs committees in the early spring.

[82] As note 80 above.

[83] *International Security Assistance Act of 1978*, Conference Report (No. 95-1546, 1978), especially pp. 8–10.

[84] Frye, *op. cit.* (*n. 22 above*), *pp. 212, 223*.

[85] Eugene Rostow in Murphy Commission 5, *op. cit.* (n. 15 above), p. 34.

[86] For background to the war powers debate, see *War Powers Legislation, 1973*, Hearings before the CFR, USS (Washington: USGPO, 1973); *Documents Relating to the War Power of Congress, The President's Authority as Commander-In-Chief and the War in Indochina*, CFR, USS (Washington: USGPO, 1970); and the excellent article by W. Taylor Reveley III, 'The Power to Make War', in Murphy Commission 5, *op. cit.* (n. 15 above), pp. 80–98.

[87] The concurrent resolution is an expression of congressional sentiment requiring a simple majority in both chambers. Unlike the joint resolution, it requires no presidential signature. Until recently, the concurrent resolution was simply used to express opinion, having no legislative or legal impact; increasingly, however, it is being used as a means of preventing or terminating presidential actions in the spheres of war powers, arms transfers and nuclear exports, thereby constituting a controversial and possibly unconstitutional 'legislative veto' against which the executive branch has no recourse. For a full discussion, see John R. Bolton, *The Legislative Veto* (Washington: American Enterprise Institute for Public Policy Research, 1977); Harvey G. Zeidenstein, 'The Reassertion of Congressional Power: New Curbs on the President', in *Political Science Quarterly*, 93 (3), Fall 1978, especially pp. 404–6. President Carter's reservations are printed in *Weekly Compilations of Presidential Documents: Administration of Jimmy Carter* 26 June 1978, pp. 1146–9.

[88] Schlesinger, *op. cit.* (n. 17 above), p. 4.

[89] See the statement by the then Secretary of State, William Rogers, before the Senate CFR on 30 April 1973, reprinted in *Department of State Bulletin*, vol. 68, No. 1769, 1973, pp. 652–5.

[90] See *War Powers Resolution*, Hearings before the CFR, USS (Washington: USGPO, 1977); *War Powers: A Test of Compliance*, Hearings before the Subcommittee on International Security and Scientific Affairs, CIR, USHR (Washington: USGPO, 1975).

[91] See especially the exchange between the GAO and Lawrence Eagleburger, then Deputy Under Secretary of State, in *Seizure of the Mayaguez: Part IV*, Reports of the Comptroller General of the United States submitted to the Subcommittee on International Political and Military Affairs, CIR, USHR (Washington: USGPO, 1976).

[92] Some of the correspondence between the State Department's Legal Advisor and certain Congressmen is published in the *Congressional Record* of 29 June 1978 (pp. S.10253–4) and 10 August 1978 (pp. H.8414–7).

[93] *Weekly Compilation of Presidential Documents*, vol. 9, No. 43, 1973, pp. 1285–7.

[94] Thomas F. Eagleton, *War and Presidential Power* (New York: Liveright, 1974).

[95] Pat M. Holt, *The War Powers Resolution* (Washington: American Enterprise Institute for Public Policy Research, 1978), p. 40.

[96] *War Powers Resolution, op. cit.* (n. 90 above), p. 8.

[97] *Ibid.*, p. 172.

[98] Robert Ellsworth, 'New Imperatives for the Old

Alliance', in *International Security*, vol. 2, No. 4, Spring 1978, p. 137.

⁹⁹ This view is argued somewhat too forcefully by Paul R. Schratz, 'National Decision Making and Military Intervention', in Ellen P. Stern (ed.), *The Limits of Military Intervention* (London: Sage Publications, 1977), p. 360.

¹⁰⁰ The initial phases of congressional involvement in nonproliferation policy are summarized by Warren H. Donnelly, 'Congress and Nonproliferation, 1945–1977', in Alan Platt and Lawrence D. Weiler (eds), *Congress and Arms Control* (Boulder, Colorado: Westview Press, 1978), pp. 135–55.

¹⁰¹ Texts are available in *Legislation on Foreign Relations Through 1977, op cit.* (n. 17 above). For a discussion of these measures by an advocate in the Congress, see Clarence D. Long, 'Nuclear Proliferation: Can Congress Act in Time?' in *International Security*, Spring 1977.

¹⁰² Reprinted in *Department of State Bulletin*, vol. 75, No. 1952, 1976, pp. 629–39.

¹⁰³ *Presidential Documents – Jimmy Carter, 1977*, vol. 13, No. 18, 1977, pp. 611–13.

¹⁰⁴ Long, *op. cit.* (*n. 101 above*).

¹⁰⁵ See, for example, *Nonproliferation Issues*, Hearings before the Subcommittee on Arms Control ... of the CFR, USS (Washington: USGPO, 1977); *Nuclear Nonproliferation and Export Controls*, Hearings before the Subcommittee on Arms Control ... of the CFR, USS (Washington: USGPO, 1977); and *The Nuclear Antiproliferation Act of 1977*, Hearings and Markup before the CIR, USHR (Washington: USGPO, 1977).

¹⁰⁶ Useful descriptions of the main provisions of the Act (PL 95–242 of 10 March 1978) can be found in Frederick Williams, 'The United States Congress and Nonproliferation', in *International Security*, vol. 3, No. 2, Fall 1978, Pat Towell, 'Legislation to Reduce Risk of Nuclear Proliferation Signed by President', in *Congressional Quarterly*, vol. 36, No. 10, 1978.

¹⁰⁷ See Thomas O'Toole and Jim Hoagland, 'U.S. Rushed Approval of Uranium Exports', *Washington Post*, 16 April 1978; two articles by Enrico Jacchia, 'U.S.-European Rift on A-Policy' and 'Bridging the Nuclear Rift', in the *International Herald Tribune* of 25 April 1978 and 15–16 July 1978 respectively.

¹⁰⁸ Quoted in *India News*, 25 April 1978 (London: High Commission of India); see also the article entitled 'U.S. Decision–A Breach of Agreement', the *Statesman Weekly*, 29 April 1978, p. 9.

¹⁰⁹ Executive Order of 27 April 1978 (text released by United States Embassy, London).

¹¹⁰ Letter from John Sparkman, Chairman of the Senate CFR to President Carter, 21 June 1978. A full account of the debate over this export can be found in *Nuclear Fuel Export to India*, Hearing before the Subcommittee on Arms Control . . . , CFR, USS (Washington: USGPO, 1978).

¹¹¹ Gunter Hildenbrand, 'A German Reaction to U.S. Nonproliferation Policy', 'in *International Security*, vol. 3, No. 2, Fall 1978, p. 54.

¹¹² For background, see Philip J. Farley, 'The Control of United States Arms Sales', in Alan Platt and Lawrence D. Weiler (eds), *Congress and Arms Control* (Boulder, Colorado: Westview Press, 1978).

¹¹³ See, for example, *U.S. Arms Sales Policy*, Hearings before the CFR, USS (Washington: USGPO, 1977); *U.S. Military Sales to Iran*, A Staff Report to the Subcommittee on Foreign Assistance of the CFR, USS (Washington: USGPO, 1976); *United States Arms Sales to the Persian Gulf*, Report of a Study Mission ... to the CIR, USHR (Washington: USGPO, 1976).

¹¹⁴ The best summary of the legislation and associated controls is in *United States Arms Transfer and Security Assistance Programs, op. cit.* (n. 80 above).

¹¹⁵ See, for example, *Proposed Sales to Jordan of the Hawk and Vulcan Air Defense Systems*, Hearings before the Subcommittee on International Political and Military Affairs of the CIR, USHR (Washington: USGPO, 1975); *Proposed Sale to Kuwait of Air-to-Air Missiles*, Hearing before the Subcommittee on International Political and Military Affairs of the CIR, USHR (Washington: USGPO, 1976); *Sale of AWACS to Iran*, Hearings before the Subcommittee on Foreign Assistance and the CFR, USS (Washington: USGPO, 1977); Richard Burt, 'Battle Lines Forming on Carter's Plan to Sell Jets to Arabs', *New York Times*, 31 March 1978, p. A2.

¹¹⁶ Dick Clark, 'The Foreign Relations Committee and the Future of Arms Control', in Platt and Weiler, *op. cit.* (n. 112 above), p. 105.

¹¹⁷ See *International Security Assistance Act of 1978*, Conference Report (No. 95–1546, 1978), especially pp. 37–8.

¹¹⁸ See, for example, *Foreign and Military Intelligence*, Final Report of the Select Committee to Study Governmental Operations with respect to Intellegence Activities, USS (Report No. 94–755) (Washington: USGPO, 1976).

¹¹⁹ The full text of the amendment, which forms Section 662 of the Foreign Assistance Act of 1961, as amended, is in *Legislation on Foreign Relations Through 1977*, vol. 1, *op. cit.* (*n. 19 above*), *pp. 162–3*.

¹²⁰ The Angolan restriction forms Section 404 of the International Security Assistance and Arms Control Export Act of 1976 (PL 94–329), the text of which is in *ibid.*, pp. 308–9

¹²¹ See S. Res. 400 (1976) and H. Res. 658 (1977).

¹²² 'United States Foreign Intelligence Activities' (Statement on Executive Order 12036 and Executive Order 12036) in *Weekly Compilation of Presidential Documents: Administration of Jimmy Carter, 1978* 24 January 1978, pp. 194–216.

¹²³ See *Rules of Procedure for the Select Committee on Intelligence USS* (Washington: USGPO, 1977), p. 5.

¹²⁴ See *Annual Report to the Senate of the Select Committee on Intelligence USS* (Report No. 95–217) (Washington: USGPO, 1977). For a different perspective (that is, one that argues that the committees have not done enough to constrain the executive), see Seymour M. Hersh, 'Congress is Accused of Laxity on C.I.A.'s Covert Activity', in *New York Times*, 1 June 1978, p. A2.

¹²⁵ Presidential News Conference of 25 May 1978 (full text in *New York Times*, 26 May 1978, p. A10).

¹²⁶ President Ford's Farewell State of the Union message (full text in *International Herald Tribune*, 17 January 1977).

¹²⁷ Proposals along this line can be found in Allison and Szanton, *op. cit.* (n. 1 above), p. 110; and in *Congress and Foreign Policy*, Hearings before the Special Subcommittee on Investigations of the CIR, USHR (Washington: USGPO, 1976), especially pp. 182–3.

38

[128] See n. 42 above.

[129] Robert S. Ingersoll, 'The Executive and the Congress in Foreign Policy: Conflict or Co-operation?', in *Department of State Bulletin*, vol. 74, No. 1911, 1976, p. 148.

[130] James Chace, 'Is a Foreign Policy Consensus Possible?', in *Foreign Affairs*, vol. 57, No. 1, Fall 1978, pp. 15–16.

[131] *Congress and Foreign Policy, op. cit.* (n. 29 above), pp. 1–2.

[132] Douglas A. Bennet, Jr, 'Congress in Foreign Policy: Who Needs it?', in *Foreign Affairs*, vol. 57, No. 1, Fall 1978, p. 45; see also the article by Lee H. Hamilton and Michael H. Van Dusen, 'Making the Separation of Powers Work', in the same issue.

[133] *Murphy Commission 5, op cit.* (n. 15 above), p. 34.

[134] See, for example, n. 127 and 131.

[135] Henry A. Kissinger, 'America's Destiny: The Global Context' (speech delivered at the University of Wyoming on 4 February 1976). Similar conceptions of the role of Congress have been expressed by one of Kissinger's predecessors, Dean Rusk (quoted in Richard F. Fenno, Jr, *Congressmen in Committees* (Boston: Little, Brown, & Co., 1973), p. 29. and by George F. Kennan, *The Cloud of Danger: Current Realities of American Foreign Policy* (Boston: Little, Brown, 1977), especially pp. 3–9.

[136] Burton M. Sapin, *The Making of United States Foreign Policy* (Washington: The Brookings Institution, 1966), p. 54.

[137] *Congressional Government, op. cit.* (n. 7 above), p. 195. See as well J. William Fulbright, 'The Legislator as Educator', in *Foreign Affairs*, vol. 57, No. 4, Spring 1979.

[138] Henkin, *op. cit.* (n. 65 above), p. 123.

[139] J. William Fulbright, *Old Myths and New Realities* (New York: Random House, 1964), p. vii.

[140] Lehman, *op. cit.* (n. 20 above), p. 214.

[141] Ingersoll, *op. cit.* (n. 129 above), p. 150.

[142] Robert McCloskey in *Congress and Foreign Policy, Hearings, op. cit.* (n. 127 above), p. 70.

ADELPHI PAPERS

NUMBER ONE HUNDRED AND EIGHTY-TWO

IISS Annual Conference Papers

Defence and Consensus: The Domestic Aspects of Western Security

Part I

THE INTERNATIONAL INSTITUTE FOR STRATEGIC STUDIES
23 TAVISTOCK STREET LONDON WC2E 7NQ

ADELPHI PAPER No. 182

The Papers presented here and in *Adelphi Papers* No. 183
and 184 were given at the Twenty-fourth Annual Conference of the IISS at Scheveningen, The Hague, The
Netherlands in September 1982.

First published Summer 1983

ISBN 0 86079 069 X
ISSN 0567-932X

© The International Institute for Strategic Studies 1983

All rights reserved. No part of this publication may be
reproduced, stored in a retrieval system, or transmitted
in any form or by any means, electronic, mechanical,
photo-copying, recording or otherwise, without the prior
permission of the International Institute for Strategic
Studies.

*The International Institute for Strategic studies was founded in 1958 as a centre for the
provision of information on and research into the problems of international security,
defence and arms control in the nuclear age. It is international in its Council and staff,
and its membership is drawn from over fifty countries. It is independent of governments
and is not the advocate of any particular interest.*

*The Institute is concerned with strategic questions – not just with the military aspects
of security but with the social and economic sources and political moral implications
of the use and existence of armed force: in other words with the basic problems of peace.*

*The Institute's publications are intended for a much wider audience than its own
membership and are available to the general public on subscription or singly.*

Printed in Great Britain by Spottiswoode Ballantyne Ltd., Colchester

CONTENTS

Introduction

CHRISTOPH BERTRAM

The Papers presented in these volumes were presented at the 24th Annual Conference of the International Institute of Strategic Studies in September 1982. It was a conference devoted to one of the most ambiguous, imprecise and elusive aspects of security: that of the domestic political factors influencing defence policies, doctrines and burdens. This is one reason why the subject has generally been unexplored in traditional strategic studies. The other is that, as long as domestic consensus on these matters existed, there was no real pressure to address them; that idyllic state of affairs no longer exists.

An important part of the public in our societies is no longer willing to trust governments or experts or even the media on matters of defence policy.

The Decline of Consensus

Many reasons can be advanced for the decline of political consensus. On a general level, our societies have become more sceptical, more half-informed, and hence more prone to doubt and question than to accept and agree. The *élites* have, as Rudolf Wildenmann and David Calleo point out, been in the forefront of this process, not mass public opinion. Moreover in all our countries, domestic priorities have acquired greater weight precisely at a time when the financial means of the state to provide a horizon of expectation have become tight, with the result that national consensus has been undermined, political forces have become fragmented, and frictions have been brought forth which in more affluent times could be lubricated away. For Kurt Biedenkopf, consensus on matters of defence and security can no longer be expected simply to derive from trust in political and military institutions. Indeed, the placing of trust in governments – with the notable exception of Japan – seems to have suffered a major setback.

But this has been a gradual, not an abrupt, evolution and cannot therefore alone explain why the decline of consensus has been a feature particularly of the past few years, or indeed why that decline has been partial, directed primarily against the nuclear dimension of Western defence. No such questioning and doubt has as yet affected conventional military efforts, although there are signs that this, too, might be drawn into the fray of controversy before too long.

There can be no doubt that nuclear issues have become more controversial, that there is now a widespread, if unjustified, fear of nuclear war, and that the beginning of the expression of this fear can be dated with some precision: to the 1979 NATO decision on introducing new medium-range missiles in Europe if negotiations for mutual limitations should fail, and the advent of the Reagan Administration in the United States. Lawrence Kaagan's Paper underlines that this is not merely a European phenomenon but an American one as well, although in the US this seems to lie more with President Reagan's bellicose rhetoric than with specific weapons decisions which have triggered public awareness and concern. There can be little doubt on this point: if nuclear deterrence is unaccompanied by a serious search for arms control, and presented in terms that suggest that governments are willing to engage in fighting rather than deterring nuclear conflict, while at the same time there is a marked deterioration in Soviet-American relations, this cannot but provoke public anxiety and fear. It may well be true that part of this anxiety follows from the decline in American power, as Samuel Huntington suggests. But even here, developments have been gradual, not abrupt: nuclear parity has been a fact of life for over a decade, and it has generally been viewed with greater calm in Europe than in the United States. In democratic societies, the way that govern-

1

ments and experts talk about nuclear weapons determines public acceptability; recent talk about nuclear weapons, starting – as Harold Brown admitted – before the Reagan Administration with the presentation of PD 59 in 1980, could not but erode that acceptability. This came at a time when public sensibilities had already been strained by the 'neutron bomb' affair two years earlier, by the NATO decision in 1979 and by the seemingly esoteric discussion over the MX missile and its elusive basing concept. Perhaps the true explanation for the outburst of concern lies here: the system was overloaded, and sensitive management of the issues involved was woefully absent.

Presentation or Substance?

It is probably no longer enough just to rely on better presentation: the substance of nuclear deterrence itself will have to be re-examined and adjusted to be acceptable for the public opinion of the 1980s. The problem will not go away. The peace and freeze movements will not disappear.

How to make nuclear deterrence more rational, more dependable and – so the assumption runs – more acceptable? There can be no real doubt that nuclear deterrence will remain essential to Western security. Nuclear weapons, just like the concerns they raise, are here to stay.

The remedies proposed remain, instead, within the system of deterrence; they involve adjustment and not radical departures. There can be no return to the sole reliance on a doctrine of mutual assured destruction, however tempting this might at times seem to America's allies. This is because it is precisely their need for protection under the American nuclear umbrella that requires the creation of options involving less than all-out nuclear strikes. Yet it is the practical translation of extended deterrence into strategic planning that has raised the concern on both sides of the Atlantic: in Europe of a limitation of conflict to the European territory; in the US of staking one's survival on a less than essential threat. Proposals for a more rational posture and doctrine must thus address these issues.

Michael Howard's call for reassurance through greater reliance on European conventional military efforts provides a coherent rationale for an Alliance less dependent on the threat of the use of nuclear weapons. Johan Holst's proposal of a posture of 'assured reflection', which emphasizes the survivability of command and control and of delivery systems rather than counter-force capability, has not only the merit of a more benign designation than that customary in strategic language, but also that of directing strategic thinking away from a fascination with the multitude of conceivable scenarios to the central task of imposing a barrier between the outbreak of war and the use of nuclear weapons. The apparent consensus that battlefield nuclear weapons could and should be scaled down is both politically attractive and in the interest of increasing control and delaying the nuclear decision in a crisis. Whether or not there should be a formal NATO declaration not to use nuclear weapons first remains an issue to be debated. But on balance the argument that there is little to gain in terms of political support, and something useful to lose in terms of the deterrence value of ambiguity and uncertainty seems to be difficult to dispute. After all, NATO finds itself today in a *de facto* 'no-first-use' situation given the potential consequences likely to follow from *any* firing of a nuclear weapon. Moreover, Soviet military planners cannot count on no first nuclear use by the West in times of war, however emphatically it is declared beforehand, while Soviet diplomacy could use such a declaration to interfere with Western nuclear decisions in peacetime.

A more rational nuclear posture is not necessarily identical with a more acceptable one. Even if the West were to decide tomorrow to adopt the Howard model, or a doctrine of 'assured reflection', if it were to do away with short-range battlefield nuclear forces, or if it renounced the first use of nuclear weapons, the basic uneasiness would remain: deterrence cannot be discussed as if it were disembodied from war and fighting, and the question what happens if deterrence should fail is not answered in these proposals.

The basic dilemma remains: deterrence has to be credible in order to deter, and that requires thinking and planning beyond the point where deterrence might fail. The pre-

2

sent school of strategic thought which emphasizes the need for discreet countervailing deterrence at every level would seem to be misguided since it is essentially open-ended and seeks to refine what is basically non-refinable, namely the crude and primitive threat of using nuclear weapons once vital interests are threatened by an aggressor. But these are, in the final analysis, differences of degree, not fundamental alternatives of how to assure deterrence through nuclear weapons. Even Michael Howard's concept of deterrence depends on 'the distinct possibility that the conflict might escalate to nuclear war'. If public opinion is worried about the possible use of nuclear weapons, no policy based on threatening their use, even *in extremis*, can reassure them. Nuclear forces, in Dominique Moïsi's phrase, tend to atomize the spirit of defence. Correcting some of the excesses of present nuclear doctrines in isolation will not, by itself, re-establish the lost consensus.

The other challenge to domestic consensus lies in the economic costs of defence. The continued willingness of all European NATO members – and, Lawrence Kaagan's poll results suggest, not only theirs – to find the money to sustain the apparatus for deterrence and defence as at present conceived and organized must be very much in doubt. This is essentially for two reasons. First, the cost pressures within the defence sector push against the ceiling of realistically obtained increases in funding. Second, governments in the West are no longer willing to incur the large deficits in public expenditure which they accepted in the past and through which they were able to avoid the tough choice between allocating resources for internal welfare and external protection.

The political consequences of these two factors are gradually emerging. In the United States, as David Calleo points out, a budgetary freeze risks a backlash not only against the expanded military budget but against the NATO commitment itself. While the Mansfield Resolutions in the 1970s for bringing American forces home were motivated by concern over America's over-extension, similar requests may soon be pushed by the concern over the overall budget deficit and the sacrifices in welfare spending that ambitious defence pro-

grammes suggest. If public opinion in practically all Western countries is today supporting present defence expenditure in the non-nuclear field, this cannot, therefore, be taken for granted in the near future. The pressures are clearly mounting. Today, the issue of nuclear weapons is in the forefront of the public doubts over the wisdom of established security policies; tomorrow it may well be the issue of defence spending as such.

This gives particular importance both to the utmost rationalization in the defence sector, and to efforts to cut costs. Sir Frank Cooper addresses these possibilities in his Paper but he does not hide the limitations. There is a need for more effective long-range planning, since rational spending becomes easier if you know how much you have to spend. Perhaps there might be ways if not to standardize equipment at least to standardize specialized military education. Much promise was seen in the concept of multi-purpose platforms, implying a basic vehicle, aircraft or ship to which specialized missions could then be attached. The lessons of the Falklands War point to the option of making much greater use of the non-military, commercial capabilities that are available in the total arsenal of the Western countries, but no major breakthrough is apparent that would reduce the costs of sustaining the apparatus of defence *as at present conceived and organized.*

It may be necessary, therefore, to go beyond defence as presently conceived and organized. This may mean, as Sir Frank Cooper emphasizes, looking at output of military effectiveness rather than input of money; examining and reorganizing existing military structures and organizations; and making a stronger assault on the 'defence culture', which at present tends to reproduce its judgments and fossilize its positions and thus to control choice by inertia. But this is a task made even more difficult by the economic recession, when the vested interests in the armed forces and the defence bureaucracies tend to dig in, preferring to consolidate rather than to risk being cut down by politicians under pressure.

Re-establishing the Context
But can greater rationality in the economic, as in the nuclear sector, do more than satisfy the

expert? Can it convince a sceptical, and perhaps increasingly sceptical, public? Can the remedies be applied, the arguments won, in isolation?

One central aspect of this question is how public arguments are shaped. This is examined in three Papers dealing with the media, their influence on defence policy, and their influence on the image of policy in the United States, in Japan, and in Western Europe. All of them, particularly those written by professional journalists, conclude that the impact of the press is fairly marginal: in the United States the press is the conveyor belt for government; in Europe and Japan it follows the fashions.

With the possible exception of the 'neutron bomb' affair of a few years ago, when one particular press story defined the public debate, no single decision on defence policy seems to have been taken or not taken because of press reporting. Yet the former journalist Lothar Ruehl, who has assumed high office in Government, was very much concerned about the quality of the press and the impact it has had on policy, not in deciding specific issues, but in narrowing options and giving respectability to opposition arguments.

There was general agreement on the limitations of the press. There is in the US an editorial system which discourages specialization and focuses instead on news stories, with editors not sufficiently concerned and informed about the issues of defence and security, and reporters keen to provide scoops rather than insights. European newsmen fared somewhat better in this *critique* than their American counterparts, for reasons that Joseph Fromm so vividly describes in his Paper.

There has been repeated concern over the impact of television. As Joseph Fromm quotes a prominent TV commentator: 'Will democracy which has uncensored TV in every home ever be able to fight a war, however just?' The electronic medium is probably unhelpful in informing the public, and this has raised questions whether some kind of censorship should not be applied to the visible media in war, as was the case in the Falklands conflict.

There is no question that an informed medium is better than the uninformed one, but consensus is unlikely to be built on co-ordination in the media. Rather, its role should remain that of raising issues for the debate, to articulate moods. In a crisis, special consideration will have to apply, but whether the handling of the press over the Falkland crisis can serve as a model must remain in doubt. It worked because the British action was crowned by success, but what if it had fallen short of that, requiring public knowledge to sustain, in adversity, public support in Britain?

Even with a more informed, expert or responsible press the problem of regenerating consensus will not be solved. The media reflects; it rarely creates events and policies. To encourage consensus, therefore, the policies must be right, and they must be convincingly defended.

A Context for Expectations

The central question, therefore, is how to achieve this. To tailor policies to what is acceptable to, or – in Michael Howard's useful term – what reassures, public opinion is as tempting as it is inadequate, for the simple reason that acceptability and reassurance, if tied to specific military programmes, are not an enduring yardstick. It is, after all, only a few years ago, as Harold Brown reminds those who have forgotten, that European governments insisted that *greater* nuclear involvement by the United States was needed to reassure them, and indeed reassurance of sceptical allies was precisely one major reason for the US to embark on the now so controversial NATO programme of nuclear modernization.

This suggests that merely to adjust specific military efforts and doctrines to become more acceptable to public opinion will not be successful. Indeed any answer given in isolation is likely to be inadequate. Rudolf Wildenmann points in his Paper to the way in which the dissent over defence and nuclear matters that arose in the 1950s was overcome and a new consensus created not by arguing in isolation the merits of weapons and missiles, but by putting the problem *in the context of European unification*. The post-war generation of the 1950s 'swallowed the frog' of German rearmament because 'it was linked to a concept of politics which put an end to wars in

Western Europe, by creating new European perspectives'.

This same theme is implicit in most of the Papers in this volume. To rebuild the consensus, so Harold Brown tells us, we need a clearer picture of what Western policy *should* be toward the Soviet Union – in military, economic and political terms. We are in a substantive crisis in the Alliance because of unsolved substantive problems rather than because of sociological phenomena, writes David Calleo. We must not see defence in isolation, writes Sir Frank Cooper. The lack of a persuasive vision of a better future for international relations is as disturbing as it is striking, according to Adam Roberts.

Indeed, the Alliance seemed in better shape, and defence expenditures and even nuclear weapons were less controversial at the time of East–West detente than they are today; it is the breakdown of that contextual framework which has brought forth the new concerns. Nuclear weapons and even defence spending for non-nuclear weapons are not in themselves sustainable by public opinion; they need to be put into a context of expectations. Only a consensus on that context will make the specific military efforts acceptable and reassuring.

If this is true, then the fight for the consensus has been badly conducted. It has only, at best, concentrated on specific issues – the number of Soviet missiles and the technical characteristics of Western missiles. It has not addressed the context for which deterrence and defence are worth having.

This inability, as Rudolf Wildenmann and David Calleo point out, is attributable to a failure of the Western elites, the results of their doubts and fashions, rather than that of public opinion at large. The public continues to believe in the Western Alliance. It is impressive – and surprising – to note the massive US support for the continuation of the European security link in Mr Kaagan's data, despite the frictions between the Allies. But, because the elites lack the confidence of a framework, they tend to narrow the debate to specific aspects which cannot alone justify the effort they demand. In isolation, consensus cannot be built on nuclear weapons, defence, the Alliance or much else.

To regenerate the consensus in the Alliance, more is needed than rational nuclear doctrines or transparent defence decisions. That is helpful, but not enough – particularly once the genie of popular doubt and anxiety has left the bottle. It also needs more than merely indulgence in the futile attempt to define defence policy by what is acceptable alone. Governments, as Johan Holst rightly reminds us, have to persuade and to listen. They are paid to lead, not to follow. They have failed in both in recent years. Leadership means the setting of the framework, of the context of security, in which destructive weapons can make sense. They will not make sense by themselves.

5

Domestic Consensus,
Security and the Western Alliance

KURT BIEDENKOPF

In an article entitled 'NATO Myths' (*Foreign Policy*, Winter 1981/82) Lawrence Freedman observes: 'Whether a strategic doctrine is acceptable to the people for whom it has been developed is as important in an alliance of democratic societies as the doctrine's ability to impress the enemy'. Democracy, in Freedman's view, is crucial to defence 'because in a real crisis public pressure will affect the implementation and success of any doctrine'.

Democratic governments, whose mandates for foreign and defence policy are derived, as those for any other area of policy, from majorities determined by general elections, have always had to give heed to domestic consensus as providing the political basis for governmental actions in the security field. Recent history is crowded with examples of the efforts that may be required to produce such a consensus or what the lack of it can do to the execution of strategies and the pursuit of political objectives which those holding public office may have considered to be important or which seem to be demanded by the national interest or to be indispensable to repel imminent dangers to one's country.

Even though the subject is thus familiar to democracies, it has recently acquired new urgency. Two factors have contributed to this change: first the absence of economic growth from which additional defence needs could be satisfied without impediment to other important political objectives; and second the special aspects of nuclear strategy. Both factors, although not necessarily related, have appeared at about the same time, and have added new dimensions to the more familiar aspects of domestic consensus in defence policy.

Economics and Defence Consensus

With the lack of economic growth, it has become necessary for governments and legislators to make choices between defence appropriations and the earmarking of public funds for other, primarily domestic, economic and social programmes. Those who are asked to approve defence spending in elections today are asked to do so at the expense of social benefits or other transferral payments which they might otherwise have received. Thus defence outlays must be justified in ways that were not previously necessary to an increasingly well-informed general public.

In an alliance such as NATO the matter is further complicated by comparisons of the relative burdens placed upon the populations of member countries. If he is asked to explain the need for certain defence expenditures to his constituency, Senator Roth observed recently, the task will become next to impossible to achieve if the relative burdens placed on his voters and on the voters of his German counterpart do not approximate to their relative income or buying power. Or, to put it differently, if the Ford worker in Detroit is asked to approve of a defence burden of 6% of GNP, his willingness to do so will drastically decline if he learns that his counterpart at Ford Cologne can get away with approving only 3% of GNP for defence although his family income may enable him to travel extensively and his country's legislation gives him protection against social and personal risks which his American fellow-worker is asked to bear personally.

Consensus and the Nuclear Question

Apart from economic considerations and a new look at long-established priorities, the growing awareness of the special dangers and risks of nuclear strategy have clouded domestic consensus with respect to defence and security matters. Before he died, President Eisenhower is said to have predicted that, in view of the menace of nuclear war, people would one day rise up and demand an end to this madness. Recently indications that this might indeed happen have appeared both in Europe and in the United States. Although differing in motives and objectives as well as organization, the so-called Peace Movements have succeeded in drawing general attention to the paradox of the policy of nuclear deterrence. The double-track decision of NATO, passed in the Autumn of 1979 and calling for the deployment of *Pershing* II and cruise missiles in 1983, if negotiations between the US and the Soviet Union in Geneva are not successful, has become a sort of catalyst for the movement in Germany and also in other European countries. In the US it has focused on demands to freeze nuclear armament in both the West and the East.

It goes without saying that such developments must affect the Alliance. As an organization for mutual defence, it is not based on an international treaty alone, which, once ratified by parliaments, is then executed by governments without further public control. The Alliance's real foundation is the support given to its objectives and strategies by the majorities of the peoples making up the Alliance.

The Nature of Consensus
As a consequence the Alliance has always been looked upon as a community of nations sharing common values and basic political objectives, united in the love for freedom and the determination to protect it. They are NATO's real charter. They have lent the Alliance its special character and cohesion. Overriding all national differences within the Atlantic Community, they have in the past successfully served as pillars on which the basic common interests rest. Most important of all they are the foundation for domestic consensus within the member countries. Freedom, democracy and human rights as common heritage and political beliefs were able to unite nations in common action that had been allies or enemies during the long course of European history.

More recently, however, this community of values and objectives seems to have weakened. Behind the political rhetoric, articulated as recently as on President Reagan's visit to Europe, more basic differences within the Alliance appear. They seem to change the nature and importance of the consensus still required in the light of the Alliance's overriding commitment to peace and the defence of freedom in Europe. Younger generations, unaware of NATO's charter experience and the continuing threats of totalitarian systems to human rights and freedom, are demanding new policies and are willing to apply new and as yet untested methods to secure peace. National interests are being restated and security priorities are being pitted against the community's interests. Apprehension is growing that the fabric of common objectives might grow weaker and no longer prove strong enough to absorb the shocks and pressures of the special interests pursued by member nations. Differences between the US and their European Allies on the strategic merits of trade sanctions imposed on the Soviet Union and the acceptability of extraterritorial effects of US administrative actions are seen by many as a rather fundamental conflict which might, if permitted to continue, threaten the very basis of the defence alliance.

NATO has certainly undergone times of crisis before. It has come through each one without permanent damage. It has adjusted to change and has proved more flexible than could ordinarily have been expected, given the rigidity of international organizations. The present developments might therefore not give cause for undue concern.

Yet a thorough re-examination of the conditions for consensus within the Alliance seems necessary. The passage of time and the arrival of new generations to shape public opinion and policy together with the sheer success of NATO in securing peace in Europe for more than three decades has not left the old consensus unaffected. What everybody has become accustomed to and learned to accept will increasingly be taken for granted. Confronted with the burden of new conflict the consensus might prove to be less stable and reliable than generally expected. A revitalization of the old consensus is therefore important but that is not enough. In addition the character and conditions of a new consensus must be developed.

If we want to reaffirm the democratic consensus as to our defence policies or to establish a new one, it is helpful to enquire how this consensus is made up and how it is brought into being. A consensus on any question of political relevance to society can be based on agreement on a policy or on support for a policy. If based on agreement, those forming the consensus agree on the substance of the policy in question. They will have studied the matter and have convinced themselves both that the recommended objectives and that the methods of accomplishing these objectives are sensible and that they can agree to them. Or they may firmly believe in the political objectives in question and therefore agree to carry them out. In either case the consensus is based on direct access to the substance of the political matter in question. People, as the saying goes, know what they are talking about. The consensus can be based either on knowledge or on basic beliefs or on common sense.

Obviously today's questions of defence strategies are not of a kind readily accessible even to the educated mind. They are the preserve of highly-trained specialists who have developed a language of their own. The rationale of their thinking and arguments is not easily understood. Indeed it is increasingly removed from those matters of political life which can be verified by personal experience.

Democratic consensus by agreement over substance is therefore rather unlikely to occur in defence matters. It can, however, still be based on public support for those who formulate defence policy, who define its objectives and requirements and who execute it. This kind of consensus is easier to establish. It does not require full knowledge and comprehension of all the intricacies of defence strategy by those who are asked to supply the political mandate for the policy. Rather consensus can be established and maintained if those voting *trust* those formulating policy to do the right things or if the majority considers the policy *plausible* in rather general terms or both. These might be described as *consensus based on trust* and *consensus based on plausibility*.

Trust

For most of the life of NATO, the defence consensus both in Europe and in the United States has been based on trust. The objectives of our common defence efforts were obvious as were the dimensions of the threat. Progress has been the password and the specialists and experts were seen as the guardians of progress. Governments were expected to assemble the best experts in the fields to master the task of formulating defence policy and were trusted to be able to do so. Matters of cost and quantity seemed relatively easy to comprehend. Basically it was enough simply to point to the dangers posed by the Soviet Union and the Communist Bloc and their holdings of men and arms in order to ensure public support for an expansion of defence outlays or such other actions as were recommended by those in authority. This willingness to trust those in authority, both politically and militarily, has however diminished. To-day it is reasonable to say that defence policies can no longer rely for their political support on consensus based on trust. This is by no means exclusively or even primarily the result of misuse of the trust previously granted. The change that we can observe has been brought about by different developments. Disappointment with the specialization is one of them but it is not the only reason why the willingness to accept formal authority as a substitute for substantial explanation has all but disappeared in most of our Western democracies.

What has basically changed since NATO was founded in 1948 are the educational standards of the population, its level of and access to information and its vastly increased sophistication in all matters of politics. What has often been described as a revolutionary change of public information through the electronic media must obviously have consequences for the establishment and maintenance of public consensus in all public matters, let alone in matters of defence. The influence of an informed public on defence and security policies during the Vietnam War revealed the extent of the change.

As a consequence, consensus on matters of defence and security can no longer be expected to arise simply from trust in political and military institutions. The policies for which consensus is asked must be *plausible*. It must make sense to a well-educated public which time and again has had occasion to doubt the

8   170

wisdom of specialists and which is supported in its quest for plausibility by the academic community and the media.

Plausibility

If plausibility of defence policy is required to bring about and maintain public consensus, then that policy must be explained. It is this need for explanation and what explanation requires that must be addressed next.

Obviously *any* defence policy only makes sense if there is a perceived need for defence. To the majority of our populations, both in Europe and in the United States, this need seems rather obvious. Even though the plausibility of the threat posed by the Soviet Union and her satellite countries may not be as strong today as it once was and may even have been reduced further during the 1970s by detente, it still prevails. In addition Soviet aggression in Afghanistan and Soviet support for martial law in Poland have helped to remove whatever doubts there may have been about the threat. But establishing a consensus on the basis of the need for defence is not enough. What is also required is public support for whatever answer to this threat is proposed. Defence policy *as such* must be plausible. It must therefore be explained also to those who share the view that it is necessary to be prepared to defend one's freedom and one's way of life.

This in turn means that some basic questions must be answered. One of them relates to the cost of defence. The cost argument has always been important. As long as there was substantial growth in the economy on which to draw, the conflicting demands on public budgets were not as incompatible as they seem today. It was possible then to satisfy both sets of demands and still avoid mounting public debts. We all know that these happy times of easy access to additional defence appropriations have passed. Today if we are to establish a consensus with respect to defence we must explain why certain additional outlays for military purposes are so important that other expectations or political objectives must give way to them.

I do not consider the competition for public funds, resulting from this development to be basically detrimental for the consensus on defence policy but it will demand more explanation and substantial rethinking within the military and the political institutions that have to make decisions. For some time many of us have wondered whether ever more sophisticated weapons systems and technologies, integrating an ever increasing variety of functions and capabilities, are really necessary to do the job that we expect the defence system to accomplish. Large organizations that are permitted to grow rapidly without meeting competitive or other resistance tend to develop waste and their cost-effectiveness declines. This is true for monopoly enterprises. It is basically true also for defence enterprises.

Even though cost-effectiveness might be more difficult to determine in the case of defence, this does not mean that it can be ignored. By being forced to compete for funds, Defence Ministries will come under increasing scrutiny both in their operation and in their bidding for funds. It follows that, although the public may be in no position to judge the merits of particular choices, they are at least assured that political control of defence expenditure is being exercised. This may in the end lead to an increase in plausibility of defence spending and thus strengthen the consensus rather than weaken it.

However this will only be true if two requirements are met: first that the military and defence establishments really accept the competitive process as an expression of political control over the military; and, second, if genuine co-operation develops between defence and those segments of the body politic that are concerned with economic and social matters.

What many see as a coming danger for both social peace and the defence consensus is the conflict between social justice and military security, developing as a result of limited resources. This can be avoided provided that both are recognized as indispensable to the existence and viability of a free society. If this is the case, no basic objection can or should be made to a competition in which defence must argue its case for modern weapon systems or more men and against the need for additional transfer payments in the social area, while those representing the social interest must

9

state their case for additional governmental action and question the wisdom of new defence outlays. Carried on in a constructive manner, this competition may both benefit and educate the general public for it is the general public which must ultimately approve.

Although an indispensable prerequisite, the establishment of the need for adequate defence expenditure is obviously not enough by itself to establish consensus. Apart from the cost, what is bought must be acceptable to the majority. In this context two questions arise which are relevant to the issue of consensus: are the means of our defence adequate to the purpose? are they acceptable as a matter of principal, that is on ethical or moral grounds? The first question is simply a statement of the old question 'How much is enough?' and thus leads to the ever present argument that we must do more because the other side does more. With few interruptions the history of NATO has been a history of the arms competition with the East for the purpose of establishing or maintaining equilibrium. The longer this process continues, the more problematic it will become in terms of establishing consensus. It is one thing to support defence spending and a defence strategy in order to maintain security. It is another to find oneself continuously frustrated by the argument that more is necessary if we are not to fall behind.

This is not only a problem of the nuclear arms competition although the issue is raised primarily in that context. It can also develop into a more general problem of acceptance, especially if we are setting out to strengthen our conventional defences in order to reduce the risk of nuclear war by raising the nuclear threshold.

In any case the plausibility of our defence strategy will be determined by the way we define equilibrium (or balance of potential) in this connection. If I read public debate and argument in my country (West Germany) correctly, we will find it increasingly difficult to maintain our defence consensus if we continue to match arms increases against arms increases and fail to find more independent standards by which to judge what is fundamental to adequate defence and what may be desirable as a marginal addition to safety.

Furthermore equilibrium (or balance) will be seen increasingly as including other factors besides the purely military. One such factor will be the *will* to defend freedom. Even the most sophisticated weapons system cannot substitute for popular will. Without it, a durable consensus on defence is impossible. If the will exists, however, and can be forcefully demonstrated to a potential adversary, it may very well have a substantial deterring effect of its own.

Another factor determining equilibrium will be the degree of consensus and internal support and control which the potential adversary can count on in case of conflict. The internal control of the armies and populations by the Soviet Union and her satellite regimes may have to be re-examined in the light of recent experience in Poland. If a totalitarian government obviously fails to keep even the children and the old women from openly demonstrating their opposition, it is difficult to assume that it would be in unquestioned control and find popular support in the case of armed conflict brought about by its own aggression.

I am fully aware of the complex issues that have to be considered in the calculations of balance. Their obvious relevance, however, demands such inclusion. The possibility of consensus will certainly be affected by the way they are evaluated.

Moral and Ethical Questions

Next to the issue of the budget, the consensus with respect to defence today is most notably threatened by the question of the moral and ethical acceptability of nuclear deterrence. Since Western security as maintained through NATO rests basically if not almost exclusively on the deterrent effect of nuclear arms, to question this defence strategy on ethical and moral grounds obviously goes to the very core of our defence consensus. Much has been said and written about this subject. The balance of terror, as Churchill called it in the 1950s, has always been seen by thoughtful students of the subject as difficult to explain. However, it seemed to have the substantial advantage of being relatively inexpensive to maintain and of avoiding the political and economic burdens connected with the conventional defence

10

of Europe. Today for all practical purposes we rely on nuclear weapons for defence. The conventional defence of Europe is such that military leaders consider that it provides no more than a 'delaying trip-wire' which, in case of an attack in Central Europe, will give them no more than a week or two to decide whether – in the words General Rogers, the Supreme Allied Commander, Europe – to go nuclear or to capitulate.

It is this situation that determines the fundamental importance of the nuclear debate for the consensus with which we are concerned. To avoid this debate would be foolish. To structure it properly and guide it to a conclusion that is both politically responsible and capable of achieving consensus is the real task before us. The following points seem to me essential:

– We must accept in principle that there is a relevant moral and ethical issue singular to the strategy of nuclear deterrence which cannot be compared with the issues involved in any other form of military defence, however devastating it may be.
– We must accept that all efforts aimed at minimizing the unique risks connected with nuclear deterrence by concepts of flexible nuclear response will not be plausible in the long run. The single most important reason for this contention is that no-one can make reasonable predictions about the possibility of controlling the process of nuclear exchange and curtailing it once it is set into motion.
– We know that we cannot maintain security through NATO for the forseeable future without reliance on the nuclear deterrent. At the same time, however, we must recognize that continued reliance on nuclear weapons for deterrence poses special problems for the consensus. The willingness to support the nuclear deterrent as a permanent basis for peace and security in Europe is diminishing. Both the Protestant and Catholic churches have declared that nuclear deterrence is only acceptable as a 'hardly bearable condition' if all efforts are undertaken to reduce nuclear arms by arms-reduction talks and to develop alternatives to nuclear defence.

– Efforts must therefore be made to develop and execute defence strategies which, while continuing to incorporate nuclear deterrence, tend to reduce the risk of nuclear exchange or the unacceptable alternative described by General Rogers. Obviously this must involve the reduction or elimination of tactical nuclear weapons and an adequate and compensatory increase in conventional defence capability. Just as obviously this also requires that real efforts be made to secure at least a semblance of civil defence in those European countries which are most exposed to possible military conflict.

I am convinced that if argued properly, and if full use is made of the moral and ethical dimensions of the issue, the development of NATO strategy in this direction and its implementation is possible. That is to say, I am convinced that it can be made plausible and thus capable of providing the basis for consensus.

Consensus and Alliance
What has been said so far about the conditions for consensus on defence policy is in principal applicable to the policies of all NATO member states. The practical conclusions that must be drawn for the policy of individual governments are largely determined by the political conditions under which these governments operate and these conditions obviously vary. Differences of considerable magnitude exist not only between the United States and their European allies. They also exist between the European members of NATO. The possession of nuclear arms or the refusal ever to exercise national control over them is one such difference. The relative proximity to possible theatres of conflict is another. Differences in the sizes of populations or in area, in historical backgrounds, in language or in orientation must also be taken into account and contribute to the plurality of conditions within the Alliance.

A defence community, however, is only viable if it is capable of defining and executing a common defence policy. If, as in the case of NATO, this community looks upon itself as a broad community of military and political interests, its defence policy must be defined in such a way as to include at least some basic common strategies in the fields of international trade, relations with the Third World and the like.

Viewed against the issue of consensus, this means that, as a *community of nations*, held together by a common political and cultural heritage, by common economic interests and by common defence purposes, NATO will have a tendency broadly to define the totality of its common interests. Made up as it is of individual democratic nations with individual sovereign governments, periodically facing elections, the consensus with respect to this community's common interests must be established within each member nation. Even if one assumes that, in defining the common policies of NATO, *national* consensus must be established, there will remain an important area of policy centering around defence and security which, because we are considering a *defence* community, must remain an area of common policy. Community policy must be supported by each national consensus.

Because the political conditions for establishing consensus on the common defence policies and strategies differ, the real challenge is to harmonize these two prerequisites of a successful defence community: the definition of a plausible defence strategy, with all its economic, political and strategic implications; and the establishment of the necessary consensus within the member states on a national basis. Since defence is one of the most important (if not the most important) expression of sovereignty and the formation of democratic consensus on defence is a kind of underpinning of democratic government, what is called for is nothing less than the harmonization of fundamental expressions of government and national existence and the foundations of the Atlantic Alliance.

It is important to realize that the plurality of interests within a community of democratic nations determines in part the level of consensus that can be attained. If consensus is to be based primarily on plausibility, whatever is defined as a political objective of the defence community must therefore be plausible also in terms of national consensus.

As long as such objectives relate to the fundamental conditions of the community, they will be plausible. This is obviously true for the commonly shared assumption that there is a need for defence or that there should be a common defence organization as long as there is to be a defence community.

As objectives become more concrete, however, their plausibility is increasingly determined by regional or national political conditions. To include them in the consensus therefore requires that they are defined in such a way as to allow room for regional or national differences. Obviously people who live close to the border dividing Germany will view certain elements of our common defence strategy differently from US citizens living in California or Canadians in Vancouver. The relative proximity to possible conventional conflict will naturally influence one's willingness to defend oneself. It will have relevance too for the support of political efforts at avoiding conflict with the possible adversary. The desirability and extent of political and economic relations with the Soviet Union will therefore tend to be viewed differently, depending on the political conditions and circumstances of the national consensuses under which alternative strategies are evaluated. This means that a durable consensus on a common defence policy can only be maintained within the defence community if this policy takes account of both the interests of the defence community itself and of regional or national conditions and particularities under which that consensus must be established and maintained. Or, to put it differently the Atlantic Alliance as a defence community based on national consensus is viable only if it succeeds in harmonizing the community's interests and the plurality of regional and national political conditions.

One way to do this is to accept the plurality of political conditions and faculties of member states as given and to use this plurality to develop the different functions of the Alliance. Plurality therefore need not be an expression of weakness with centrifugal forces harming the cohesion of the Alliance. Rather, if properly understood, it can serve to strengthen the strategic and tactical means of the defence community. It can broaden the community's scope of action and increase its plausibility at the same time.

12

If accepted as an opportunity, plurality can thus permit us to define the different contributions made by individual member states to the common objectives of the Alliance as being of equal significance. This can be very important when trying to overcome the problems of determining comparative burdens and the appropriate contributions that each should make to the Alliance. It would, for instance, allow us to accept that maintaining defence consensus in the immediate face of the enemy and the acceptance – under such circumstances – of the stationing of nuclear arms over which one has no control on one's own territory could be regarded as an assumption of a special political burden, to be recognized when enquiring into the equality of burden sharing.

If we are prepared to recognize the plurality of political conditions and regional interests within the community as relevant for the maintenance of consensus, we pay tribute to the fact that an Alliance of democracies is possible only to the extent that its members are capable of establishing the requisite national consensus. At first sight this may seem to be an inherent disadvantage of an alliance of democratic nations when compared to a totalitarian alliance. Indeed there has always been a tendency within NATO to view Western plurality in this way and this is especially true for the military side of the Alliance. More than once have the military leadership of the Alliance felt restrained in the execution of what seemed plausible in military terms by the need to establish plausibility in political terms.

Yet plurality properly applied can be a distinct advantage for the Alliance. Not only does it widen the scope of the tactical and strategic activities of the Alliance but it also increases its flexibility and thus its ability to adapt to meet new challenges and opportunities. If properly correlated with the common objectives of the Alliance, plurality can also broaden the consensus on which the Alliance is based. If individual countries within the Alliance find their own political identities represented in the pursuit of common objectives, the plausibility of consensus is increased. Consensus on defence policies within the defence community can thus be assured if the structural characteristics of the Alliance of democratic nations are properly recognized. This requires that no individual country tries to define its own interests as community interests.

Disregard for this structural condition of the Atlantic Alliance is at the heart of the present dispute between the United States and her European allies on the gas pipeline issue. It is not so much the controversy on the feasibility of sanctions that threatens to divide the Alliance, but rather the way that the United States seems to be trying to impose on the Alliance as a community interest what must appear to the other member states as a national interest of one member. The notion that what is good for General Motors is good for the United States has never been accepted in America. Within the Alliance the same may be true for the relationship between the leading member and its European Allies. What is good for the US may not be good for NATO as a whole.

European consensus on the objectives of the Alliance will thus be determined by, among other things, our readiness to respect and make constructive use of the plurality which exists within the Alliance. If we act properly, all will benefit from whatever increased plausibility and thus political strength the Alliance will gain as a consequence.

Public Opinion and the Defence Effort:
Trends and Lessons
The United States

LAWRENCE KAAGAN

By the middle of 1982 it was possible to describe three salient themes which underlay American public opinion with regard to defence and foreign affairs. Deriving from these themes were a wide range of attitudes regarding allies and adversaries, support for and opposition to specific policy initiatives, and the presumed foreign policy mandate which the public has (or has not) offered the Reagan Government. The themes, stated most broadly, are:

- The American public, buffeted by domestic and international events which have shaken presumptions of hegemony, eminence and even potency in world affairs, have been rudely awakened to a world in which the United States can neither dictate nor dominate, and perhaps not even arbitrate. Yet no coherent set of principles has been offered by any recent Administration which would help the public to shape its expectations under these new circumstances. In a variety of situations, bombast has filled in where consistent policy was absent, and the inadvertent result over the period of the last six years is a public mood which is alternately assertive and angry, or disappointed and sullen. There is an inherent instability in a public whose psychology is simultaneously apprehensive and extrovert.

- The American public, starting at its fringes but working quite rapidly through the heart of the body politic, is having new thoughts about the definition of the phrase 'national security'. The decade-long trend, with a brief diversion during the Vietnam War, was to equate higher levels of military spending with higher levels of national security. This trend was accelerated by several traumatic events of 1979 and 1980, principally the taking of diplomatic hostages in Iran, the aborted raid in an attempt to rescue those hostages, and the Soviet invasion of Afghanistan. But since 1981 there has been evidence of second thoughts in the public mind concerning this equation. These second thoughts were prompted by two separate but related developments. The first has been the deep recession afflicting the American economy, and the sharp focus on economic policy during the first half of the Reagan Presidency, including the trade-offs between defence build-up and other national goals brought to light during that time. The second has been an almost uncharacteristic questioning of the premise that 'more is better'. While anxious to have the 'best defence that money can buy', Americans are now less than certain that current or anticipated outlays are in fact buying the 'best', or that throwing money at an arms race is any more likely to buy national security than the same behaviour directed at social welfare programmes is likely to produce 'the Great Society'.

- The third broad theme is closely connected to the first two, but contains such enormous psychological and political potential that it must be isolated and identified in its own right. For the first time, we are seeing the breakdown of what had been a hitherto unexplored popular assumption of American strategic invulnerability. While there is not yet any credible, stable measurement of the proportion of the American public which accepts President Reagan's assertion of Soviet nuclear superiority, his statement, and those of others, have at least awakened a dormant public to the reality of nuclear parity. By a curious logic, the doctrine of Mutual Assured Destruction (MAD), for the years it lasted, was soothing to the national psyche. The all-or-nothing character of the doctrine seemed to dictate that, so long as maniacs were kept away from the button, the world lay suspended between the options of total annihilation and heavily-armed peace, with the latter choice the only reasonable one for both sides. However, since 1981, the American public (and the world public) have been confronted by official statements emanating from Washington which contained talk of nuclear 'warning shots', 'limited' nuclear war, a European nuclear battlefield, and 'winnable' extended exchanges. These concepts have absolutely no credibility with the American public, and have unleashed deep fears where only a short time ago there were complacent assumptions of vague threat. In short order, the invincibility of nuclear hegemony disappeared, the stable protection of MAD disappeared, and for better or worse, the strategic dialogue solely among expert 'mandarins' has disappeared as well. This changed consciousness rippling through the American public is of such magnitude that it is likely to remain until the issues are addressed in a manner the public understands and accepts – not an easy task.

Related to these three themes are a number of other observations about stability and change in US public opinion on international and defence issues. The connection between military budgets and domestic economics, the willingness to apply American force of arms in various circumstances, and the public opinion context of efforts to control and reduce nuclear arms, have all evolved separately but all should be seen in the light of the above mentioned themes.

Public Support for Defence Spending

For the first peacetime period in the nuclear age, the American people are really thinking about the economic impact of large-scale defence spending. Surveys show us several swings in mood from tempered isolationism to what Lloyd Free has recently called 'moderate extrovert internationalism'. And we have seen pre- and post-Vietnam fluctuations in what was considered 'morally' appropriate levels of defence spending. There has been a resurgence of support for a conscripted army and for bilateral reductions in nuclear weapons. Nevertheless, the phrase 'guns versus butter' has clearly taken on new meaning in the arena of American public opinion.

Post-war changes in public support for defence budgets have proved to be among the most dramatic indicators of attitudes towards a US posture in foreign affairs. In 1971, with the war in Vietnam still weighing heavily on the national mood, only an 11% minority of the public said they thought the Pentagon had too little to spend. A decade later in 1981, after becoming disenchanted with a period of detente which seemed to benefit only the Soviet Union, a 51% majority said that the American government spent too little on military and defence needs (see Table 1).

Table 1: Opinion of Defence Spending

In its spending on defence and military purposes the government in Washington spends:

	1982	1981	1976	1973	1971	1969	1960	1953
Too little	19%	51%	22%	13%	11%	8%	21%	22%
Too much	36	15	36	46	50	52	18	20
About the right amount	36	22	32	30	31	31	45	45
No opinion	9	12	10	11	8	9	16	13

Source: Gallup Poll Index 199, 1982

Table 2: Orientations Toward Defence

The US Government's emphasis on defence is:

	1982	1981	1980	1979	1978	1977	1976	1975
Too great	25%	11%	12%	17%	17%	12%	20%	29%
About right	48	35	33	47	41	51	41	41
Too little	22	47	47	30	35	31	32	21
Don't know/no answer	5	7	8	6	7	6	7	9

Source: Yankelovich, Skelly and White Surveys, 1982

Table 3: Defence Spending

Given all the international, defence and economic considerations, there should be:

	1982	1981	1980	1979
A reduction in defence spending	40%	17%	23%	40%
An increase in defence spending	51	76	65	50
Don't know/no answer	9	7	12	10

Source: Yankelovich, Skelly and White Surveys, 1982

Table 4: Defence Trade-Offs

A.	Solution:	*More government spending on defence.*		
	Sacrifice:	*Some social welfare programmes may have to be cut.*		

	1982	1981
Acceptance	23%	42%
Rejection	40	22
Net	−17	+20

B.	Solution:	*More emphasis on defence programmes.*		
	Sacrifice:	*Less resources to rebuild American industry.*		

	1982	1981
Acceptance	20%	29%
Rejection	45	25
Net	−24	+ 4

C.	Solution:	*More government spending for defence.*		
	Sacrifice:	*Higher taxes, inflation.*		

	1982	1981
Acceptance	15%	26%
Rejection	57	34
Net	−42	− 8

Source: Yankelovich, Skelly and White Surveys, 1982

16

But in the trend studies by the Gallup Organization, from which these data are taken, support for expanded defence spending has recently collapsed. In Gallup's most recent 1982 reading, only 19% felt that Washington spends too little on defence, a 32% decline – the most precipitous one-year change with respect to this issue since the Korean War.

The nature of this change is reflected in responses given to trade-offs, or sacrifice-versus-solution questions. Public sentiment is coming to regard military expenditures in a nuclear age not merely as a requirement of a super-power, or at least as an uncomfortable necessity without which national and international security might be threatened, but as a threat in its own right, and as an unacceptable economic hardship as well. The perception of the threat is demonstrated in a survey conducted for *Time* magazine in March 1982, in which the public split down the middle on whether further spending on nuclear weapons weakens the national security (45%) or strengthens it (48%).

In particular, the juxtaposition by the Reagan Administration of proposals for massive increases in defence spending and for broad reductions in spending on social programmes has had a sharp impact on public opinion regarding the acceptability of military budgets (see Table 4). In early 1981, when the Reagan proposals were simply the translation of a candidate's promise into a budgetary realignment, a 2 to 1 margin of the public (42% to 22%) accepted the proposition that some social welfare programmes might have to be cut in order to increase spending on defence. A year later, after absorbing the first of widely reported human costs of social welfare reductions in the midst of a recession, there was a 2 to 1 public margin (40% to 23%) *rejecting* the trade-off. Similarly, in 1981 a narrow majority accepted the idea that a renewed emphasis on defence programmes might diminish resources available to rebuild American industry. In 1982, a 2 to 1 margin rejected this trade-off as well.

Responding to what Americans saw as a long string of post-Vietnam humiliations, infringements and threatening developments, public opinion measurements recorded a virtual surge in approval for enlarged defence expenditures. Analyzing public opinion changes in their book *State of the Nation III*, William Watts and Lloyd Free called public support for defence spending in 1976 'little short of phenomenal'. That intensity continued to grow through 1980, and the assertive mood it represented helped to propel Ronald Reagan into the White House.

What we see now, however, is the fragmenting of consensus on defence spending that is almost equally phenomenal. And while the growth in public consensus was in large part tied to developments in the international arena, its fragmentation is attributable in an impressive degree to the traumas associated with a faltering domestic economy.

Episodes in American Involvement and Aversion

Over the past decade, a short inventory of events and episodes has helped to shape the current climate of US public opinion on international and security issues. The climate thus created became itself an interpretive filter through which the public viewed other events which drew the US into the world arena.

The first category of episodes are those which elicited from the American public a desire to be assertive and involved. This desire, which did not find a satisfying outlet in each instance, drew upon a wide range of civic emotions, including sympathy and altruism, patriotism bordering on jingoism, righteous wrath, stifled rage and frustrated impotence. Among the incidents falling into this category are:

– *The Panama Canal Treaties.* Despite nearly a decade of bi-partisan negotiations and support from most of the nation's military and diplomatic community, public response to the signing of the Panama Canal Treaties in September 1977 was ambivalent at best, hostile at worst. A significant part of public opposition to the Treaties was based on an incomplete knowledge of the purposes or contents of the agreements. (See 'Farewell to "President Knows Best"', *Foreign Affairs,* Vol. 57 No. 3, 1979). A vigorous campaign by the Carter Administration succeeded in gaining Senate ratification of the Treaties and in correcting widespread public misconceptions, but an equally large, or perhaps larger, ingredient in public opposition was the matter of national pride. A majority of Americans said they did not want to 'give away' something that 'rightfully' belonged to the US; and the logic of 'we built it, we own it' was strongly endorsed (65% in an October 1977 Harris survey) right up until the time of ratification. Even though there has been little polling of public attitudes on the Canal Treaties in the past few years, and the issue remains salient only to the most extreme conservatives, there is almost certainly a residue of dormant public resentment concerning this episode in which many Americans felt their country had been 'pushed around'.

- *The Overthrow of the Shah and the Rise of The Mullahs.* Americans had been conditioned to see the Peacock Throne as an important locus of American influence – if not power – in the Middle East. The Shah's regime had received considerable support from successive American Governments and, despite some public qualms about the human rights record in Iran, the modernizing, Westernizing rule of the Shah was viewed as a positive force. The overthrow of the Shah, and his replacement by the vehemently anti-modern Muslim clergy, devoted to the image of Uncle Sam as the devil incarnate, was a profound shock to the American people.

- *The Hostages.* The shock of the Shah's fall paled in comparison to the American public's response to the seizing of 52 US diplomatic hostages by Iranian militants in the American Embassy in Tehran. This event, as no other, riveted public attention to the vulnerability of Americans overseas, to the nuances of Middle East political affairs of which Americans had little knowledge and over which the US had no control and, with each passing week, to the impotence of the American military and diplomatic efforts to free the hostages. Concern for the welfare of the hostages barely suppressed the humiliation and outrage of the American public and, while there was little public clarity at any time during the crisis as to what measures should actually be taken, survey respondents agreed that the episode had

diminished US prestige abroad and consolidated the sentiments of Americans at home.
- *The Rescue Raid.* The public anguish over the hostage episode only deepened the longer it continued, and became a gaping wound when, in April 1980, the raid intended to release the captives was aborted after a series of calamities. An already troubled national psyche was further troubled by the loss of the services of a respected diplomat when Secretary of State Vance resigned in disagreement over plans for the raid, and by the double trauma of a military mission failing in its purpose and of equipment and personnel appearing not to have been sufficiently co-ordinated to avoid catastrophe.

- *Afghanistan.* Coming in the wake of these developments in Iran was the Soviet incursion into Afghanistan. If President Carter was surprised by the boldness of the Soviet move, the American public seemed less so. Afghanistan proved to be the catalyst for a trend in public opinion which had for several years been growing more suspicious of Soviet behaviour under detente and, along with the Iranian situation, crystallized public sentiment for a tougher stance generally in world affairs. Military action was foresworn by both the Carter Administration and the NATO Allies, and economic sanctions had little impact except on American farmers. Public opinion reacted again with gnawing frustration as the US seemed impotent to counter Soviet aggression with anything but denunciations but support for higher levels of defence spending spurted after the invasion, as did support for the reinstatement of military conscription.

- *Cuba.* In the past few years, Americans have felt tricked, embarrassed and abused by a small island ninety miles off their coast. In 1979 the disclosure of the presence of Soviet combat units in Cuba caused more of a flurry of press coverage than of genuine strategic concern, but the public was once again forced to ponder whether the US was powerless to do anything about provocative Soviet acts, even within sailing distance of American shores. But somehow more galling to the public than the tenure of Soviet troops in Cuba was the arrival of 100,000 Cubans in Florida in May 1980. What was first seen as a 'boat lift to freedom' soon took on the aspect of a humiliating example of strategic 'people dumping'. The majority of Americans came to see the arrival of Cuban refugees as a successful attempt by Fidel Castro 'to make us look foolish', and to burden the US with an additional economic millstone when the nation could least afford it.

– *Poland.* The sympathies of the American public are with the people of Poland and Americans are convinced that the Poles are waging an heroic struggle against Soviet-enforced oppression. The public would also like to believe that some action, taken by the US alone or in concert with Western Allies, would have the desired effect of easing that oppression and restoring some measure of self-determination to the Polish people. However the pipeline issue did not engage public attention to any serious extent, and there is a sense in the public that, in this episode too, the US was in no way effective, either with threat of force or with the weight of economics, in affecting Soviet behaviour.

On the other side of the ledger are what might be called 'negative' episodes, those which draw most prominently on the 'lessons of Vietnam' on the American public's suspicions of bad management by its own Government, and on latent or overt fears of the consequences of precipitous actions in the internal sphere. These are situations in which, either convulsively or on some reflection, the public has shown some concern for taking a definition of 'the national interest' into its own hands.

– *Vietnam.* The most significant single imprint on the national psyche remains the experience of the Vietnam War, for it was in that morass that the American public first came to grips with the limits of super-power status. From the Vietnam experience, Americans took a series of lessons about US strategic interests and no-end-in-sight involvements, some of which continue to influence popular responses to a proposed

American role in trouble spots around the world.

– *Angola.* When the Soviet Union and their Cuban surrogates began their most visible activity in Angola, the American people were in the early spasms of post-Vietnam self-doubt and apprehensiveness. Angola bore the stamp of the Vietnam *débâcle*, and neither popular nor congressional support for countering Soviet adventurism was forthcoming. The very idea of deploying American troops into what appeared to be a civil war on alien terrain was just too much for the American public in 1974 and 1975.

– *El Salvador.* Despite obvious hemispheric considerations to the contrary, El Salvador loomed in 1981 and 1982 as the first 'prospective Vietnam' for the Reagan Administration. The American public suspected that in El Salvador President Reagan had chosen his arena to 'get tough', regardless of the strength or weakness of El Salvador's claim to be a dispute which engaged vital American interests. The public rejected the claim, though there were, and are, abiding concerns about the stability of the Latin American region. So adamant were public sentiments against direct American intervention in El Salvador that, in one particular survey, a majority (51%) announced support for defiance of military conscription if troops were to be called up for deployment there.

– *The Economy.* As outlined in the previous section, the high costs of building, modernizing, maintaining and deploying a military and defence system have become concerns uppermost in the mind of the American public in the past year. The Reagan Administration's calls for a dramatically increased military budget while making substantial reductions in social spending, all in the midst of deep recession, have made the public acutely aware of the dollar costs of the defence establishment. Sensitivity to waste and cost-overruns is high, and the media's attention to a nearly item-by-item accounting of the cost of ships, missiles, planes and even fuel during the recent British-Argentine engagement in the South Atlantic has further sharpened the public's 'money response' to military affairs.

– *Nuclear War*. The American public is acquiring a new, or revived, level of consciousness about the threat of nuclear war. The orientation is not pacifist, nor is it unilateral in focus. It *is* a growing concern about 'omnicide' or the 'fate of the earth'. In rejecting the idea of a winnable nuclear war, or controlled exchanges, of effective civil defence, or normal postal service within the blast zone, the public has not eschewed the need for a strong military or an assertive national posture, but there are now doubts about leaders who speak of winning – rather than preventing – nuclear war. Their judgement in matters of war and peace is likely to be subjected to closer scrutiny.

The American Public

Public disposition towards the use of American military forces abroad is a special case, and is a function of several factors, none of which has become more important recently than the public's own *clear* perception of a threat to a *genuine* US national interest or moral obligation, and the public's belief in the truthfulness of US government representations of the situation in question.

Despite the sometimes turbulent economic and political relationship between US governments and those of Western Europe, Japan and other industrial democracies, the American public is not only disinclined to a 'divorce', but shows a rather strong loyalty to allies, particularly in cases of hypothetical attack.

Since the mid-1970s, pluralities and then the solid and growing majorities of the American public have sanctioned the use of American military force to assist friends under attack. The crucial element here is the word 'friends', for it is the existence of security commitments commingled with deeply-felt public affinities which account for a willingness to send troops overseas. In surveys by Gallup and Potomac Associates in 1975, 48% of the American people agreed that, if a major European ally were to be attacked by the Soviet Union, the US should use force in the defence of that ally. By 1980, Americans had become somewhat disillusioned with the theory that detente had reduced world tensions; instead they saw it providing a screen behind which the Soviet Union had become more expansionist. A 74% majority supported the view that US military action should be taken to repel a Soviet invasion of Western Europe. Similar dramatic growth occurred in public willingness to defend Japan in the event of an hypothetical attack on her by either the Soviet Union or China. Between 1975 and 1980, willingness to use US military force in such circumstances increased from 42% to 68% (see Table 5).

Yet the public clearly distinguishes between the use of force in defence of substantial allied commitments and the insertion of a US military presence merely on the orders of an administration in Washington. As the experience in Angola in 1975 demonstrated, the American public and the Congress had learned how to avoid the traumas of the Vietnam quagmire. Again in 1982, despite Government assertions to the contrary, Americans saw a Vietnam analogy in El Salvador.

El Salvador provided a litmus test of the public's ability to discriminate between those policies judged to be in the national interest and those which their Government put forward as necessary and proper. In late March 1982, 8 in 10 Americans interviewed in one survey said that they disapproved of the US sending any troops to fight in El Salvador. In the same survey, when asked whether they thought the Reagan Administration was telling the truth when it stated it had no intention of sending troops, 42% of the public said yes; 42% said no. Against this background, nearly two thirds (64%) said that they fully expected that the United States would send troops to El Salvador anyway, if the Government there does not win its own war against rebel insurgents (see Table 6). This public suspicion of the way in which the Reagan Administration determines the 'national interest' in world affairs has already begun to shadow public attitudes on another and more vital issue. The most fateful of questions, the future of arms control and of the war- and peace-making intentions of governments, is moving to centre stage in the arena of American public opinion.

Nuclear Awareness

The threat posed by international instability and even more deadly nuclear weapons and

Table 5: Should the US use Military Force to Defend X (if attacked by Y)?

			1980	1979	1978	1976	1975	1974	1972
1.	One of the US's major	*Agree*	74%	64%	62%	56%	48%	48%	52%
	European Allies	*Disagree*	19	26	26	27	34	34	32
	(if attacked by USSR)	*Don't know*	7	10	12	17	18	18	16
2.	Japan (by USSR	*Agree*	68	54	50	45	42	37	43
	or China)	*Disagree*	28	35	35	37	39	42	40
		Don't know	4	11	15	18	19	21	17
3.	South Korea (by	*Agree*	38	32	32				
	North Korea)	*Disagree*	51	56	52				
		Don't know	11	12	16				
4.	Taiwan (by China)	*Agree*	43	34	32				
		Disagree	42	51	48				
		Don't know	15	15	20				
5.	Thailand (by	*Agree*	30						
	Vietnam)	*Disagree*	55						
		Don't know	15						
6.	Australia (by an	*Agree*	70						
	enemy of US)	*Disagree*	21						
		Don't know	9						
7.	Philippines (by an	*Agree*	65						
	enemy of US)	*Disagree*	25						
		Don't know	10						
8.	China (by USSR)	*Agree*	45						
		Disagree	42						
		Don't know	13						

Source: Gallup Organization; Potomac Associates in *Americans Look at Asia*, Watts, 1980

Table 6: US Role in El Salvador

1)   The Reagan Administration has said it has no intention right now of sending American soldiers to fight in El Salvador. Do you think the Reagan Administration is telling the truth about that or not?

Yes, Administration is telling truth	42%
No, Administration is not telling truth	42
Don't know	16

2)   Just your best guess, if the El Salvadorean Government cannot defeat the rebels, do you think the United States will eventually send American soldiers to fight in El Salvador or not?

Yes, US will send troops	64%
No, US will not send troops	27
Don't know	9

3)   Would you approve or disapprove of the United States sending troops to fight in El Salvador?

Approve	18%
Disapprove	79
Don't know	4

Source: ABC/Washington Post Poll, March 1982.

delivery systems has become, at last, a public issue. While it is not likely that a large portion of the US public will become more knowledgeable about MIRV, MARV or throw-weights, it is virtually certain that the nuclear Pandora's box is now open and, as far as the American public is concerned, it is not likely to be closed until there are clear signs that progress is being made on arms limitations, reductions and safeguards.

For the American public at least, support for a nuclear freeze of any type, or support for any other formulation of nuclear arms control, should not be equated with a reversal or softening of an essentially assertive public posture on US foreign affairs. Rather, such support represents, as did public opinion with respect to proposed government policies towards El Salvador, a substantial erosion of consensus on what a valid national security stance actually is or ought to be. Survey questions couched in terms of a desire for 'toughness' or a desire to 'reduce tensions' show growing sentiment for co-operation on arms control. However a significant trend, dating from the middle of the 1970s, embodies a 'don't tread on me' outlook which continues to underlie American public opinion.

Support for specific arms-control proposals has not congealed in any way which would demonstrate that the public feels that it has (or should) pre-empt Presidential prerogatives at the negotiating table. But, unlike the early days of tentative protest against the war in Vietnam, the American public has rejected the idea that it does not 'know enough' to be concerned or to have a valid opinion, or that 'experts' should necessarily be left alone to decide the proper national posture in reducing the threat of nuclear weapons.

In fact it was the public pronouncements of a number of these 'experts' which gave rise to the re-born anti-nuclear movement in the US. Some of the early foreign policy and defence statements of President Reagan, as well as Secretaries Haig and Weinberger, led many Americans to see the present Government as bellicose, and too likely to push the world beyond confrontation and into a nuclear war. As public confidence in President Reagan's grasp and handling of foreign affairs began to slip, so rose the fortunes of the anti-nuclear movement.

As with El Salvador, the public was disinclined either to trust or believe statements made by the Government on what constituted the best policy. In an April 1982 survey by the *Washington Post* and ABC News, a 57% majority said that they did not feel that government officials could be trusted to make the 'right decision' about a nuclear freeze policy without being subjected to public pressure. By an even larger margin (64%) the polls showed that the public believed that it was pressure for a freeze that had given arms-control negotiations a higher priority within the Reagan Administration.

Underscoring what is clearly a gap between the Government and the governed is the public's sense that this Administration may not be seriously interested in reducing the threat of nuclear war. A 53% majority in an early Summer 1982 Harris poll rated the President negatively for his posture on arms-control negotiations with the Soviet Union, and 48% in the survey cited above (ABC/*Washington Post*) said that they felt that President Reagan had not done all he should to reduce the international build-up of nuclear weapons. Only 17% in a survey in May 1982 by the Associated Press and NBC accepted the proposition, often presented by the Administration that 'limited' nuclear war is both possible and winnable.

The arena in which the American debate – or struggle – over nuclear disarmament is taking place is generally described as containing two participants or sets of actors. The first can be thought of as the Department of Defense, adherents of the Defense Guidance Plan, etc. Without impugning the morals of this group, it is possible to conceive of them as the 'pro-nuclear' movement. On the other side, there is the anti-nuclear movement, advocating a freeze and disarmament measures. In some cases they, like their counterparts in the European movements, play down or discount Soviet intentions, both conventional and nuclear, and focus their attention on the reduction of US and NATO nuclear forces.

Each of these sets of actors, in presenting argument, testimony and public witness, speaks and acts as a surrogate of the public, taking it for granted that they speak in their best interests, and with the will of the people behind them.

Both sides are wrong. There is a third actor, and the third actor shares some of the perspectives of the first, and some of the second, but is accurately represented by neither. The third actor is the general public, and now that the public has begun thinking about the unthinkable, there is not likely to be a national consensus on nuclear arms policy until *three*, not *two* voices are listened to.

In sympathy with the anti-nuclear movement, the public wants to take steps towards reducing the threat of nuclear catastrophe. With these activists, the public feels that no conceivable dispute is worth destroying the world for, and that the realists on this issue are those who favour the control of nuclear weapons, not those who devise strategies for the use of the tools of omnicide.

Yet, along with the defence and foreign policy establishment, the public also firmly believes in the existence of a Soviet threat to world peace and thus to the American way of life. While seeking parity with, rather than clear superiority over the Soviet Union, the public nevertheless feels that the US some-how lost ground during the period of detente, and has become a less potent actor in world affairs than in decades past. With the defence establishment, the public feels in its heart that, despite the huge stockpiles of nuclear weapons at US disposal, it is not as well-protected in a dangerous world as it might be – and should be.

In response to a shifting rhetorical framework presented by political leaders, large segments of the American public have begun to question – and to challenge – the prerogatives of the strategic community on the issue of nuclear weapons and nuclear war. Under the pressure of a tight economy and government policies which reduce social services and increase military expenditures, the issues of strategic modernization and the cost of military procurement overall have begun to generate public resistance. Taken together, these two developments have begun to shake the public consensus which has supported the structure and direction of American – and Western defence efforts in the past. If there is a lesson to be learned, it is that the time for a new, constructive consensus-building dialogue among leaders, experts and the public has come. It has come, that is, unless it has already passed.

Public Opinion and the Defence Effort: Trends and Lessons

Europe

RUDOLF WILDENMANN

For many years now public opinion in industrialized countries, as identified and measured in surveys, has followed a reasonably set pattern of clearly defined policy goals and, with only a few exceptions, it continues to do so even today. It is not surprising that between 50% and 70% of the population ask for an improvement in economic policies, with the emphasis at the moment on employment policies. Social security and related issues follow employment with concern over law and order also playing important roles. While different age cohorts and social groups may show varying degrees of emphasis on certain subjects, such variations do not significantly change the basic pattern.

What is remarkable about public opinion today is that defence does not figure at all as a policy goal. On the other hand the issue of 'peace' (as distinct from 'defence') has managed in the past few years to secure about 20% support from the general public and much more from the younger age groups. This is an extraordinary phenomenon. It is generally the educated section of the population which advances the issue of peace, not the blue-collar workers, and their definition of peace more or less completely rejects military defence.

Today's pattern also holds true if we divide mass public opinion into groups according to knowledge, political interest and political participation. We may identify five groups[1] within European countries and the US: 'activists', 'reformists', 'conformists', 'inactives', and 'fundamentalists' ('protesters' in the terminology of Barnes and Kaase). The degree of information they possess or the structure of their knowledge may be different but there is no decisive change in the pattern of their goals. It is also clear that the priorities of

peace provide a base from which the various peace movements work, with their strength varying according to whether they are Catholic or Protestant.

Topics which play an important role in the high level political discussions (such as energy, economic policies, the role of the law in society, etc.) are hardly of concern to publics. Moreover, the relation between democracy and defence, which is after all what fundamentally underpins NATO, does not now appear to constitute a basic consensus in Western societies.

Since there is no comparable data available besides the three positional elite studies carried out in West Germany[2], we have to take results from these studies as *pars pro toto*, in order to identify patterns in elites, acknowledging, of course, that there might be significicant differences from nation to nation. In our studies we found the following rank-order of issues (scale from 0 to 10): *energy* 8.4; *fundamental rights* 8.4; *freedom of mass media* 7.8; *social market economy* 7.7; *full employment* 7.6; *detente* 7.5; *prices* 7.5; *foreign trade balance* 7.5; *law and order* 7.4; *good relations with USA* 7.4; *defence* 7.4; *European unification* 7.3; *social security* 7.2; *budgetary debts* 7.2; *terrorism* 7.0; *environmental conservation* 6.8; *economic growth* 6.6; *education* 6.5; *house construction* 6.5; *relations with USSR* 6.0 (and some others below that scale).

The greatest variation between political groups (clusters) can be found with respect to the social market economy and the assessment of detente. Each elite sector has its own, slightly different, rank-order of importance for policy issues but these patterns are very different from those of the mass public, and this situation has not changed dramatically since

24

1968, except that the issues of detente, European unification and education were then somewhat more strongly emphasized.

In a modern form, these differences in terms of interest, insight and emphasis between élites and the mass public reflect Alexis de Tocqueville's idea that democratic societies tend to be primarily concerned with their domestic well-being, whereas only elites ('aristocracies' at this time) concern themselves with the pursuit of long-term foreign or defence policies.

The following generalizations can be put forward on this basis of analysis:

- The mass public (almost by necessity) concentrates on its individual security in social life – on the family, occupation and employment, the well-being of its children, its idiosyncratic interests and hobbies.
- We should not complain about the lack of political interest on the part of the mass public or its poor judgment, but we should look rather into the socio-political structures and kind of 'political education' (in the sense of Walter Bagehot) which prevails.
- Opinions and attitudes (including non-attitudes) on the part of the mass public result largely from the influences of political leadership. If defence is presented in an unfavourable light or is not presented as an important policy goal to the public or if there is a lack of basis consensus, then this indicates a failure on the part of political leadership.
- The combined policy goals which seem to have been linked and fundamental in the late 1940s and 1950s – namely, stable economic conditions, social security, European integration and defence – seem today neither to be linked nor any longer to be fundamental. Without this combination of policies which appealed to the imagination of the younger generation 30 years ago, the policies of the 1950s would not have succeeded. If there is now a lack of consensus, we need to question the abilities of governmental machinery and party systems to resolve problems. Last but not least, we need to question the pattern used for the selection of party leaders.

Unfortunately there are many methodological errors in the surveys relating to the mass public and one of the most frequent is to put questions to them which only 'experts' are in a position to answer. Those carrying out such surveys then find themselves left with a mixture of reliable information, artefacts, and non-attitudes, simply because people feel compelled to answer questions even if they have no real insights or are simply not informed about the survey topic. It is therefore hardly useful to turn such answers into impressive tables and graphs.

Reliable information is most likely to be available when people are questioned as to their sentiments. For example, we could take as reliable the sampling of opinion as to the deterioration of trust in American governments, as distinct from trust in the United States herself. In many European countries this trend is obvious (as it is in the United States). We may conclude, too, that the fear of nuclear weapons and the risk of war is increasing everywhere in Western Europe, with the possible exception of France. Yet there still remains a strong feeling of necessity to be allied with the US through NATO (except again in the case of France) and, varying according to group, there is no trust of the USSR. The invasion of Afghanistan or the events in Poland have in fact increased distrust of the USSR, even if by and large they did not increase the fears of the risk of war in Europe, although in most countries the use of military force in the case of an attack still has the support of the majority. Negotiations with the East are regarded as being either useful or desirable or both. Trade with the USSR is seen as a means of maintaining a situation of non-war.

One theme comes through quite clearly. There is no desire whatsoever to engage in a war with the USSR. Peace should be maintained. War is not the way to solve differences within Europe, yet there are considerable differences of opinion as to how to avoid a war – which is not very different from the debates amongst policy-makers.

If we turn now to surveys of expert opinions and attitudes, only those carried out in West Germany[3] are available. Some of the important results are as follows:

- Very differentiated opinions are expressed *inter alia* on the usefulness of *détente* policies, on MBFR, on the implications of deterrence, on the production and location of new nuclear weapons, on the evaluation of political and military developments in the USSR and on the global versus European approaches to security. Major variations appear between governmental parties (then SPD and FDP) and the opposition (then CDU) including other sectors related to these parties (clusters). These variations are similar to variations found among elites with respect to defence or detente.
- The complicated nature of defence relations is mirrored in a diversification of policy assessments and possible goals. There is *no* general consensus as to what should be the underlying rationale for defence policies – as was once the case in the 1960s – except that there is a consensus in preventing war.

In 1950, the then Minister of Internal Affairs of the first Adenauer Cabinet, Gustav Heinemann, resigned when the question of German rearmament was favourably considered by Konrad Adenauer. In his letter of resignation, he pointed out that 'social rearmament' was necessary, not 'military rearmament', and that West Germany should aim at peaceful unification with East Germany and neutrality between the powers. Later, he founded his own party, the GVP, which was merged in 1956 with the SDP, and many of the GVP's leaders (for example Eppler, Rau, Posser, Heinemann) later became prominent figures in the SPD-dominated government. As President of the Republic, Heinemann was himself very active in the creation of the German Society for Conflict and Peace Research, even though he was no longer then directly involved in policy formulation. The former policies of the GVP have had a considerable influence on the contemporary SDP's positions, and on part of the FDP, as well as on other important political formations.

Military versus social spending is thus not a new problem in West Germany, and a number of politicians (and scientists), having now become members of German elites, are still very active in pursuing a different course in politics

to that of the SPD/FDP when they were in power.

However, the question of 'butter' instead of 'guns' is not as simple as it may appear. All NATO countries are facing similar issues; the anti-nuclear movements reflect, in varying degrees, environmental, anti-nuclear and neutralist sentiments.

In the case of West Germany, the strength of the movement is also due to the fact that neither the governing parties nor the opposition took the movement seriously when it first appeared in the mid-1970s, even though empirical evidence was already available that about 15% of the population was sympathetic to such ideas.[4]

Several aspects of the phenomenon came together and there are several political dimensions of their possible consequences. Only those which are most central will be considered.

As Max Beloff remarks in his *New Dimensions in Foreign Policy* (London: George Allen and Unwin, 1961), it is hard for a democratic society not to escape the latent dangers of international relations. In the case of very protracted conflicts that are difficult to comprehend and require steady, reliable and rational policies, democratic societies in their perceptions tend to minimize these conflicts. Although the belief that democratic societies are bound always to say no at the wrong moment (as Walter Lippman in his 'Public Opinion' once contended – no at a time when armaments are needed and no at a time when the pursuit of peace is necessary) may not be correct today, it does seem true that the desire for European Unification (Hamilton Fish Armstrong) correlates with the perception of 'danger' from the USSR. It would also seem that democratic societies remain more concerned about the development of justice, liberty, freedom and welfare than about armaments.

It is becoming increasingly difficult to convince the younger generation that democracies need to be defended, that resources are scarce and that priority should be given to increasingly costly weapons when there seems already to be an abundance of them. In contrast, the post-war generation of the 1950s 'swallowed the frog' (D. Sternberger) of West German rearmament, simply because rearmament was linked to political concepts which foresaw an end to wars in Europe by the creation of new European perspectives and institutions. Such goals are no longer placed before today's younger generation. On the contrary, Europe seems to them to be on the point of stagnation wtih endless bureaucratic struggles about subsidies, market regulations and protective tariffs. One indicator for this disillusion was the very low electoral participation of the younger generation in the Direct European Elections.

This younger generation was raised in a period of prosperity and convincing democracy, when the capacity of democracies to resolve problems seemed to be immense. The 'restless generation', a term Max Kaase and I used in 1968, was very exposed to democratic socialization in schools and society. The more exposed, the more 'restless' it became (R. Wildenmann/M. Kaase, *Die unruhige Generation*, 1968). A rising percentage of each age group is receiving a higher education, and educational expectations are still on the increase. What M. Rainer Lepsius terms the *Versorgungsklasse* (the class of people provided for by the state) is to a very large extent independent of economic growth and takes it for granted that the reallocations of resources will be in its favour. Higher education resulted also in a greater interest and participation in politics. It widened the gaps between the various strata of society in terms of their respective influence over policy – it did not narrow them.[5]

In their writings M. R. Lipset and Stein Rokkan, analysing the rise of political structures in the second half of the 19th and early 20th centuries, stated that political and party systems were aligned along the lines of the political cleavages of these times. Transformed into a general approach this means that the following cleavages were covered:

- The reproduction of tangible and intangible capital in society, namely, productivity and natural science research and technology, mainly by the 'conservative' parties in Europe;
- Communication and social mobility as well as solidarity in society, in concrete terms, by the development of the Welfare State, mainly by social-democratic or liberal parties.

This leaves the problem of the relationship between man and his environment, as well as the problem of 'creativity', especially with regard to the capacity of developing new political structures – whether domestic or international. These new issues in democratic societies are now put on the agenda by the environmental and peace movements which are strongly in the interest of the *Versorgungsklasse*.

It is evident that, if democratic societies are to formulate a convincing foreign policy (especially with regard to defence), there must be reconciliation between these opposed forces. Unfortunately most political elites seem to identify problems after things have gone too far by which time it is difficult to resolve them by mutual agreement. Moreover there is still no attempt to establish a more systematic solution to the problem which Ferdinand A. Hermes defined as 'the people's peace and the tyrant's war' (1944, Notre Dame), in other words to create a variety of international institutions and procedures to control or resolve conflicts and (gradually) replace the uncertainties of a deterrent strategy and of the arms race.

The results of this brief investigation into public opinion both of the masses and positional elites strongly indicates that an extensive debate on defence should have taken place a long time ago. Given the enormous difficulties of formulating and carrying out a multidimensional defence policy under present conditions, and given that long-lasting emotional stability and solidarity are required in order for such policies to be successful, the failure of elite judgment as to these issues in the last 10 or 15 years becomes apparent. This applies both to the domestic and foreign policy dimensions of the problem. Western industrialized states managed to adapt their institutions and their political processes after the Second World War in order to meet the enormous problems of the day. They also attempt to create a European constitutional structure and were quite successful until the 1970s. Neither are adequate any longer. To regain the confidence of our public and political elites in defence policies, we must find a very different approach to today's fundamental challenges.

NOTES

[1]See Edward N. Muller, *Aggressive Political Participation* (Princeton: Princeton University Press, 1979); and Samuel Barnes and Max Kaase *Political Action: Mass Participation in Five Western Democracies* (London: Sage Publications, 1979).

[2]1968: Wildenmann *et al*: 1972: Kaltefleiter/Wildenmann et al; 1981: Wildenmann/Kaase *et al.* In each case the sample consisted of top positional holders across society; in 1981 there were 1,750 respondents from a total of 3,150 top position holders.

[3]Schössler/Schmitt/Jung, Mannheim: SIPLA 1978-1981, three studies on 'Sicherheitspolitische Planung' carried out on about 600 'experts' participating in security policies.

[4]Regular yearly surveys 1976–1980, partially published.

[5]Muller and Barnes/Kaase *op. cit.* in note 1.

The Media and the Making of Defence Policy: The US Example

JOSEPH FROMM

Over the past decade the media in the United States have acquired a reputation as a major force in shaping national policy, credited with bringing down one President in the Watergate affair and forcing another to end American combat involvement in a war in Vietnam.

Nevertheless, the tangible influence of the American press and television on the decisions of government today is a subject of widespread and continuing controversy. There is no doubt that the spread of television into virtually every home has transformed the communication of news, information and ideas, with results that have yet to be accurately measured. It is a vehicle that has been utilized by the civil rights movement and the anti-Vietnam war movement successfully to proselytize a nation and ultimately to bring about a radical change of course. Conversely, it also has been exploited by Presidents, with varying degrees of success and most notably by Ronald Reagan, to win support for their policies.

In some areas of government affairs, it is possible to cite specific examples of the direct impact of the media on political decision-making or behaviour.

The 'supply-side economics' policy pursued by the Reagan Administration is a classic example. This controversial and unconventional theory of economic management was embraced by Reagan, as a candidate, largely as a result of the proselytzing endeavours of Robert Bartley, editorial page editor of the *Wall Street Journal*, and Jude Wanniski, his deputy.

On a different level, David Gergen, the President's Aide in charge of communications, told the *National Journal* that the press was responsible for the Reagan Administration's quick retreat from a plan to grant tax-exempt status to racially-segregated schools. The White House, he said, had responded to 'the warning flags . . . first published in the columns, opinion pieces and editorials'.

In foreign policy, Presidential Counsellor Edwin Meese told a group of journalists earlier in 1982 that the impact of the media is especially noticeable. 'The press', he said, 'acts as intermediary between the public and the government as a national interpreter of events'. He pointed to El Salvador to illustrate the practical effects of this.

'The very fact', he said, 'that the press keeps asking if the President is going to send troops to El Salvador makes it an issue even though Mr Reagan has stated he is not planning such action'. The upshot, said Meese, was that Senate Minority Leader Robert Byrd sought to 'tie the President's hands'.

While one must resist the temptation to draw unwarranted general conclusions from these examples, they do illustrate the sensitivity of the government – particularly in the White House – to popular opinion as reflected by the press and television. One authority on the subject has concluded that the 'news media have become such pervasive forces that from a public affairs viewpoint, many events don't really take place unless they are covered by television, newspapers or news magazines'.

Nothing could illustrate the point more vividly than the emergence of the 'nuclear freeze movement' as a political force. It was only when television and the press 'discovered' the movement early in 1982, many months after it had established itself at grass-roots level across the country, that the political leadership in Washington took note and reacted by displaying greater enthusiasm for renewed strategic arms negotiations with the Soviet Union.

29

Marginal Direct Impact

Against this background, it might seem logical to assume that defence policy is influenced as much if not more by the news media than policy in other areas – given the vast sums of money devoted to the armed forces and the implications not only for the nation's security but for the economy as well. In fact, defence appears to be something of a special case.

Systematic analysis of the subject is almost totally lacking. In attempting to calculate the influence of the media in the shaping of defence policy one must rely on personal experience, random interviews with representative journalists covering defence affairs and officials involved in the decision-making process and an examination of some of the more controversial national security issues.

A paradoxical conclusion emerges from such an inquiry. The direct impact of press and television on weapons decisions and strategy is marginal: yet the evidence indicates that the media may exercise a critical influence on the ultimate issue – the use of the armed forces to engage in war.

First then, it is necessary to examine the limited impact of the media on routine decisions – those involving the choice of weapons, manpower policies and strategic planning. One of the most respected television journalists assigned to the Pentagon offers this explanation: 'Strategic issues are too esoteric, weapons systems too complex and public understanding inadequate for the media to play a significant role. On high priced weapons systems, the press and television may force greater accountability but cannot force a change in the decision itself'.

James Reston, the distinguished *New York Times* columnist, provided another explanation for the limited impact of the media on specific policy decisions. 'When you talk about the media's impact', he said, 'you have to define what you mean. For example, the impact of ideas and criticism in the daily and periodical press is indirect. The criticism may bubble over policy on defence or policy on El Salvador and be argued in the press. But it is only when the other branch of government, in Congress, picks up that criticism that the press begins to have an influence since we do not have the power to subpoena'.

Among Pentagon correspondents and academic specialists in the defence field there is agreement only on a single weapons decision in recent years that may have been decisively influenced by the media – President Carter's April 1978 decision to defer production of the neutron warhead. Details of this episode bear recalling briefly.

On 6 June 1977, the *Washington Post* published a front page article by Walter Pincus under the headline 'Neutron Warhead Buried in ERDA Budget' with this opening paragraph: 'The United States is about to begin production of its first nuclear battlefield weapon specifically designed to kill people through the release of neutrons rather than to destroy military installations through heat and blast'.

Even though funds for neutron warhead development had been budgeted previously for some years without stirring controversy or even attracting notice, the Pincus article triggered an international furore that took the Carter Administration by surprise. Whether intended or not, the article set the tone of the controversy not only with the inference that there was something especially sinister about a weapon that killed people without destroying property but also with the hint that the Administration may have been guilty of deception by 'burying' the funding for the project in the budget for Energy Research and Development Administration (ERDA). The controversy was sustained by the American press as well as European media and, of course, Soviet propagandists.

The upshot was doubtless the most lamentable chapter in the four-year history of the Carter Administration's conduct of alliance diplomacy. After his top national security aides had negotiated what was considered an acceptable compromise with the European Allies on production and deployment of the neutron warhead, the President could not bring himself to make the final decision. On 7 April 1978, to the consternation of all concerned – and especially his closest advisers – he announced that manufacture of the weapon would be deferred.

What is noteworthy is not that a newspaper may have contributed significantly to the derailing of the neutron warhead but rather that the incident is generally regarded as unusual if not unique. This is not to suggest that the press and television do not play a role – indeed, a most significant one – in the formulation of defence policy in the United States.

Shaping Popular Perceptions

Their influence can be defined in two ways. First the media, while not among the major players in the national security debate, serve as a conveyor-belt of information – and possibly misinformation – ideas and arguments calculated to influence the principal participants. Second the press and television contribute materially to popular perceptions that have a critical bearing on defence policy.

Taking the question of perceptions first, it is probably a safe generalization to assert that in determining the broad thrust of American defence policy – whether the budget should be greatly increased or curtailed, whether more super-carriers should be built or troops withdrawn from South Korea – nothing is more important than the popular perception of the Soviet threat and of the nation's preparedness to cope with it.

How radically and quickly American attitudes on these issues of national security can oscillate has been amply demonstrated in the past few years. In November 1976, the electorate, disillusioned by the failure of American military power in Vietnam, chose as President an obscure former Georgia Governor, Jimmy Carter, who pledged to reduce defence spending, withdraw American ground troops from Korea and – as he spelled it out later – to end 'the inordinate fear of communism'.

Four years later Ronald Reagan was elected, in a landslide, to replace Carter as President with a campaign that promised a massive increase in defence spending to finance modernization and expansion of the armed forces and held the Soviet Union responsible for all major international troubles.

Needless to say, the choice in both elections was influenced primarily by domestic affairs and, to some extent, personalities. But not to be discounted was the drastic change in the electorate's perception of the Soviet threat and American defence needs. Opinion polls show that, whereas in 1977 a large majority of Americans perceived the US ahead of the Soviet Union in military power, in 1981 the ratio was reversed. And while 63 per cent in 1977 felt that military spending should be maintained at the current level or reduced, in 1981 89 per cent favoured the current level or an increase – with no fewer than 61 per cent supporting higher defence outlays.

What accounted for this extraordinary turnaround – and what part did the media play? While disenchantment with super-power detente was apparent early in the Carter Administration as the result of Soviet-Cuban adventures in Angola and Ethiopia, the radical transformation in attitudes toward military readiness is widely ascribed to four events which occurred in 1979:

- The Senate debate on the SALT II Treaty which focused national attention more on the shortcomings of America's defence posture than on the virtues of arms control.
- The fall of the Shah of Iran which brought home to Americans the vulnerability of Persian Gulf oil supplies and the failure of US policy designed to guarantee the security of the region with a surrogate power.
- The Iran hostage crisis seen by most Americans as humiliating evidence of the impotence of US military power – a perception that was powerfully reinforced by the rescue fiasco and the spectacle of a burnt-out helicopter in the Iranian desert.
- The Soviet invasion of Afghanistan viewed as the first conclusive demonstration of Soviet willingness to use her armed forces overtly outside the Soviet bloc.

These events – the overthrow of the Shah and the marathon hostage crisis above all – had a profound impact on the public consciousness in the United States, thanks in large part to the manner in which they were projected by the media. The torrent of news reports, commentaries, photographs and film concerning developments in Iran throughout 1979 and 1980 was overpowering.

The perception that became pervasive was that of the United States as 'a helpless giant' – powerless to save her most valued ally in the

Persian Gulf, to protect her diplomats imprisoned by Moslem revolutionaries in the American Embassy in Tehran or to rescue the hostages.

The cumulative impact of the events of 1979 as projected by the media produced a striking increase in popular support for additional defence spending and for action to overcome what was widely perceived as a position of military inferiority. The change was signalled most vividly in the Senate late in the Summer of 1979 by a revolt against the Carter Administration's defence budget and a vote allocating billions more for the military than requested by the Pentagon.

That this mood persists today is evidenced by continued Congressional support for high levels of defence spending and the Administration's success in resisting significant cuts in its Pentagon budget at a time when social welfare funding is being reduced sharply in an effort to narrow a $100-billion-plus federal government deficit.

Thus, while no methodical study has yet been undertaken to ascertain the impact of the media on the perceptions of the American public and Congress with respect to national security, it seems safe to conclude that it is critical. But a qualification is required: the influence of the press and television is exerted not as a result of deliberate positions they take on issues of defence but primarily through their normal activities in covering the news and through the pervasive role of television that brings news in its most graphic form into almost every home.

Transmission-Belt for Leaks
Similarly, in their role as transmission-belt of information, the media rarely exert influence in an overt or direct fashion but rather as a vehicle that is used by the actual players engaged in the game of formulating defence policy. To grasp what this means, it is important to understand the unique US system of decision-making in the national security field.

In contrast with most other countries – including most democracies – where defence policy is a virtual monopoly of the defence establishment and the Executive branch with little if any input by the Legislative branch, in the United States the role of Congress is im-

portant and has expanded greatly in recent years. The defence budget and programme are debated and approved by the Appropriations and Armed Services Committees in both Houses of Congress and certain specific aspects of national security – such as arms sales and aid – are scrutinized by other committees. This protracted and open process of examining defence issues obviously encourages efforts to influence the judgment of Members of Congress.

Another feature of the American policy-making process is the proclivity of the several branches of the armed forces and other competing forces in the defence community to utilize the media aggressively to advance their arguments and influence decisions. Finally, there is probably greater willingness by the media in the United States to publish 'secrets' than in any other country.

In this system, those who shape defence policy – in the Pentagon as well as in the Congress – look to the press to a remarkable extent to keep them informed about what is happening inside their own bureaucracies. The Air Force publishes twice daily a comprehensive reprint of virtually all articles related to defence and summaries of television comment. The first edition of this *Current News* is printed on yellow paper and is appropriately dubbed 'the yellow peril' because it often brings bad news to top officials at the Pentagon.

The system places a high premium on 'leaks' and the deliberate planting of information as a device for influencing policy. Representative Les Aspin of Wisconsin, among the most knowledgeable Congressmen in the ways of the Pentagon, says that Defense Department officials plant stories in an effort to influence, not the public, but decision-makers. He explains: 'Leaks come through bureaucratic wars – somebody who doesn't like a plan thinks that by leaking the existence of it, he will kill it; somebody who does like the existence of a plan thinks by leaking it, he will encourage it. . . . There are lots of games going on in this town and the press is the conduit for a whole lot of them'.

One of the most striking recent examples of leaking to influence the decision-makers involved an embarrassing disclosure concerning the defence budget. The story that appeared

32

on the front page of the *Washington Post* on 8 January 1982, reported that a secret session of the Defense Resources Board had been warned that the Reagan defence programme as translated by the Joint Chiefs of Staff 'could cost $570 million more than his administration had budgeted over the next five years . . . dramatic evidence that defence spending threatens to run out of control'.

The leak, in the midst of a battle over major cuts in federal spending, was apparently intended to strengthen the hand of those who were critical of misleading projections of the cost of the military build-up and advocating tighter control of the programme. Although the Administration succeeded in warding off attacks on Pentagon military spending, a full-scale investigation was mounted that subjected all participants in the Defense Resources Board meeting to lie-detector tests.

The final stage of the neutron warhead controversy in the Spring of 1978 was marked by an aggressive campaign of leaking that was calculated – unsuccessfully – to induce President Carter to reverse or modify his decision to defer production of the weapon. A more successful campaign of leaks was waged in the Autumn of 1981 at a critical juncture in the Senate debate over the sale of AWAC (Airborne Warning and Control Aircraft) to Saudi Arabia. In this case, officials – presumably with the blessing of the Administration – provided reporters with information designed to demonstrate the limitations of America's most advanced air-borne early-warning system. The purpose was to allay fears that the Saudis could use the plane to attack Israel. The Senate approved the sale.

With rare exceptions, students of government in the United States say that the Administration is able to utilize the media more effectively than its critics in any controversy over a defence issue. Through his news conferences or speeches, the President can convert the press and television into a platform to present his point of view. The Secretary of Defense and other ranking officials also have easy access to the media to argue their case, an advantage not so readily available to their opponents.

Navy Secretary John Lehman provided a classic demonstration of what one authority on national security termed 'the pre-emptive strike' in the controversy over the sinking of the British destroyer HMS *Sheffield* in the Falkland Islands war. Within hours of the ship going down, Lehman, cutting short a trip to Europe, flew back to Washington to seize the initiative in the debate. At a meeting with a hand-picked group of Pentagon reporters, he advanced the argument that the sinking of the *Sheffield* demonstrated the indispensability of big-deck aircraft carriers to provide adequate defence against long-range missile attacks. In so doing, he went far to seize the high ground in advance against critics claiming that the episode proved the vulnerability of surface vessels and super-carriers in particular.

Leslie Gelb, the *New York Times* National Security Correspondent, who has held positions in the Defense and State Departments, maintains that 'any half-way competent and disciplined Administration can get its story published pretty much the way it wants'. The fact is that American Administrations have almost invariably won endorsement of their major defence decisions, however controversial they may have been and whatever treatment they have received by the media. That was true of the Nixon Administration's proposal for an anti-ballistic missile (ABM) system, the Carter Administration's decision to cancel the B–1 bomber, the Reagan Administration's decision four years later to revive the B–1, President Carter's 'race track' basing plan for the MX missile and the subsequent rejection by President Reagan of that scheme.

The Impact of Television

The role of television requires special attention. Upwards of 70 per cent of Americans rely on television as their principal source of news but the other 30 per cent include the best educated with the highest income in the population, and thus presumably the most effective in terms of influencing national policy.

Furthermore, of all forms of communications, television is probably the least suited for dealing with news and information on the complex questions of defence. Imagine the daunting challenge facing a reporter attempting to explain the 'dense pack' basing mode for MX in 90 seconds or two minutes. Dan

Rather, now anchorman on CBS Evening News, told an interviewer that television news 'tends to be a headline service, not an in-depth service'. He went on: 'Anybody who just watches TV news cannot be well informed. You have to read'.

The only systematic study available tends to underscore the inadequacy of television as a medium for informing the public about defence. On the basis of a survey of Walter Cronkite's CBS-TV Evening News programme in 1972 and 1973, Ernest W. Lefever concluded: 'An attentive American viewer relying wholly on the Cronkite show for 1972 and 1973 would have received a partial and highly distorted picture of the dangers confronting the country, the government's response, and the opposing views on national defence. The show carried almost no news on growing Soviet military might in missiles, aircraft, warships or manpower'. Lefever found also that the programme 'painted an overwhelmingly negative picture of US military developments' with 69 per cent of the stories casting the defence establishment in a negative light.

It should be noted that, if Cronkite struck an anti-military posture on his programme, he was doing little more than reflecting the mood of the day – with the nation still scarred by the Vietnam debacle and sentiment against the defence establishment running strong. How far the CBS programme stimulated or reinforced popular attitudes or influenced decision-making is another matter.

A better basis for judging the influence of television on defence policy is provided by a more recent series that CBS-TV screened in June 1981. The series of five, one-hour programmes at prime time – *The Defence of the United States* – was promoted as 'the most important documentary project of the decade'. The overall message questioned the seriousness of the Soviet military threat and raised doubts about the magnitude and direction of the massive defence build-up that the Reagan Administration was initiating. In short, it ran contrary to the mood of the nation in June 1981 – a mood characterized by profound concern about the Soviet military build-up and wide support for greatly increased Pentagon spending.

The avowed aim of the CBS series was to 'stimulate a debate' at the grassroots across the country on the Administration's rearmament programme. What is striking, given the extraordinary scale of the CBS-TV effort, was the apparently inconsequential impact. In fact, if this television blockbuster affected support for the Reagan defence programme among the public or in Congress it was not evident in opinion polls a year later and even less in the national security policy espoused by the Administration.

Negligible as the impact of television appears to be on the formulation of US defence policy generally, in one sense its influence may be crucial. The experience of Vietnam, the Iran hostage crisis and, more recently, the Lebanese War have raised serious questions as to whether, in the television age, the United States can use her armed forces in a foreign war – in particular, in undeclared wars – without tight censorship.

Although a subject of continuing controversy, there seems little doubt that the nation's attitude towards the Vietnam War and the decision to liquidate the US commitment to it was profoundly influenced by the fact that television brought it all into the American living room. To quote James Reston, the *New York Times* columnist: 'Maybe the historians will agree that the reporters and the cameras were decisive in the end. They brought the war to the people . . . and forced the withdrawal of American power from Vietnam'.

Similarly, live television coverage of the early months of the hostage crisis in Tehran – with the mobs chanting outside the beleagured American Embassy night after night – and Walter Cronkite's nightly reminding of viewers of the number of days the crisis had run – had a significant effect on the Carter Administration's policy, especially the decision to mount the doomed rescue operation. Hodding Carter, State Department spokesman at the time, said in an interview: 'That constant reminder of the failure to resolve the crisis had to have magnified the pressure. It had a definite effect on the process'.

More recently, television coverage of Israel's siege of West Beirut had a dramatic effect on public opinion in the United States –

and apparently on President Reagan personally – with the result that traditional support for Israel was sharply eroded and pressure developed for sanctions to force Israel to call a halt to her attacks.

The extreme sensitivity of decision-makers to the potential impact of television in conflict situations was illustrated by deliberations within the Reagan Administration over the commitments of US troops to a peace-keeping force in Lebanon. A participant at a National Security Council meeting weighing the decision reported that much of the time was devoted to debating how the public would react if the Marines were caught up in hostilities that were screened live by TV.

The implications for future American policy of the prospect of televised warfare are a matter of concern among those responsible for national security and especially among military officials. General William C. Westmoreland, who commanded American forces in Vietnam, said recently: 'Vietnam was the first war ever fought without any censorship. Without censorship things can get terribly confused in the public mind. Television is an instrument which can paralyze the country'.

It might be argued that Westmoreland is a biased witness, given his unhappy Vietnam experience. But his concern is felt, too, in media circles. Roger Mudd, a prominent television commentator, reflected the anxiety by raising the question whether a 'democracy which has uncensored TV in every home will ever be able to fight a war, however moral or just'.

Conclusions

There appears to be an exaggerated perception overseas of the direct influence of the media on American defence policy. The impact of the press and television on concrete decisions involving weapons, strategy and manpower is limited but they do make a major contribution to the 'national atmospherics' – popular impressions about the Soviet threat and American readiness – that, in the final analysis, determines the amount of resources the country is willing to devote to defence.

A controversy over the role of television in conflict is likely to develop in view of the concern that the US – or any democracy – may be hamstrung in the use of its military power, even in pursuit of interests deemed vital by the government. The stringent censorship imposed by the British in the Falkland Islands campaign will in all probability be studied – and debated – as a possible model for future US policy.

The Media and the Image of Defence Policy:
Europe

LOTHAR RUEHL

The Press has always sought to remark on the remarkable and to find fault with official explanations of the ordinary. The control that the Press (and in later days, the electronic media of mass communications) can exercise over the political process is that of an outsider and thus bound to be provocative. Without provocation, without the revelation of hidden facts and unorthodox or at least unconventional explanation of these facts the media cannot fulfill their purpose which is to satisfy curiosity, to arouse interest and to draw attention to issues that would otherwise go unremarked. Yet some ask more: they would wish the media at the same time to clarify issues and to respect their real proportions in order not to distort their meaning. This, however, is to ask too much for the Press has never been able to show things as they are without a measure of arbitrary distortion. Distortion is the price that has to be paid for bringing into focus complex and ambiguous issues.

Since war and peace, foreign and defence policy, international security, armaments and arms control are all highly complex and ambiguous matters, the media rarely manage to do justice to the issues involved. This difficulty is increased by the media's own business interests: they must try to win the public and that often means limiting the public's exposure to issues which are both unfamiliar and difficult to understand, otherwise the public will desert the media.

In former times, war and the military were taken for granted: every generation in most countries of Europe was expected to have to fight at least one war and preparation for war was part of national policy. If a generation was spared a war, they were considered lucky. War reporting in the eighteenth and nineteenth centuries, when the Press emerged as a permanent phenomenon in Western Europe, was no different from reporting a fire or an earthquake. Everyone expected such calamities. Moreover, war was widely seen as a means of policy. War reporting, therefore, was nothing more than observing and analysing the use of armed force. The legitimacy of that use was rarely questioned. War correspondents accompanied armies and navies in order simply to tell a story.

Three of the bloodiest wars of the last century and early in this were widely reported in the Press, albeit with a considerable measure of compassion for the ordeals of soldiers and victims: the Crimean War, the American Civil War and the Russo-Japanese War. War was identified with the noble image of 'Nations in Arms' and national feelings had generally accepted war as a national duty once national interest seemed to be at stake and the war 'just'.

This 'alliance' held more or less until the end of the First World War, despite the growth of Christian, liberal and socialist philosophy strongly condemning war and postulating general disarmament. However, the European Press reflected this unease and, when World War I broke out in 1914, there was articulate opposition to the general popular surge towards war. The traumatic experience of the war itself reinforced the moves towards disarmament and pacifism, and this was reflected in the European Press. Scepticism and criticism of the military establishments, defence and armaments blossomed in the liberal, democratic and socialist newspapers.

World War II again appealed to patriotism, and the 'just war'. Mass mobilization and mass suffering demanded that the war effort be identified with the highest national and humanitarian purpose. Fascism and Hitler made it easier to make that identification

36

among the Allies. In the Soviet Union, Poland, Yugoslavia and Greece, it was not much different whereas in Germany war and national defence had been discredited.

In the post-war period a strong initial impetus for peace and disarmament was finally overcome by fear of a new aggression, this time from the East. For almost three decades, public discussion of security affairs was reduced to general expressions of reservation and the democratic left of Europe (and in the churches) and by technical descriptions of deterrence and defence on the centre and right. The European Press dealt with these matters in a strangely ambiguous and veiled manner. Latent scepticism combined with enthusiastic reporting on the new arms technologies, on the modern armed forces, on alliance politics, and on the strategy of deterrence by controlled escalation and flexible response – all highly abstract and complex subjects, difficult to deal with in the pages of the smaller newspapers in the 1960s and 1970s and almost impossible to present with any claim to reality and objectivity on television. There were some brave attempts to explain nuclear deterrence, escalation and conventional defence but more often the tone was one of breathless admiration for technical mastery.

In 1970, Helmut Schmidt, then Defence Minister, called the Bundeswehr an industrial organization that 'produces security' and the media accepted, by and large, the official explanations of deterrence. There was not much controversy until the late 1970s and criticism was confined to compulsory military service, where it existed, to the high cost of armaments and to the absurdity of armed East-West confrontation. The era of negotiations tended to deflect criticism of the military but such debate as took place was a privileged communication between a few specialists in the media and within the bureaucracies and legislatures. The central issues were not debated. They were insulated and widely misunderstood by the general public – like modern works of art: complex, ambiguous, awesome, and, at times, awful. The media employed few specialists and had little interest in defence, armaments and arms-control policies, strategy and security. Editorial staffs

were therefore ill-prepared when the old controversies of the 1950s over the rearmament of West Germany, nuclear arms in Europe and deterrence exploded again in the late 1970s and swiftly engulfed significant parts of the educated public – in churches, at universities and in high schools with many teachers leading the opposition against nuclear arms and NATO policies.

This lack of preparation was due mainly to the latent opposition within the media against military security and nuclear weapons. Since the late 1960s, many former participants in the student revolt against the Vietnam War and American policies had joined the editorial offices of television and radio stations, newspapers and the wire services. In West Germany many of them had invoked the constitutional privilege of declaring themselves conscientious objectors to conscription and had carried on a propaganda campaign against military service. The ground was prepared for the setting up of organized resistance to the State's laws on military service and to the politics of military security in Europe.

The Impact of Detente
The years of detente after 1966–67 had changed the perceptions of the 'potential enemy' or 'potential aggressor' in the East. The Harmel Report on the Future Tasks of the Alliance had declared that the relaxation of tensions with the East was compatible with and even complimentary to defence and deterrence. But this combination, while entirely rational as a policy, was ambiguous as to precisely how the Soviet Union and the other Communist-governed countries of Eastern Europe were to be approached for limited cooperation and a security partnership. The central proposition of the Harmel Report was neither understood nor accepted by large segments of West European Society. Detente had been looked upon by many politicians, academics and journalists as an alternative to East-West confrontation in Europe – much as arms control had been understood as a substitute for armaments and defence. If the Soviet Union and her allies in Eastern Europe were to be considered as prospective partners, why should they then be looked upon as 'potential aggressors' to be countered by NATO

with new arms and defence measures? The basic concept remained that of qualitative superiority of the West over the East in military forces and arms technology. The West European Governments relied on this assumed qualitative superiority in order to limit defence efforts and, in particular, military expenditures beyond an agreed and rather modest level. NATO relied on stabilizing security by mutual and balanced force reductions (MBFR) and the Vienna Negotiations encouraged expectations for arms control in Europe as the Conference on Security and Co-operation in Europe (CSCE) had done since 1973. Detente policies were invoked to justify opposition to conscription, to armed security and to defence expenditures. The democratic left in Europe was particularly impatient with the East-West confrontation and NATO programmes and its many supporters within the media transmitted this impatience to the public, as did many teachers in schools and the proponents of peace research at academic institutions. Social-democratic Governments in Western Europe came under relentless criticism from within their own parties, from trade unions, from their youth organizations and from the churches for their alleged lack of awareness of the risks of confrontation and the dangers of war resulting from armaments programmes and the high levels of military forces. The traditional pacifism of the European left, embedded in all the Socialist and Social-Democratic Parties of Western Europe (and in large segments of the Liberal Parties as well) was revived by the hopes of the detente period and the aim of detente was anticipated as reality long before the process had time to develop and arms control to be established. The 'Spirit of Helsinki' was often taken for a fact, whereas in reality it still remained simply a promise of better times to come.

The media, never well-equipped for dealing with complex matters of international relations and by tradition emotional rather than capable of detached examination of unpleasant facts, had left reporting and commenting on military and security affairs to a very few specialists. These were considered by the editors with a mixture of awe, condescension, suspicion and mild neglect yet they held a near monopoly. Privileged they

may have been but their impact was sharply limited by the space and time the editors made available for them. Thus a strange situation had emerged: a small number of professional journalists of varying quality virtually controlled all information and commentary on defence and security affairs but they did little to shape editorial policies. This became evident when the first epic controversy arose over 'the neutron bomb'.

As far as personnel were concerned, many of the correspondents who had covered World War II survived into the post-war period. These professional journalists specialized in war and military affairs but the interest shown by their editors has varied sharply. For example, the last war the French press really covered in depth was the Algerian War of Independence 1954–62.

The Vietnam Legacy

The war in Vietnam changed things. It became a permanent subject of newspaper and television interest in most of Western Europe with ideological and political factors tending to dominate both the reporting and the evaluation. This led observers generally to wrong conclusions about the nature and the eventual outcome of this war. By 1965 it was generally proclaimed that this Second Indochinese War could not be ended by a military victory and that therefore only a political solution could end the struggle. Reporting and comment tended to reflect this dominant conviction in Western Europe, in particular in the French media but also in Germany, Scandinavia, Italy and the Netherlands. The effect of this general conviction was to underestimate the significance of the strategic equation, the balance of military forces after the withdrawal of US forces in 1973, the impact of the arms support given to North Vietnam by the USSR and China, and the strain of combat on the forces of South Vietnam and the population. Last not least, reporting underestimated the political significance of armed combat in the strategy and psychology of the Vietnamese Communists. When South Vietnam collapsed this belied the forecasts of ten years of reporting in the Western press. The interdependence of political and military factors had been wrongly interpreted in favour of an assumed permanent military stalemate that left only a negotiated settlement as an outcome. European public opinion, however, shaped by the media and by the elite in universities, churches, humanitarian institutions and political parties, did not correctly perceive the lessons of the event, namely that it was the physical and moral exhaustion of the forces of resistance in the South that had finally led to collapse under military pressure.

The image of the Vietnam War on television has shaped the ideas relating to military security, the use of armed force, national defence and the role of violence in politics of an entire generation. Although the reporting of European television and the higher quality press was by and large correct, preconceived notions were not shattered by the evidence on the ground. Even the advance of the columns of North Vietnamese tanks into the city of Saigon did not dissipate the false impression that South Vietnam had been smashed by its own people in revolt, helped, but not led by the North. The subsequent annexation of the South by the North and the later military invasion of Cambodia by the Vietnamese have been treated only with cursory interest. The War was over and that was what counted in European perceptions.

Since the Vietnam War, the problems of peace and military security in the East-West context and in Europe itself have been overshadowed by the reporting of more distant wars. Nevertheless the constant reference to war has affected public attitudes to nuclear deterrence and military defence in Europe. The continuous reporting of human suffering and damage impresses the horror of war on peoples' minds and tends to identify defence and military security with war in Europe. The emotional reaction of the media to armed conflict elsewhere, irrespective of the causes and the course of events, has reduced the determination to defend even one's own country and Western Europe against a possible threat from the East. The reporting on all wars since Vietnam has followed the same pattern: war is senseless; it can serve no rational purpose; it must end in catastrophe; and there is no legitimacy in using the military instrument for any political end including the defence of freedom

and independence. One can observe this 'anti-war' reporting in the case of the Gulf War between Iran and Iraq, in the Lebanese War and in the conflict between Britain and Argentina over the Falklands. Reporting has tended to concentrate on the cruelty and senselessness of war, which can be expressed visually or written about descriptively. While this is to be commended from a humanitarian and philosophical point of view, it does not help to distinguish the causes of war and hence between defence and aggression and between deterrence and war-fighting. The European media seem to have the most serious difficulties in this respect. There is an exception: the British media coverage of the conflict in the South Atlantic. The reporting here reminded one of traditional war reporting: confidence that the cause of their country was right and pride in performance. While interesting in itself, that may not be an attitude that is helpful in explaining the need to defend Western Europe against a superior military force.

Erratic Coverage

Coverage, then, tends towards the spectacular and the spectacular dominates not only the television screen and the headline but also the understanding of defence and security, often equating them with war and insecurity. Second, only very few media organizations employ professional journalists specializing in military and security affairs. For many years in West Germany only two nationally-distributed daily newspapers – the *Frankfurter Allgemeine Zeitung* and *Die Welt* – published articles and reports on defence and security issues. Even today regular, systematic reporting and comments on these subjects can be found only in these two newspapers, while others, such as the *Süddeutsche Zeitung* of Munich and the *Frankfurter Rundschau*, tend to keep up their reader's interest by a certain amount of copy dealing with security, arms control and defence. The weekly press is represented especially by *Die Zeit* of Hamburg and, with some qualifications, by *Der Spiegel*.

Third is the question of regularity. Only the *Frankfurter Allgemeine Zeitung* offers substantial continuous coverage of security and defence matters. The bulk of the press and the radio programmes address defence and security if and when there is a public debate, usually a controversial one, and when the issue can be easily defined. This was the case with the 'neutron bomb'. It is also the case with such issues as chemical weapons, nuclear arms, NATO strategy or when there is discussion of the possibility of a limited war in Europe or limited use of nuclear arms in Europe. Television on the other hand has screened a number of informative and explanatory films on nuclear arms and strategy, on the balance of forces, on arms control and on the military threat to Western security.

West Germany may not be typical of all Western European countries. Others probably do less since national defence is unlikely to have the same degree of urgency and the same controversial character as in a frontier country, where destruction would first occur in the case of conventional or limited nuclear war. Moreover in Germany the traumatic experience of a lost war dominates whenever the use of military force is discussed. Responsibility for war and for preparations for war weigh heavily on the consciences of many politicians, churchmen, journalists, and academics. It is the main theme of any discussion of the ethics and morality of national defence and deterrence, since the nuclear fact, as Professor Kurt Biedenkopf has pointed out, imposes on people a state of extreme psychological tension bordering on the unbearable.

For this reason alone arms-control proposals are followed closely in public once the issues have been clearly shaped and recognized by the media. However, the public attention span is short and this is why the media have not consistently featured long drawn out negotiations like MBFR or SALT very prominently; the subjects are too complex and detailed knowledge indispensable if one is to understand what these discussions are all about. Occupation with such themes is even less in evidence in such countries as Britain, France, Italy and Spain. The Nordic countries, the Netherlands and Switzerland, on the other hand, seem to resemble the situation in West Germany. Great occasions in international politics, such as summit meetings, can confer some sudden interest on the

subjects under discussion but the treatment given usually consists of a resumé of the record prior to the event and of the problems encountered. The British and West German media generally do quite well on such occasions. The MBFR and SALT negotiations, for example, have been rather well reported since they began and CSCE has been adequately reported. On the other hand, French, Italian and Dutch reporting has been less frequent and continuous during the last ten years or so, although the NATO 'dual track' decision of 1979 and the problems of its implementation related to the INF (Intermediate Nuclear Force) negotiation have received considerable attention in the media of nearly all West European countries.

Influence in Concrete Cases

One can single out four particularly critical and significant cases of media influence on the political decision-making process during the last few years:

- the 'neutron bomb' decision;
- the storage of chemical warheads;
- the storage of nuclear warheads;
- the *Pershing* II and GLCM deployment decision of 1979.

These and other related issues (such as 'no first use') have much to do with the perception of the East-West theatre balance in Europe, the perception of threat from the East, the concept of extended deterrence and the Alliance strategy of flexible response by controlled escalation. In other words, the issues are complex and highly technical. They are not easy to understand and to discuss.

Public debate lives on simplification and hence the media have simplified and often oversimplified the issues as have many politicians taking part in the debates. The peace movement in Europe has generally adopted a clearcut and summary formulation of the issues and has largely falsified the original propositions as they did in the case of the 'dual track' decision. Soviet propaganda has seized the opportunity offered and its disinformation campaign has been and is being manipulated by internal communist agitation within the peace movement in several West

European countries. The media, of course, have acted as media tend to do: they support or at least record the opposition to Government policies and strategy. In this respect the affiliation of a certain number of journalists with parties of the Democratic Left, with the labour movement, with churches and with student groups tends to reinforce the position taken by those organizations or groups. In such cases the media no longer act independently but rather under external influence.

One can argue, of course, that this is how most information or at least most elements of opinion are reported. However, there have been examples of rather biased programmes produced with the help of those in opposition to government policies and dominated by the 'counter-experts' of the peace movement without government or independent contributions arguing a genuine case in objective terms. Spokesmen for the Soviet Government have been granted easy and generous access to programmes for interviews and lengthy statements where spokesmen for the Government have been excluded or not been offered the same conditions. In fairness such manipulation has by and large remained the exception. On the whole the media have represented both sides in the debate even if they have tended to lean towards emotional explanations and to be critical of official policy and they have mostly featured the danger and the horrors of nuclear war where the issue was, and remains, one of deterrence and arms control.

The most spectacular case is that of the Reduced Blast/Enhanced Radiation (RB/ER) weapon or 'neutron bomb'. The coining of the label 'neutron bomb' decided the shape of the issue and the explanation offered first in the *Washington Post*, according to which this weapon would kill humans but would spare property, decided the terms of the debate. Europe rejected the 'neutron bomb' almost out of hand with public statements by politicians, churchmen, academics and journalists, few of whom had more than the vaguest idea of what this weapon was intended to do. The debate has since been clarified and broadened but not entirely in favour of NATO policies. In 1977–78 public opinion in Western Europe, in particular in West Germany and the Netherlands, had suffered a shock when first confronted with the neutron weapon. Discussion of its characteristics and significance for deterrence and defence brought out a clearer picture of its purpose but did not lead to the desired quietening of public opinion. The neutron weapon remains a highly sensitive and divisive political issue, invariably spoken of in press reports and on television in the context of its use by NATO in the early stages of a war in Europe.

During that first phase of public discussion, the 'neutron bomb' overshadowed all other nuclear weapons and the entire issue of Theatre Nuclear Force (TNF) modernization. However, no sooner was the neutron issue taken off the political agenda as a result of President Carter's decision in the Spring of 1978 to defer production when public attention turned to TNF. From 1979 that issue was fuelled by the 'dual track' decision on the modernization of long-range TNF (or INF – Intermediate Nuclear Forces). Soviet propaganda paired the neutron weapon with the ground-launched cruise missile (GLCM) and later also with the *Pershing* II. The press and television generally questioned the usefulness or desirability of new TNF systems. Press and other media commentary together with the arguments of the opponents to these NATO options in public debate created an unfavourable environment for the implementation of NATO plans. In 1981 – 82 the neutron weapon issue was revived by US procurement decisions. On this occasion it became clear that no West European government or parliament would accept deployment in their countries. In retrospect, it can be seen that the neutron weapon issue changed the entire psychological climate for TNF modernization.

The debate on the 'dual track' decision and hence on LRTNF modernization has also changed since the end of 1979. While there has been no general rejection of GLCM and *Pershing* II deployment in some parts of Western Europe, the issue has become dominant in domestic politics in West Germany and in the Netherlands and is a latent problem for any Belgian Government. The situation in Italy and in Britain seems less critical. In West Germany it is expected that the public debate in 1983, the year in which first deployment of both missile systems is envisaged, will be conducted in an emotionally charged atmosphere. The arguments have already been formulated, political parties have taken positions (some of them only provisional) conditional on the expected results of the Geneva INF negotiations. The press is in possession of more facts and figures than ever before and the Government has given more information and more political guidance for the understanding of the problem than in any other matter on public debate concerning security. In the press at least this is still an open issue – while the case of the 'neutron bomb' is politically closed.

Attention has turned also to nuclear and chemical weapons stockpiled in Europe. Some magazines, like *Der Stern* in Germany, have featured articles on these stockpiles prominently for some time and thus created an issue, seized upon by the peace movement. The stockpile issue has come up again and again in political debate at regional and local levels. The peace movement and, in particular, action groups of the extreme left (such as the Communist Party and other persuasions of the radical ecologist factions) have prepared 'peaceful sieges' of US and German nuclear weapons sites and have placed obstacles on the roads. *Der Stern* published a map of such sites in West Germany in 1981, although the sites marked were partly wrong and markedly in excess of the real number. *Der Stern* had pictured West German territory as a nuclear weapons launching pad and this bellicose picture of West Germany has been taken up both by the Communist and left-wing radicals and by official propaganda and information media in East Germany.

In this way all the issues mentioned above have been linked in order to present a kind of deadly network covering West Germany likely to attract pre-emptive strikes on a territory already overburdened with nuclear arms and delivery systems even without additional deployments. The fact that 1,000 nuclear warheads have been withdrawn since 1979 as part of the 'dual track' decision and that the replacement of *Honest John* by *Lance* has resulted in a reduction of systems and operational warheads has hardly been mentioned in media reports.

While Soviet propaganda did strongly influence part of the press and the electronic media it appears on the strength of current evidence, that this influence is reducing.

One must conclude that the media in Western Europe and particularly in West Germany have played a considerable role in determining public opinion on the issues in question. The interplay between the media, the peace movement, certain politicians and academics as well as 'counter-experts' opposing official policies and NATO programmes has been remarkable and certainly not without impact on the public, as the mass demonstrations of October 1981 and June 1982 showed.

Conclusions

Defence and security, foreign policy and military policy have become the object of closer if not always serious scrutiny by the media. The nature of the media offers easy access to dissenting opinion, all the more so since it can present itself as non-conformist and can call official policy into question. The opposition groups can raise artificial or irrelevant issues through the media and make unrealistic arguments without proper correction since those working in the media have only general knowledge and experience. Unless debates are arranged with competent representatives of Governments or advocates for the official policy, 'counter-experts' go unanswered. Since radical minorities are committed to agitation and organized to carry it through, entire audiences can – and on occasions have been – seen or heard to support the most extravagant arguments and alternative policies, such as the replacement of military defence by 'social defence', by which is meant passive resistance to a foreign occupier instead of fighting a defensive war. Deterrence is being systematically attacked as counter-productive and as leading to a general war without any evidence offered other than historical 'lessons' that 'armies will always wage war in the end'. The Press is less exposed to organized manipulation by dedicated groups than the television and radio networks but the press remains particularly wary of official explanations and statements of fact. Both have to be scrupulously correct and at the same time plausible to be accepted. Since to divulge military secrets no longer deters indiscretion among officials or investigative reporting by journalists, the debate can be dominated by selective reporting and by artificial constructs of strategy, arms programmes and defence.

The general lesson for official information policy is clear: Governments and NATO must cope with the new realities of the political process. Neither the media nor the general public can handle or absorb the information on which decisions must be based. The result is confusion and polarization on artificial, irrelevant or falsified issues whether these are nuclear policies, NATO's strategy of deterrence or the military requirements for effective defence. Governments must recognize that the media suffer great difficulties in explaining the background to political decisions to the people. The necessary clarity is often submerged by abundant or even overabundant flows of news, the relevance of which cannot always be recognized and the quantity of which can no longer be absorbed.

This makes selection paramount and confers on the media the privilege of choosing between items and arguments, entirely at their own discretion. The selection of news has always been the major editorial task but guidance when needed could be obtained by reference to established opinion, to the accepted authorities and by reference to debate between differing opinions in appropriate fora. Today the concept of national interest is no longer accepted as a matter of fact, nor can Alliance decisions be translated into national policy simply after a debate in Parliament and government decision. Nor do the media have the space or time necessary for explanation since the subjects of defence, security, arms control, and strategy do not appeal to the larger public. Hence proper selection and formulation, presentation and research become all the more important for correct reporting and balanced argumentation.

Modern journalism in Europe is not exactly conducive to such an approach, since it tends to focus on the expression of personal opinion and to side with minorities. The minorities in question claim the role of a legitimate opposition. They stake their claim in the name of non-conformism and as representatives of the citizens, who do not feel properly represented in parliaments. This claim alone makes them interesting and attractive to the media. They also make good journalism by promising spectacular scenes and lively debates which make for good political entertainment. In this way the reasons behind official decisions can be overburdened with controversy. The public begins by being confused and is then exposed to their distinct propaganda message: opposition to official policy in the guise of 'struggle for peace' and 'peace festivals' are arranged by popular 'artists for peace'. Political propaganda programmes are shown on television or broadcast on the radio carrying a message against NATO's 'dual track' decision or the 'neutron bomb' or nuclear stockpiles and usually against all of them at the same time. The Press reports favourably on such happenings, unable to see through false appearances. Part of their public, in particular the younger generation, feel in any case sympathy for the cause propagated. The media in turn follow what they perceive to be a general feeling or preference. In this way the media tend to neutralize themselves and to lose influence. In short, they are being manipulated in their desire to follow what they take to be the fashion. Governments and defence establishments that have long dominated the news and impressed the public with their authority must now make greater efforts to get across their part of the news and the truth. Education of journalists is both necessary and difficult because of concern in the media that journalists might be manipulated by Governments. The establishment of independent fora for the education of media representatives which would help to draw them into discussions on security, defence, arms control, strategy and military policy generally would seem to be the most promising approach. Media representatives must be trusted to perform the role of watchdogs. To do that effectively they should not be left alone with the committed agitators. Yet it is not easy for the media fully to explain matters, for the need to restrict classified information often results in counter-productive denial of news or lack of explanation. This has been the case with the Soviet SS–20 deployment. Not only are there differences of opinion within the community about the number but even simple counting difficulties contribute to the confusion. They cannot, therefore, be held entirely responsible for the programmes or articles they produce. It has to be recognized that the media can neither be used to justify nor to explain Government decisions. Governments must explain and defend their policies themselves and compete with those who would oppose these policies. It is not possible or desirable in a democracy to attempt to exercise control over the media even in the cause of national security. On the other hand, media sympathy for the cause of disarmament can be easily obtained since this is a natural sentiment and a sensible attitude towards war and peace. Governments must see to it that this inclination is not exploited by those who think only of disarmament without due regard for security and who are in no position to influence the policies of those powers on the other side of the East-West divide with whom they seek security through adaptation.

The Media and the Image of Defence Policy:
Japan

MASASHI NISHIHARA

In every mass society, the press and television have become major actors in the political arena and Japan is no exception. The media exerts an important political influence, first by disseminating facts or selecting from facts those that it chooses to disseminate and, second, by encouraging the public to adopt certain political values through editorials, commentaries, and even through the tone given to the headlines of news articles. Much of the credit for the successful anti-nuclear campaigns in Japan during the first half of 1982, aimed at influencing the UN Special Conference on Disarmament, should go to the mass media.

Political leaders, while utilizing the media to disseminate their views, often run the risk of being exaggerated or distorted by the media. Opponents and critics readily use the views reported to attack them and, on occasion, even to force their resignation. Because of newspaper *exposés*, many Japanese Government leaders, including several Heads of the Defence Agency (equivalent to a Defence Minister) and of the Joint Staff Council, have experienced political difficulty. Press coverage may relate to views on the Constitution, on the Japan–US Security Treaty, on nuclear issues, on the Self-Defence Forces and other defence issues, not to mention occasional political scandals. Successive Cabinets have made their defence policies deliberately ambiguous, hoping thereby to minimize the effects of media criticism.

While the mass media's political role is thus unquestionably important, there are very few cases, at least in postwar Japanese politics, in which the mass media have clearly influenced the public views on defence issues and led the public to demand that the Government shift its policy. For the past thirty years, some major newspapers have persistently criticized the Liberal Democratic (Conservative) Government for its conventional rearmament programmes, begun in 1954, and pressed their pacifist or 'dovish' views. But that has not prevented the Liberal Democrats from forming the Government for the entire postwar period, except for the sixteen months after June 1947. The Government survived in 1951 over the issue of the Peace Treaty with the Allied Powers, in 1960 over the problem of a revised Japan–US Security Treaty, and in 1972 over the matter of regaining control of Okinawa from the US. Despite the bitter attacks by the press of a government policy that has steadily increased defence spending in spite of an economic recession, Prime Minister Suzuki's Government retained much popular support for its policy during its lifetime.

There are therefore clear limits to the political influence of the Japanese media and this raises questions of how the media, particularly the press and television, function, why they have tended to be 'dovish', and how they have presented certain specific issues.

The Big Five

More than half of some 120 daily commercial newspapers, national and local, have morning and evening editions. This may be an additional factor contributing to their influence although, since they have to compete with television news programmes in the evening, the evening editions have substantially smaller circulations. Nevertheless the total circulation, counting morning and evening editions as two, amounted to some 66.3 million copies a day in 1980.[1] If morning and evening editions are counted as one set, the total circulation was still 46.4 million copies and, if this latter figure is adopted, there were some 400 copies for every 1,000 people in Japan. This compares well with other countries such as the Soviet Union (397 copies per 1,000 population), Great Britain (388), West Germany (312), the United States (287), France (214) and Italy (113).[2]

45

Five daily newspapers with nationwide circulation enjoy uniquely dominant positions in the world of Japanese news media. None of them support any particular political party nor are they supported by any party. The 'big five' are *Asahi* (7.5 million copies for morning editions in 1980), *Mainichi* (4.6 million), *Yomiuri* (8.4 million), *Nihon Keizai* (1.8 million), and *Sankei* (1.9 million). Between them they have 53 per cent of the total newspaper circulation, national and local. Although *Yomiuri* has now become more centrist, it used to carry, together with *Asahi* and *Mainichi*, almost uniform layouts and similar 'dovish' editorial views and reporting preferences but the fact that *Yomiuri*'s circulation now outnumbers those of *Asahi* and *Mainichi* has much less to do with its editorial policy shift than with its aggressive sales and promotion policy. *Nihon Keizai*, equivalent to *The Wall Street Journal* or *The Financial Times*, emphasizes the reporting and analysis of economic affairs, but still treats major political events at great length. It is considered to be a well-balanced, high-quality paper. *Sankei* is the most 'hawkish', stressing the importance of a stronger defence posture and closer ties with the United States. It also tends to be alarmist about Soviet military power and Communist ideology.

In the Tokyo area there are seven television stations (two public and five commercial) running programmes continuously from six in the morning until midnight or later. Although 98.2 per cent of Japanese households own colour television sets, the television news programmes appear to have a very limited impact on the public. Television networks in the Tokyo area, for instance, allocated in 1980 only 10 per cent of their time for news reporting and commentaries, in contrast to 60 per cent allowed for entertainment.[3] Only 7 to 10 per cent of those polled watched news and commentary programmes. In contrast, over 70 per cent of the adult population read a newspaper every day, and about 92 per cent read newspapers with varying degrees of frequency.[4] Also relatively high are the percentages of those who always read the 'serious' pages: editorials (25.6 per cent); politics (46.0 per cent); and foreign news (22.3 per cent).[5] A survey conducted in Tokyo in 1975 produced

some interesting statistics: asked why they made use of different types of media, about 60 per cent of those surveyed said that they read newspapers 'to learn of trends in public opinion and acquire their own basis for judgements and opinions', while only 30 per cent relied upon television for such purposes.[6] This is because television, while providing news analysis, rarely gives strong opinions. The exceptions are a few popular commentators such as Ken'ichi Takemura and Ryūgen Hosokawa. Both happen to put over conservative views. One media survey showed that there was 'substantial public support to make Takemura Prime Minister'.[7]

Why is the Press 'Dovish'?

The 'dovish' editorial policies of *Asahi, Mainichi* and *Yomiuri* can to a considerable extent be explained by their history. Founded at the time of the Meiji Restoration of 1868, they established the role of government critic and believed that they should enlighten the public on how Japan should be modernized. They did not see their role to be that of reporting events and analyzing them in a balanced manner.[8] Papers which supported particular governments tended to be damaged when that government fell. On the other hand, the government often attempted to control a critical press by using the security police to harass editors and writers and by controlling the amounts of paper available. Clashes between the government and the press continued until the 1930s when the government adopted strict censorship and intervened directly by interfering with press personnel management.

The journalists' failure to fight the government's control of the press in the pre-war years left them with a sense of guilt. They felt that if only they had fought harder, they might have prevented Japan from getting involved in an unwinnable war. This feeling persists today.

A constant point of reference in post-war Japanese debates on defence policy is Article 9 of the Constitution, originally drafted by the Occupation Authorities in February 1946 and put into effect in May 1947. This Article renounces Japan's right to belligerence 'as a means of settling international disputes'. When, in 1947, General Douglas MacArthur,

46

then Head of the US-dominated Allied Occupation Forces, talked about Japan becoming a neutral, peaceful country like 'a Switzerland of the Orient', the majority of Japanese endorsed his views. The Government, the press and the public all agreed. However, when the Cold War developed, Prime Minister Shigeru Yoshida, often referred to as the 'Adenauer of Japan', took a more realistic view of Japan's security by approving US foreign policies. The press immediately suspected that this was the beginning of the road to Japan's rearmament and began to warn the public of the danger. For the Socialists and Communists, as well as for most journalists, pacifism became an ideology, and they failed to give pragmatic consideration to Japan's national interests. All security issues, including Article 9 itself, have been debated between the idealists (or, as Masamichi Inoki has called them, the 'utopian pacifists') and the realists.

The occupation authorities naturally encouraged a free press, although they did censor press coverage of the occupation policies. They also encouraged the formation of labour unions in the newspaper companies' work force. Workers, now led by the Socialists or Communists, began to criticize their newspapers' editorial policies and to demand the removal of all those in positions of authority who were suspected of having supported the Government during World War II. The *Yomiuri* Company in particular had a series of serious labour disputes starting late in 1945. The disputes ended in victory for the Company in the following year, but only with the help of the occupation authorities. Many other newspapers also encountered the same difficulty, and their editorial policies have tended ever since to be affected by the ideological leanings of their workers. *Asahi*, for example, is often labelled 'red' partly at least because of its strong leftist unions.

The Pacifist Argument

Issues related to defence are naturally wide-ranging, and they are often compounded with problems of international security, foreign policies, and budgetary priorities. What is unique to the Japanese press is that their analyses of major East-West tensions treat American policies much more critically than Soviet policies. Moreover almost all defence issues are debated on legal grounds, the basis of which is Article 9 of the Constitution, rather than on pragmatic assessments of security needs. At the risk of over-simplification, typical press arguments on current issues may be summed up as follows:

1. The Reagan Administration's military programme intensifies East-West tensions and demonstrates a lack of seriousness about arms talks with Moscow. The road to peace lies through positive reductions of forces, including unilateral reductions. Japanese defence build-up is against the wishes of peace-loving peoples.

2. The USSR 'military threat' in the Western Pacific has been exaggerated by the US, which plays down Soviet internal weaknesses such as low economic productivity and ethnic tensions. The Japanese defence build-up provokes the USSR.

3. The Polish crisis has been aggravated by the Administration's policies of sanctions against General Jaruzelski's Poland and the Soviet Union. Japan should not support President Reagan's policies.

4. The Suzuki Government's policy of increasing defence was a step to military power. It was against the Constitution. Spending over one per cent of GNP for defence will lead Japan down a dangerous road.

5. Japan's economic power should be used for peace, not for war. Japan's security can be maintained externally by friendly relations with all major powers and internally by solid welfare and education programmes.

6. The Self-Defence Forces (SDF) should be placed under strong civilian control, to avoid any resurgence of their political power. Japan has to be set an example of anti-militarism. The Falkland War showed how silly the military of both Great Britain and Argentina were in fighting over such a useless, unpopulated island.

7. For Japan's SDF to participate in UN international peace-keeping forces

47

would be a dangerous step towards involvement in international conflicts. It too is against the Constitution. Japan has to show the world its strong, sincere desire for peace.

8. Japan should not possess any 'offensive' weapons. It also is against the Constitution. The Government should not give in to American pressure for greater defence efforts. Siding with the US is a dangerous course.

9. The American military presence in Okinawa can easily involve Japan in regional and global conflicts. It should thus be reduced to a minimum. Japan should have tighter control over the movement of US troops and arms in and out of the island.

10. Japan is the only victim of an atomic explosion. This should be the basis of Japanese peace diplomacy. The introduction of US nuclear weapons, including transit through Japanese waters of US ships carrying nuclear arms, should never be allowed.

In short, the leading daily newspapers attempt to present two views: that the Japanese should wish to see a militarily weak Japan contributing to world peace by not siding with major powers and by using its economic power constructively; and that successive Conservative Governments, being reactionary, are driving the nation along a wrong and dangerous road. These arguments are not just made over editorial pages but also in columns (Op-Ed pages) to which selected writers are invited to contribute and through the somewhat sensational wording used in news article headlines. *Asahi*, for instance, often carries a series of special reports, such as 'Japan Turning to the Right', 'Is the "Soviet Threat" Real?' and 'The Tilt to Military Expansion'. Every Summer, most newspapers run a series of anti-nuclear articles to commemorate the Hiroshima and Nagasaki disasters in August 1945. Every Autumn (and particularly in the last two years) the news media have paid special attention to how new budget allocations are decided for defence items.

The press also seems to have been 'outraged' by President Reagan's military programmes and alarmed by the neo-conservative political trends in Britain, Canada and Japan (and, should one also add, in Mitterrand's France?). In 1982, journalists of pacifist inclination have been encouraged by the success of the peace movements in Europe. Disproportionate coverage has been given to anti-nuclear campaigns. During the Spring of 1982, *Asahi*, for instance, had almost daily news articles, columns and editorials about the 'grassroots' anti-nuclear movements in Japan. They reported how many local communities had declared themselves to be 'nuclear-free' communities and that groups such as writers, theatrical performers, academicians, religious believers and housewives had taken part in joint petitions against nuclear weapons. As a climax to these campaigns, some 27 million signatures were collected on a petition to be presented to the UN Secretary General in early June 1982.[9] Yet *Asahi*'s headline read: 'One Hundred Million People's Petitions Submitted to UN'.[10]

Limits of Influence

Despite this activity, an examination of Japan's post-war political history clearly demonstrates the limits to the actual impact of such pacifist editorial policies upon the defence policy of the country. While raising the controversial issues (such as 'Will the Japan-US Security Treaty Endanger Japan?') and enlightening the public about such issues, most national newspapers have failed to weaken Conservative Governments or to force them to adopt more pacifist foreign and security policies. Several examples may be cited.

The constitutionality of a proposed Self-Defence Force (SDF) began to be debated soon after the Korean War broke out in 1950. The media and the opposition parties criticized the Government and maintained that the Constitution prohibited the Japanese from exercising the right to self-defence. The Government interpretation was that the Constitution did not prohibit self-defence, and they went on to establish the SDF in 1954. Despite press editorials critical of the SDF, a *Mainichi* poll taken in September 1953 showed that 48 per cent supported rearmament, while only 33 per

210

cent opposed it.[11] This issue of constitutionality subsequently came up on countless occasions, notably in a number of well-known court cases. Major newspapers have pointed to the ambiguous constitutional basis of the SDF but popular support for it has gradually increased over the years and, by 1978, as many as 86 per cent of those polled recognized the SDF as necessary for the country.[12]

The Japanese-US security relations have also caused anxiety with the major newspapers. The issues involve nuclear deployment, US military bases, defence co-operation, joint exercises, and military technology co-operation. They often pertain to legalistic arguments as to what is or what is not possible under the existing legal framework. There have been several occasions for tension. For instance, US sources, whether intentionally or unintentionally, have claimed that US warships have visited Japanese ports with nuclear weapons on board, despite the Japanese Government's persistent denials and its policy of not allowing such visits. The latest such incident was a casual claim to that effect made in May 1981 by Edwin Reischauer, who was US Ambassador to Tokyo during the 1960s. As it was printed in *Mainichi*, it became a political bombshell.[13] The major daily newspapers implied that the successive Japanese Governments had been intentionally hiding the facts from the people who, they claimed, totally opposed the visits of nuclear-armed US warships to Japan. However, a subsequent poll by *Asahi* revealed that 33 per cent of those polled supported such transit visits and 10 per cent even favoured US-sponsored nuclear deployments on Japanese soil.[14]

Perhaps the greatest impact that the Japanese press has had on the public has been its constant opposition to the revised Security Treaty between the two countries, signed in January 1960 and ratified in June of that year. Opposition groups, primarily Socialist and Communist Parties, left-wing labour unions and student organizations, were able to make their presence felt to the point that President Eisenhower had to cancel his visit to Tokyo at the last minute, causing him considerable embarrassment. This climate of opposition to the Treaty was certainly fostered by the mass media, which maintained that, if the new Treaty were ratified, Japan would be drawn into dangerous Cold War conflicts. In a pre-ratification *Mainichi* opinion survey of March 1960, 22 per cent favoured the Treaty; in a post-ratification *Mainichi* survey (August 1960), only 15 per cent favoured it, although 34 per cent thought they could not avoid accepting it.[15] Despite the opposition, despite such luke-warm support and despite the resignation of Prime Minister Nobusuke Kishi, he was in fact replaced by Hayato Ikeda, from the same ruling party, who carried on basically the same defence policy. This demonstrates the limits to the impact of the media.

Defence expenditure is currently one of the most contentious security issues in Japanese politics. The ratio of the defence expenditure to GNP is treated by the opposition parties and in the pacifist newspapers as a symbolic criterion for the Government's defence posture. Until 1965 the ratio was over 1 per cent and in 1955 it was as high as 1.8 per cent. As GNP increased sharply, the ratio went below 1 per cent, although the defence expenditure itself still increased in real terms. Late in December 1981, the Suzuki Cabinet increased its defence budget from 0.91 per cent of GNP for FY 1981 to 0.93 per cent for FY 1982. *Asahi*'s headlines included, 'Another Step Toward a Military Power', 'A New Era of Military Expansion', and 'Suzuki Selling Out to US'. It also criticized the fact that the planned rate of increase for the welfare budget over the previous year was lower than for the defence budget. The same newspaper invited liberal sceptics and opposition party leaders to give their comments, which were naturally critical.[16] Yet the public has basically accepted the government's policy for gradual defence improvement. All polls taken during the recent years of defence increases have revealed that the majority of respondents accept 'the present level' of SDF strength. The people appear generally to recognize that Japan cannot forever depend upon another power for her survival.

Conclusion

The news media certainly play a vital role in drawing the public attention to the issues, but, at least in Japan, they have failed to persuade

49

the public to adopt their editorial views. For some 20 years after 1945, the majority of Japanese were attracted to 'utopian pacifism', but, since about 1965, they have outgrown pacificism much faster than the press and appear to accept the world as it is with a mixture of cynicism and sophistication. Perhaps the Japanese people have been impressed that, despite the newspapers' constant warnings about the dangerous consequences of having a Security Treaty with the United States, Japan did manage to stay clear of the Vietnam debacle. Japan has not been involved in conflict since 1945. What is more, Japan has successfully overcome economic difficulties including the the two oil shocks of 1973 and 1979. The public seems to have been convinced that much of the credit for this should go to the distinctly conservative leadership of the Liberal Democratic party. *Yomiuri*'s gradual shift to editorial moderation is considered to be an attempt to conform to this change in popular climate. The fact that Takemura, the popular television commentator mentioned earlier, publicly criticizes *Asahi*'s views and expresses his own pro-Government views, emphasizes this conservative political climate. The people are opposed to nuclear weapons, but they seem to sense that demonstrations alone do not bring peace.

Japanese politicians and officials are extremely cautious in their remarks and in their conduct for they know that they will be extensively reported in the press and that any press criticism may be used by the opposition parties to attack them. Consensual decision-making, characteristic of Japanese political practice, requires a minimum level of co-operation from the opposition parties. The Government and the governing party, while enjoying a clear majority in the Diet, have still to move slowly on defence issues. It is in this sense that the role of the press in forcing a slow change in defence policy implementation is likely to remain important in the future.

NOTES

[1] *The Japanese Press 1981* (Tokyo: Japanese Newspaper Publishers and Editors Association, 1981), p.62.

[2] *Ibid.*, p.15. This publication actually cites '570 copies per 1,000 Japanese people', based on the figure of 66.3 million copies rather than 46.4 million copies. The writer feels that the figure of 46.4 million should be used because morning and evening issues should be counted as one newspaper copy rather than two. That would be more comparable internationally.

[3] *Japan 1981: An International Comparison:* (Tokyo: Keizai Koho Centre), p.68; and *Asahi nenkan 1979, bessatsu*, p.437.

[4] Young Kim, *Japanese Journalists and Their World* (Charlottesville, Va: University Press of Virginia, 1981), p.18. This is based on the 1969 survey, conducted by the Japan Broadcasting Association (NZK).

[5] *Ibid.*, p.19. This is based on the 1974 survey.

[6] *Ibid.*, p.21.

[7] John Marcom, Jr., 'Japan's Leading Pundit Gains Fame with Tidal Wave of Gab on the Airwaves', *The Wall Street Journal*, 11 May, 1982.

[8] *Asahi* started in 1879, *Mainichi* in 1872, *Yomiuri* in 1874, *Nihon Keizai* in 1876 and *Sankei* in 1933.

[9] *Asahi*, 1 May, 1982, morning edition. Buddhist groups claimed that they would collect 70 million petitions. *Asahi*, 1 June 1982, morning edition.

[10] *Asahi*, 11 June 1982, evening edition.

[11] *Mainichi nenkan 1979, bessatsu*, p.114.

[12] *Bōei Handobukku 1981*, p.391.

[13] The circumstances under which this incident occurred are well described by a *Mainichi* journalist, Yoshihisa Komori, who interviewed Reischauer. See his *Kaku wa mochikomareta ka* (Have nuclear arms ever been brought into Japan?) (Tokyo: Bungei Shunjū Sha, 1982).

[14] *Asahi*, 14 June, 1981, morning edition.

[15] *Mainichi nenkan 1979, bessatsu*, p.114. For the 1960 incident see, for example, George Packard, III, *Protest in Tokyo; The Security Treaty Crisis of 1960* (Princeton, N.J.: Princeton University Press, 1966).

[16] E.g. *Asahi*, 27 December, 1981, morning edition.

50

The Management of Defence Expenditure

SIR FRANK COOPER

This Paper is intended as a basis for international discussion – no more, no less – not least because of the variations from country to country of government institutions, procedures and attitudes. Inevitably the Paper reflects to a significant degree experience within the British system but it deliberately covers a wide area of ground.

Defence is – amongst other things – a major enterprise. In many countries defence ranks high on the list of public spending agencies; it is frequently the largest single management authority, particularly if account is taken of both military and civilian personnel; it often stands at the forefront of purchasing organizations both nationally and even more so within Government where it accounts for a very high proportion of central Government purchases of supplies and services; and it frequently operates large industrial undertakings of its own and has a significant impact on the fortunes of defence-related industries and on employment prospects in them.

The management of defence expenditure is superficially akin to that of a large, international conglomerate. Many of the same kind of characteristics exist – for example, international issues, major investment questions, and the deployment of a wide variety of personal professional skills. It is also true that the difference between 'policy' and 'management' is frequently incapable of disentanglement except in the most arid sense. Yet there is one overriding difference – there is no profit and loss account. The defence tests are either success through the preservation of peace coupled with the maintenance of a successful foreign policy or failure through the outbreak of war due either to inadequate force structure, which represents a failure in the management of defence expenditure, or to a political failure to convince a potential adversary that what may be an adequate structure will be brought to action. Beyond these lie the ulti-mate test of the success or failure of arms in battle.

There are many constraints on defence and its management. It is worth identifying some of them.

Constraints on Management

It would be as well to say a brief word first about the old question of whether the allocation of resources to defence should be determined by the threat and commitments or by what nations believe they can afford. Historically it is difficult to dispute the proposition that the threat only dominates when national interests – almost national survival – are perceived to be at serious risk. This is not to approve or applaud such a stance but to recognize that, particularly in Western democracies (not least in time of economic recession), there is a strong tendency for the electorate and Government to go down the road of what can apparently be afforded without disturbing too much the general tenor of national life. This path is arrived at by some alchemic process of subjective judgement rather than by logical argument. There is no objective way of deciding the size of a defence budget. Total resource allocation is neither a science nor an art.

The essence of democracy is choice. There is a constant interplay between external and domestic factors and within the domestic economy. Two of the most important choices that democracies have to make are the size of the public sector in relation to the private sector and the distribution of resources and expenditure between the various programmes that make up the public sector. Most public programmes have a definite and clearly desirable output – for example, schools, hospitals and roads. Defence expenditure is seen as more akin in the public eye to expenditure on insurance. It differs, however, very significantly from the payment of an insurance

213

premium in that it actually reduces the probability of the disaster against which it seeks to insure. Nevertheless, like many private citizens, Governments are sometimes tempted to under-insure – all the more so when economic growth is low or non-existent.

It is this background which tends to encourage medium and small democratic countries to look at each other and gives rise to suggestions that the level of a country's defence expenditure should be determined by the proportion of GDP that its allies devote to defence. This approach is a fallacy, one that is manifestly illogical and ignores the fact that what matters is the quantum of defence that is required.

There are many factors which bear directly upon the management of defence expenditure. It may be helpful to list briefly some of the major ones:

- The national system of government
- International commitments and obligations
- Good or bad intelligence
- The clarity with which defence strategy and objectives are defined
- National political priorities and public attitudes to defence
- The current politics and problems of governments (almost invariably dominated by the short-term)
- The long-term nature of defence exemplified by the emphasis on long lead times and heavy forward commitments
- Government procedures – notably, in the budgetary area:
  decision-making procedures
  availability of funds – single or multi-year basis
  annuality or flexibility of funding
  public accountability
  public purchasing policy
- The scope of the defence industrial base and scientific base and availability or otherwise of industrial competition
- The impact of factors partially or wholly outside national control such as the world economy, oil prices, foreign exchange, availability of manpower, inflation
- Rising costs of technology and the nature of modern weapon systems

- Manpower – availability, cost, skill
- The military life-style and tradition
- The nature of a country's history, its experience of warfare and military affairs
- The irresistible urge to replace existing defence systems
- The competence of the military/civilian bureaucracy
- Vested interests

This list is not remotely exhaustive and the weight of the various factors varies from time to time and from nation to nation. It is not intended to examine each item in turn. It is simply intended to illustrate some of the problems – some real, some artificial – that inevitably play a significant part in the management of defence expenditure. The central practical problems in defence management rest in relatively few areas – particularly rising real costs and the measures to deal with them; major investment decisions; and the reconciliation of the long-term nature of defence with short-term political and economic pressures. Yet ever present are other dimensions, not least the politics of national priorities, the state of the domestic economy, international obligations and public support. There are too the practical problems connected with resource allocation.

How are the resources to be devoted to defence determined? Most countries seek to plan a national programme over a period of years within the framework of a system which combines analysis with dialogue and debate founded upon a central assessment of how the economy is likely to perform over the period of the plan. In recent years many countries have been faced with difficult defence management problems because of high rates of inflation (which has made full inflation-proofing nigh on impossible), lower rates of growth than expected, and rises in public expenditure either relative to the private sector or in absolute real terms, or both. Cash flow has become increasingly important and more difficult to control. For the defence manager this has resulted in the need to make continuous short-term revisions, often of an undesirable nature. These revisions of necessity fall upon capital investment items, stocks, and military activity levels.

These difficulties can be made even more severe by the rules of public accounting which do not always harmonize with the demands of a long-term capital programme. Any business would be extremely difficult to run if it had no cash reserves or overdraft facilities. There is a strong case in the modern world for all defence managers to have a degree of flexibility, approved by the legislature, in managing the cash resources allocated to them.

How is the allocation of resources within the defence budget to be managed? There is no serious alternative to the production of a long-term plan and updating and costing it at regular intervals. Such a plan has to take account of internal and external factors. It depends crucially on the assumptions fed into it, and, with an alliance, on the successful reflection or reconciliation of national and international aspirations and priorities.

There is no one currency in which the output of a defence programme can be measured. In consequence there is no way of proceeding from data to decision through scientific and quantifiable processes. These can and will illuminate some of the choices; but the ultimate decisions are a matter of judgement, often as much political as military. There has to be a continuing dialogue and full debate, and this is provided for through detailed procedures – frequently time-consuming – within and between governments.

Rising Real Costs

The continuing rise in the real cost of defence equipment is well known. It is more than doubtful whether the consequences in terms of policies or management have been adequately studied, let alone turned into constructive attitudes for the future.

The principal reason for these cost rises can readily be identified. At their head stands the demand to exploit the outburst of advanced technology which poses new threats and demands new responses. In particular much entirely new technology has been introduced into warfare (for example, guided weapons in ever-increasing variety, computerized fire control systems, thermal imaging, satellites and nuclear propulsion). There have been major new twists in technology (switching to short-take-off/vertical-landing flight capability (V/STOL); turning torpedoes into true guided weapons; and towed array sonar). And there is real cost growth as each mark or generation of equipment becomes more complex and improved.

From studies done in the British Defence Ministry it seems that something like 60% of the equipment budget is likely to experience growth in real terms of 6–10% per annum in terms of capital and production costs. It is dubiously profitable to seek more accurate figures for the subject is detailed and complicated. The problems of comparing like with like, of weighting for multi-role or changed role, the effect (not necessarily positive) of changes in reliability and maintainability and the measuring of effectiveness obviously present formidable difficulties. Nevertheless, the increases are real. Some typical consequences are shown in Table 1.

Table 1: Relative Production Costs of Successive Generations of Equipment

Example	Nth Generation	N+1th Generation	Years Between In-Service Dates	Multiplication (Real Cost)	Average Real Annual Rate of Increase
Frigate	Leander	Type 22	14	3.0	14.0%
FGA Aircraft	Hunter F6	Harrier GR1	16	4.0	19.0%
Trainer Aircraft	Gnat Mk1	Hawk Mk1	19	1.5	2.6%
Helicopter	Wasp Mk1	Lynx Mk2	12	2.5	12.5%
Infantry Vehicle	FV 432	MCV 80	20	3.5	12.5%
Guided Missile	Sea Cat	Sea Wolf	13	3.5	19.0%
Artillery Shell	5.5 in.	155 mm L15	11	2.0	9.0%

Source: Statement on the Defence Estimates 1981: Cmnd 8121-1, HMSO, April 1981

53

This type of problem further manifests itself in terms of the investment costs of research and development (R&D) compared with money spent on production. In general the overall ratio of production to development is low – typically three or four to one. The ratio tends to become even less favourable as the planning stage is replaced by real time development.

It must be broadly true that a higher production to development ratio represents good investment. But this generalization needs to be treated with some caution. The overall ratio says nothing about total procurement costs of particular equipments or the availability of alternatives. High development costs aimed at reducing subsequent production costs could be advantageous; likewise a high production ratio could reflect unsatisfactory increases in production costs. Above all, the ratio says nothing about relevance and effectiveness.

Another phenomenon which affects the defence manager is the impact of the defence Relative Price Effect (RPE). RPE is imperfectly understood. Public sector costs tend to rise faster than prices in the economy generally and the rate varies from programme to programme. Defence prices are no exception. The main reasons appear to be: a). changes in labour productivity in manufacturing industry generally compared with defence industries; and b). movements in import prices relative to domestic costs per unit of output.

The defence RPE tends to rise when manufacturing labour productivity has improved and when relative import prices rise – and vice versa.

Historical data from a number of Western countries who reported sophisticated defence deflators covering the 1970s suggests that defence prices increased at a faster rate than general inflation, the difference being an average of 1.3% per year over the period as a whole. Substantial sums are involved and present a significant problem for the managers of defence expenditure which can only be dealt wwith either by increasing the resources allocated to defence or by adjusting the defence programme.

Manpower costs have also risen in real terms. Again quoting from British experience over the last 20 years, there was a definite upward and real trend at an average annual rate greater than 3%. However, in the latter part of the period increases have moderated to between 1% and 2%.

The major consequence of these factors taken together has been substantial reductions in the number of equipments it is possible to maintain in service. This is most noticeable in terms of ships and aircraft. If one takes 1960/61 as the base year (= 100), by 1980/81 aircraft were 50 and destroyers and frigates 45.

Meeting the Challenge of Rising Costs

Real cost escalation has been with us for many years. It seems unlikely that any Government will be able to fund over a long period of years real cost escalation on the scale indicated. Hitherto, defence managers have reacted by cutting commitments, reducing the quantities of equipment, abandoning some equipments, keeping equipment in service longer, and improving the efficiency of defence management. Inevitably, with the passage of time the room for manoeuvre diminishes.

Britain has at least been successful in a sustained drive to invest a larger percentage of the defence budget in equipment. In particular, the number of United Kingdom based civilian staff has over the last six years been reduced by more than 50,000 (up to 20% of the total) and much has been done to reduce overheads in many areas. In consequence the percentage of the defence budget devoted to equipment has risen spectacularly and so too has the real amount spent as shown in Table 2.

What more can be done? There are a number of relatively conventional initiatives which are being pursued: avoiding over elaborate operational requirements; using commercial equipment; collaboration with allies; more emphasis on sales potential; reducing through-life costs; sensitivity analysis; improved contracts procedures; exploiting stretch potential; and continuing the drive to cut overheads of all kinds.

Yet it seems unlikely that these initiatives will result in solutions which will halt the trend. Are real solutions in sight? Are they possible? External and internal pressures on defence managers almost invariably tend to aim at the replacement of an existing weapons

54

Table 2: British Defence Expenditure

	74/5	75/6	76/7	77/8	78/9	79/80	80/81	81/2*	82/3*
Percentage of defence budget devoted to equipment	31	34	35	38	40	40	44	44	46
Spending on equipment at constant 1982 prices (£m)	4025	4489	4411	4511	4683	4899	5542	5604	6005

* Estimated

system. What kind of new ship, tank, or aircraft? But is this the right question to ask? Is this the way to solve the problems of the next century? An alternative formulation might, for example, be what kind of equipment will be required in the next century to execute that part of the land battle which is currently undertaken by tanks? But even this formulation may not be fundamental enough since it needs to be related to opportunity costs in other parts of the defence programme and the overall balance of capabilities required to fulfil defence objectives and ensure defence effectiveness. What is to be feared is that conventional and conservative questions will produce conventional and conservative answers and that these, coupled with rising real costs, will inevitably diminish the quantity of defence to a point where, however high the quality, it cannot provide an effective defence posture.

Where does the answer lie? There is almost certainly no single solution. One major factor could, of course, come from measures of multilateral disarmament but the possibilities of progress are at best uncertain. Is it perhaps inevitable that the range of capabilities provided by a single nation will diminish and that increasing measures of specialization will be enforced either by *force majeure* or by deliberate intent? Military specialization in terms of capabilities and tasks has been canvassed over the years. Progress so far is not encouraging. Countries have been more prepared to give up capabilities than to exchange them with others. There is no sign of early results on a significant scale. Indeed many will argue strongly that diversity is a source of strength.

In recent years greater effort has been devoted to equipment collaboration. There are a number of good examples of both joint development and joint production in a variety of forms. Another approach is the so-called 'family of weapons', where two or more countries agree to undertake the separate research, development and production of associated weapons. This has much to commend it but it does require a degree of international reliance and trust which are not always easily found.

Will economic pressures and costs bring about further measures of industrial specialization? For example, some countries have given up manufacturing various types of aircraft and other equipment. Is there scope for specific specialization arrangements, where two or more Governments agree to depend on one another for the supply of certain types of equipment with the goal of eliminating duplication in Government-funded technological and industrial capability? Such an approach might produce considerable dividends, though it would be difficult to achieve in practice. It may be that pressures on the industrial market can achieve more than Governments. For example, firms engaged in similar fields could merge their activities to form a single international company. Governments would contract with a single company leaving the international division of work to the company. Again firms might join together to establish temporary or permanent international consortia to supply particular equipments. Such consortia would arrange for different parts of the work to be undertaken in different countries. No doubt arrangements of this kind would need to overcome a number of difficulties not least in the legal, contractual and procedural fields.

Another form of specialization is for two or more countries to make reciprocal purchases without commitment to permanent and long-term specialization. Thus country A might meet its needs for certain types of armoured vehicles by placing an order with country B, while country B might make a reciprocal purchase of helicopters from country A. Are these possibilities not worth pursuing? One particular difficulty is that most countries seek to define their operational requirements in obsessively detailed and elaborate terms. There could be an advantage in countries specifying their requirements in shorter and simpler terms, stating the problems and objectives but leaving the solutions unspecified. They could also on occasion set a target cost for the project.

Solutions such as these could share out R&D, achieve longer production runs, and lower unit costs through larger volume production, but it is difficult to believe that they will resolve the dilemma of rising costs or, as James Farrow put it, the *Quality/Quantity* quandary.

Is there a real way forward? The only safe statement is that sticking to one's last is the way to disaster. Change is difficult but change is necessary and possible. It demands hard questions and receives harder answers.

There is, however, a further area which is as yet inadequately explored, namely that it does seem very possible to make much better use of assets not exclusively devoted to defence. Virtually all countries have ships, aircraft and vehicles in use for commercial and other purposes. Given the development of modern technology, there does seem a real prospect of enhancing military capability at a marginal rather than full cost. Adaptation for alternative use seems not merely practicable but highly desirable. Many examples spring to mind – the use of container ships for the operation of helicopters or vertical take-off aircraft; the ability to adapt commercial shipping rapidly for helicopter operations and refuelling at sea; the conversion of civil aircraft to the in-flight refuelling role; and the widespread opportunities for the use of civil aircraft, helicopters and vehicles for defensive purposes and the relative ease with which a variety of military equipment – particularly missiles – could be fixed to them. Special training and special legislative powers might well be required but proposals of this kind do seem to offer a real prospect for the future. Put simply, if it is not possible to afford all the defence-dedicated systems that the planners require, is it not possible to turn modern defence technology to advantage by making use of non-dedicated assets?

Setting Priorities

This leads on to the endemic difficulty of changing defence priorities in short order despite the natural predilection of most democratic governments for short-term measures. Defence equipment programmes are long-term and involve substantial forward commitment of resources. The British position with respect to major equipment projects (some 60 per cent of all equipment expenditure) shows a more or less linear decline in planned allocations remaining from about 92 per cent at the end of year one to 40 per cent in year ten, assuming that the programme is already in full development or has entered the production phase at the start of year one.

This is not to say that commitments cannot be changed but the cash cost will be high with considerable disruption to R&D and production programmes. Moreover, major projects require massive capital investment and the further they get down the road, the more they acquire a certain momentum of their own which is difficult to stop – even if it were right on policy grounds to do so.

Increasingly manpower, both military and civilian, inhibits changes in priorities. The need to recruit and train skilled personnel also involves considerable lead times and high investment costs both in people and in the facilities to train them.

Treaty obligations and other commitments tend to militate against change and to 'institutionalize' relationships. This situation is not necessarily undesirable in itself for, where defence relationships between countries and between *blocs* are institutionalized, change can be destabilizing. Changes in weapons technology are inevitable and can in themselves, on occasion, be destabilizing.

Nevertheless, it is the task of a defence manager to see that expenditure is used to produce an effective defence posture and programme. Budgetary and administrative controls – which are increasingly the norm – have a negative rather than positive effect. Alliances provide a forum for debate, dialogue and consensus and they can offer a monitoring system over members' programmes albeit through somewhat laborious processes. The real problem of the next twenty years remains, namely how to sustain an effective defence against the background of real cost rises and exploding technology. How is the problem to be tackled?

Two suggestions are put forward with some diffidence. It can be said with reasonable safety that those who take major investment decisions now are unlikely to be in positions of authority when the investment matures. They rarely have to account for them. It might be a salutary discipline if, when these decisions were taken, it became mandatory to ask and answer two questions. What alternative would be adopted if this decision were not taken? What could be done to improve existing systems? In both cases the answers should be made part of the public decision-making process.

Secondly, there is a need for both international and national policy reviews. Virtually all planning is conservative and incremental. As a general rule it is a war which stimulates imagination and innovation – and results in change. Reviews should not be frequent – this would be totally against the long-term nature of defence – perhaps once a decade. They need to concentrate initially on strategy and major defence objectives before looking at defence equipment, manpower and infrastructure. Aims and standards should be formulated. There is much to be said for such reviews being undertaken by groups specially assembled for the task and therefore able to take a rather more dispassionate look than those immersed on a day-to-day basis of defence management.

Public Confidence

Defence to be effective requires public support and needs to command public confidence. It is doubtful whether any democracy with a disunited people could sustain a war. Public confidence is crucial to the question of allocating resources to defence. The tradition-al pattern in most Western democracies is for the executive to submit proposals for the defence programme and the consequential expenditure to the legislature. The form of the debate and approval varies from country to country but no legislature regards defence expenditure as anything other than a major area of interest.

Arrangements for overseeing the efficient disbursement of money are also important. The legislature, frequently with strong and independent professional support, exhibits a deep concern for ensuring that money has been spent on the purposes for which it has been provided and increasingly exhibits also an interest in probing wider questions of efficiency and economy.

The level of public understanding and debate of defence issues is frequently low. Too often issues are distorted by being presented as quarrels between interested parties: between the fighting Services; between Ministries; between the United States and Europe; between East and West; and between government and defence industry. Except in contexts of this kind, it is often the case that little attention is paid to management and resource allocation issues, perhaps because they are not of particular interest to most of those not engaged in the process.

There are, of course, constraints to any debate. Military secrets should not be passed to potential adversaries. Nor should advanced technology. There is also the much ignored fact that discussion tends to be inhibited by the closed nature of society in many non-democratic countries. Open discussion is denied to the closed societies of the East, whose legislatures and citizens do not have the same opportunities to consider the form and scale of their government's defence policies. This is a vital difference between the West and East. In the long term, a knowledgeable and informed public opinion throughout the world is one of the best guarantors of peace.

There are those who argue that public debate demonstrates weakness, lack of direction, uncertainty, lack of will, and simply provides information to potential adversaries. The true counter to this argument is that in a democratic nation its defence policy, its defence programme and its effectiveness in war depend on public understanding and support from those who foot the bill. It is also relevant that governments have a monopoly in defence – though doubtfully in wisdom. That monopoly needs to be probed, prodded and questioned – otherwise it will not command public support nor will it be efficient or effective.

Among the worst features of the management of defence expenditure are its frightening complexity, its inability to simplify, its continuing search for consensus, and the fact that it apparently only becomes really creative as a result of war. It finds difficulty in explaining itself to itself let alone to the ordinary citizen.

Further changes are inevitable and great skill will be required to identify the objectives to be sought and the policies to be pursued. Hard and innovative thought is needed. The demand on national resources has to be fully justified and accounted for in an open and proper way. The crucial points need to be identified and action taken.

Nevertheless, an attempt must be made to simplify issues in such a way that they are comprehensible in broad terms to the individual citizen and stand a reasonable chance of commanding his support. The almost inexhaustible store of weapons technology, rising real costs, the vicious effects of inflation, and the element of genuine incredibility which lurks about many defence issues argue strongly for seeking simplicity. The support of the nation is an essential part of defence management.

Conclusion

This Paper raises more questions than it answers. The reason is straightforward – there are no quick or easy answers. The practitioner in defence management knows full well the complexity of the defence environment in which he works. He knows the sensitivities of national and international politics, the influential weight of national history and military experience, the impact of economic growth (or lack of it), the clash between competing national priorities, the pressure of industrial policy, and the efforts that countries within an Alliance must make in order to be sure of adequately understanding each other. It is factors such as these which produce a lively debate, force out facts and encourage analysis. Controversy and argument about defence in a democracy are a source of strength not weakness and are an essential part of earning public support.

ADELPHI PAPERS

NUMBER ONE HUNDRED AND EIGHTY-THREE

IISS Annual
Conference Papers

Defence and Consensus: The Domestic Aspects of Western Security

Part II

THE INTERNATIONAL INSTITUTE FOR STRATEGIC STUDIES
23 TAVISTOCK STREET LONDON WC2E 7NQ

ADELPHI PAPER No. 183

The Papers presented here and in *Adelphi Papers* No. 182 and 184 were given at the Twenty-fourth Annual Conference of the IISS at Scheveningen, The Hague, The Netherlands in September 1982.

First published Summer 1983

ISBN 0 86079 070 3
ISSN 0567-932X

© The International Institute for Strategic Studies 1983

All rights reserved. No part of this publication may be reproduced, stored in a retrieval system, or transmitted in any form or by any means, electronic, mechanical, photo-copying, recording or otherwise, without the prior permission of the International Institute for Strategic Studies.

The International Institute for Strategic studies was founded in 1958 as a centre for the provision of information on and research into the problems of international security, defence and arms control in the nuclear age. It is international in its Council and staff, and its membership is drawn from over fifty countries. It is independent of governments and is not the advocate of any particular interest.

The Institute is concerned with strategic questions – not just with the military aspects of security but with the social and economic sources and political moral implications of the use and existence of armed force: in other words with the basic problems of peace.

The Institute's publications are intended for a much wider audience than its own membership and are available to the general public on subscription or singly.

Printed in Great Britain by Spottiswoode Ballantyne Ltd., Colchester

CONTENTS

Introduction

CHRISTOPH BERTRAM

The Papers presented in these volumes were given at the 24th Annual Conference of the International Institute for Strategic Studies in September 1982. It was a conference devoted to one of the most ambiguous, imprecise and elusive aspects of security: that of the domestic political factors influencing defence policies, doctrines and burdens. This is one reason why the subject has generally been under-explored in traditional strategic studies. The other is that, as long as domestic consensus on these matters existed, there was no real pressure to address them. But that idyllic state of affairs no longer exists. An important part of the public in our societies is no longer willing to trust governments or experts or even the media on matters of defence policy.

The Papers in this volume are devoted to the task of defining to what extent this lack of trust is justified, to what extent it is inherent in a doctrine of nuclear deterrence, and to what degree it may be remedied by more rational concepts for nuclear weapons than those that enjoy currency today. But it may be that there is no answer that can be given in isolation but that the context is all-important. Indeed, the Alliance seemed in better shape, and defence expenditures and even nuclear weapons were less controversial at the time of East–West detente than they are today; it is the break-down of that contextual framework which has brought forth the new concerns. Nuclear weapons and even defence spending for non-nuclear weapons are not in themselves sustainable by public opinion; they need to be put into a context of expectations. Only consensus on that context will make the specific military efforts acceptable and reassuring.

If this is true, then the fight for the consensus has been badly conducted. It has, at best, concentrated on specific issues: the number of Soviet missiles, the technical characteristics of the Western missiles. It has not addressed the context for which deterrence and defence are worth having.

This inability, as Rudolf Wildenmann and David Calleo point out, is attributable to a failure of the Western elites, the result of their doubts and fashions, rather than that of public opinion at large. The public continues to believe in the Western Alliance. It is impressive – and surprising – to note the massive American support for the European security link in Mr Kaagan's data, despite the frictions between the allies. But because the elites lack the confidence of a framework, they tend to narrow the debate to specific aspects which alone cannot justify the effort they demand. In isolation, consensus cannot be built on nuclear weapons, defence, the Alliance, or much else.

To regenerate the consensus, more is needed than rational nuclear doctrines or transparent defence decisions. That is helpful but not enough, particularly once the genie of nuclear doubt and anxiety has left the bottle. It also needs more than merely to indulge in the futile attempt to define defence policy by what is acceptable alone. Governments, as Johan Holst so rightly observes, have to persuade and listen. They are paid to lead, not to follow. They have failed in both in recent years. Leadership means the setting of the framework, of the context of security, in which destructive weapons can make sense. They will not make sense by themselves.

The Critique of Nuclear Deterrence

ADAM ROBERTS

The purpose of this Paper is to enumerate some of the main grounds for concern about nuclear deterrence and also to try to suggest where the critique of nuclear deterrence leads.

The ambitious title suggested for this Paper is, of course, simplistic. There is not a single critique of nuclear deterrence: there are several. Arguments about nuclear weapons are always, like other arguments, shaped by their intellectual roots and their national environment.

The most 'successful' anti-nuclear arguments so far – in the sense of leading to decisions by particular states not to manufacture or deploy nuclear weapons when they could have done so – have for the most part not been critiques of absolutely *all* nuclear deterrence: often they have had a less fundamentalist character, stressing particular aspects of a state's situation which might indicate a preference for a non-nuclear or at least a less nuclear approach. Such limited prudent arguments, important as they are, are not the main focus of this Paper.

It is the somewhat more general arguments against nuclear weapons and deterrence that form my subject here. At various times since the Second World War there has been, particularly in the NATO countries and also in Japan, a great deal of public criticism of reliance on nuclear weapons. There have also been many detailed written critiques, both of nuclear weapons generally, and of the paraphernalia which has surrounded them: strategic doctrines, delivery systems, alliances and so on. In this Paper I cannot do full justice to all these critiques, but they do have enough in common to make some crude attempt at synthesis and analysis possible.

In looking critically at nuclear deterrence, this Paper focuses mainly (but not exclusively) on Western Europe. This is not just due to the parochialism of the writer: in the past few years several issues relating to nuclear wea-pons have arisen particularly in, or in relation to, the Western European member-states of NATO; and it has been there that public expressions of concern about nuclear weapons have been most evident.

As far as the NATO member countries in Western Europe are concerned, generalizing wildly one can say that their governments have relied on two principal types of nuclear deterrence: the extended (and probably over-extended) deterrence involving the US nuclear forces in the defence of Western Europe; and the less extended deterrence provided by the national nuclear forces of Britain and France. Both types of nuclear deterrence have for a long time involved an element of threat to use nuclear weapons first in the event of massive attack – an approach which is increasingly criticized. But many critiques of a rather more limited character have been made of one or other of these types of deterrence. Such critiques, often focused on the one issue of credibility, were used largely to justify a different but still definitely nuclear approach. Thus critiques of extended deterrence contributed significantly to the development and maintenance of the British and French national nuclear forces, while McNamara's 1962 critique of national nuclear forces was connected with his advocacy of a particular type of extended deterrence. While *both* critiques may have been correct, the example confirms the obvious: that not all critiques of nuclear deterrence are necessarily compatible with each other; and that it is desirable to be reasonably clear as to whether a critique applies to nuclear deterrence in general, or just to a particular form or application of it.

My focus in the Paper on the more sweeping anti-nuclear position – the one to which I am closest – does not imply any easy assumption that the total abolition of all such weapons is a realistic possibility. The argument that nuclear weapons have been invent-

2

ed, and that man, having eaten of the fruit of this particular tree of knowledge, cannot now disinvent them, is reluctantly taken as read in this Paper. Indeed, it seems clear that the existence of nuclear weapons (being large in their effects, but relatively easy to conceal) makes general and complete disarmament an even more unattainable goal than it was before. But it is not obvious what corollary follows from the assessment that, for the foreseeable future, we will live in a world of nuclear weapons. We also live in a world where concentration camps, napalm, torture, chemical and biological weapons, and heroin have all been invented: yet most states and individuals manage to avoid relying on most of these things most of the time, and they have been brought under various kinds of national and international control. Nuclear weapons are already subject to several types of restraint and control, but perhaps, if we are going to go on living with them, further limitations will have to be accepted.

Deterrence vs. Nuclear Deterrence

The subject of this Paper is *nuclear* deterrence, not all deterrence. The distinction is especially emphasized here because, in contemporary parlance, including even some professional usage, the concept of deterrence (like that oft-misused adjective 'strategic') is still sometimes equated in a facile way solely with nuclear weapons. This is especially so in the US, which happened to assume a wide range of international responsibilities in the very years, after 1945, when she happened to have a temporary monopoly of nuclear weapons.

However, deterrence can be found at many levels of animal and human life, and in many conceptually quite distinct forms. If deterrence is defined as being no more than the clear threat of sanctions in the event of violations of territory or of basic norms, then it can assume forms that are very specific (making punishment fit the crime); and its forms may not necessarily in every case be physically violent. However, the concept of deterrence does more normally contain an element of violence and even terror.

A very strong case can be made for many forms and uses of deterrence, and it would be intellectually absurd to criticize them all collectively. Many forms of deterrence have proved very enduring over time, and are to be found in countries with very different ideologies and political cultures. In many cases, such forms of deterrence have a clear and even positive social function.

However, as bases for regulating the behaviour of individuals and groups, at least some forms of deterrence have long, and perhaps increasingly, been recognized as having severe limitations. In many countries, the progressive reduction of the types of crime subject to the death penalty may be a case in point. In many spheres of activity the most extreme threats are not necessarily the most effective: hence the curious necessity, recognized in many countries, to make people wear car seat belts under pain of summary legal action rather than under pain of death. The observation of some criminologists, that deterring crime successfully depends more on the certainty of being caught than on the extreme character of the threatened punishment, may have wider application.

In international relations, deterrence is usually, and quite reasonably, associated with the threat of using violence, and it is very deeply rooted in the system of states. For better or for worse, the world of sovereign states which we inhabit is a world in which the survival of states, or at least of their governments, depends to a significant degree on their ability to discourage or to defeat foreign military attack if they fail to discourage it. True, there are many lightly-armed states (Iceland and Ireland are just two examples), but they may in some cases owe their security either to geographical accident or to deliberate accommodation with a greater power: just as the fact that most citizens are unarmed does not mean that force has no role in society, so the existence of some relatively lightly-armed states does not itself prove that factors of power balance and of deterrence are not important in international relations.

But a state's efforts to discourage attack do not have to assume the form of threatening to retaliate on a massive scale with indiscriminately destructive weapons against the adversary's society. Historically, deterrence has often been the product of a threat to inflict losses on an attack locally: to deny an attacker victory on the ground; to ensure that any victory gained by an attacker will have few, brief or bitter fruits; to retaliate against hostages specifically taken for the purpose; or to retaliate against an attacker's homeland, but with conventional rather than nuclear means. Deterrence before Hiroshima did not consist only of that airpower element about which George Quester has written eloquently[1], but also of many more ancient military forms and methods.

Today, when considering deterrence, it is well to remember that the great majority of states in the world are neither nuclear powers themselves, nor members of nuclear alliances. While many of these states have themselves been involved in war (as too have all the nuclear powers), and many are hardly cases for emulation, there may be something to learn from at least some of them about how non-nuclear deterrence can still operate in the nuclear age; how nuclear blackmail seems in practice to be less of a threat than the theoreticians would have us believe; and how a state, even today, can manage its security policy effectively and with public support.

Non-nuclear deterrence has by no means always worked in international relations. Its failures may be a matter of considerable historical dispute, but the fact that there have been some is hardly in doubt. There was a good deal by way of deterrent threats before the First World War, but war broke out nonetheless. Moreover, conventional military balances are often very unstable. The point here is not to eulogise non-nuclear deterrence, but simply to register that it is a pervasive phenomenon, that it existed before 1945, and that it continues to exist today.

Just as a serious (but by no means flawless) case can be made for deterrence in general, so such a case can be made for nuclear deterrence in particular. The record of the nuclear powers and alliances is itself a powerful if not unimpeachable argument: World War III has been frequently forecast, and its history has been written many times, but it has not actually happened. Even if every nuclear doctrine so far developed can be shown to be flawed – containing such embarrassing impurities as patent bluff, gross political sim-plification, moral dereliction, and unwitting invitations to the adversary to take countermeasures – nuclear deterrence itself may still have, as intended, a certain frightening and impressive quality. It is no part of the argument of this Paper that nuclear deterrence can be easily abandoned by all the states which at present rely on it. The strengths as well as the weaknesses of nuclear deterrence have to be recognized.

Limitations of Critiques

At least where matters of defence and security are concerned, intellectual critiques of existing policies can represent no more than the beginning of a long journey. It is quite easy to criticize almost any defence policy as having crippling defects but the exercise will be condemned to futility unless there is something else to offer in place of the policy being criticized.

There is ample evidence from other fields of human activity that simply telling people about the perils of their situation, or advising them what *not* to do, is of distinctly limited value. If criticism of an existing policy is to be effective, there has to be a reasonably clear alternative, or at least a plausible vision of one. If there is no alternative policy in sight, then through a process of psychological denial people may well reject all evidence of the danger of their situation.[2]

The evidence of the public opinion polls tends to confirm the inadequacy of simply opposing an existing policy. Despite the obvious dangers of nuclear weapons, one poll after another, both in Britain and other countries, suggests that although particular weapons systems may be opposed by a higher percentage, a simple unilateral rejection of nuclear weapons and alliances never gets much above 30 per cent support – about the same as pacifist movements got in the 1930s. This would seem to point to the need to move the framework of debate away from the somewhat sterile single issue of multilateral v. unilateral disarmament.

Some may argue otherwise, and may say that there is political or intellectual merit in criticizing nuclear deterrence irrespective of the question of alternatives. Thus Philip Green, in his book *Deadly Logic*, made a spirited attack on nuclear deterrence, and on its theoreticians, particularly in the US:

> The false attribution of expertness to an intellectual elite, which has in effect passed a test of political acceptability, narrows rather than enlarges the channels of influence. Pseudo-science such as that of deterrence theorists thus constitutes a disservice not only to the scholarly community, but ultimately to the democratic political process as well.[3]

However, he specifically stated that it was not the job of the academic to propose what should be put in the place of the nuclear deterrence which he castigated. While one can well understand the anxiety of the American academic in the 1960s not to get caught up in the Washington policy advice shuttle, the consequent reluctance to propose any policy direction at all does look like intellectual escapism.

There is a second limitation of many critiques of nuclear deterrence, namely that they sometimes contain quite serious elements of inconsistency. Take for example the question of minimum deterrence. In Britain, some anti-nuclear writers have criticized US nuclear forces for being far larger than a minimum deterrence policy would require; and have then dismissed the British nuclear force on the grounds that it is a pathetic symbol of her fading imperial grandeur, quite lacking in any practical strategic value. While these two statements may not be logically compatible, there is a tension between them which is seldom, if ever, explored.

Anti-nuclear critiques often appear to be inconsistent on a more fundamental point. Absolute arguments may be presented against nuclear weapons, but the inevitable and depressingly hypothetical follow-up question, 'Should the US (or USSR) give up these weapons unilaterally?' often produces a cautious, even equivocal answer. Such inconsistencies appear not just in political exchanges, but also in state-to-state relations. Thus Japan, an almost allergically anti-nuclear country which has repeatedly stressed her three anti-nuclear principles, has been involved in a close security relationship with the US ever since the post-Second World War occupation.

Advocates of nuclear deterrence are no less guilty of inconsistency. For example, many of them are poor at explaining why it is good for their country to have nuclear weapons, but bad for other countries to do so; and at explaining whether, or in what circumstances, they would 'press the button'.

Such inconsistencies, on both sides of the nuclear debate, are a tribute to the complexity of the problem, and amount to an unintended confession of the partial and inadequate character of our various prescriptions for tackling it. One might end up accepting inconsistencies, in the spirit of Walt Whitman: 'Do I contradict myself? Very well then I contradict myself.' At all events, the reader is warned that some degree of inconsistency may be inevitable in a critical exercise of this kind.

Headings of Criticism
Below are listed (not in any order of priority) some of the main headings of criticism of nuclear deterrence. They seem to me to be the most serious lines of criticism; and some lines which I take less seriously (e.g. that there is no possible threat to any of the nuclear states, and therefore nothing that needs to be deterred) I have simply omitted. There is considerable overlap between the different headings.

1. Where Does It All Lead?
However impressive the achievements of deterrence in general, or those of nuclear deterrence in particular, may have been so far, this nagging question remains. To critics of nuclear weapons, it is saying that what nuclear deterrence has worked up to now is the equivalent of the man who has fallen from the top of a skyscraper saying 'So far so good' as he passes the tenth floor. Even if some past gloomy prognostications have been proved wrong, and even if one does not foresee imminent major war, the question remains: How long states can rely on nuclear deterrence without there being a conflict involving the use of these weapons? As Lawrence Freedman has written:

> An international order that rests upon a stability created by nuclear weapons will be

5

the most terrible legacy with which each succeeding generation will endow the next. To believe that this can go on indefinitely without major disaster requires an optimism unjustified by any historical or political perspective.[4]

The sense of unease about the ultimate direction of nuclear weapons policies is apparent in many statements and actions of governments of nuclear weapons states. For example, the three nuclear powers which were the original parties to the 1963 Partial Test Ban Treaty (PTBT) stated in the preamble;

Proclaiming as their principal aim the speediest possible achievement of an agreement on general and complete disarmament under strict international control in accordance with the objectives of the United Nations which would put an end to the armaments race and eliminate the incentive to the production and testing of all kinds of weapons, including nuclear weapons...

Five years later, the 1968 Non-Proliferation Treaty (NPT) not only reiterated this language in the preamble, but also stated in Article VI of the body of the Treaty:

Each of the Parties to the Treaty undertakes to pursue negotiations in good faith on effective measures relating to the cessation of the nuclear arms race at an early date and to nuclear disarmament, and on a treaty on general and complete disarmament under strict and effective international control.

Such statements, which go far beyond the modest references to disarmament in the UN Charter itself, are perhaps one type of indication that the nuclear powers at least feel the obligation to pay lip-service to the possibility of a better world. It is all reminiscent of George Orwell's discovery, when writing *Down and Out in Paris and London*, that none of the tramps he met actually called himself a tramp: they were always gentlemen 'temporarily in difficulties'.

Even if one rejects the theory that arms races inevitably lead to war, the lack of any persuasive vision, especially perhaps in Western countries, of a better future for international relations is as disturbing as it is striking. For as soon as even the possibility of nuclear disaster begins to loom in people's minds, the whole armaments process can easily seem like a series of small decisions, each in its own terms perfectly rational, which leads only to the utter irrationality of genocidal war.

2. The Catastrophic Character of a Nuclear War

It is absurd that it should have become necessary, over a generation into the nuclear age, to reassert the obvious: that a nuclear war between the super-powers would be a catastrophe, not just for this or that country, but for human civilization. But it needs to be said. Even if attempts were made to limit such a war, it would still be an unparalleled disaster, and perhaps most of all in Europe – both East and West. Alexander Pope's lines might become horribly applicable:

Now Europe's balanced. Neither side prevails
For nothing's left in either of the scales.

The widespread and justified feeling that nuclear war represents a vast and looming threat, greater than any issue which might be in dispute between the Eastern and Western Alliances, and that it is reliance on nuclear deterrence which has made nuclear holocaust possible, leads on to the conclusion that it would be better to accept the possibility of foreign attack and occupation than to risk the destruction of civilization. The slogan 'better red than dead' is a somewhat simplistic encapsulation of this position: since socialist states tend to be fairly heavily militarized and have even got into armed conflicts with each other, it is more doubtful than ever whether 'red' and 'dead' are real alternatives. Overall, one cannot be happy about the narrow and simplistic depiction of choices which leads to such conclusions and slogans. Simply to make a state vulnerable to occupation by a nuclear superpower is not a very attractive proposition in itself, and might not in the end contribute greatly to international stability. All this points to the need for (though it does not

6

establish the possibilities of) non-nuclear means of defence, to which reference is made at the end of this Paper.

But as long as defence is presented as an essentially nuclear matter, based on the threat to unleash total war, it is inevitable that at times of international tension or crisis, or at times when new weapons decisions are under discussion, many citizens will conclude that such a defence is worse than the evil against which it is supposed to protect them.

3. How Much Stability Has Been Achieved?
Public scepticism about nuclear deterrence may owe something to doubts as to how much stability has in fact been achieved by these weapons, whether such stability as exists may be due to other causes as well, and whether stability really is supremely desirable as a goal.

The evidence that international relations today are unstable, while it should not be exaggerated, is indeed plentiful. The Soviet intervention in Afghanistan in December 1979, the continuous stream of wars in the Middle East, and the Argentine invasion of the Falkland Islands in April 1982 (the most flagrant attack there has yet been against a territory held and administered by a nuclear power) have all been reminders that we still live in a world in which norms against resort to force are far from strong. Of course deterrence theorists can reply, in each of the cases cited, that if only deterrence had been stronger, if only commitments had been clearer, if only the politicians had had more sense than to negotiate with the adversary, if only a few warships had been sent in time . . . These arguments have considerable merit: but so, too, does the perception that some degree of muddle, confusion, and misunderstanding may be inevitable in politics and international relations, and that the causes of some conflicts are very deep-seated.

True, it was never claimed for nuclear deterrence that the possession of nuclear weapons by a few states could bring about general stability. But in the US some claims very close to this were made, and apparently believed, at the height of East–West detente. Now, almost a decade later, talk of a 'generation of peace' and of a five-cornered structure

of power all sounds hopelessly dated. The considerable confusion in US foreign policy-making in the past few years – in part the consequence of the rival foci of power in the State Department, the Pentagon and the White House – has contributed greatly to the sense that, in tackling nuclear problems, man has more power than wisdom at his disposal.

For all the concern about international stability, and about the means by which governments reach decisions, Europe seems remarkably stable; and the argument that nuclear weapons have contributed to this stability is serious. The continent which was the cockpit of two world wars in thirty years has now experienced no major war for over thirty-five years. Part of the explanation for this may be that Europe is where the two great nuclear Alliances meet. But there is something absurdly simplistic in the oft-repeated contention that it is nuclear weapons which have kept the peace in Europe. In the past, for example in the nineteenth century, Europe has had long periods of peace, which was hardly due to nuclear weapons. Today, other factors may be involved. It is possible that Europe has been kept at peace not so much by nuclear weapons in particular, as by the general presence in Europe of two major outside powers; that the memory of two past World Wars, both sparked off in Europe and largely fought there, is itself a deterrent to war; and that the remarkable internal political stability of most European countries has contributed to international stability. Certainly the wide range of factors contributing to European stability needs to be borne in mind: where such factors are not present, nuclear deterrence may be inapplicable, as witness the distinctly lacklustre results of (and disappearance of) NATO's Asian clones, CENTO and SEATO.

European critics of nuclear weapons sometimes make a rather different argument: not that these weapons have contributed relatively little to stability, but that they have contributed too much, that the Cold War, now descending on us again, has frozen Europe into an absurd and brittle condition of ideological division. Undoubtedly, part of the attraction of the European Nuclear Disarmament (END) movement has been its appeal to a vision of Europe which, however vague, represents a sharp move away from what is perceived as the thraldom to the two major blocs. Edward Thompson expressed the matter with characteristic pithiness when he said:

I am not quite sure how the third, European, perception so suddenly emerged, although we did something about it ourselves. It is this. We are pig-in-the-middle while an interminable and threatening argument between born-again Christians and still-born Marxists goes on above our heads.[5]

The case of Poland is sometimes cited as proof of the deleterious consequences of the division of Europe into two nuclear blocs. The political developments of 1980–81, sparked by the growth of Solidarity, symbolized to many people a reassertion of a European political culture against super-power control; and the introduction of martial law in December 1981, after very heavy pressure from the Soviet Union for a restoration of order, seemed as clear a triumph of the bloc principle as had the military *coup d'état* in Chile eight years earlier, in 1973. A few people in the West, including some theoreticians of nuclear deterrence, had before December 1981 expressed rather frankly their concern that a greater degree of Polish independence could be bad all round for international stability, especially if it served to encourage neutralism and unilateralism in the West. Thus in his 1981 Reith Lectures Laurence Martin said that 'the Polish crisis is dangerous for NATO as well as the Warsaw Pact'.[6] No statesman in the West reacted to the imposition of martial law in December 1981 quite as cynically as Louis Philippe in 1831, who said of the suppression of the Polish revolt in that year: *'L'ordre règne à Varsovie.'* But the thought may still have been there in some form.

The very mention of Louis Philippe is a reminder that international solidarity among conservatives pre-dated the invention of nuclear weapons and the emergence of NATO and the Warsaw Treaty Organization. One cannot lay the blame for the order, such as it is, now reigning in Warsaw entirely at the door of nuclear weapons: almost any imaginable security system, whether autonomous or within an alliance, is bound to place some premium on order. But a conception of order which sees a threat in a non-violent workers' movement with limited goals is vulnerable to the charge that it reduces the possibilities of peaceful change, and thwarts assertions of national independence and political freedom.

4. Instability in Weapons

Alongside the general instability of international relations, there is a more particular instability of a technical character, Neither weapons nor the cost thereof has stood still. In the NATO countries in the past few years there has been a succession of bitter controversies surrounding new nuclear weapons and delivery systems: the neutron bomb; cruise missiles and *Pershing* II; the British *Trident* programme; and the MX missile. Whatever the technical explanations for them, these weapons give rise to quite genuine concerns: the 'neutron bomb', that it is a nuclear 'solution' to a conventional problem (massed tank attack) and is thus a first-use weapon; cruise and *Pershing* II, that they are nuclear weapon systems whose deployment was decided upon in haste before they had been tested, that they are of a type and range bound to be regarded as a direct threat by the USSR and to be targeted accordingly, and are to be located on land in densely-inhabited parts of Western Europe; the British *Trident* programme, that its expense involves some de-emphasis on conventional forces, and that it was bought 'off the shelf' with an offensive power vastly greater than the Ministry of Defence wanted; and that the MX missile, originally intended for an elaborate new basing system, is perhaps the first major weapons development in history which has nowhere to go.

It may be regrettable that so much of the public debate has centred on these new weapons, rather than on underlying issues of overall defence policy, or on existing weapons which may be even more dangerous, such as the so-called 'battlefield' nuclear weapons in Europe. But there are reasons for the attention given to the new weapons systems, not least that their accuracy seems to fit in with certain ominous statements about nuclear 'warfighting'. Moreover, the argument made for

8

some of these new systems, that they are absolutely essential to the maintenance of deterrence or to the credibility of the Alliance, serve as unintended reminders of the weaknesses of nuclear deterrence. If the whole nuclear house of cards is as fragile as some of the experts would have us believe, small wonder that some want to demolish the house rather than replace or add to the cards.

The number and scale of recent weapons developments, both in the East and the West, do seem to demonstrate a dangerous dynamism in the technology of nuclear weapons and delivery systems. As in the Cuban Missile Crisis of 1962, so also with the Soviet Union's SS–20 missile programme today, new weapons deployments seem themselves to contribute to an increase of tension between states. To the extent that this is so, and it is of course far from being a complete explanation of international tension, the arms competition between East and West may have the character of a self-perpetuating process, not only continuously producing new weapons, but also the condition of tension which is needed in order to justify the defence efforts of states.

The deployment of multiple independently-targetable re-entry vehicles (MIRV) has been a sad example of the destabilizing effects of new weapons systems. In the mid-1960s, when they were being developed, many warned that they might create a situation where each side had more means of nuclear attack than the other side had nuclear targets, a situation in which ideas of pre-emptive blows are bound to flourish. Such warnings have been more than amply fulfilled in the intervening years.

5. Disturbing Trends in Strategic Thinking

It is not just in the hardware itself, but also in the purposes and strategies attached to it, that there is evidence of inner dynamism and restlessness. Deterrence and war-fighting can never be totally distinct modes of thought, and perhaps one should not be surprised at the re-emergence of a war-fighting approach. What is particularly odd and alarming about this re-emergence is that it includes an element of faith that one side might prevail in a nuclear war, or that such a war once started might be geographically limited.

Before pointing to particular disturbing trends, one general observation about contemporary nuclear strategic thought should be made: much of it, for understandable reasons, has a highly mathematical and technical character. Strategists working out how many MIRV can be got into an ICBM may be the modern equivalent of mediaeval theologians working out how many angels can be got on the head of a pin. To the layman much of this exercise seems academic in the worst sense, not least because the actual conflicts in the world never involve such neat numerical balances, and always involve a large political element. While academic strategists, who have largely taken over from bishops the role of blessing the bomber, discuss multiple warheads which they hope will never be used, in Afghanistan tribesmen fight a nuclear super-power with weapons which might be from the Imperial War Museum.

The current disturbing trends in strategic thought have their origins in an earlier failure. The attempt to reach a stable state of nuclear deterrence, based on the concept of Mutual Assured Destruction (MAD), suffered successive blows not just because the Soviet Union developed other ideas, but also because MAD itself seemed to have several built-in flaws. For military men it is a somewhat bleak and depressing approach, and for civilians it is hardly better. MAD seemed to a few Western Europeans to foreshadow an era in which the nuclear forces of the two super-powers cancelled each other out, leaving the Soviet Union with a preponderance of conventional military power in Europe; and some Americans had even stronger objections to it. The return by the United States to a declaratory policy of counter-force has been due to many factors, but also produces its own problems. If counter-force is better than MAD in that it is more discriminate, it is worse in that it seems to put a premium on acting pre-emptively, and to require continuous quantitative and qualitative improvement of nuclear arsenals. This argument, though hardly new, is still persuasive.

In the past few years, there has been particular instability in matters of strategic doctrine. The various US statements on the possibility of a limited nuclear war in Europe, or indicating that a nuclear war might be less than a catastrophe for the United States, may have been intended to strike fear into the hearts of the Soviet leaders (and may indeed have done so), but their principal visible effect has been to cause alarm and despondency in Western Europe and in the United States herself.

A related but even more ominous sign of the instability of weapons and strategy has been evident in the 'window of opportunity' theory. It is true that the idea of a 'window of opportunity' can help to explain at least the timing of the outbreak of some past conventional wars. As far as nuclear weapons are concerned, the 'window of opportunity' theory presumes that one side might exploit a temporary preponderance in nuclear weapons to attack the nuclear forces of the other side – or at least to use the threat of such an attack as a lever for exerting very heavy pressure on the adversary. This theory has always been questionable, because it implies a decision to launch an enormously risky adventure for reasons which seem more technical than political, which are difficult to square with almost any ideology or ethical system, and which in any case seem to take little account of the degree of confusion, malfunction and muddle (to say nothing of mass murder) likely to attend such an exercise.

However wrong-headed they may be, the various American (and Soviet) statements indicating some degree of willingness to fight a nuclear war, and some expectation that one side might prevail in such a war and recover within a few years, may be an outcome not only of the warped minds of their authors, but also of a more general belief that in order to maintain nuclear deterrence it is necessary to talk tough and even to accept openly the possibility of a nuclear war. One could conclude, therefore, that the heightened fear of nuclear war in the past few years is an inevitable consequence of nuclear deterrence itself. Many would challenge this, including the late Bernard Brodie, who argued eloquently that 'the balance of terror is decidedly *not* delicate'.[7] But military doctrine as well as deployments seem to have been informed, especially in recent years, by a more restless and Manichaean spirit than Brodie's.

6. Risks of War by Accident or Miscalculation

The possibility of war occurring as a result of some technical accident – the mis-reading of radar information, computer malfunction, the freak detonation of a nuclear weapon in a plane crash – has been the subject of much attention since at least the early 1960s.[8] Numerous precautions have been taken by the nuclear powers to guard against such dangers, and the evidence would appear to be that these precautions have been effective. However, the continuing stream of reports of accidents involving nuclear weapons, and of control computers malfunctioning, suggests that an accidental or unauthorized detonation of a nuclear weapon is by no means impossible. Moreover, any regression to situations or strategies placing a high premium on pre-emption or quick reaction could heighten the risk of an accident degenerating into an accidental war.

War arising from miscalculation, rather than from a technical accident pure and simple, seems more plausible. Indeed, there has been a strong element of miscalculation in the outbreak of many past wars: for example, miscalculation about the capacity of one's own forces or those of an adversary, about the likely reactions of third parties, or about the degree of commitment of an adversary to a particular cause or piece of territory. Rival involvements of the super-powers in Third-world countries, especially those with political systems or frontiers whose legitimacy is contested, may offer particular risks of a war arising at least in part through miscalculation. Kissinger's fears that the Middle East of the 1970s might be like the Balkans in the decade before 1914 was one expression of the concern about the wisdom of super-powers hitching their wagons to unstable stars in troubled areas.

7. Possibly Indecisive Character of Nuclear Weapons

Although immensely destructive, nuclear weapons may not be quite so decisive. True, the evidence is persuasive that they did help to end the War in the Pacific in 1945, though in circumstances where it was clear that Japan's defeat was inevitable anyway, due both to the military victories of US forces, and to the entry of the USSR into the war.[9] Like strategic bombing, of which they are the logical and terrible culmination, nuclear weapons may perhaps sometimes be more effective in hurting an adversary's society than actually stopping his forces from fighting.

In peacetime, the threat of use of nuclear weapons seems to be a blunt and largely unusable instrument. In the period since the Second World War there have been relatively few cases in which their use has been threatened in any way as a means of securing a particular change of policy, and these threats do not seem to have been outstandingly successful. The success of US policy in the Cuban Missile Crisis is perhaps the most striking exception, but it owed much to local naval preponderance. The idea that non-nuclear countries must necessarily be vulnerable to nuclear blackmail finds relatively little validation in the actual events of the past thirty-seven years.

8. Nuclear Deterrence and Obstinacy
It is frequently asserted that nuclear weapons have made states cautious, and there is some evidence for this. But it is by no means the whole truth. Nuclear weapons may also have a particular tendency to lead to obstinacy in the foreign policy-making of the powers which possess them. The US persistence in remaining in the quagmire of Vietnam appears to have owed much to a belief that a superpower has to demonstrate its steadfastness, commitment and resolve, otherwise its willingness to use its forces (including nuclear forces) on behalf of other allies around the world might be doubted. The whole problem of great powers being concerned with face, and with demonstrating *urbi et orbi* their determination or willingness to use force, is scarcely new, but it may have been made more difficult by the development of nuclear weapons.

9. The Particular Problems of Extended
   Deterrence
One of the reasons for the current concern about nuclear weapons is that many US commitments to distant territories – commitments which have traditionally been of great concern to western strategic writers – pose especially sharp problems now that the Soviet nuclear forces are so large. The scope of these problems of extended deterrence is peculiar to the US: no other nuclear power has them in so clear or extensive a form. The issue is not simply the distance of commitments from America herself, but also that they involve the issue of first use. The arguments over extended deterrence are numerous and complex, and one may dismiss some of the more extreme attacks on the idea. The French view, that because it would not be logical for the US to risk nuclear war for the sake of Europe, she will therefore not do so, betrays a curious faith that what is illogical must therefore be impossible. But if extended deterrence cannot be written off by logic alone, the attempts to resolve the obvious problems of extended deterrence by new strategic doctrines or new weapons have something of the air of the attempts to make the Ptolemaic system credible by the frenetic adding of epicycles. It is possible that one partial resolution of the problem might come from a recognition that nuclear weapons are not the centre of the strategic universe, and cannot do very much more than cancel each other out. This raises the difficult question of 'no-first-use' policies, discussed below under a separate heading.

The problem of extended deterrence today, at least in the European context, is simply an extreme version of the classic problem of nuclear deterrence itself. Either it seems all too credible, to the extent that it frightens allies and leads to counter-action by adversaries; or it does not seem credible enough. The fears being expressed simultaneously in Europe, though for the most part by different people, that the US would be all too willing to fight a so-called theatre nuclear war in Europe, and also that the US nuclear guarantee is hardly credible, confirm this. Although the idea of extended deterrence is not yet by any means dead, its evident weaknesses so far as Europe is concerned may suggest the need to find solutions going beyond the inevitable Alliance fudge-words of 'flexible response'.

10. Nuclear Weapons and the Laws of War
The relationship between nuclear weapons and the Laws of War is an area of vast com-

plexity and deep moral ambiguity in which the layman fears to tread.

The use of nuclear weapons against most targets, and especially of course their use against cities, would obviously risk running counter to the most basic principles of the Laws of War: discrimination, protection of non-combatants, and general prohibitions of the use of weapons which are particularly inhumane. The immediate carnage resulting from such use of nuclear weapons would on its own be enough to justify such a statement. The long-term after-effects – psychological and physical – have been well documented in Hiroshima and Nagasaki. Weapons which have severe after-effects, even when the conflict in which they were used is long over, have traditionally been restricted under the Laws of War.

Yet there are in fact relatively few formal international legal prohibitions which explicitly govern the use of nuclear weapons in war (as distinct from their testing and deployment in peacetime, which comes under the rubric of arms control). As a class, nuclear weapons have escaped the kind of formal international prohibition on use which has been applied (mainly through the 1925 Geneva Protocol) to gas and bacteriological weapons. The failure of states to conclude any binding multilateral agreements explicitly restricting the use of nuclear weapons in war is remarkable, especially in view of the fact that in the nuclear age some eleven major multilateral agreements on various aspects of the Laws of War have been concluded. In relation to 1977 Geneva Protocol I, additional to the 1949 Geneva Conventions, Britain and America have gone so far as to state explicitly in reservations that the terms of this Protocol do not apply to nuclear weapons. However, in a number of statements the US has recognized that the principles of law relative to the use of weapons in war 'apply as well to the use of nuclear and similar weapons'.[10]

The reason for the dearth of laws-of-war type controls over the use of nuclear weapons is that there is a degree of tension between the underlying ideas of the Laws of War on the one hand, and of nuclear deterrence on the other. The Laws of War seek to limit war: in particular, to reduce its cruelty, and to ameliorate its effect on non-combatants, on persons who are *hors de combat*, and on neutral states. Most forms of nuclear deterrence, by contrast, seek to prevent war by making it so utterly frightful that states will fear to resort to it. Thus these two major approaches to the control of war appear to clash irreconcilably.

One may doubt whether in fact the clash between ideas of deterrence and the Laws of War has to be so absolute. The two approaches can be compatible in some respects. To accept certain principles of limitation of the use of force does not necessarily make the outbreak of war more likely, and indeed it may make it less so. If war does break out, the Laws of War may combine with deterrence to keep the war limited: for example, in Europe in the Second World War, explicit deterrent threats, clearly articulated on several occasions, underpinned the 1925 Geneva Protocol's prohibition on the use of gas and bacteriological weapons. Indeed, that agreement, including the reservations appended to it by many states, has the character of a 'no-first-use' agreement, although it also goes beyond this.

There are respects in which a laws-of-war approach may not be altogether incompatible with nuclear deterrence, but this is not necessarily in every case an occasion for rejoicing. Because assured destruction of an adversary's society is plainly in conflict with the Laws of War, a laws-of-war approach could easily be used as a subtle argument for counter-force strategies, the disadvantages of which hardly need further elaboration here.

So far, however, nuclear deterrence has not been effectively integrated into the laws-of-war stream of thought, and it appears indeed to largely reject this major traditional approach to the control of armed conflict. For all the limitations of the Laws of War, so sharp a rejection of an approach which is still deeply imbued in much of our thinking about the problem of war is itself a reasonable basis for criticism of nuclear deterrence.

11. Continued NATO Reliance on First Use
Under the rubric of 'flexible response', NATO has continued to rely on a policy of possible first use of nuclear weapons – a policy which

is increasingly questioned, not least by soldiers and ex-soldiers.[11]

If nuclear weapons have to be developed and deployed, the most obvious restriction on their employment would appear to be a policy of no first use. This could be a matter of unilateral deployments and declarations, or of multilateral agreement of the laws-of-war type. The most recent expression of a no-first-use commitment was contained in the message from President Brezhnev which was read out by Soviet Foreign Minister Gromyko in his speech at the United Nations on 15 June 1982. Since China has also made some no-first-use declarations, of the five recognized nuclear powers it is only the three NATO members which do not have such a declaratory policy.

The reasons why NATO has not felt able to accept a declaratory policy of no first use need to be recognized. Partly they are the outcome of history and inertia. In an era of US nuclear dominance, and European exhaustion following the Second World War, the idea of reliance on possible first use was more understandable than it is today, at least in the sense that it posed far fewer practical problems. Today, granted that the aim of NATO is to deter all war (not just nuclear war) between East and West in Europe, the adoption of a no-first-use policy would not be at all easy – especially as the Warsaw Pact states have numerical advantages in some categories of conventional weapons, and geography, as in Berlin, does not favour a purely local defence. The idea underlying NATO's approach to deterrence – namely that *any* aggression must be seen to risk incalculable consequences – seems to go against the grain of the no-first-use idea. Moreover, it is often doubted whether 'no first use' statements amount to very much more than paper promises.

While these objections are serious, they are far from being conclusive. Even if the idea of a formal no-first-use declaration is rejected, there is still a powerful case for moving away from a strategy of actual dependence on first use.

However, many reasons can be advanced for supporting not merely an avoidance of dependence on first use, but an open policy of no first use. NATO threats to use nuclear weapons first are increasingly incredible, because of the extreme vulnerability of Western European societies to retaliation and the uncertainty as to whether any nuclear war could remain limited. Moreover, in any European conflict, any NATO decision to use nuclear weapons would be far more likely to divide the Alliance than unite it, and might thus achieve the opposite effect from the intended one. To get away from reliance on first use might also reduce the need for at least some of the land-based nuclear weapons systems in Western Europe, the presence of which has caused great public concern. Furthermore, no-first use policies might, by clarifying the limited nature of the role of nuclear weapons, assist public acceptance of the need to maintain or increase a non-nuclear defence capacity. There have been some proposals, which might or might not involve negotiated agreements, to try to link a NATO no-first-use approach to certain reductions in Warsaw Pact forces, and such proposals might offer a means of tackling the admittedly difficult problem of a perceived imbalance in conventional forces. Words are important, and statesmen go to great lengths to explain the purposes and intentions behind the enormous power they possess. Clearly enunciated policies limiting first use, accompanied by necessary changes in military deployments, might contribute both to a sense that nuclear weapons are subject to some reasonably clear governing idea, and also to East–West stability. The failure to move in this direction confirms the general impression that the nuclear arms race has a dynamic of its own, unrestrained by human intellect or purpose.[12]

12. The Limits of Arms Control

For over twenty years, arms control has been widely regarded as the best available means for keeping weapons development, especially in the nuclear area, under some kind of limitation while at the same time maintaining a balance of power. This approach has a serious and well-articulated rationale.[13] Moreover, many important arms-control measures have been agreed, including the 1963 Partial Test Ban Treaty, the 1968 Non-Proliferation Treaty, and the 1972 SALT I Accords. However, these and similar agreements can be criticized on many grounds, and they have plainly been an inadequate brake on the momentum of the arms race. By the beginning of 1982, with the SALT II Treaty still in difficulties, and with other negotiations on nuclear and conventional arms control apparently becalmed, some of the hopes held out for arms control a decade or two earlier seemed to have been disappointed. Whether anything can be salvaged in the various negotiations now proceeding – including the talks on intermediate-range nuclear weapons in Europe, and also START – remains to be seen. But the limited nature of the achievements of arms control so far, and its failure to improve East–West relations in a lasting way, add to the sense that arms control has delivered rather less than was once hoped of it.

The accusation made against arms control is not merely that it has failed to tame the tiger of the nuclear arms race, but also that in some respects it has whetted the tiger's appetite. It does seem to have contributed to the current preoccupation with numbers and equivalences; and it has also contributed to the idea of bargaining chips – weapons projects developed so as to form a kind of currency to be used in arms-control talks. Because of these factors, arms control may even have contributed to the arms race it was intended to curb.

This is not to suggest that arms-control talks should be abandoned. For one thing, the criticisms summarized above do not apply equally to all arms-control negotiations and agreements. Moreover, the first eighteen months of the Reagan Presidency have been an object lesson in the folly and political costliness of soft-pedalling arms control. What the criticisms above do particularly suggest is that arms control, although it may help at the margins, is not likely on its own to improve political relations, to stop the arms race, or to offer a way out of the dilemmas of nuclear deterrence.

13. Moral Criticisms of Nuclear Deterrence
The application of moral principles to international relations is notoriously strewn with pitfalls, and the old saying, that the road to hell is paved with good intentions, might yet be proved more literally true than its anony-

mous author can ever have intended. The question of the morality of nuclear deterrence is by no means simple, and no course proposed is free of moral difficulty.[14] But the moral problems involved in reliance on nuclear weapons are serious and need to be faced. Although morality is sometimes perceived or presented (particularly in discussions about the problem of war) as a series of absolute and abstract rules imposed from outside, it is perhaps better seen as a necessary condition of human existence in a world which has always been dangerous; and as a means of asserting general interests as distinct from purely individual ones, or long-term interests against short-term ones. Hence moral considerations are not, and certainly should not be seen as, separate from practical ones.

The recent increase in public concern about nuclear weapons does have a moral element, a sense that to base a defence policy on the threat of genocide is wrong. Even though plenty of criticisms can be made of the adequacy of this position, it does have a strong basis and it does exist as a powerful political fact. One could put it even more strongly: a policy which could involve us in the roles of Nazi and Jew at the same time has unique moral defects. Moreover, a policy which explicitly relies on the possible first use of nuclear weapons is particularly questionable on moral grounds, especially where (as in the case of NATO) such a policy is the result of a reluctance to make necessary efforts in the field of non-nuclear defence.[15]

Although the idea that nuclear weapons are uniquely evil is vulnerable to criticism (other means of warfare also being indiscriminate, and some imaginable uses of some nuclear weapons being quite discriminate), there is a moral and practical case for trying to prohibit or in other ways restrict the use of nuclear weapons as a class. As many have remarked, there is simply no firebreak in war anything like as clear as that between non-nuclear and nuclear weapons.

14. The Economic Costs of Nuclear Weapons Systems
The question of the costs of nuclear weapons has featured prominently in recent public debates, especially in Britain where the cost of

14

the *Trident* D–5 programme is a particularly sensitive matter. It is certain to take a larger slice of the defence budget than did the *Polaris* system it is due to replace. The old idea that nuclear weapons offer a cheap form of defence – 'a bigger bang for a buck' – is not easily sustainable today. The evidence on this is not just that the nuclear weapons states (China perhaps excepted) also happen to have defence budgets which, whether expressed in dollar equivalents or as a percentage of Gross National Product, are somewhat above the international average. It is also that nuclear weapons systems, being basically unusable for almost any rational purpose, have not proved a substitute for more conventional air, naval and ground forces. Nuclear weapons and their associated delivery systems are simply one more claim on already stretched defence budgets and, because of budgetary constraints, the pursuit of nuclear deterrence may, for some states at least, involve some inevitable degree of reduction of conventional defence and deterrence.

15. The Failure to Protect Populations

It is an odd fact that the western states which are either nuclear powers themselves, or are closely allied to nuclear powers and are likely to have nuclear targets on their territory, have done relatively little to protect their populations from the effects of nuclear attack. This is particularly clear in the cases of the US, Britain and France. One might also note in passing that there are no anti-nuclear civil defence preparations whatsoever today in the city of Hiroshima. All this does not prove that democracies are incapable of planning for the worst. The highly developed civil defence preparations of Sweden and Switzerland suggest that something can be achieved.

What is the explanation for this paradox, that some non-nuclear and neutral states have made a serious effort to protect populations whereas the Western nuclear powers have not? In nuclear powers there seems to be some official reluctance to admit that the seamless web of nuclear deterrence might fail. When the governments of these powers have tried to introduce civil defence programmes (as in Britain and the US in the early 1960s, and again in the last few years) they have done so

in an amateurish way, and have run into a deadly combination of apathy and opposition, based in part on a concern that precautions against war looked like preparations for it. The considerable professional disagreements about how much, if anything, civil defence measures could salvage from the catastrophe of a nuclear war have added to the reluctance of many governments to go in for more than half-hearted half-measures where civil defence is concerned.

All these considerations apply less strongly in some of the non-nuclear states, including Switzerland and Sweden. It is less difficult for them to concede the obvious, that nuclear deterrence might fail. Since they are non-nuclear, their civil defence policies can hardly look provocative. To the extent that they might not be nuclear targets in a war, there are greater possibilities of protecting the population, for example from hazards such as fall-out. A further significant factor is that the countries which now take anti-nuclear protection seriously have long traditions of interest in civil defence, pre-dating the invention of nuclear weapons; and their defence policies, overall, are of a kind which is comprehensible to the population.

Within nuclear states, by contrast, the position regarding civil defence is peculiar and ugly. The populations lack even those elementary forms of protection which might at least help in the event of a major nuclear weapons accident. By contrast, the governments are reasonably well protected. A system of nuclear deterrence which leads to such a bizarre outcome is not easy to defend.

Where Does the Critique Lead?

The preceding headings – which are certainly incomplete – involve several distinct strands of criticism. There is the danger of nuclear weapons accident and of nuclear war, concern about which must be at the heart of any critique of nuclear deterrence. There is the lack of confidence that any war, and especially any nuclear war, between East and West could remain limited. There is the sense that the calculations of strategic planners, both East and West, have acquired a logic and momentum of their own. There is the doubtful morality of relying on essentially indiscriminate weapons, and the doubtful practicality of relying on what amounts to a threat to commit mass suicide. There is the uncomfortable fact that nuclear deterrence has not led towards stable super-power relations, or to extensive measures of arms control. Because of the criticisms enumerated, nuclear deterrence does not seem to be a system which should inspire much confidence even in the relatively short term, let alone *sub specie aeternitatis*.

But any attempt to proceed beyond this point must start by acknowledging the inadequacies of what one might call the politician's fallacy: the assumption that because one can denounce the faults of an existing system, therefore one's own preferred nostrum must work. To a large extent we have got into the present situation precisely because the possible alternatives were widely deemed to have failed, or to be inadequate. The mere reiteration of shop-soiled ideas is not likely to achieve very much.

Thus the well-known deficiencies of the idea of general and complete disarmament are not reduced – indeed they may in some respects have been increased – by the development of nuclear weapons. As for the idea of world government, some of the very problems that have made the nuclear situation worse – the extreme distrust between the superpowers, and their commitment to unilateral arms build-ups as a means of achieving security – also have had the effect of ruling an international security authority even more firmly off the agenda than it was in the first place.

Because of the difficulties and defects of such multilateral approaches, a thoroughgoing critique of nuclear deterrence cannot avoid pointing in a unilateral direction. But this does not mean that the debate has to be framed around the one idea of unilateral disarmament as conventionally conceived: i.e. a single act of renunciation, in which it is perfectly evident what kind of defence which is rejected (nuclear deterrence), while that which is to take its place is not so clearly defined. Moreover, the conventional argument for unilateral disarmament, that the moral gesture by one country would be likely to affect other potentially nuclear countries, may reasonably be doubted.

To formulate defence policy on the basis of a single anti-nuclear moral imperative is questionable, both because there are bound to be accusations of continuing to rely, consciously or unconsciously, on another state's nuclear umbrella; and because the usual unilateralist emphasis on a single country acting alone seems to down-play the value of a collective attempt, which could be within the framework of existing alliances, to get away from the present and questionable state of affairs where defence is largely equated with nuclear weapons.

As distinct from unilateralism as traditionally presented, a different approach, justified as much on prudential as on moral grounds, needs to be considered: namely the attempt to develop non-nuclear policies for defence and deterrence, relying to the greatest extent possible on conventional military forces, or on militia-territorial type forces, or on organized civil (i.e. non-violent) resistance as a means of discouraging attack or resisting occupation. Thus the choice presented here is not just between nuclear deterrence on the one hand, and conventional deterrence on the other, but may involve an element of unconventional defence and deterrence. This could involve the use of resistance in depth, at least in populated areas, against possible foreign attack and occupation. Such resistance might assume either guerrilla or non-violent forms.

However, I have written on such approaches elsewhere,[16] and must observe my own warning against shop-soiled ideas. There is no use putting a greater burden of weight on such approaches than they are capable of carrying. To take civil resistance, it has occurred (and continues to occur) in a quite wide variety of circumstances, not least in occupied areas. Its successes, though few, have not been entirely negligible. However, there are many fundamental difficulties in trying to make this technique the sole basis of a state's defence policy, and it rather has the character of being a special option for special circumstances.[17] As for a territorial-militia type of defence, this does have considerable strengths, as Yugoslavia's maintenance of her dependence since 1948 has demonstrated: yet this case also shows that such an approach is not necessarily a total escape from involve-

16

ment with nuclear powers: Yugoslavia has at times sought a modest degree of reinsurance with the US. Moreover, the Yugoslav approach would not easily be transplanted to the very different geographical and social terrain of Western Europe. But other ideas for a non-nuclear defence might have greater validity there, including some which have been put forward for a re-vamped conventional defence with greater reliance on the much-vaunted precision-guided munitions and on territorial forces.

Whatever the difficulties of such approaches, and they are undeniable, it is well to remember that the overwhelming majority of states muddle through in one way or another without nuclear weapons, and the problems of non-nuclear defence, though serious, should not be exaggerated.

The fact that many states have remained non-nuclear does not mean, however, that a completely non-nuclear world is a realistic possibility. For the foreseeable future it is not. Even a complete renunciation of all nuclear weapons by the western states alone is not only exceedingly unlikely but also – if one is to be frank – not necessarily to be desired. The fact that nuclear deterrence has crippling weaknesses does not mean that it has no validity whatsoever.

At this late stage one important observation, both methodological and substantial, should be made. Even though the emphasis throughout this Paper has been on general criticisms of nuclear deterrence as such, inevitably, by the mere act of searching for evidence and thinking about issues, one focuses not on the general, but on the particular. To a large extent, it is particular ideas about the role of nuclear weapons which one questions, particular strategies which one criticizes, particular nuclear weapons or deployments about which one is most concerned. It is not only inevitable, but also right, that concern with the general issue of nuclear deterrence should not be at the expense of attention to more particular and limited issues.

So far as NATO member states are concerned, many of the criticisms of nuclear deterrence enumerated in this Paper might point to particular and limited conclusions which can be briefly encapsulated as follows:

- It may well be that, just as civil nuclear power generation has not lived up to all the early hopes for it, so also nuclear weapons have introduced considerably less of a revolution in warfare than has often been thought, especially in the NATO member states. To a large extent, though perhaps never completely, nuclear weapons simply cancel each other out, and other forms of military preparation and deterrence have not lost their importance.

- The idea that only the most extreme threats deter, or that they are particularly effective in doing so, is fallacious. The most extreme threats, and the weapons which go with them, may not only inspire the adversary to take counter-measures, but may also deter us as much as potential adversaries. This is a particularly serious consequence because the primary mechanism by which NATO deters is simply by hanging together, and it cannot do so on the basis of making threats which are, and will remain, internally divisive.

- Naïve doctrines of prevailing in a nuclear war, and misleading justifications of civil defence conveying the idea that nuclear war might be less than a catastrophe for civilization, are evidence of the bankruptcy of much nuclear deterrence theory, and should be abandoned.

- The issue of a 'no-first-use' policy regarding nuclear weapons, and the changes in deployments to go with it, needs to be reconsidered. While the difficulties of this approach, and its inherently meliorist character, are evident, it could make possible the introduction of a defence system which had a higher degree of credibility, which was understandable to the public, which reduced the pressure for new and controversial nuclear weapons deployments, and which reinforced the crucial firebreak between nuclear and other weapons.

- In order to deter attack effectively without resorting to the threat of first use of nuclear weapons, the conventional military forces of some NATO countries need to be restructured or even increased; and preparations for unconventional forms of defence, which also have some deterrent power, deserve to be more fully considered within NATO than they ever have been in the past.

- Despite all the difficulties of so doing, the continuing validity of the underlying principles of the Laws of War (especially the avoidance of the use of particularly inhumane weapons, and the protection of non-combatants) needs to be vigorously asserted. The issues raised by this approach are not simple, but cannot be ignored in view of the obvious necessity of maintaining clear limits on the use of arms in a century which has already seen far more deaths in war than any other, and in a world which is grossly over-armed and seems likely, for better or for worse, and to a greater or lesser degree, to remain so.

NOTES

[1] George H. Quester, *Deterrence Before Hiroshima: The Airpower Background of Modern Strategy* (London: John Wiley, 1966). For an interesting discussion of pre-nuclear deterrence more generally, focusing mainly on events before the First World War, see particularly Richard Rosecrance, 'Deterrence and Vulnerability in the Pre-Nuclear Era', in Christoph Bertram (ed.), *The Future of Strategic Deterrence* (London: Macmillan Press, 1981), pp. 24–30.

[2] For an interesting essay arguing this point, see Lester Grinspoon, 'The Truth is Not Enough', in Roger Fisher (ed.), *International Conflict and Behavioural Science*, (New York: Basic Books, 1964), p. 238*ff.*

[3] Philip Green, *Deadly Logic: The Theory of Nuclear Deterrence* (Ohio: Ohio State University Press, 1966), p. 276.

[4] Lawrence Freedman, *The Evolution of Nuclear Strategy* (London: Macmillan Press, 1981), p. 399.

[5] E. P. Thompson, *Zero Option*, (London: Merlin Press, 1982), p. 37.

[6] Laurence Martin, *The Two-Edged Sword: The Reith Lectures 1981* (London: Weidenfeld and Nicolson, 1982), p. 33.

[7] Bernard Brodie, *War and Politics* (London: Cassell, 1974), p. 380.

[8] See for example the report, *Accidental War: Some Dangers in the 1960's*, prepared under the auspices of the Mershon Center at Ohio State University in 1960, and published in Britain by Housmans, London 1962.

[9] See for example the account of the Japanese decision to surrender in L. Giovanetti and F. Freed, *The Decision to Drop the Bomb*, (London: Methuen, 1967), pp. 275–95.

[10] US Delegation to UN General Assembly, Press Release, 10 December, 1968.

[11] See for example, Field Marshal Lord Carver *A Policy for Peace* (London: Faber and Faber, 1982), pp. 11, 58–60, 101–6.

[12] For recent advocacy of a no-first-use policy for NATO, see McGeorge Bundy, George F. Kennan, Robert S. McNamara and Gerard Smith, 'Nuclear Weapons and the Atlantic Alliance', *Foreign Affairs*, Spring 1982. See also the reply by Karl Kaiser and colleagues in the Summer issue, and Michael Howard's letter in the Fall issue.

[13] See for example Hedley Bull, *The Control of the Arms Race* (London: Weidenfeld and Nicolson, 1961).

[14] For some excellent discussions of these issues, see Geoffrey Goodwin (ed.), *Ethics and Nuclear Deterrence* (London: Croom Helm, 1982).

[15] For a discussion of nuclear weapons in relation to the 'just war' tradition, and proposing a no-first-use approach, see James Turner Johnson, *Just War Tradition and the Restraint of War: A Moral and Historical Inquiry*, (Princeton: Princeton University Press, 1981), pp. 357–65.

[16] In the volume I edited, *The Strategy of Civilian Defence: Non-violent Resistance to Aggression* (London: Faber, 1967); and in my *Nations in Arms: The Theory and Practice of Territorial Defence*, (London: Chatto and Windus, 1976).

[17] This was my conclusion in *Total Defence and Civil Resistance: Problems of Sweden's Security Policy*, a report prepared for and issued by the Research Institute of Swedish National Defence, Stockholm, 1972, pp. 151–81.

18

Domestic Consensus and Nuclear Deterrence

HAROLD BROWN

The Breakdown of Domestic Consensus on Nuclear Policies

Over the past eighteen months, a substantial breakdown has taken place in the domestic consensus on nuclear policies in Europe and the United States. In Europe, mass demonstrations have occurred against the deployment of new US cruise and *Pershing* II ballistic missiles. These include not only young protesters, ecologists, ’ and other cause-adopters. Many middle-aged, middle-class, conservative Europeans have also joined. Especially among the Protestant churches, leaders have condemned in ethical and religious terms the development and possession of nuclear weapons, nuclear deployments, nuclear strategy and nuclear deterrence.

Somewhat later, parallel phenomena have appeared in the United States. One movement to educate the public about nuclear war is led by physicians, galvanized by the realization that destruction of civilization includes destruction of physicians. Another is the Ground Zero movement. That makes no prescriptions, but tries to awaken the public to what the effects of a nuclear war would be and to the importance of taking steps to prevent nuclear war. Respected public figures, many of them well experienced in defence, foreign policy and arms-control matters, urge a nuclear freeze or a ‘no-first-use’ doctrine or both. The Conference of Catholic Bishops in the United States is considering a pastoral letter on nuclear issues. In its early draft, it asserts a ‘no-first-use policy’ as a matter of pastoral doctrine. It denies the morality of retaliation in kind to nuclear attack if that retaliation is aimed at or collaterally inflicts massive civilian casualties. And it questions the morality of retaining a nuclear capability at all.

The present protest movement exceeds in size anything yet seen in the United States, and equals that of the nuclear disarmament campaigns in Europe in the late 1950s and early 1960s. Moreover, it may well have more influence in electoral politics. Non-Communist parties in Europe either sharing power or with a chance of coming to power (the British and Dutch Labour Parties, the ‘Greens’ in West Germany, and segments of the Dutch Christian Democratic Appeal Party (CDA) and German Sozialdemokratischepartei deutschlands (SPD) not only oppose the 1979 NATO decisions but also favour unilateral disarmament, at least in terms of a denuclearization of their own territories. Some of these positions are rather imprecise. Others might not be implemented by their present proponents if they come to power. Nevertheless the public protests and party positions indicate severe disquiet about situations and about policies. These include the nature and direction of the nuclear arms competition, the nuclear doctrine of the Western Alliance, the policy of nuclear deterrence, and the delegation of decisions on these matters to the experts, professionals and political leaders who now have that responsibility. Domestic consensus has clearly eroded in most Western countries with respect to national and alliance nuclear policies. Why?

First, US-Soviet relations have markedly deteriorated. Indeed, they are now worse than at any time since the Cuban missile crisis, perhaps since the death of Stalin. Some observers and publics see Soviet assertiveness and expansionism (in Poland and in Afghanistan, and previously in various parts of Africa) as increasing the chance of a nuclear war. Others perceive an increase in the willingness of the United States to take risky military action as having the same effect. The former view is based on Soviet actions; it continues to dominate US opinion. The latter is held by many in Europe. They point to the Reagan Administration’s own policies and to its

19

rhetoric about Soviet intentions and behaviour.

Second, the prospects for arms control appear bleak. A major element in public unease is the failure of the United States to ratify the SALT II Treaty, even though that can be attributed largely to the Soviet invasion of Afghanistan. Another is the absence in US security policy under the Reagan Administration, until recently, of an arms-control and reduction component. In the past a serious commitment on the part of the United States and other Western governments to negotiations on nuclear arms has offered hope to publics in the countries of the Alliance. (Some opponents of arms-control negotiations would claim it has been a false hope.)

The Reagan Administration has now made a commitment, still rather ambiguous, to continue to observe SALT II. It has resumed strategic arms talks in the form of START, and continued negotiations on intermediate-range nuclear forces (INF). These actions have helped to limit suspicions that arms control no longer plays any part in US policy. To the extent that US proposals have been seen as reasonable, they have operated to lever the US position among informed European publics back up the precipice over which it was falling. But there is still uncertainty on both sides of the Atlantic as to how serious this commitment to negotiations is. Moreover, the setting forth of negotiating positions in the form of public speeches, however necessary under the circumstances, is unlikely to be helpful to the negotiating process.

The problem of perceptions of fairness of US positions is not eased by the inadequacies in Soviet proposals. The USSR is not expected by many among Western publics to make fair proposals – or rather, many Western commentators see fairness in Soviet proposals whose reciprocal equivalents they would find unfair if made by the United States. While it is not realistic to see arms control as a road to peace separate from the resolution or habituation of major political differences, arms control can and should stabilize military balances. The new barriers in that road are, therefore, a significant concern.

Third, governments have in their nuclear strategies appeared to give more emphasis to fighting rather than to preventing nuclear wars. Numerous declarations by various officials in the Reagan Administration, which the President himself has lately been careful to avoid, have been a significant factor in public disquiet both in Europe and in the United States. These include statements, or implications, that nuclear wars can be won, or that they could well be limited in geography or intensity, or that even all-out nuclear wars can be survived given enough shovels. Some Europeans have expressed particular concern that geographical limitation could mean limitation to Western and Eastern Europe with the United States and the USSR as sanctuaries. Failures and malfunctions of warning systems have heightened public fears that nuclear war could occur, if not by plan then by accident.

In short, a reversal has taken place since 1979 of what had been an easing of concerns in the United States and Europe about nuclear weapons through most of the 1970s. That relaxation had developed from an expectation, realized to a significant extent during that period, that budget limitations, arms-control efforts and nuclear strategies would all act to limit the Soviet–American competition and reduce the risk of nuclear war. During the 1980s, publics have with good reason come to be less confident about the effectiveness of each of these limits. When further reminded about the real existence, and presence in their midst, of nuclear weapons by the proposals for new missile deployments, their concerns have been transformed into a major political force.

At the same time, another public in the United States and in some cases also in Europe has become increasingly worried since the early 1970s by the build-up of Soviet forces and what they consider the failure of the United States and the Allies to meet the challenge. They are concerned about the possibility that the USSR might undertake what it may see as limited nuclear wars or a winnable all-out nuclear war. While the claims by these groups and their opinion leaders about US strategic nuclear inferiority are at best misleading, the concerns polarize the publics and further undermine domestic consensus on nuclear policy. These groups press to have nuclear capabilities that exceed and doctrines that match what they consider to be those of the USSR. They and the officials who share their positions widen the spread of views and make it less likely that any particular doctrine or programme will be generally accepted. Moreover, the unlimited force requirements and costs that could be derived from such an approach deepen the divisions in the electorate.

In the US, in Europe, and in Japan as well, there is a widespread perception that the Soviet Union is ahead of the Alliance in strategic nuclear, medium-range nuclear and conventional forces. On both the left and on the right, proponents respectively of social welfare programmes and of greater military strength push for a choice of one at the expense of the other. The more extreme among them exaggerate the real need for choice between the two as much to reduce the activity they oppose as to increase the activity they support. Although this conflict is, in my judgment, more a political one than the consequence of a genuine and sharp economic limit, it further polarizes public opinion and makes agreement on all defence programmes more difficult. The cost of nuclear forces is about one-quarter that of conventional forces. But the concern in the countries of the West is greater about nuclear than conventional war. Moreover, the question of 'how much is enough?' can be more sharply posed to publics with respect to nuclear forces. For both reasons, real or overstated competition for funds with non-military needs can hit sharply at nuclear force programmes. Continuing economic distress – 'stagflation', unemployment – intensifies these effects. That has significantly eroded support for nuclear programmes in conservative business circles in the US, and I would judge in Europe as well.

PD-59: The Role of Public Views

In the past, public attitudes have not been given much attention in the definition of US and NATO nuclear policies. A recent example is the formal US adoption in PD-59 of the countervailing strategy. This refinement in US nuclear strategy was prompted by several concerns. The first was the major build-up in Soviet offensive nuclear capabilities. But the emphasis in Soviet writings on nuclear warfighting and war-winning strategies also

played a part. So also did the planning and programmes for protection of Soviet political and military leadership in case of nuclear war, and perceptions, however questionable, of a massive Soviet civil defence programme.

In the countervailing strategy, the United States would put at very high risk the elements of Soviet power and society believed to be held as valuable by Soviet leadership. Thus either in limited or all-out nuclear war the Soviet leadership would stand to lose more than it could possibly gain. By these steps, including the ability to respond to the unlikely contingency of a limited attack in a (believably) limited way, the US aim has been to continue to deter both limited and all-out attack by the USSR. The method of this deterrence is to be through persuading Soviet planners that they could not win a nuclear war at any level because both sides would lose.

Thus the policies embodied in PD-59 were directed primarily toward planning for US strategic nuclear forces, and the deterrence of Soviet attack on the United States. They were, however, consistent with NATO's plans for the use of nuclear weapons in either selective attacks or all-out nuclear war. The studies and analyses which formed the basis of PD-59 were completed in 1979. An outline of the proposed doctrinal refinements was presented in the unclassified January 1980 Annual Report of the Secretary of Defense. It had been foreshadowed in earlier public statements, and was subsequently discussed both in closed Congressional testimony and in NATO Ministerial Meetings. Those presentations had been accepted as rather routine

The public announcement of PD-59 was delayed until the Summer of 1980 primarily because other events in Iran and Afghanistan took priority. The August 1980 public statements made all the doctrinal points described above. At the same time, the Carter Administration attempted to use this modest refinement in US nuclear strategy as a response to charges that the USSR had achieved strategic nuclear superiority. It hoped thus to gain support from (primarily US) publics who were swayed by those changes. To a degree, this backfired. It encouraged widespread though mistaken interpretations by the public and by some experts in the United States and Europe that PD-59 signified a major step toward a strategy and plan for fighting a limited nuclear war. Moreover, few hardliners were impressed. Thus the handling of PD-59, by trying to gain the support of conflicting constituencies, lost more than it gained. The ground should have been more carefully prepared among journalists and non-governmental experts.

Overstatements by some officials, in describing PD-59, of belief in the feasibility of fighting nuclear war helped to increase public fears that governments take the prospect of nuclear war lightly. Perhaps the saddest aspect of all was the failure of the following Administration to learn from the effects of the inadequate emphasis, in its predessors' public handling of the matter, on PD-59's overwhelming concentration on deterrence rather than warfighting. Instead, Reagan Administration officials appeared to clasp nuclear warfighting to their bosoms. The public reaction, in the US as well as Europe, was predictable.

Steps to Rebuild the Consensus
In the future, political leaders and governments will have to pay more attention in defining and articulating their nuclear policies, to re-establishing and sustaining public support and confidence.

First, they will need to be sensitive to understandable concerns, and be prepared to respond directly to rational arguments about the possibility and potential consequences of nuclear war. Moderate and reasonable publics in the United States, Europe and Japan have such concerns and express such arguments.

That the nuclear arsenals of the super-powers could end civilization not only for them but for the countries of Europe and Japan as well is a legitimate reason for public alarm, even though it is not a new reason. The damage to society that would result from use of the nuclear arsenals is no greater than it was ten years ago; indeed it may be marginally less. The increase in popular concern derives more from a public perception that such a war has increased in likelihood.

The deterioration of US–USSR relations that drives that perception is also real, and serious. Yet the enormous destructive potential of the nuclear capabilities of both sides, in a continued approximation to parity, continues to introduce caution into the policies of both super-powers. Just as before, their nuclear arsenals act as a strong deterrent to Soviet–American military conflict. Moreover, in Europe and the Far East, the existence of US conventional and theatre nuclear forces, and the mutual Alliance commitments, make any Soviet adventure too dangerous to be undertaken at all lightly. In South-west Asia, where US forces remain offshore, nuclear force is – properly – more remote, and a political-military security structure is lacking, the potential danger of war is probably greater. But in the light of the enormous complexity of the regional political situation in South-west Asia and the great variety of its rivalries and hatreds, both the USSR and the West will have a number of non-military options to promote their interests. As a result, they may not feel driven to undertake military actions. In any case, neither super-power could have great confidence that such actions would succeed in the light of the military and political uncertainties.

Yet, even if these concerns of publics are addressed, the fundamental problem of the threat of nuclear war will still exist. In order to retain or regain public support for national and Alliance nuclear policies, political leaders must convince their publics that they are doing what can be done *to minimize the chances that a nuclear war will occur.*

All Western nuclear policies should continue to have deterrence as their central objective. Essential strategic nuclear equality is also a requirement, politically even more than militarily. Other objectives, such as escalation dominance, warfighting, or successful defence against a nuclear attack, are very unlikely to be at all feasible. Actions or doctrines seen as pursuing them as major goals could not only undermine deterrence but would probably further erode public support for nuclear policies. However, Western nuclear policies should seek to maintain and improve deterrence of Soviet aggression by creating and declaring the existence of various nuclear responses appropriate to the nature of a nuclear attack. Thus the US would not be limited to an all-out response, against all classes of targets and with the entire forces, independent of the nature of attack that prompts the response. These options should pose likely costs to the USSR that outweigh reasonably foreseeable gains to her. The nuclear forces must therefore provide capabilities for attacks of various magnitudes against a variety of classes of potential targets. It is also of critical importance that the nuclear forces should have a high degree of survivability and should not require either quick decisions on their use or plans for launch under attack.

Arms-control initiatives can also serve to reduce the possibility and risks of nuclear war. The actual achievements of arms control have been modest, but they have not been a trap. The United States and the Allies need to pursue control, limitation, and reduction efforts seriously and forcefully. This will test whether the Soviet leadership is prepared to accept equitable and verifiable agreements. A more explicit acceptance by the current US Administration of the SALT II provisions as upper limits on forces would give some reassurance to publics on numbers of launchers, warheads, fractionation, and numbers of new missile systems permitted to be developed. Freezes of particular categories of weapons should not be excluded from consideration, though, because deterrence has complex ramifications, my own view is that a general freeze has serious pitfalls. For example, to freeze nuclear-armed bombers and cruise missiles but non-nuclear air defences undermines the stability of deterrence. Even major reductions in present forces on both sides would reduce public concerns more than they would reduce the damage potential of nuclear war but, if carefully crafted, such reductions could improve the stability of deterrence, which should continue to be a major goal of strategic weapons programmes and arms control alike. Thus efforts towards nuclear arms limitation and reduction remain urgent, but publics must not be deceived into thinking that arms-control efforts – even the most successful that have been achieved, such as the ABM Treaty and the SALT Agreements, or conceivably achievable by the START negotiations – will remove the threat of nuclear destruction.

The West needs also to define a set of technical, political and military security policies more effectively aimed at reducing the incentives for nuclear proliferation. These will not be easy to devise, still less to implement. A world with more nuclear states would not necessarily (though I think it likely to) increase the risk of nuclear war between the super-powers but surely the interactions of all states would become more precarious and complex. The super-powers share a common interest in postponing the spread of nuclear weapons.

To reduce the risk of nuclear escalation from a conventional war, Western governments need to design a strategy and programme for improving conventional military forces.

Many difficulties stand in the way of programmes to improve the conventional balance. The industrialized democracies can surely afford the economic costs of such a posture but they will confront major political inhibitions, at a time of slow economic growth, to even marginal changes in the allocation of resources. Moreover, the governments differ in their attitudes toward the threat posed by the Soviet Union. They vary in their views of the appropriate division of military responsibilities in Europe, the Pacific and elsewhere. Major splits mark their perceptions of the nature of the problems in South-west Asia, and of the proper balance between political and military responses to those problems.

The patchy progress in meeting the force structure, equipment, and development objectives agreed to in the NATO Long-Term Defence Programme (LTDP) by heads of government at the 1978 Summit is hardly encouraging. Moreover those improvements in the NATO-Warsaw Pact balance continue to be needed, along with further concentration on concepts that might radically improve tactics, training and force utilization.

Despite its difficulties of achievement, a more reassuring conventional balance is, paradoxically or not, one of the major ways to reduce dependence on nuclear deterrence and in turn to reduce the chance of a nuclear war. It would raise the nuclear threshold and provide an incentive for reductions in nuclear weapons both unilaterally and in arms-control agreements. It would also create some basis for a believable no-first-use commitment. Whatever its dangers (which could well still predominate in that case) such a commitment would have advantages in gaining support for security policy in general. An improved conventional balance could at the same time even produce a greater acceptance of present nuclear doctrines and programmes by publics in Europe, in Japan and in the United States.

To reduce the pressures for the early use of nuclear weapons in case of a war, NATO needs to readdress the requirements for battlefield nuclear weapons. Consideration should be given to reducing their number as the new artillery rounds are produced, and to their eventual replacement by systems of at least one or two hundred kilometres range. These replacements would need to be assigned to the same categories of targets. Their accuracy, yield and target acquisition systems would have to be the same, in order to pose the same threat to massed attackers. All of those features are technically feasible. Organizational and command arrangements may be more difficult but the greater range and the higher level of control would, advantageously, reduce the risk of being overrun and the pressure for devolution of release authority. Automaticity of use would be reduced. Some may argue that would reduce the effectiveness of deterrence. I believe the reduced risk of escalation to nuclear war substantially outweighs that fear and such a shift would surely increase public confidence that nuclear war had been made less likely.

To reduce the chance of nuclear war through misperception or a misunderstanding of intentions or actions, the US and the Soviet Union need to improve their procedures for crisis management. A hotline exists but it needs to be upgraded in reliability and function. It is not clear that procedures exist at both ends to ensure prompt delivery of messages to a level where decisions can be made.

One possibility is the establishment of a joint US–USSR operations centre. It could be staffed by military officials and diplomats of both nations, able to communicate with their own headquarters in respective capitals, and thus, in times of crisis, to explain ambiguous events or apparently threatening actions. They could share intelligence when it was decided by their superiors that doing so would reduce risks of war through misunderstanding.

But these actions could be taken only on higher authority. Such an arrangement could thus confuse matters by setting up a parallel chain of communication. Moreover, where would the centre be located? And what about problems or deception? These and other objections properly generate a degree of scepticism, and would have to be examined closely. So far the thought remains only an interesting speculation.

A less far-reaching step would be the establishment of regular consultations between senior defence officials of the US and USSR, both ministerial and professional military. This was proposed at the Vienna Summit in 1979 but Soviet actions in Afghanistan and the US failure to ratify SALT II aborted the prospects of such a development. Such consultations and exchanges are particularly needed when super-power relations are bad. It is precisely then that they are most difficult to establish. Therefore they should be initiated on a regular basis whenever a modest easing of the present state of affairs allows.

The US has given considerable attention to eliminating the possibility of the use of nuclear weapons through accident, unauthorized action, or mistaken perceptions of being under attack. Computer malfunctions have given false warnings, and individual sensors have given mistaken signals. But confirmation from separate sensors and circuits is required for substantial movement even toward recallable actions and no irreversible actions can be taken without human judgments at the highest political level. Past malfunctions are indeed reason enough for serious concern and system revisions have been made but in fact US nuclear forces have never begun to come at all close to being launched in a retaliatory mode.

Improvements can be made in other ways to reduce the chance of accident. Better security against conventional attack or hijacking of field-deployed tactical weapons are examples. Another is continuing improvement of mechanical controls that prevent firing without insertion of the correct code. Increasing the distance of stationing of ballistic missile

24

submarines and intermediate range missiles from each other's capitals, to lengthen their flight time and increase warning time, has also been suggested. Verification poses difficulties, but the idea is worth exploring.

Ultimately, the West needs a policy for relations with the Soviet Union which, accepting the almost certain continuation of competition and risk of confrontation, includes political and economic incentives for constructive behaviour, as well as disincentives for disruptive behaviour. All of this is a very large order. And in the end, the adversary nature of the relations between the Soviet Union and the industrialized democracies, together with the existence of substantial numbers of nuclear weapons, means that the catastrophe of nuclear war will continue to remain a real possibility. The world will remain a correspondingly dangerous and frightening place. This limits what can be done by Western leadership in banishing the shadow of nuclear war. But publics are entitled to assurance that, insofar as it lies within the power of Western leadership, what can be done to reduce these dangers is being done.

Public Presentation
Political leaders will also need to discuss forthrightly with their publics both all the requirements and all the ambiguities of nuclear deterrence.

With respect to strategic nuclear doctrine and forces, the public must be persuaded, or repersuaded, about deterrence. Two propositions must be embodied in the case thus made. First, deterrence is, under any reasonably foreseeable circumstance, a necessary pillar of security. Moreover, it is also the only available strategy that carries reasonable confidence of success – even though it has elements of ambiguity and uncertainty, and includes contingency planning for morally repugnant behaviour. The ethical dilemma of threatening the destruction of a hundred million ordinary people in retaliation for a similar attack on the West as a way of deterring such an attack cannot be avoided: it has had to be lived with over the past quarter of a century. The practical dilemma created by nuclear weapons systems whose principal purpose is served only so long as they are not

used, indeed which will have succeeded as effective instruments of policy only so long as they are not used, will also remain.

It is not easy for publics to grasp the way in which a perceived 'overkill' in nuclear capability in the form of a very large stockpile could be transformed, through vulnerability to preemptive attack, poor command, control and communications, and loss of capability to penetrate defences, into an inadequate deterrent. Such analyses need to be better explained. Publics need to be educated as to why nuclear systems must be able to survive a surprise attack and be capable of control for scenarios other than a single spasmodic retaliatory strike. This can be done without Western planners succumbing to the delusion that protracted nuclear wars are likely, that a nuclear war can be planned with any confidence, or that limited nuclear wars, tactical or strategic, are likely to remain so.

Nuclear plans and credible nuclear response options should be explained to Western publics in terms of their intended purposes, along the following lines. These plans are to convince the USSR that she cannot hope to gain military or political advantage by having plans or capabilities for which the West has no appropriate response. Moreover, Western political leaders are more likely to make sensible decisions in a crisis or in case of an actual nuclear attack, of whatever nature and size, if such options exist beforehand and have been thought through and considered in exercises. Nothing could be more irresponsible than the creation of a situation in which a limited attack is detected as being in progress and Western political leaders are told that the only available choices are no response or an all-out nuclear retaliation, because it had previously been decided that such an attack was impossible.

Convincing publics along these lines is bound to be more difficult than the explanation of the simple deterrence of an all-out Soviet attack on the United States through the threat of all-out retaliation.

Most analysts, planners, parliamentarians, publics and political leaders have come to recognize the existence of a state of approximate equivalence in the Soviet–American strategic nuclear balance. Inevitably, the utility of US nuclear forces in deterring Soviet nuclear or conventional aggression in Europe or against Japan has correspondingly diminished. What de Gaulle said in the 1960s and Kissinger in 1979 may or may not have been true at the time, but has come increasingly to be so, perhaps in part because they said it. There remains, in my view, a penumbral area of extended deterrence. It makes both superpowers substantially more cautious in taking steps that they consider to have a substantial probability of causing their own conventional military forces to become engaged with the conventional military forces of the other. It rests on the belief that the coupling of conventional and nuclear (theatre and strategic) forces of the super-powers is sufficiently close that such conventional conflict would have a high risk of escalating into a nuclear war – but that is a rather far cry from the way in which extended deterrence was once declared to function, with conventional aggression in much of the world substantially deterred by the threat of US nuclear retaliation. Moreover, in a state of nuclear parity, when the balance of conventional forces is marginal or unsatisfactory, opportunities for political intimidation as well as for military attack will arise.

US nuclear forces deployed in Europe represent a special and intense case of public interest. Analysts, strategic thinkers and political leaders in Western countries – and this applies particularly in Europe – need to be able to present publics with a more clearly explained and believable rationale for their purpose, deployment and potential use. This will be particularly difficult because few if any scenarios for their employment are convincing. Such forces do, however, continue to function as a powder train, acting to assure whatever penumbral effect exists of extended deterrence. Battlefield or longer-range nuclear weapons have, by their very existence, had an effect on Warsaw Pact conventional forces, including their tactics and deployments. The Warsaw Pact must spread out these forces, thus reducing their ability to crack allied defensive lines by massing armour. The possibility of Soviet political intimidation based on a threat to confine a nuclear war to Western Europe is reduced through the existence of US intermediate-range nuclear missiles with the capability to strike targets in the Soviet Union. These US missiles also provide reassurance for Europeans who may believe that the US would be reluctant to use her strategic forces in an initial response to a nuclear attack on Europe.

Finally, political leaders need to pay more attention to the goal of increasing public confidence that US and allied policies are directed toward reducing the chance that a nuclear war will occur. NATO missed an opportunity in this regard when it gave little publicity to the decision made in 1979 to withdraw 1,000 nuclear warheads from Europe. As the United States implements her current plans for a further withdrawal of more than a thousand air defence and older missile warheads, she should emphasize the reduced NATO emphasis on nuclear defence. The public also needs to be made more aware of the widespread deployment, both in tactical and strategic forces, of Permissive Action Links (PAL), which mechanically prevent the launch of nuclear systems or their explosion in the absence of the receipt of the proper coded signal along with the authorization for their use.

Conclusion

In summary, Western publics consider themselves more secure insofar as they believe that Western military strength is adequate, that it is under responsible control, and that their leaders are informed, wise and sensitive to the concerns of their citizens. But the ambiguities and paradoxes of the nuclear age must be accepted and lived with along with the imperfections of leaders in democracies. Publics must come to understand that, although there may be some easing of, there is no escape from, the threat of nuclear annihilation so long as nuclear weapons exist in large numbers in an atmosphere of adversarial relationships between East and West. Neither of these circumstances is at all likely to change in the coming decades, even if there were a complete freeze on the production and deployment of nuclear weapons, a significant reduction in the nuclear stockpiles, and a sincere expression of an intent not to be first to use nuclear weapons.

Public officials responsible for national security will have to be prepared to address the entire complex of nuclear policy and related issues described above. Public debate will be necessary with those who have various concerns or contrary views. The thirty-year diffusion of nuclear policy consideration and formulation from official through academic and intellectual to journalistic and public circles is now irreversible. The debate will have to be carried out in public at a level comprehensible to publics and to conclusions they can afterwards support.

The declaratory policies of Western governments must mirror actual nuclear policies more closely than has been the case in the past. Nuances may separate the ways in which US nuclear doctrine and planning appears to or is described to various audiences. Indeed, the nuclear planners and political leaders themselves may not see their policies in exactly the same light as any of the parties at whom their declaratory policy is directed – domestic publics, allies, neutrals or potential adversaries. Blatant contradictions however are another matter. By presenting adversaries with unreal dangers or opportunities, they risk unintended crises. By confusing domestic publics, they lose the political support necessary to maintain realistic security policies.

Political leaders in the industrialized democracies will continue to confront enormously difficult issues in designing an effective nuclear posture. They will now face the additional task of re-establishing a domestic consensus about the role of nuclear weapons in their overall security policies. Creating a consensus to this end, unified beyond the domestic constituencies to encompass the whole of the global alliance, will be even more challenging. But the genie of public involvement and discussion, like the genie of nuclear weapons, is already out of the bottle. There is no alternative to living with both.

Domestic Concerns
and Nuclear Doctrine: How Should the Nuclear Posture be Shaped?

Defence Policy and Consenus

In democratic societies, defence policy must be socially acceptable in order to remain viable and credible. Sharply controversial policies are prone to erosion by political opposition and therefore tend to be less credible and predictable than those which command broad support. Social acceptance does not imply unanimous support nor does it suggest a need for enthusiastic endorsement. Broad consensus on the basic features of national security policy and the assumptions on which it is predicated is necessary, however, for democracies to be able to maintain a steady course in a turbulent and uncertain world. Frequently, public attitudes to arms policies are volatile and harbour many inconsistencies. Nevertheless, governments must strive to fashion policies which are reasonably coherent, stable and consistent. Governments are, however, subject to constraints imposed by existing commitments, economics, technology and competing interests. They are invariably and justifiably concerned about re-election. They should ignore public concerns at their peril. But governments also have an obligation to lead, to choose a course of action under conditions of uncertainty, to focus on long term consequences and options rather than simply succumb to short-term expedience. However, if they lack public support they will fail. They must persuade and listen. Communication and dialogue between government and the governed, between state and society are keys to effective policy-making in democracies.

The complexity of modern weapons and the esoteric nature of nuclear strategy make real public dialogue about defence policy extremely difficult. Alienation and frustration often shape attitudes, demonstration tends to replace conversation. The dialogue tends to assume Chekhovian qualities as the participants talk past each other and stop listening. The problems are compounded by changes in Western society. The arrival of material plenty has shifted emphasis away from a primary concern with material well-being and physical security toward greater emphasis on less tangible qualities of life.

A mood of discontent has been stimulated by a waning belief in the idea of progress, in the blessings of technology and in man's ability to avoid catastrophe. War has become an abstract notion which has been delegated to experts. In terms of experience, war is something which happens to other people in distant lands. At the same time a subliminal fear of a repetition of the carnage of the Second World War permeates and shapes the European sense of vulnerability. Societies crave for reassurance against the perils of war as such. Nuclear war appears to be a greater danger than the political ambitions or misjudgments which could unleash it. The welfare state and discontent with it are transformed into fears about the possible emergence of a warfare state. A growing fear of war coincides with an economic crisis which exacerbates the choices between guns and butter, between social welfare and insurance against warfare, between deterrence and detente. At the same time the educational revolution has produced a larger section of society which is interested in national and international politics and which is seeking participation in decision-making at this level. It enables many to engage in what Ronald Inglehart calls 'elite-challenging' as opposed to 'elite-directed' activities.[1] Public opposition is spearheaded by 'counter-elites'. The intelligentsia is capable of challenging the details of policy-making, thus forcing governments to engage in esoteric discourse which is beyond the comprehension of the ordinary citizen. Basic purposes and irreducible dilemmas get lost in a cloud of technical ornaments of a baroque quality which increases the sense of alienation and anger.

The emergence of single issue political movements constitutes a challenge to the established institutions for the integration of competing interests and objectives in our societies, such as parliaments, political parties and governments. The 'peace movement' contains an institutional challenge in addition to questioning the premises and priorities of Western defence. It constitutes an example of expressive politics, enabling and encouraging citizens to express concerns and attitudes towards the policies of governments which must be moved by instrumental concerns about the consequences, costs and risks of specific courses of action, about the relationships between ends and means and the constraints on options imposed by competing interests and wills. Nevertheless expressive political movements are often needed in order to foster realignment of the priorities and calculations between society and the state. We are not confronted, however, by a simple phenomenon of the 'people' against 'establishments'. Popular movements are spearheaded by counter-elites, by the would-be establishments and sometimes by members of former establishment elites. The new intelligentsia appears to harbour a certain proclivity for 'conformist opposition'.

The public argument is shaped to some degree by a decline in the perceived legitimacy of hierarchical authority and reduced confidence in established institutions. The younger generations of Europe have never experienced invasion and war in their homelands. There is a discontinuity of experience across the generations in Europe. We should note also that class voting is declining in Western democracies. Support for parties of the left may increasingly be coming from the middle classes. Their claims to political participation will frequently derive from an issue-oriented approach rather than a desire to support a given group of leaders. The issues on which the counter-elites will mobilize are difficult to bargain over as they do not have the incremental nature of economic issues, but tend instead to assume a moralistic tone making compromise very difficult. The nuclear weapons issue is a key case in point.

This paper does not attempt to analyze the sociology of the peace movement nor its political basis and purposes. The movement encompasses a variety of views and prescriptions. Some ambiguity is necessary in order for the movement to stay together. The protest is to some extent inchoate. Nevertheless, it does represent and reflect a broadened concern in our societies about the dangers of nuclear war. The intensity of its expression may oscillate, but the basic concern is likely to persist and re-emerge in connection with specific decisions concerning nuclear weapons in the defence posture of the West. It is easy to attack the peace movement for being one-sided, for focussing on Western decisions and actions while being rather muted in its reaction to Soviet arms policy. However, we should accept that the peace movement is now part of the political culture of Western democracies. It is part of our political process and will direct its energies and attention towards affecting decisions to which it can obtain some access. (Incidentally, it should be noted that policy-makers and analysts in the West frequently approach defence problems with little attention to how the recommended actions may be perceived 'on the other side of the hill'. All evidence suggests that ethnocentric propensities are even more pronounced and pervasive on the Soviet side).

The defence postures in the West and their associated doctrines have evolved incrementally through the post-war era. It would be surprising if the accumulated results of a long and varied history were coherent and consistent, and we can claim no such surprises. It is difficult, moreover, to establish criteria and yardsticks for measuring effectiveness and consistency. Defence postures serve tasks beyond that of containing the aspirations of would be adversaries. In coalitions they become currencies for the management of political relations, for the marking of commitments, and preservation of options for future change. Particular weapons and deployments assume symbolic significance which affects the cost of whatever reconfiguration is necessary to enhance credible deterrence. Defence postures and doctrines are relevant, in other words, to shaping the conditions of the political order, present as well as future. Such impacts and relationships are, however, rather abstract and conjectural. Complexity, contingency and uncertainty are hard to convey and still harder for the concerned citizen to fathom. The physical realities and prospective horrors of nuclear devastation seem more tangible and real. In addition, political perspectives and priorities may differ within coalitions of states, as indeed they are likely to do within the Western Alliance in the years ahead. Continued domestic strife over the shaping of defence policy may amplify and exacerbate political differences within the West, particularly with regard to policies towards the East. There are strong reasons therefore to undertake a basic reconsideration of the whole structure of Western defence with a view to restoring broad domestic and inter-Alliance consensus. In addition there are important considerations of strategy which point towards the need for changes in the posture and doctrine of Western defence. Some of the key issues which relate to the structure and purposes of the nuclear posture will now be examined.

Shifts in the Nuclear Posture
The following discussion will lead to three normative propositions concerning the shifts which *ought* to take place in the Western nuclear posture as a result of restructuring and possibly by negotiated agreement with the East:

- The *size* of the nuclear arsenals (both in terms of warheads and delivery systems) should be markedly reduced.
- The *pressures for early use* of nuclear weapons should be markedly reduced.
- The *reliance* on nuclear weapons should be markedly reduced.

The basis for these propositions will be developed with regard to strategic nuclear forces, battlefield nuclear weapons and intermediate range nuclear weapons respectively. The changes needed derive from the evolution of the arsenals and deployments over the last twenty years, and particularly from the changes in the relative capabilities between East and West and in the present and prospective weapon technologies.

The issues will be dealt with conceptually rather than technically, although it must be recognized that technological and operational feasibility will constrain implementation of the basic reforms which are proposed. It is necessary, however, to create a conceptual framework for a consideration of the defence posture rather than having the latter be driven by available technology. Such an approach may suggest priorities also with respect to technological development. Furthermore, while declaratory policies serve important functions in projecting intentions and shaping expectations, they will be but empty shells unless they are buttressed by changes in the posture which emphasize the intentions conveyed. The discussions of a no first use of nuclear weapons policy has been unsatisfactory so far because, to the degree that it has focussed on changes in the existing posture, it has dealt almost exclusively with the perceived need to strengthen options for conventional defence and left out of consideration the changes which would be needed also in the nuclear posture.

In dealing with changes in the nuclear posture it is important to distinguish between three basic avenues of approach: negotiated agreements on arms reduction and limitation (arms control); national (and Alliance) defence policy; and confidence-building measures (CBM). A new balance has to be struck in order to develop a viable system of management which is able to exploit synergistic relationships among the three approaches.[2] Nations have been trying to do too much through arms-control negotiations, engaging in negotiations about the detailed shaping of defence postures. In future, negotiations should aim to establish broad parameters of constraints, primarily through agreements on force reductions and qualitative limitations rather than provisions for detailed regulation. The parties should be left free to mix forces within the negotiated parameters. Negotiations have tended to have a built-in political bias in favour of symmetry, and detailed regulation has implied symmetry in detail. Such agreements are difficult to negotiate and to verify and they tend to produce a great deal of controversy due to the variety of assessments which detailed regulation stimulates. The approach collides also with the different traditions, service interests, technological choices and geographical circumstances which shape the deterrent postures which states adopt. It tends also to increase pressures for matching the forces of the adversary and to aim for high ceilings. The detailed structuring of defence postures should be the task of prudent defence policy. Such policies should be enlightened by a practice of mutual restraint and by recognition of the perceptions and conditions of the other side. CBM may be viewed as the connecting link between national defence policies and negotiated arms-control agreements.[3]

The Strategic Nuclear Posture
The size of the American strategic missile force was essentially determined early in the Kennedy Administration. We do not know how the Soviet force levels were defined and to what extent those definitions were influenced by American decisions. The American levels were the result of political compromise rather than the derivation of 'an internally consistent strategy and compatible targeting plans'.[4] Doctrine, however, provided an *ex post facto* rationalization for prior decisions concerning size, and provided a framework for combating pressures for expansion.

It is commonly believed that the Soviet Union and the United States have been engaged in an accelerating strategic arms race. This particular belief is incompatible with the facts.[5] The size of the US strategic forces is smaller today than at the end of the 1950s when it included almost 1,500 medium bombers of the B-47 variety, a delivery vehicle which was MIRVed in the sense that each aircraft carried several nuclear bombs each of which could be directed to separate targets. The number of nuclear warheads in the American nuclear stockpile has actually decreased by twenty-five per cent over the last

fifteen years while the total megatonnage has dropped by a factor of four. While the US nuclear stockpile decreased by some 6,000 warheads, the Soviet stockpile reportedly grew by some 8,000, causing the overall Soviet stockpile to exceed the American. Still the size of the total stockpiles on both sides is awesome and it includes some 24,000 weapons on the American side alone. It can legitimately be asked if deterrence requires such enormous destructive potential or if it could not be assured at substantially lower levels.

The size of the strategic forces must reflect a variety of considerations, including such factors as expected reliability, survivability, penetrability, targeting policy and target structure. The basic considerations revolve around the concept of deterrence: how to relate the size and shape of strategic nuclear forces to the task of dissuading a would-be adversary from undertaking specific actions. Deterrence, as has often been noted, is basically a psychological phenomenon. It is not susceptible to precise calculation. Any quantified expressions of how much is enough for deterrence are at best tools for analysis in planning force postures. It is possible to calculate the marginal utility of additional forces for accomplishing a given mission. However, any quantified expression of the destruction which is postulated to deter is basically arbitrary. Deterrence must inevitably reduce to the question about who is to persuade whom not to do what in which set of circumstances.[6]

Technology will influence calculations about the relative effectiveness of weapon systems and identification of potential options for deployment or employment of weapons but the political calculus will remain intractable. The dilemmas are awesome and inescapable. It is very hard to imagine any American or Soviet leader being persuaded that a nuclear war could now be won with 'acceptable' damage. Political leaders know from experience and by instinct that something always goes wrong and, precisely because things may go wrong, they cannot commit the future of their nations to an unqualified presumption that deterrence will not break down. Here we confront the basic dilemma of choices between 'assured destruction', 'controlled response' and 'war-fighting capability', the choices that governments make and which influence the size of their forces.

The notion of assured destruction has a deceptive clarity and neatness. The problem of deterrence is reduced to being able to confront a would-be adversary with an ability to retaliate in an unacceptably destructive manner with high confidence after having been attacked. Admittedly the detailed questions of design and planning are not easy. The survival of sufficient forces for retaliation has to be assured, it cannot be assumed. Choices must be made concerning warning, dispersal, protection and command and control. However, basically it is not possible to determine how much assured destruction will assure deterrence. In most instances a reasonable chance of having to suffer but a fraction of the destruction which has been established as a planning objective would suffice. The problem is, however, that choices are unlikely to present themselves very neatly in terms of retaliating or not retaliating. Decisions are likely to be more incremental and cumulative than that. They could come at the end of a process which narrows the alternatives and creates almost irresistible momentum; accidents and miscalculation may trigger and channel the momentum. Governments therefore cannot ignore the question of what to do if deterrence fails. As a minimum they should invest in capabilities for reflection, negotiation and eventual termination short of absolute catastrophe. Responses have to be controlled and measured rather than constitute simply reflexive wrath. However, the ability to withhold action and to tailor the response to circumstances carries on its back the temptation to go further and develop capacities for conducting extensive limited nuclear war campaigns as a matter of deliberate policy, including first-strike options. The question is again one of deciding how much is enough and to be able to cut off at a level of ambition which is clearly on the side of prudential insurance against the breakdown of deterrence and not on the side of an open-ended chase of a war-winning posture. The dilemmas are real and troublesome. They must be resolved not only in the abstract through intellectual analysis; choices must be made which will have sufficient resilience against pressures for re-

duction and addition in the policy-making processes. They must be viewed also from the point of view of the perceptions of allies and adversaries.

Domestic Support for Strategic Deterrence
What choices are likely to command domestic support? Any answers to that question must necessarily be conjectural and value-loaded. One assessment may be summarized in the following way: a simple posture and doctrine of assured destruction is not a viable choice. Public confidence in the ability of governments to do their job has been declining and scepticism is likely to persist, even from that perspective which equates the avoidance of war with the promise of massive destruction and which seems risky in the extreme. If defence is associated with the purpose of effecting large-scale destruction, it will remain a highly controversial aspect of public policy.The deliberate targeting of cities, a posture which holds citizens as hostages for the good behaviour of their governments, will not and should not receive broad social support. There is a difference between accepting the possibility of large-scale destruction as a consequence of war and accepting its deliberate creation as a legitimate purpose of policy in the event of war.

The very idea of mutual assured destruction is abhorrent and inconsistent with even a rudimentary ethical perspective with respect to the purposes of statecraft and the international security dilemma in the nuclear age. It ignores the many ways in which wars may break out, ways which are beyond deterrence or on the margins thereof. One could agree with Fred C. Ikle who has observed: 'The jargon of American strategic analysis works like a narcotic. It dulls our sense of moral outrage about the tragic confrontation of nuclear arsenals, primed and constantly perfected to unleash widespread genocide. It fosters a current smug complacence regarding the soundness and stability of mutual deterrence. It blinds us to the fact that our method for preventing nuclear war rests on a form of warfare universally condemned since the Dark Ages – the mass killings of hostages'.[7]

The first order of business then is to move away from the distorted dogma that deterrence must be based on a threatened response involving the mass killing of people. Furthermore, there appears to be no reason why the response has to be prompt and instant. That presumption points towards the logical perversity of 'launch on warning', when enormous political decisions have in effect been delegated to machines. Instead I would argue for a doctrine of deterrence based on 'adequate retaliation' and 'assured reflection'. There is no absolute way to determine what measure of retaliation would be adequate. Therefore flexibility must be built into the strategic force posture, allowing the political authorities to make that judgment concretely. Clearly a capacity for adequate retaliation requires survivable and controllable forces but the absolute size of the forces could be substantially lower than at present.

The second element in a preferred doctrine is based on the notion that deterrence may fail in spite of the best attempts to assure it. In that event the military posture should be designed to support deliberate attempts to avoid and limit destruction. Therefore the concept of 'assured destruction' should be replaced by a concept of 'assured reflection', enabling governments to assess the situation *after* the outbreak of war and to hold and measure responses with a view to terminating the war. A posture of 'assured reflection' will include a highly reliable system of command, control and communication (C^3) and a strategic nuclear force which is sufficiently invulnerable to pre-emptive immobilization to pose with high confidence the threat of second strike retaliation, and sufficiently accurate to be launched against military targets, but not necessarily against hardened missile silos. Such a force could be significantly smaller than existing forces but bringing down the levels requires agreement between the United States and the Soviet Union for reasons of domestic politics as well as because of the impact on survivability of substantial numerical disparities.

Strategic Posture and Force Levels
The current round of negotiations on the reduction and limitation of strategic nuclear forces should therefore try to shape a more stable balance at substantially reduced levels.

Deep cuts of some thirty to fifty per cent would amount to a salient reversal of the trends of the last decades and contribute to the recreation of public confidence in the commitment and ability of governments to avoid the trap of an open-ended competition leading to constantly changing and generally expanding arsenals of strategic weapons. Stability can be enhanced by a combination of explicit provisions and implicit incentives. Unfortunately, the 'MIRV genie' is out of the bottle. However, agreed limitations on the total number of warheads are likely to diminish incentives for the further fractionation of the payload of each missile out of concern for the ability of the delivery vehicles to survive a first strike. Limitations on the total number of delivery vehicles, combined with freedom-to-mix, are likely to increase incentives to move missiles to sea, particularly as such missiles acquire accuracies which enable them to threaten fixed land-based missiles. Dispersal in smaller submarines rather than increased concentration of missiles in large submarines may make sense, in operational as well as in economic terms. It is part of the established wisdom that strategic forces should not be concentrated in one basket; different systems should present an adversary with separate sets of uncertainties. However, the concept of a 'strategic triad' sometimes appears to be designed less with a view to enhance deterrence than in order to protect a multi-service solution to its maintenance. Apparent simplicity of design will improve the chances of gaining public confidence; conspicuous complexity is likely to stir concerns about malfunctions and fears of the tyranny by machines over man as has been shown by the controversies in the United States over successor systems to the *Minuteman* ICBM. Sea-based systems, however, pose particular problems of command and control which consequently require close examination.

The posture must be compatible, of course, with a strategic doctrine which is credible and supportable. In the past many have confused the *de facto* existence of an 'assured destruction posture' with the attainment of a desirable and stable conclusion of human endeavour. We may be temporarily trapped, but to elevate such entrapment to a permanent principle of international relations is short-sighted at best and seems certain to stimulate desperate attempts to escape. There are too many ways that things may go wrong. History does not warrant the placing of confidence in the indefinite functioning of particular arrangements for nuclear deterrence, even if these arrangements have proved themselves more robust than initially expected. An assured destruction posture tends to focus public attention on the destructive horror of nuclear war, causing rejection rather than viable proposals for modification. The state becomes associated with unacceptable destruction and governments must be concerned about the consequences of a break-down of deterrence. There must be a serious problem of credibility during crises if the only alternative to surrender is self-destruction. Immobility and fear are not likely to contribute to resolution or defusing of crises or permit gracious disengagement from confrontation.

A Seminar on Strategy

A posture of 'assured reflection' would certainly carry with it the danger of being extended to encompass a variety of limited nuclear war-fighting options. However, acceptance of rough parity and an active pursuit of force reductions should contribute to the containment of such impulses. In addition, mutual confidence between the United States and the Soviet Union could be enhanced by the institution of a systematic dialogue about strategic doctrine and postures. We are not arguing for the negotiation of common strategic doctrines but rather for the establishment of a Seminar on Strategy, with the appropriate acronym of SOS, which would enable the parties to explain the rationales behind their defence postures and to voice any apprehensions which may exist about the motives of the other party and the implications of its policies. Hence, the SOS could presumably serve to alleviate fears about the pernicious consequences of specific choice and make both sides more sensitive to the concerns and outlooks of each other. The SOS could take place within the framework of the Standing Consultative Commission (SCC) which has been established in connection with the SALT I Agreement.

Extended Deterrence

What would be the consequences of such an approach for extended deterrence? Threatening to blow up the cities of your adversary in order to protect your allies will always beg questions of credibility and proportionality. In future, deterrence is likely to be viewed less as a result of the certain prospects of unacceptable destruction than as a result of substantial residual uncertainties concerning the progress of events if the major nuclear powers should clash at points of vital interest.

Extended deterrence in its simple form was based on strategic superiority. Real strategic superiority is for all practical purposes now unattainable. Extended deterrence therefore must be based more on the projection of common political purposes and an ability to resist aggression at the point of challenge than on the threat to initiate strategic nuclear war. In order to maintain public support and confidence in Alliance defence in the years ahead, a viable conventional defence option is needed, permitting European societies to become real subjects with respect to their own protection rather than the objects for threats of nuclear destruction. Part of the reasons for the present malaise is the perception that control over the destinies of European society has been abdicated to Presidents of the United States and the Soviet Union whose political acumen and wisdom do not invariably inspire trust and confidence. Indeed the differences in political style and culture between the United States and Western Europe will constitute a heavy burden on an alliance relationship which makes defence depend primarily on decisions about nuclear response in Washington. Such an arrangement is likely to stimulate the propensity which General Bernard W. Rogers (currently Supreme Allied Commander, Europe) has warned against, that of placing the super-powers on the same moral plane and at the same time applying double standards to the two.[8]

Battlefield Nuclear Weapons

Nuclear weapons are not, of course, only deployed in the territories of the United States and the Soviet Union. In the present analysis, however, the French and British nuclear forces will be excluded. The analysis will concentrate on the nuclear force posture of the United States. The number of theatre nuclear weapons in Europe reached a maximum of 7,000 during the Kennedy Administration. It has recently been reduced by 1,000, primarily by the withdrawal of warheads for obsolete *Honest John* short-range missiles. The relationship between the present force posture and NATO defence doctrine is both tenuous and controversial. Even after the withdrawal of the *Honest John* warheads, more than half of NATO's theatre nuclear weapons are associated with systems which have a range of under 30 km, namely nuclear artillery and very short-range missiles. About one third are associated with medium-range (150–1,500 km) systems, primarily nuclear bombs for dual-capable aircraft. The balance is made up of nuclear munitions for air defence missiles, atomic demolition munitions (ADM) and anti-submarine warfare (ASW) weapons. The nuclear munitions are stored in Special Munition Sites (SMS) of which there are some 90 when the air defence sites are excluded. Some 20,000 US and Allied personnel are probably associated with the SMS. Most of the sites are rather vulnerable to attacks even with conventional munitions, and the short warning time which is likely to prevail makes dispersal of the nuclear munitions very difficult. Considerable attention has been devoted to improving the safety, security and survivability (S³) of the SMS. However, the measures are often mutually exclusive. For example, a particular measure designed to improve safety could result in reduced survivability.

The functions of NATO's theatre nuclear forces (TNF) have varied over time; some have been added and their relative importance has changed. They include: deterrence of large-scale conventional attack; compensation for inferiority in conventional forces; deterrence of the first use of nuclear weapons by the other side; and the provision of links to American strategic nuclear forces.

The Employment of Battlefield Weapons
The doctrine for nuclear employment is based on the strategy of flexible response as embodied in NATO document MC 14/3 encompassing the triple functions of direct defence,

deliberate escalation and general nuclear response. Employment is constrained by agreed political guidelines beginning with the Athens Guidelines of 1962, the Guidelines Concerning Consultation Procedures of 1969, Guidelines for Initial Tactical Use of 1970, the ADM Guidelines from 1970, and the 1972 Guidelines Concerning the Theatre Nuclear Strike-Role Concept.[9] Nuclear release has to be authorized by the American President (and that applies to all nuclear weapons which are deployed to Europe under Programmes of Cooperation (POC), in consultation with Allies in the North Atlantic Council (NAC) according to agreed procedures. Once a 'package' of theatre nuclear weapons has been released, its tactical use is controlled by a corps commander, sub-package employment can be delegated to divisional level, but, generally, not further down.[10] A corps package reportedly could, but need not, consist of between 100–200 nuclear weapons and the time-frame for employment may be restricted to from several hours to a day.[11] According to American doctrine, five general categories of constrained theatre nuclear employment may be distinguished: demonstration; limited defensive use; restricted battle area use; extended battle area use; and theatrewide use.[12]

SACEUR's Nuclear Operation Policy (NOP) includes prepared selective employment plans as well as a general strike plan in coordination with the American Single Integrated Operation Plan (SIOP). Battlefield weapons are not included in the prepared attack options. It is significant to note, however, that NATO has not managed to agree on guidelines for follow-on use of nuclear weapons if a first attempt to communicate NATO's intentions through a controlled demonstrative detonation does not suceed in persuading the adversary to halt hostilities. Discussion on this topic has proceeded for more than ten years. The failure to agree reflects some of the basic political dilemmas and difficulties with the current nuclear posture in Europe. Operational plans for follow-on use do, however, exist.

The present posture gives cause for concern from the point of view of public acceptability as well as operational effectiveness and reliability. The heavy reliance on short-range battlefield weapons in forward areas is inconsistent with the objective of reducing pressures for early use of nuclear weapons. On the contrary, it is likely to generate precisely such pressures as the nuclear assets in forward locations may be in danger of being overrun by advancing enemy forces. Tactical situations may thus come to exercise strong pressures on the political decisions concerning the conduct of a war. Once the nuclear threshold has been crossed, the possibility of limiting a nuclear war in Europe with current arsenals seems remote in the extreme. Hence, it is arguable that current defence arrangements fail to provide plausible protection.

The dilemmas are many and complex. Generally speaking it is easier to employ theatre nuclear weapons early rather than late, due to the inevitable confusion on the battlefield. Command, control and communication will constitute formidable problems. Furthermore forward defence based on short-range battlefield weapons forces NATO into rapid reactions with imperfect knowledge against a very complex and dynamic target cycle. Rigid control may limit close-in use, generating pressures for delegation. Furthermore, it is going to be very difficult to slow the battle tempo and enemy advance by attrition only; such employment does not change the shape of the battlefield.

NATO's present reliance on nuclear weapons involves a serious danger of political immobilization in a crisis or in war. The problem has been graphically depicted by Fred C. Ikle:

> In the context of a conventional war, it would take but one nuclear detonation somewhere – a 'warning shot' or an accident – to propel the horror of nuclear destruction into public consciousness in every Western country. And if a large-scale conventional war in Central Europe broke out, it might not even require the emotional impact of a nuclear detonation to bring into consciousness the terror of nuclear war. Enormous pressures would be mobilized and brought to bear on government leaders – through parliaments, the media and other channels – to avoid at almost any price the risk of large-scale nuclear war.[13]

It should be recalled here that it is NATO strategy to use nuclear weapons for demonstration in the event of a decision to use them first. It is not at all clear that such employment would demonstrate resolve as much as consternation, nor that the effect would be pressure on the enemy to halt rather than on NATO governments to seek accommodation. Again one could agree with Fred C. Ikle who observed that in a crisis 'the long-standing reliance of NATO governments on the nuclear back-up to a conventional defence would suddenly turn from an asset to a liability . . . Far from bolstering a full-scale conventional defence, NATO's nuclear threat of first use could turn inward to unravel the Alliance in the hour of crisis'.[14]

'No First Use'
The option of a 'no-first-use' pledge has recently received increased public attention. Such proposals clearly capture a mood and indicate a desirable direction of change but the changes which are needed in the nuclear posture for such declarations to be convincing have not been sufficiently examined.[15]

A 'no-first-use' commitment could serve to widen and strengthen the fire-break between conventional and nuclear weapons. It could reduce expectations that armed conflict would inevitably escalate to the nuclear level. It is arguable that such changed expectations would weaken deterrence. However, the impact need not be very significant. Residual uncertainties would be very large and no party could be confident that it could push the other against the wall without causing him to abrogate his commitment. The importance would lie in the direction of the change involved – reduced reliance on nuclear weapons, particularly on their early use.

As has been observed above, extended deterrence can no longer be based on the assumption of American strategic superiority. Hence coupling between theatre forces and strategic forces becomes more complex. It should be recalled also that, during the 1970s, the Soviet Union eliminated NATO's advantage in theatre nuclear forces. It is likely, as has been argued above, that a commitment to first use could unravel the Alliance in an extreme situation, irrespective of the coupling to

American strategic forces. Again one should avoid treating the issues in black and white, as 'either-or' questions, because residual uncertainties would be enormous and the continued existence of powerful nuclear forces would certainly affect the propensity to push to the limit.

The change in doctrine which is involved in a 'no-first-use' pledge is not in fact as large as all that. NATO has already moved away from a 'first-use' doctrine to a 'not-necessarily-first-use' doctrine. The difficulties in agreeing on guidelines for follow-on use after a demonstration shot indicate that it may be very difficult indeed for the Alliance to agree on first use in war. However, the posture in Europe is such as to exercise strong pressures for early, and possibly massive use, of nuclear weapons. Any change in declaratory policy should therefore be associated with some basic restructuring of the Alliance's theatre nuclear posture. It is probable that a restructuring of that posture should be associated with a further shift in doctrine to 'no early first use', recognizing that the definition of 'early' may be ambiguous but, more importantly, in order to allow more time for consideration of the changes needed in the conventional force posture in order to accommodate reduced reliance in nuclear response and lend credence to a 'no-first-use' intention. We are not arguing in favour of a negotiated agreement with the Soviet Union about 'no-first-use' of nuclear weapons. Such agreements could permit contentious claims of *droits de regard* in respect of the defence arrangements on both sides which are unlikely to contribute to East–West tranquillity or domestic harmony. Formal pledges could also stir up differences and tensions within the Alliance which could possibly be contained by moving instead towards an implicit pledge as a result of restructuring of the theatre nuclear posture so as to reduce the pressure for *early* use. In any event, a formal pledge must follow rather than precede a process of restructuring.

The changes in the theatre nuclear posture (intermediate-range nuclear forces will be treated separately) which should be implemented in order to permit a shift towards 'no-(early) first use' of nuclear weapons by NATO include the following:

- withdrawal of battlefield nuclear weapons from forward areas in Europe;[16]
- reduction by several thousand of the nuclear battlefield weapons in Europe;[17]
- cessation of nuclear air defence systems (the existence of such systems stimulates pressures for the early use of nuclear weapons and the pre-delegation of authority to fire them. NATO is currently in the process of reducing reliance on nuclear air defences. The successor system to *Nike-Hercules*, the *Patriot*, will be conventional only);
- withdrawal of ADM. While such weapons have not been 'prechambered' in Europe, their existence could involve pressures for early deployment in order to stop conventional offensives and, in addition, once they had been emplaced they would impose a rigidity on operations which could lead to rapid escalation;
- a stand-down of quick-reaction–alert forces. A small number of aircraft and *Pershing* I missiles are specifically withheld for rapid nuclear strike missions and are permanently loaded with nuclear munitions, ready for instant launching;
- re-evaluation of the commitment of dual-capable aircraft to nuclear roles. The ambiguity posed by dual-capable aircraft could provide incentives for extensive pre-emptive actions by the adversary. The need for enhanced conventional air-power combined with the vulnerability of tactical aircraft to nuclear or conventional pre-emption suggest that stability might improve with a reordering of missions, relying on missiles for nuclear strikes over medium ranges. More importantly, improved conventional munitions may substitute increasingly for nuclear munitions.

The Implication of Re-structuring
This proposed restructuring of NATO's theatre nuclear posture in Europe should be implemented unilaterally as part of an Alliance defence policy designed to bolster the firebreak between conventional and nuclear weapons and to reduce pressures for early use of nuclear weapons, including pre-emption by the adversary. Desirable changes in NATO's nuclear deployments should not become hostage to Soviet consent to reciprocation.

It should be emphasized that neither the purpose nor the result of the changes proposed would be to make Europe 'safe for conventional war'. Indeed the current discussion of nuclear weapons has reminded us that the overall European concern is that of preventing war of any kind in Europe. Modern warfare is enormously destructive; the pictures from Beirut in the summer of 1982 carried convincing proof of that assertion. Europeans have in part resisted building up their conventional defences to higher levels out of fear that it could indicate a readiness to accept the consequences of a major conventional war in Europe. However, the social circumstances in Western Europe as well as basic changes in the Soviet–American strategic nuclear balance necessitate a reconsideration of earlier positions. Credibility in the 1980s requires the initiation of changes involving reduced reliance on nuclear weapons.

Planning assumptions in NATO have been largely separated from assumptions about how a war might actually break out. It is difficult to discuss the possibilities for fragmentation in a crisis but the issues cannot be assumed away. A real crisis will test the ability of the Alliance to respond to ambiguous warning. The present posture is not well suited to provide the basis for unified responses, nor can heavy reliance on early use of nuclear weapons provide a basis for repeatable responses to ambiguous signals of heightened danger. In addition the present nuclear posture may prove destabilizing in wartime due to points of vulnerability which may invite Soviet pre-emption. Incentives for Soviet pre-emption may even increase with the expectation of a NATO resort to early use of nuclear weapons,

It makes little sense, of course, to consider the theatre nuclear problems in Europe separately from the conventional defence tasks. Somewhat different perceptions exist with respect to how much additional effort is needed in order to create a viable conventional defence option. However, its feasibility is not questioned provided the resources are made available.[18] That, of course, will always be a key problem, particularly in a period of economic difficulties. This Paper is limited to considering the nuclear posture. The threat of

nuclear weapons has led the Soviet Union to disperse and deeply echelon their forces. The result is that greater time is required for second and third echelon forces to follow the initial thrust. We must consider therefore whether the threat of the first Alliance use of nuclear weapons is not needed in order to maintain a high risk of the massing of forces. Again the answer would seem to be that the Soviet Union could never rely on NATO's abstaining from resort to nuclear weapons if faced with a massive and unambiguous Soviet offensive. It should be recalled that this Paper has not argued for the denuclearization of NATO's defences, only for a major reduction in numbers and a restructuring which would involve the preferential withdrawal of battlefield systems. It should be considered whether any nuclear artillery is needed and if so how much is required simply in order to impose desirable constraints on the offensive operations of an adversary. The emphasis should probably be on a *small* force of highly survivable and controllable theatre nuclear systems of medium range, always recognizing that survivability for land-based systems in Europe is inherently difficult to attain. It is more attainable, however, if it is fixed as a characteristic in the design of the weapon system beforehand rather than treated simply as an additional requirement to be met after a decision has been taken in favour of deployment.

A shift in the direction of a 'no-first-use' posture is usually predicated on a commitment to improve conventional defences. Such improvements are clearly desirable and restructuring, redeployment and re-equipment of NATO's conventional forces should be considered and implemented. However it is less clear that reliance on 'early-first-use' of nuclear weapons makes sense under present conditions nor that early resort to nuclear weapons can compensate for conventional inferiority. In fact it has never been demonstrated how NATO could defeat an attack by nuclear weapons if it was not able to defeat it by conventional force.

The ambiguities which exist about the relationships between the deployment of theatre nuclear weapons in Europe and NATO's employment doctrine may have served to avoid damaging disagreements in the past but the nuclear posture and associated dilemmas have now become a source of public restiveness. Ambiguity can create a serious lack of confidence. In addition we have to be concerned about the ability of the Alliance to respond to a broad variety of possible contingencies in the complex world of the 1980s. Heavy reliance on early use of nuclear weapons is likely to increase tension and disagreements within the Alliance in the event of ambiguous warning and limited conflict of uncertain nature and scope. A viable conventional defence, on the other hand, should bolster the ability of the Alliance to cope with military challenges. If such an effort should not receive social support, our societies are even less likely to support decisions to initiate the use of nuclear weapons, from which they would suffer inconceivable destruction.

In order to enhance conventional defence more effort should go into improving the firepower of in-place forces, improving and diversifying the capacity for mobilization, expanding territorial defence forces and into developing an effective capacity for holding second and third echelon forces at risk. It should be noted here that there is a difference between improved conventional capabilities and a conventional defence option. Furthermore, improvements which are designed to fill gaps in the existing conventional force posture may not coincide with the measures which would be undertaken if the goal is that of shifting emphasis from reliance on nuclear to conventional means. It should be possible, however, to identify and exploit synergistic effects. Adoption of the 'Airland Battle' concept, with its heavier emphasis on mobility as opposed to a linear defence orientation with emphasis on attrition, may enable NATO to be more imaginative and effective in its defence but reduced reliance on nuclear weapons will tend to increase NATO's reliance on the safe passage of reinforcements across the Atlantic, which will in turn increase the interdependence of the Central Front and the NATO's Northern Flank.

Intermediate-range Nuclear Forces (INF)
The INF issue has occupied centre stage in East–West relations and in the domestic controversy over defence policy in Western

Europe in the last few years[19]. It involves fundamental issues of political balance and equity in Europe.

It is true that the Soviet Union has 'traditionally' deployed a rather substanial continental-range nuclear strike capability against Western Europe. However, the SS-20 should not be considered solely as a replacement for obsolescent SS-4 and SS-5 missiles. It should be considered in the context in which its deployment was initiated. That context was essentially different from that of the 1950s and 1960s as the Soviet Union had achieved essential equivalence, or parity, in intercontinental-range nuclear strike systems during the 1970s. The arrival of parity was formally recorded in SALT. The SS-20 deployment coincided also with growing concerns about the relative vulnerability of land-based strategic missile forces. Moreover, the SS-20 did not fit into the previous context of a 'balance of imbalances' so it raised several basic questions with respect to Soviet long-range intentions in Europe, about the purposes of the Soviet Union's continued investment in special capabilities for holding Europe as a nuclear hostage. In other words, the role and position of the Soviet Union in the political order in Europe was at issue, as was the position of Europe in the context of super-power relations.

If the challenge inherent in the SS-20 deployment had not been met, it is arguable that the widening asymmetry between the Soviet Union and Western Europe in the broader context of super-power parity could have a stronger, more lasting and even more polarizing impact on the domestic politics of the states in Western Europe than that which followed in the wake of the dual-track decision in NATO in 1979. Almost all the states of Western Europe, it should be recalled, are *capable* of producing nuclear weapons. If unattended to, the SS-20 could also have given rise to new tensions within the Western Alliance concerning the credibility and efficacy of extended deterrence.

The political issues were compounded by the special characteristics of the SS-20 and by the coincidental deployment of a new generation of short- and medium-range nuclear systems by the Soviet Union. In addition to having improved accuracy and multiple warheads (MIRV), the SS-20 maintains a much higher state of readiness than the SS-4/-5 (a set-up time of about an hour compared to more than a day). Hence, it provides options for rapid attack in support of military operations. The number of special munition sites and major airfields in Western Europe is not very large compared to the number of SS-20 warheads deployed. Moreover, the SS-20 seemed to fit into a broader process of force modernization designed to provide an enhanced warfighting capacity.

Fundamentally, the issue at stake in the NATO decision on INF modernization was that of creating some symmetry of territorial vulnerability in Europe by weakening the sanctuary position of the Soviet Union *vis-à-vis* Western Europe.

The Soviet Union has in fact been caught applying double standards. On the one hand the Soviet Union seeks co-equal status as a super-power with the United States (The Khrushchevian task of catching up with and surpassing (*dognat' i peregnat'*) the rival super-power may have blinded the Kremlin to the European implications of certain weapon decisions). On the other hand she seeks acceptance as a major power within the European political order. Such acceptance, however, depends critically on reassuring Western Europe that the USSR does not have hegemonic aspirations. The political balance in Europe cannot be reduced to a simple derivation from the balance of deterrence between the US and the USSR. It depends on acceptance of the principle of the equality of states and the need for reciprocal restraint. Soviet insistence on including US Forward-Based Systems (FBS) in Europe in the INF negotiations because some of them in principle could reach Soviet territory, while refusing to include similar Soviet systems which threaten targets in Western Europe, illustrates the duality. From the point of view of Western Europe, Soviet forward-based missiles and aircraft of medium range could provide functional threat equivalents to SS-20 missiles and *Backfire* aircraft deployed to the Soviet rear. American sea-launched cruise missiles (SLCM) could produce similar problems for the Soviet Union. Hence a treaty on INF limitations would probably have to include agreement on collateral constraints to protect the Treaty against circumvention.

The NATO decision on INF modernization was motivated also by considerations relating to Alliance cohesion, such as the need to couple American strategic power more closely to the direct defence of Europe in the context of strategic parity and a broad build-up of Soviet theatre nuclear forces. It could be viewed also as a means of providing capacities for threatening Soviet second and third echelon ground forces in the event of a major attack in Europe. Such tasks, however, may perhaps be accomplished more credibly by modern conventional weapons.

The Zero Option

The zero option proposal for reciprocal reductions which has been put forward at Geneva is consistent with the proposition that the issues posed by INF are primarily *political* issues which relate to the structure of the political order in Europe. The precise calibration of that option must, of course, be determined through negotiations. The important consideration will be that Soviet levels should be drawn down considerably below the 1979 level and fixed by mutual agreement. The NATO numbers were never designed to match Soviet INF numbers.

It is arguable, of course, that the Soviet Union lacks strong incentives to bargain on the basis of an agreement involving substantial reductions in existing forces in return for NATO's abstaining from a deployment which may in any case be prevented by domestic opinion in Western Europe. The stakes are very high, however. Failure to carry through with deployment in the absence of concrete results from negotiations would cause a major crisis of confidence within the Western Alliance. Governments have much at stake in the decision and Soviet intransigence is likely to affect attitudes among the Western publics. A lost opportunity to turn the tide could change the climate of East–West competition in a manner which would be a real burden on and bring real risks to the Soviet Union in a period of serious economic constraints and a still unsettled succession. The simplicity and salient fairness of the Western position also

40

constituted an advantage. However, that advantage would evaporate quickly if it came to be seen as a piece of propaganda and gamesmanship rather than as providing a serious negotiating platform.

The composition and scale of the INF deployment which was decided by NATO was designed to communicate defensive intentions. Cruise missiles are too slow-moving to constitute a first-strike threat against the Soviet Union. 108 *Pershing* IIs hardly constitute a first strike potential against Soviet strategic and intermediate-range forces. The flight time is, however, short (comparable to that of the SS-20 against targets in Western Europe) and it could constitute a threat to Soviet command and control installations. Their vulnerability could be reduced by hardening and dispersal, and by a negotiated agreement which eliminates or bounds the threat. In any event the idea of instant retaliation is unsettling in the extreme. We have a dangerous situation if a difference in warning time of some twenty-five minutes has a major impact on the Soviet response. It is possible that an INF agreement has to be constructed in phases, starting perhaps with an agreement involving a reduction of SS-20 to levels below the 1979 levels and a commitment to forego the deployment of *Pershing* II coupled to an agreement on the parameters of the second phase negotiations about substantial reductions in cruise missiles and comparable aircraft on both sides as well as the residual force of SS-4/-5 and SS-20 missiles. The phasing of the negotiations and the shape of the agreements need to be considered in conjunction with the phasing and shaping of an agreement about strategic arms reductions (START). British and French submarine-launched missile forces may be taken into account in START and the (relatively few) French land-based intermediate-range missiles in the second phase of the INF negotiations.

We should therefore be looking towards a negotiated outcome which essentially eliminates intermediate-range nuclear forces as a major determinant of the political order in Europe by establishing very low ceilings. Negotiations, like deployments, should be phased in order to permit the two sides gradually to knit a web of reciprocal restraints with regard to the deployment of intermediate-range nuclear forces capable of reaching targets on the continent of Europe. That web would clearly have to extend also to cover the forward and seaward deployment of nuclear systems of shorter or similar range. It would seem important too to protect options for enhancing conventional capacities, or at least to identify them so as to be able to assess the costs of their abrogation. At the same time particular attention should be devoted to enhancing the survivability of *Pershing* II and GLCM in the event that it should prove impossible to negotiate a 'zero' solution.

The Broader Perspective

There is no escaping from the dilemmas posed by nuclear weapons. They do not lend themselves to disinvention but nor should they be accepted as 'just another weapon'. They are different. That difference is an important consideration in any responsible approach to force planning and the development of doctrine. They will always inspire awe and revulsion. Hence, nuclear deterrence will never be a popular aspect of modern statecraft. Nor should it be. But it is a necessary part of the burden of responsibility in our times. It is to be hoped that it will be but a temporary expedient in the history of mankind. It should never be considered a desirable end-point. Political organization and technology should, in the long run, enable man to transcend the almost arcane logic of nuclear deterrence.

It has been argued here that residual uncertainty has a considerable impact on deterrence, on the threat which implicitly leaves much to chance due to the limits of prediction and control, and this is a general feature of the predicament in the age of nuclear weapons. In force planning, attention must be paid to the size of the uncertainty. Deterrence will not work automatically, nor will it work invariably.

Some would contend that even a conditional intention to use nuclear weapons is as immoral as the use itself but as Geoffrey Dunstan, a noted theologian, has observed: 'The intention in possessing a nuclear "deterrent" force is *not* to use it, but to restrain a potential enemy from the first, provocative use. The *intention* is, by maintaining, a credible threat, to prevent any occasion for its use – to deter the other side from the first immoral act, the nuclear strike'[20]. Here is another argument in favour of moving towards a 'no-first-use' posture and for the adoption of a doctrine of 'assured reflection'. For, if deterrence should fail, we may not choose to copy the immoral act.

NOTES

[1]Ronald Inglehart, *The Silent Revolution: Changing Values and Political Styles Among Western Publics* (Princeton, N.Y.: Princeton University Press, 1977).

[2]For further elaboration see Johan Jørgen Holst, *Arms Control Revisited: An Exploratory Essay*, NUPI/R–63 (Oslo: Norwegian Institute of International Affairs, December 1981).

[3]For a discussion of CBM see Johan Jørgen Holst, *Confidence Building Measures: A Conceptual Framework* NUPI/N–253, Oslo, Norwegian Institute of International Affairs, September 1982.

[4]See Desmond Ball, *Politics and Force Levels: The Strategic Missile Program of the Kennedy Administration* (Berkeley, Los Angeles, London: University of California Press, 1980), p. 209.

[5]See Albert Wohlstetter, 'Racing Forward or Ambling Back?', *Survey*, (314) Summer/Autumn, 1976, pp. 163–217.

[6]The best discussion is still Ithiel de Sola Pool, *Deterrence as an Influence Process* (Cambridge, Mass: Center for International Studies, Massachusetts Institute of Technology, 1963).

[7]Fred Charles Ikle, *Can Nuclear Deterrence Last Out the Century?*, California Arms Control and Foreign Policy Seminar, January 1973, p.14.

[8]Speech by General Bernard W. Rogers, Supreme Allied Commander Europe, to the 35th Congress of the Inter-Allied Confederation of Reserve Officers in Washington, 9 August 1982.

[9]See *The North Atlantic Treaty Organization. Facts and Figures*, Tenth Edition, Brussels, NATO Information Service, Chapter 13, pp.152–4.

[10]John P. Rose, *The Evolution of U.S. Army Nuclear Doctrine, 1945–1980*, (Boulder, Colorado: Westview Press, 1980), p.175.

[11]*Ibid.*, p.172.

[12]*Ibid.*, p.170.

[13]Fred Charles Ikle, 'NATO's Nuclear Use: A Deepening Trap?' *Strategic Review*, Winter 1980, p.20.

[14]*Ibid.*

[15]For an early and systematic analysis see Richard H. Ullman, 'No First Use of Nuclear Weapons', *Foreign Affairs*, 50 (4) Spring 1972, pp. 669–83. The present debate was initiated with the publication of McGeorge Bundy, George F. Kennan, Robert S. McNamara and Gerard Smith, 'Nuclear Weapons and the Atlantic Alliance', *Foreign Affairs*, 60 (4) Spring 1982, pp. 735–68. A German response was presented in Karl Kaiser, George Leber, Alois Mertes and Franz-Josef Schulze, 'Nuclear Weapons and the Preservation of Peace', *Foreign Affairs*, 60 (5) Summer 1982, pp. 1,157–70. See also various exchanges in 'The Debate over No First Use', *Foreign Affairs*, 60 (5) Summer 1982, pp. 1,171–80. The most rigorous analysis to date is probably that by Fred C. Ikle, *op. cit.* in note 13.

[16]This recommendation was made by the 'Independent Commission on Disarmament and Security Issues'. See *Common Security: A Programme for Disarmament* (London: Pan Books, 1982), pp.146–9.

[17]This recommendation parallels that of Senator Sam Nunn (although his is explicitly predicated on prior agreement and the start of implementing measures to create a viable conventional defence). See *NATO: Can the Alliance be Saved?* Report of Senator Sam Nunn to the Committee on Armed Services, United States Senate, 97th Congress, 2nd Session, 13 May 1982, p.13.

[18]E.g., General Bernard W. Rogers, 'The Atlantic Alliance: Prescriptions for a Difficult Decade', *Foreign Affairs*, 60 (5) Summer 1982, pp. 1,145–56; 'Do you sincerely want to be non-nuclear?', *The Economist*, 284 (7248) 31 July 1982, pp. 30–32. John J. Mearsheimer, 'Why the Soviets Can't Win Quickly in Central Europe', *International Security*, 7 (1) Summer 1982, pp. 3–39, and Robert W. Komer, 'Is Conventional Defense of Europe Feasible?', Unpublished paper (Second draft 13 May 1982).

[19]This section is adapted from the author's article 'Arms Control in Europe: Towards a New Political Order', *Bulletin of Peace Proposals* 13 (2) 1982, pp. 81–9. See also Johan Jørgen Holst, 'The Future of East-West Relations: Some Policy Perspectives', *Naval War College Review*, (Forthcoming).

[20]G. R. Dunstan, 'Theological Method in the Deterrence Debate', In Geoffrey Goodwin (ed.), *Ethics and Nuclear Deterrence* (London: Croom Helm, 1982), p. 50.

42

IISS Annual
Conference Papers

ADELPHI PAPERS

NUMBER ONE HUNDRED AND EIGHTY-FOUR

Defence and Consensus:
The Domestic Aspects
of Western Security

Part III

THE INTERNATIONAL INSTITUTE FOR STRATEGIC STUDIES
23 TAVISTOCK STREET LONDON WC2E 7NQ

ADELPHI PAPER No. 184

The Papers presented here and in *Adelphi Papers* No. 182
and 183 were given at the Twenty-fourth Annual Conference of the IISS at Scheveningen, The Hague, The
Netherlands in September 1982.

First published Summer 1983

ISBN 0 86079 071 1
ISSN 0567-932X

© The International Institute for Strategic Studies 1983

All rights reserved. No part of this publication may be
reproduced, stored in a retrieval system, or transmitted
in any form or by any means, electronic, mechanical,
photo-copying, recording or otherwise, without the prior
permission of the International Institute for Strategic
Studies.

*The International Institute for Strategic studies was founded in 1958 as a centre for the
provision of information on and research into the problems of international security,
defence and arms control in the nuclear age. It is international in its Council and staff,
and its membership is drawn from over fifty countries. It is independent of governments
and is not the advocate of any particular interest.*

*The Institute is concerned with strategic questions – not just with the military aspects
of security but with the social and economic sources and political moral implications
of the use and existence of armed force: in other words with the basic problems of peace.*

*The Institute's publications are intended for a much wider audience than its own
membership and are available to the general public on subscription or singly.*

Printed in Great Britain by Spottiswoode Ballantyne Ltd., Colchester

CONTENTS

Introduction

CHRISTOPH BERTRAM

The Papers presented in these volumes were given at the 24th Annual Conference of the International Institute for Strategic Studies in September 1982. It was a conference devoted to one of the most ambiguous, imprecise and elusive aspects of security: that of the domestic political factors influencing defence policies, doctrines and burdens. This is one reason why the subject has generally been under-explored in traditional strategic studies. The other is that, as long as domestic consensus on these matters existed, there was no real pressure to address them. But that idyllic state of affairs no longer exists. An important part of the public in our societies is no longer willing to trust governments or experts or even the media on matters of defence policy.

The Papers in this volume are devoted to the task of defining to what extent this lack of trust is justified, to what extent it is inherent in a doctrine of nuclear deterrence, and to what degree it may be remedied by more rational concepts for nuclear weapons than those that enjoy currency today. But it may be that there is no answer that can be given in isolation but that the context is all-important. Indeed, the Alliance seemed in better shape, and defence expenditures and even nuclear weapons were less controversial at the time of East–West detente than they are today; it is the breakdown of that contextual framework which has brought forth the new concerns. Nuclear weapons and even defence spending for non-nuclear weapons are not in themselves sustainable by public opinion; they need to be put into a context of expectations. Only consensus on that context will make the specific military efforts acceptable and reassuring.

If this is true, then the fight for the consensus has been badly conducted. It has, at best, concentrated on specific issues: the number of Soviet missiles, the technical characteristics of the Western missiles. It has not addressed the context for which deterrence and defence are worth having.

This inability, as Rudolf Wildenmann and David Calleo point out, is attributable to a failure of the Western elites, the result of their doubts and fashions, rather than that of public opinion at large. The public continues to believe in the Western Alliance. It is impressive – and surprising – to note the massive American support for the European security link in Mr Kaagan's data, despite the frictions between the allies. But because the elites lack the confidence of a framework, they tend to narrow the debate to specific aspects which alone cannot justify the effort they demand. In isolation, consensus cannot be built on nuclear weapons, defence, the Alliance, or much else.

To regenerate the consensus, more is needed than rational nuclear doctrines or transparent defence decisions. That is helpful but not enough, particularly once the genie of nuclear doubt and anxiety has left the bottle. It also needs more than merely to indulge in the futile attempt to define defence policy by what is acceptable alone. Governments, as Johan Holst so rightly observes, have to persuade and listen. They are paid to lead, not to follow. They have failed in both in recent years. Leadership means the setting of the framework, of the context of security, in which destructive weapons can make sense. They will not make sense by themselves.

1

Domestic Priorities and the Demands of Alliance: An American Perspective

DAVID CALLEO

Vietnam and Watergate revived the old question of whether US domestic politics and priorities are compatible with her international role. Worsening economic conditions and rising military costs have kept the topic alive.

The subject remains many-sided and hard to grasp. Analytically, the distinction between foreign and domestic goals is often elusive. Many domestic aims depend closely upon a certain kind of international order. Alliances are almost inevitably enfeebled when principal members suffer from deteriorating and neglected domestic economic and social conditions. Prescribing the appropriate sum and balance of foreign and domestic claims, even when such claims are distinguishable, depends upon answering numerous complex questions: abroad, what are the nation's appropriate commitments and acceptable ways of meeting them? At home, what level of prosperity and welfare is needed to sustain a stable social and political system solidly committed to democratic values? At what point does diverting resources from civilian purposes undermine growth and long-range strength? Can the burden of external commitments be shared through the international economy? What are the consequences for economic and political stability? Analysing why policy reaches the answers that it does requires an understanding of the perspectives and dynamics of US mass and elite opinion, the political process with all of its structures and mobilized groups, the economic trends and expectations, and the role of foreign pressures. Analyses of such matters are highly controversial in themselves, let alone in conjunction.

The Traditional View

The issue of domestic versus external goals is not only inherently complex, but difficult for students of international relations to approach without distorting preconceptions. Those who study and practice foreign policy are strongly inclined to regard interfering domestic priorities like psychosomatic causes of bad health – unfortunate and unnecessary. Their natural inclinations towards the primacy of foreign policy are strongly reinforced by certain widely-prevailing views about recent history. The Second World War is blamed on Europe's 'appeasement' of Hitler a policy traced to the domestic self-indulgence of democracies with provincial leaders.

Alongside this common view of European appeasement is an equally traditional picture of American isolationism and its international consequences. In this traditional historical view, the United States should have taken up the indispensable role of world manager as Britain grew progressively enfeebled. The *Pax Britannica* should, it is said, have been sustained by being transformed into a *Pax Americana*. Instead, the isolationist inclinations of its masses kept America aloof. The disintegrating world balance led to two world wars, neither of which could be resolved until internationalist-minded elites manoeuvered the United States out of her domestic self-preoccupation. Thanks to the Cold War after World War II, America's elites, with transatlantic help, were able to keep the country's attention on international responsibilities. The post-war *Pax Americana*, NATO in particular, was a sort of benevolent and successful conspiracy of transatlantic elites against an erratic American public. Populist isolationism revived, however, with Vietnam. America's policy, and the world's stability, have been seriously undermined ever since.

However valid this isolationist paradigm may seem for the past, it is irrelevant to the Alliance's current problems. The American public is not opposed to foreign commitments, least of all to America's European commitments. The current quarrel is not between the public and its elites but among the transatlantic elites themselves. Those in charge of foreign policy in Europe and America do not agree over the shape of the future world system. Increasingly, they do not agree on how to deal with the Soviet Union, or with the Third World, or with their own relationship. On the American side, at least, the springs of this conflict are not to be found in the popular heartland, but in elitist Washington. If American foreign policies are more and more 'unilateral', by which it is usually meant that Europe does not approve of them, the blame should not be laid on the American public's domestic preferences.

Public Opinion and the Alliance
Measurements of public opinion over the past few years confirm the continuing mass support for using American troops against a Soviet attack in Europe. According to one set of data,[1] a post-Vietnam bottom of 48% in favour was reached in 1974–5, with 34% opposed. Support began rising by 1976, with a temporary post-war high of 74% in favour with only 19% opposed in July 1980, following the invasion of Afghanistan by the USSR and the seizing of American hostages in Iran. Polls in 1982 show support down to a more normal 56% in favour and 25% opposed. Logically enough, the public also supports keeping troops in Europe. A Gallup poll in February 1982, showed half the American public favouring American European forces at their present level, and 16% wanting an increase, while 10% favoured a reduction and 11% wanted the troops out altogether.[2] But even in 1974, with anti-Vietnam feeling still running high, 52% favoured retaining the same troop levels, with 3% wanting an increase, while 25% favoured reduction and 12% elimination.

Rising support for the European commitment after the mid-1970s was paralleled by sharper increases in support for defence spending. In various polls from the late 1960s to the mid-1970s, one third to one half the respondents regularly found US defence spending excessive, whereas those who found it insufficient ranged 9% to 17%. By 1975, an NBC poll recorded 41% who still found spending excessive, but 25% who believed it

insufficient. The trend thereafter changed the ratio dramatically. By 1980, various polls showed only 5–14% who found spending excessive and 46–76% who found it insufficient.[3] By March 1982 the huge Reagan defence proposals seemed finally to have produced a public reaction. A CBS/*New York Times* poll showed 49% favouring defence cuts against 41% who did not.[4]

Such surveys hardly reveal an American mass opinion chronically disposed to place domestic goals above military needs and obligations. On the contrary, even in the wake of Vietnam and the more sanguine view of Soviet-American relations prevailing in the heyday of Kissingerian detente, public support for NATO remained strong, with a near majority even at its lowest point in the mid-1970s.

Today's revived public support for external commitments is, however, selective. The strong majority found to favour NATO in Europe in 1982 diminishes slightly for the American commitment to Japan (54% in favour to 30% opposed) and dwindles into a minority of one-third (with 51% opposed) for South Korea.[5] Support for Central American interventions is almost non-existent. The public also seems increasingly wary that the Reagan Administration's foreign policy is too belligerent and undiscriminating. A Harris poll of 17 June 1982 shows 52% worried about Reagan 'getting the country into a war', with 45% not worried, and 53% giving the President 'negative marks on his nuclear weapons negotiations with the Soviets', with only 41% positive.[6]

When nuclear weapons are mentioned, even public support for European defence looks more ambivalent. An NBC poll in October 1981, showed 52% opposed to America's using nuclear weapons in reply to a Soviet nuclear attack on Western Europe. Only 29% favoured either a limited or an all-out American nuclear response; 78% felt neither side could win a nuclear war.[7]

Even if public support for the Alliance has always remained strong, it has nevertheless varied considerably over the years but other issues of foreign and defence policy have seen even wider swings. What mechanism governs changes in public opinion?[8] On foreign policy

3

issues, public opinion as a whole generally appears less volatile than the opinion of what might be called its 'upper stratum', those occupying high occupational, economic and educational status. Mass opinion tends to follow this upper stratum but with a smaller fluctuation. The upper stratum, for example, turned against the Vietnam War and defence spending earlier and more sharply than the general public. It also seems to have grown fearful of declining American strength earlier than the public at large.

Opinion in this upper stratum is said to be particularly sensitive to the treatment of foreign policy events in the media. The media themselves reflect the foreign policy elites – Administration leaders and other politicians, bureaucratic 'experts', vigorous interest groups, as well as a sizeable band of private pundits and research centres.

At the present time, criticism of the Alliance in foreign policy circles has grown intense and is already amply represented in the media. Upper-stratum and ultimately mass opinion may thus be affected. Mass opinion seems already well aware of the current transatlantic friction. An NBC poll in early 1982 revealed 72% who saw Western European allies not supporting US sanctions against Poland sufficiently and 80% who saw insufficient support for American policies in general.[9] Should such disappointments and irritations ultimately disintegrate popular support for the European commitment, however, the shift would not fit the traditional isolationist paradigm. An autonomous and fickle mass drift to neo-isolationism would not overpower the internationalist elites. Instead the mutation in public support would follow debates initiated among elite policy-makers and private experts in which the Alliance lost ground and the consequences gradually filtered into mass opinion.

Cultural Community

Transatlantic recrimination among foreign policy elites has, of course, been frequent since the NATO Treaty was signed in 1949. Yet the public has remained faithful. An intense cultural community, close economic inter-action and a myriad of personal connections are thought to form a community of identity and perception that shields military and political ties from the inevitable collisions of national interest. The political benefits of cultural interpenetration may, of course, be exaggerated. Intense inter-dependence has characterized relations among European states throughout much of their history without preventing innumerable European wars. Post-war Europe and America, however, have had the crucial advantage of being able to define their common values and interests in relation to an obvious common enemy. Yet detente has now made European-American-Soviet relations more ambiguous and, in addition, many people perceive a corresponding attenuation of transatlantic cultural ties.

Factors like cultural sympathy and mutual identity are difficult to define or measure. Relationships that can be counted do not in fact reveal diminishing transatlantic interactions. From 1962 to 1977, for example, the number of Europeans studying in America in any year increased nearly four times, while nearly twice as many Americans were studying in Europe. From 1960 to 1977, the annual number of European visitors to the United States increased almost tenfold, while the number of Americans visiting Europe more than doubled.[10]

The quality of relations may deteriorate, of course, even as the frequency increases. Changes in education can make Europeans and Americans know each other less well even as they see each other more often. American elite education, once heavily oriented toward European history and culture, has entered into a time of relative proliferation and disarray, with greater sensitivity to non-European aspects of America's heritage.[11] Education in Europe, too, has undergone a democratic revolution of its own. Serious knowledge or interest about America seems less common. Many young Europeans, moreover, are intrigued by a Third World where, in the Leftist perspectives that dominate much of European education, America has been cast in a heavy and unsympathetic role – a part the Reagan Administration seems ready to play. As a result, what was close identity in the last generation threatens to become only ritualized nostalgia in the next. If so, the problem is not the quantity of communication but its

4

substance. Present uneasiness over the quality of cultural bonds suggests both the need for careful thought on how they may be reinforced and less complacency about their capacity to compensate for deep political differences.

Domestic Pressure Groups:
The Anti-Nuclear Movement
To affect policy, public opinion needs to be mobilized. In political systems as open and unstructured as the American, well-organized interest groups can give minority views greater weight than the widespread but inert predispositions of the broader public. Apart from the essentially economic pressure groups discussed below, two groups seem particularly relevant to America's external commitments: the renascent anti-nuclear movement and the long-standing Israeli Lobby.

The recent rise of a militant mass movement against nuclear weapons seems to belie the stability of popular support for America's external commitments, particularly in Western Europe, where a nuclear deterrent is widely thought essential to compensate for an imbalance in conventional forces.

America's mass anti-nuclear movement is sufficiently recent, sudden and diffuse to resist easy generalizations. Its rise can be most plausibly explained, not as a spontaneous defection from old commitments, but as a popular reaction to the Reagan Administration's massive arms build-up and bellicose rhetoric.[12] Not unreasonably, the public fears not only nuclear war but men in power who appear to anticipate it with complacency.[13] Logically, an American fear of nuclear war could easily turn into hostility toward the Atlantic Alliance. Renewed American interest in European conventional defence, for example, is driven by fears not only that regional deterrence in Europe may be inadequate, but also that the United States may thereby be drawn into a nuclear war.[14] As more radical experts occasionally suggest, America's nuclear risks would greatly diminish without her NATO commitment.

Whether the anti-nuclear group's momentum will carry it from condemning nuclear war to advocating withdrawal from nuclear commitments remains to be seen. European agitation over the dangers of American missiles on European soil may, of course, resonate to America but assuming a link between the anti-nuclear movement and isolationism seems premature. The logical affinities, however, suggest the importance of making public sense out of military strategies and official positions on arms control. An intemperate and insensitive official posture risks provoking an organized wave of public mistrust that may greatly inhibit external commitments in the future. No doubt experts will then blame neo-isolationism.

Ethnic Lobbies
Of America's lobbies claiming to represent ethnic groups and pressing particular foreign policy goals, the Israeli Lobby is the most ambitious and effective. Not only American Jews but a large part of the general public feels a special sympathy and obligation towards Israel. For several decades a coalition of diverse agencies and individuals has effectively mobilized and brought this support to bear on Congress and the Administration. Pro-Israeli influence has been felt not only on American policy toward the Middle East but also toward the Soviet Union. Soviet persecution of dissenters, plus support for Syria and the PLO, have in recent years encouraged a certain coalescence between pro-Israeli and anti-Soviet perspectives. This coalescence has played its part in the deterioration of Soviet–American detente. In particular, the Jackson–Vanik Amendment, hoping to constrain the Soviet Union to permit more emigration, became a serious obstacle to building up Soviet–American trade.

Some of Israel's American supporters have also grown increasingly critical of Europe. In an American perspective combining support for Israel with loathing for the Soviet Union, European states can easily be criticized for 'Finlandization' at home, a pro-Arab bias in the Middle East, and a generally fatuous complacency about revolutionary movements in the Third World. European inclinations to appease this criticism have declined and European disapproval of current Israeli policy has grown more vehement. With most European states increasingly alienated from Israel, how significant for American–European relations is this coalescence of pro-Israeli, anti-Soviet and anti-European perspectives?

An American foreign policy opposing detente in Europe while condoning Israeli militancy in the Middle East clearly was not formulated with European sensibilities in mind but, if popular antipathy against the Soviet Union remains strong in America, support for Israel's present militant course seems on the wane, not least in the American Jewish Community itself. Even Americans deeply attached to Israel and sympathetic to the dilemmas involved in 'appeasing' the Arabs must wonder at the cost to the United States of a policy that progressively alienates not only the Arab states but also the European Allies. Such sentiments are widespread among foreign policy elites and surface more and more frequently in the media.[15] If the American public is unlikely to renounce concern for Israel, the escalation of the diplomatic costs should make future support less unconditional and sweeping. Logically, a certain coalescence of American and European views on the Middle East is more imaginable than formerly. At least one source of transatlantic friction shows some possibility of diminishing.

Economic Constraints on Foreign Policy
Every Western state has a multitude of powerful economic interest groups. Deteriorating economic conditions intensify their vigour and competitiveness. Greater competitiveness between domestic economic goals and foreign commitments seems logical, even if the distinction is often elusive.

Examining tensions between domestic interests and foreign obligations involves looking at both macro-economic and commercial policy. In macro-economic policy, the size of the defence budget is the most self-evident foreign policy issue. Defence spending obviously has its domestic beneficiaries but since the state's resources are not infinite, a bigger defence budget appears to mean a smaller civilian budget. Whether a particular defence budget seems adequate obviously depends upon estimates of the foreign commitments that national security requires, the forces needed to meet the commitments adequately, and the reasonable cost of such

forces. Someone who believes that the United States should be the 'world's policeman', with a secure first-strike capability against the Soviet Union and the capacity to fight two or three major conventional wars simultaneously, requires a different sum and balance of domestic and foreign spending from someone with more limited external requirements.

Comparing American with Soviet, or NATO with Warsaw Pact military spending is one obvious, if misleading, index of military adequacy. The difficulties of such comparisons are well known. Straightforward comparisons do not, however, show an overall imbalance unfavourable to NATO. In 1980, before Reagan's major build-up, the US defence budget was $142.6 billion. Published CIA calculations have the Soviet Union spending the equivalent of around $185 billion. The rest of NATO, however, spent well over $98.2 billion, as opposed to roughly $16.7 billion for the rest of the Warsaw Pact. The West also has slightly more men under arms in peacetime (4.93 million as opposed to 4.78 million).[16] Such comparisons, obviously crude, nevertheless help to put into perspective the widespread notion of the Warsaw Pact's superior military resources. That NATO should be able to outspend and outnumber the Warsaw Pact should not be surprising. The West is far superior in population, industrial infrastructure and technology.

Despite its inherent superiority in resources and its explicit superiority in spending and manpower, many analysts find the West's effective combat strength markedly inferior, particularly for conventional war. Logically enough, some trace this putative inferiority to a misallocation of resources. Its critics, for example, often find American defence planning without an adequate military doctrine to link commitments, tactics, weapons and forces. In this view, official planners, bemused by technology, know more about weapons than about fighting. Reagan's build-up is seen merely as an extravagant shopping list of new weapons, in many cases without serious military justification. The United States lacks not money and men but the brains and imagination needed for adequate doctrine and organization. Even if critics are more convincing when pointing to defects rather than to alter-

6

natives, America's low ratio of combat forces makes the criticism plausible.[17]

The inability to formulate coherent and efficient military doctrines does not in itself indicate a scarcity of material resources. Rather the opposite is true. Nor do budgetary politics in recent years suggest a squeezing of defence spending. From 1960 to 1980, American military outlays increased 7% at constant prices. The rate, to be sure, was uneven. A compound annual growth rate from 1960 to 1970 of 2.7% was followed by a 1.9% compounded annual decline from 1970 to 1979. The American decline in the 1970s, however, was more than matched by compound annual increases of 1.8%, 3.3%, 2.8% and 3.5% for Britain, France, Germany and Italy, respectively.[18] In any event, the Carter Administration had already reversed the American decline. The Reagan plans announced in 1981 called for defence expenditures to rise from $161 billion in fiscal year 1981 to $343 billion in fiscal year 1986 – a gradual increase to an annual level $181 billion higher.[19]

Despite the straitened economic circumstances and prolonged congressional budgetary struggle of 1982, the new defence programme emerged virtually unscathed. In the end, Congress abandoned not the military build-up, but any prospect of moving toward budgetary equilibrium. Despite all the rhetoric about fiscal responsibility, the Administration proposed and the Congress accepted an overall budget that would predictably lead to a deficit of well over $100 billion.[20]

The 1982 budget battle was simply a more theatrical version of an annual American performance.[21] Once more, Congress proved unable to reconcile domestic and foreign claims within the resources it was willing to make available. True, in the face of a tax cut and substantial military increases, the annual rise in civilian expenditures was slowed; it nevertheless continued to grow and a record deficit became unavoidable. Resolving the budgetary dilemma through a large deficit has, by now, become the normal state of affairs. Except for 1969, the US Federal Budget has been in deficit every year since 1960.

Deficits are not cost-free. Depending on whether monetary policy is generous or tight, perpetual and substantial fiscal deficits generally mean either inflation or else a shortage of capital for private investment. The United States has now experienced both forms of cost. Until recently, Congress's traditional aversion to high interest rates meant financing deficits with easy money. Hence we have seen a steady rise of inflation along with a weak and often depreciating dollar. Given the dollar's international role, much of the inflation was exported, adding significantly to the inflationary problems of most advanced capitalist countries. The cost of America's deficit was thus shared throughout the Alliance.

Tighter American monetary policy since 1979 has meant more financing from real savings borrowed in the capital markets. Unfortunately, this shift to tight money has coincided with a severe cyclical recession and Reagan's greatly increased fiscal deficits. Unprecedented interest rates and a dramatically appreciated dollar have made it difficult for either the American or other economies to recover. Unemployment and bankruptcy have reached levels unknown in the post-war era. Few predict a sustained recovery under present circumstances. In short, the deficits once paid through inflation are now being paid through deflation.

The political distress of prolonged recession could easily force either a new round of excessive monetary creation, and hence renewed inflation, or else a new drive toward fiscal equilibrium, and hence a serious battle for fiscal priority. Either course poses real difficulties for the Reagan Administration.

Renewing inflation is the traditional and perhaps the easiest tactic. Some analysts believe the Federal Reserve and Treasury, fearful of world-wide depression, financial collapse and protectionism, were already following such a course by the autumn of 1982. If so, a new and even more exaggerated cycle of 'boom and bust' may be expected to follow. Whether this traditional stop-go pattern can be continued through another round without a major breakdown may be doubted. The alternative of trying seriously to move toward fiscal equilibrium means either raising taxes or cutting spending. Congress did impose considerable tax increases during the early autumn of 1982, but increasing taxes sufficiently to restore some semblance of fiscal

7

balance would threaten the Administration's basic 'supply-side' economic strategy and might well prove self-defeating in a recession. Moving toward balance by cutting expenditures, on the other hand, means a heightened confrontation between civilian and military spending. With the recession boosting welfare costs and draining the Administration's political support, success in cutting civilian budgets grows increasingly improbable. Since American defence expenditures are already much higher than Western Europe's, and US welfare expenditures are relatively meagre, a budgetary squeeze risks a backlash not only against the expanded military budget, but against the NATO commitment itself.[22] Such a reaction, logical and widely feared, might sorely test the public's long-standing devotion to the Alliance. In 1982, it bears repeating, it is still the foreign-policy elites and not the general public who are most exercised over the 'free-riding' allies.

Whatever else may be said, the Reagan Administration's economic policies cannot be construed as domestic priorities over-riding foreign commitments. Wisely or not, the Administration, supported by the public, has refused to cut back its ambitious plans for the increased defence spending it believes vital for national security and world obligations. In effect, economic policy has been sacrificed to defence policy. If some of the consequences have been as unpopular abroad as unfortunate at home, they must be blamed on an excess of internationalist zeal rather than a rebirth of isolationist domesticity.

Protectionism and the Alliance
Whereas the international significance of America's domestic fiscal and monetary policy has only gradually been recognized, commercial policy has always seemed crucial to Alliance relations. Liberal trade has long been thought essential to foreign political and military ties. Liberal trade, of course, is not a foreign obligation necessarily honoured at the expense of domestic priorities. Many domestic interests depend on foreign markets for their prosperity. Among these are the farmers – with many of the industries tied to agriculture – and the multinationals in general – including the big banks.

The notable economic disruptions of the 1970s were widely expected to threaten liberal trade with a rebirth of protectionism. Rich Western economies would seek to insulate themselves, it was thought, against an increasingly erratic and unfavourable international environment. Even internationally-minded economic firms would limit their horizons to more predictable home or regional markets. But, despite inflation, oil shocks, competition from newly industrializing countries and increasingly severe business cycles, trade remained remarkably open in the 1970s. In the 1980s, however, with unprecedented recession and unemployment in both Europe and America, and several basic industries in deep structural difficulty, commercial barriers have been proliferating. As the recent transatlantic conflict over steel imports illustrates, the American Government has great trouble controlling protectionist forces.

The change is less abrupt than it seems. The liberalism of commercial exchange in the 1970s was to a considerable extent illusory. Generous monetary policy, unbalanced fiscal policy and the dismantling of capital controls meant a periodically declining dollar, which the Government refused to defend.[23] Demands for trade barriers were thus appeased by a regularly depreciating dollar. The combination of policies gratified both the nationalist and the internationalist wings of the American economy. Unprecedented freedom to export capital was a boon to internationally-oriented business, banks in particular, while a steadily depreciating dollar helped to keep home-based manufacturers competitive, despite their inflating costs. Such a policy was as 'mercantilist' as formal protectionism. But it did make direct trade barriers unnecessary and, one way or another, concealed and diffused the costs of America's inflation to her partners. When the accumulating costs of inflation finally forced a tightening of American monetary policy, and the dollar thereby began to appreciate sharply, American products lost their continually renewed competitive advantage. In a depressed economic climate, pressure for direct protection was bound to increase. In this perspective, the new American protectionism of the 1980s is not a shift toward mercantilism but merely a change in its form. American manufacturers and workers now expect tariffs to export the domestics costs of deflation as formerly they expected a declining currency to export the domestic costs of inflation.

A return to genuine liberalism seems improbable so long as American monetary policy is condemned to oscillate from exaggerated inflation to exaggerated constraint. A more stable monetary policy would require re-establishing control over fiscal policy, an unlikely achievement without some reconciliation between the American Government's resources and the domestic and foreign goals it pursues. Until this elementary equilibrium is achieved, the West can look forward to mounting economic disorder. Like some deep inner sickness, America's fiscal imbalance may be expected to generate a shifting and accumulating variety of noxious symptoms.

The significance of the military budget in the overall American budget, and the weight of the NATO commitment in that military budget, together link the Alliance directly to America's fiscal problem. Any serious attempt to achieve American budgetary equilibrium may well involve a showdown in NATO over respective defence costs.[24] For obvious reasons, such a confrontation would constitute a major political challenge. Understandably, European governments would prefer to avoid it. From a broader perspective, however, significant adjustments in the responsibilities and costs of European defence may seem not only beneficial but essential. For the United States, to achieve fiscal equilibrium, and hence monetary stability, cannot be counted a selfish domestic goal pursued at the expense of foreign obligations. America's fiscal disorder has contributed heavily to the World's inflation, unemployment, financial over-extension and general economic disarray of the past few years. Those 'burdens' have been shared in a way that military costs have not. Economic conditions that steadily sap the West's productive vitality and undermine its social peace are no less real a threat than a Soviet invasion of Western Europe. Americans may certainly be criticized for failing to tax themselves adequately. Such criticism, however, does not sit well from rich allies whose own territory is directly menaced but whose defence spending is disproportionately less.

Democracy and Foreign Policy

What broad conclusions can be drawn about the relationship between America's domestic priorities and her Alliance obligations? In direct military and political obligations the traditional isolationist paradigm does not seem to apply. Isolationism is not deeply rooted in the masses, nor does internationalism depend upon the elites. The general public has supported America's European commitment and the military budgets demanded to sustain America's external role, a willingness no doubt made easier by America's relatively underdeveloped civilian demands and compulsive fiscal deficits. Present US dissatisfaction with Europe stems, if anything, from the foreign-policy elite itself. The issue, moreover, is not priority of domestic over foreign goals but a different international strategy.

In economic relations, a different picture emerges. Rising American protectionism clearly suggests a conflict for priority between domestic and foreign claims – between preventing further unemployment in home-based industry and sustaining an open international economy. This growing protectionist pressure is not a populist mutation, but results logically from present economic policies carried out under present circumstances. The chain of causes that ends with turning away from internationalism in trade passes through a macro-economic policy of perpetual fiscal imbalance. For over twenty years, the American political system has failed to reconcile the sum of the resources it is willing to raise with the civilian and military budgetary claims it insists upon meeting. The accumulating consequences have seriously undermined Western economic prosperity and progressively soured transatlantic political relations. The resulting pressure to end American fiscal instability also feeds a quarrel within the Alliance over military budgets. A long-standing structural imbalance between respective national resources and military responsibilities has itself played a considerable role in that American fiscal imbalance which lies at the heart of the economic deterioration. From this perspective, the Alliance might be

9

better off today if the American public had long ago insisted more firmly on its domestic priorities and been less fond of its foreign obligations.

The analysis may perhaps be put in more general terms. Over the past two decades, neither the United States nor the states of Western Europe have come to terms with their changed situation. American wealth and power, the initial foundation of the post-war system, has inevitably diminished in relation to both America's adversaries and her allies. America's relative decline represents not a failure of long-standing policy, but its logical consequence. Under the circumstances, preserving the highly integrated and relatively stable post-war order, of which the Atlantic Alliance has been the keystone, requires a more plural sharing of cost and control. This means a substantial adaptation of roles and general perspectives within the Alliance itself.

To ask whether American public opinion would comprehend and support such an evolution seems premature. American leaders have never presented the public with a realistic view of the country's changing world position. Nor, it must be confessed, have its foreign policy and political elites been fertile sources of appropriate new policies. Instead, official America has been bemused first by unrealistic notions of detente and now by an unrealistic nostalgia for hegemony. The result has been a progressive renunciation of serious efforts at accommodation with the Soviet Union, followed by a progressive alienation from Western Europe. As more sensitive pollsters suggest, it is not the public that is demanding unilateral world hegemony. Unfortunately, failures in American leadership are not without their analogue in Western Europe. If American policy may be accused of wanting detente or hegemony 'on the cheap', present European policy might be dubbed 'self-determination on the cheap'.

In America, at least, it is the elite and not the public that has failed. At the moment, public education in foreign policy falters for lack of a suitable curriculum. Blaming the bankruptcy of elite policies on the domestic constraints of democracy seems a judgment mistaken in its analysis, evasive in its prescriptions, and dangerous in its implications.

NOTES

[1] Surveys for Potomac Associates kindly provided, along with much good advice, by William Watts. See his 'The United States and Japan: How We See Each Other', speech delivered on 28 May 1982 in Tokyo, p.14. Also Lloyd Free and William Watts, 'Internationalism Comes of Age . . .Again', *Public Opinion*, April/May 1980, p.46. For interpretations I take to be along the broad lines developed here, see also Daniel Yankelovich, 'Cautious Internationalism: A Changing Mood Toward U.S. Foreign Policy', *Public Opinion*, March/April 1978, p.12; Daniel Yankelovich and Larry Kaagan, 'Assertive America', *Foreign Affairs, America and the World*, 1980, Volume 59, Number 3, pp.696–713; Bruce Russett and Donald R. DeLuca, 'Don't Tread on Me: Public Opinion and Foreign Policy in the Eighties', *Political Science Quarterly*, 96, Number 3, Fall 1981, pp.381–401; a broad view which has influenced my thinking is John Lewis Gaddis, 'Containment: Its Past and Future', *International Security*, Volume 5, Number 4, Spring 1981, pp.74–102.
[2] International Poll by Gallup-Affiliated Institutions during February 1982, for *Newsweek International*, and other European news organizations.
[3] Various CBS/*NY Times*, NBC and AIPO surveys as summarized in Table 1 in Russett and DeLuca, *op.cit.* in note 1.
[4] CBS/*NY Times* Poll, 18 March 1982.
[5] William Watts, *op.cit.* in note 1.

[6] Harris Poll, 17 June 1982.
[7] NBC Poll, 10 November 1981 (taken in October 1981).
[8] Bruce Russett and Donald R. DeLuca, *op.cit.* in note 1.
[9] NBC Poll, 5 February 1982.
[10] Derived from various years of *UN Statistical Yearbook* and UNESCO, *Statistics of Students Abroad*.
[11] See David P. Calleo. 'The Alliance: An Enduring Relationship?', *SAIS Review*, Number 4, Summer 1982.
[12] For a comprehensive recent survey, see Fox Butterworth, 'Anatomy of the Nuclear Protest', *New York Times Magazine*, 11 July 1982, p. A13. For public opinion on whether the Reagan Administration is too bellicose, see note 6.
[13] See, for example, two articles by Robert Sheer, 'Civil Defense Program to be Revised: Reagan Seeks to Counter Possible Attack by Soviets', *Los Angeles Times*, 15 January 1982, Section I, p.1; and 'U.S. Could Survive War in Administration's View', *Los Angeles Times*, 16 January 1982, Section I, p.1; also Judith Miller, 'Panel Angered by Failure of Aide to Testify on Civil Defense Plans', *New York Times*, 17 March 1982, p. A16, and her 'Civil Defense Notions Change but the Skepticism Remains', *New York Times*, 4 April 1982, p. 6E.
[14] See McGeorge Bundy, George F. Kennan, Robert S. McNamara and Gerard Smith, 'Nuclear Weapons and the Atlantic Alliance', *Foreign Affairs*, Spring 1982.
[15] Polls in early July 1982, assessing public reactions to

Israel's Lebanon invasion varied widely. For a sensitive analysis of growing anti-Israeli sentiment, see Stephen S. Rosenfeld, 'Anti-Semitism and U.S. Foreign Policy', *Foreign Policy*, 47, Summer 1982, pp. 172*ff.*

[16] International Institute for Strategic Studies, *The Military Balance 1981–1982, passim.*

[17] For a survey of Congressional and other critics of military budgeting, see Richard Halloran, 'Criticism Rises on Reagan's Plan for 5-Year Growth of the Military', *New York Times*, 22 March 1982, p. 1; James Fallows, *National Defense* (New York: Random House, 1981) mounts a comprehensive attack on the defence budget. Concern about NATO's effectiveness among Congressional leaders generally worried about defence can be found in Senator Sam Nunn, *NATO: Can the Alliance Be Saved?*, Report to the Committee on Armed Services, United States Senate, 13 May 1982 (Washington DC: USGPO, 1982). For a recent newspaper survey of NATO's deficiencies, see Neil Ulman. 'An Out-gunned NATO has Much to Discuss at its Summit in June', *Wall Street Journal*, 26 May 1982, p. 1. Specialist literature on military issues is extensive. Representative American critiques of present doctrines and force structures are Steven L. Canby, 'Territorial Defense in Central Europe', *Armed Forces and Society*, Volume 7, Number 1, Fall 1980, pp. 51–67; or William S. Lind, 'Some Doctrinal Questions for the United States Army', *Military Review*, Volume 17, Number 3, March 1977, pp. 54–65. For sharp critique of the critics, see John J. Mearsheimer, 'Maneuver, Mobile Defense, and the NATO Central Front', *International Security*, Winter 1981–82, pp. 104–122. A survey assessing and synthesizing contrasting positions is Colonel T. N. Dupuy, U. S. Army, retired, 'The Nondebate Over How Army Should Fight', *Army*, June 1982, pp. 35*ff.*

[18] IISS, *op. cit.* in note 16, p.110.

[19] *New York Times*, 5 March 1981, p.A1. An updated request can be found in Department of Defense, *Annual Report to the Congress: Fiscal Year 1983*, January 1982.

[20] For a detailed account of the Senate debate, see Pat Towell, 'Defense Authorization Bill Passed by the Senate after Trims Made to Meet Budget Goals', *Congressional Quarterly, Special Report*, 15 May 1982, pp. 1,155*ff.* For the flavour of the House debate, see Margot Hornblower, 'House Backs Reagan on Military Spending', *International Herald Tribune*, 31 July–1 August 1982, p.1. For various estimates of the deficit, see 'U.S. Aides Downplay Report on Economy', *Ibid.*

[21] For an extended version of this argument, see David P. Calleo, *The Imperious Economy* (Cambridge and London: Harvard University Press, 1982), chapter 9.

[22] In 1980, defence expenditure as a percentage of GNP for Britain, France, Germany and the US were 5.1%, 3.9%, 3.2% and 5.5% respectively. American social security expenditures are, in proportion to GNP, about two-thirds those of Britain and roughly half those of France and Germany. IISS, *op.cit.* in note 16, p.112. Social security figures are from the Comparative Studies Staff, Office of International Policy, Social Security Administration, and are spelled out in Calleo, *op. cit.* in note 21, p.96.

[23] Calleo, *ibid.*, chapters 4 and 8.

[24] David P. Calleo, 'Inflation and American Power', *Foreign Affairs*, 59, Spring 1981, pp.781–812.

11

Domestic Priorities and the Demands of Alliance: A European Perspective

DOMINIQUE MOÏSI

Introduction

In his memoirs, 'Die Welt von Gestem', the Austrian writer Stefan Zweig described the period before World War I as the 'Golden Age' of security. The guns of August 1914 were to destroy that age, maybe forever. Yet, thanks to the protection of the American nuclear umbrella and to the logic of nuclear deterrence during a period of US nuclear superiority, the Europeans were able to enjoy for more than twenty years – from the death of Stalin to the Yom Kippur War – a feeling of relative security. They had the illusion that Europe, no longer at the centre of World History, could live in a prosperous and comfortable cocoon, in relative isolation from the sound and fury of a violent world. Crises did of course occur, such as over Berlin and Cuba, but their resolution simply confirmed a climate of security that gave birth to the word detente. The crises that did develop inside the Alliance were reflections of its success. The aim of security achieved, however, many in the US now consider the price of the Alliance economically too high, while many in Europe feel the political cost too heavy.

It has been the disappearance since 1979 of that feeling of security that gives a new significance to the troubles of the Alliance, and makes some observers question its very survival in its present form. Since the Soviet invasion of Afghanistan there has been the sensation of living in a state of permanent crisis; the use of military force to impose political solutions is becoming the rule and is no longer the exception. The past is now evoked to stress the danger of the present and the fear of the future. Analogies with 1914 and 1939 recreate a link with history of the kinds of crisis and wars that the existence of nuclear weapons seemed at one time to render impossible. The evolution of the balance of forces of the Soviet Union, the multiplication of opportunities for crises and the dual revolution of nuclear technology (precision added to miniaturization) has seemed to add rationality to these new fears.

The divisive impact on alliances of the logic of nuclear war, denounced in the 1960s by de Gaulle and his followers, has now taken on a new validity. How can the Americans, who are not even sure of having enough weapons to defend themselves, protect Western Europe? European fears over the inadequacy of US military capabilities are reinforced by frustrations with US political behaviour.

The Nature of the Crisis

The present crisis of the Alliance is preoccupying not only because it takes place within the context of a different balance of forces but also because it translates into the conflicting interests of the respective governments and the divergent evolutions of societies' historical and national emotions. These two evolutions meet and reinforce each other. The constellation of values that constituted the basis of the Atlantic Alliance is slowly eroding. The 'troubled partnership' no longer places France in opposition to the United States, as it did in the 1960s, but now it opposes all of Western Europe against America, something which could only be interpreted positively if it were to lead to real European solidarity.

Nor is the current crisis of the Alliance any longer limited either to quarrels over its internal fabric (as under de Gaulle) or to crises occurring beyond its geographical boundaries. As demonstrated by the 'pipeline' issue, the very essence of the origins of the Alliance and its justification has come under fire in the debate over the type of relation the West should have with the East.

12

Both in Western Europe and in the United States, the present crisis could be summarized as the tendency to give priority to domestic considerations over international ones, to national interests over the concerns of the Alliance. From a gallocentric perspective one could smugly describe this phase as a posthumous triumph of a *Gaulliste* view of the world. When the German Director of the IISS refers to attitudes of the Federal Republic of Germany as '*Gaullisme* in a minor key' and when a well-known French commentator accuses the present US Administration of 'Californian *Gaullisme*', they describe the growth of what can only be called a 'new nationalism' in the Western World. This new nationalism is assertive in the US and in France. It is an inward-turning nationalism in most nations of Northern Europe including the FRG. The French and the Americans want to carry out what they consider their historical mission. The rest wish rather to be left alone, out of the limelight and tempest.

The return to nationalistic attitudes is understandable in a world rediscovering such 'classical' concepts as the use of military force, and the predominance of national actor states over transnational groupings. We may be witnessing a progressive divorce between the economic and political realms. Yet, even if it exists as a temptation, real protectionism is no longer a possibility in a truly interdependent world economy.

This rediscovery of nationalism erodes the Alliance's solidarity not only at the political and economic level but, more seriously, at the level also of culture and society. This is not the place to discuss the issue but one could here evoke in parallel the erosion of the ideals of the European Community.

To analyse the political and psychological dimensions of what I here call a crisis and the growing conflict between domestic priorities and the demands of Alliance, it is necessary to examine the roots of anti-nuclear, pacifist and neutralist forces in Western Europe. The words used to describe them are either too simplistic or too ambiguous. Moreover, it is difficult to make generalizations for historical, geographical, religious and cultural differences render any such attempts treacherous but it is nevertheless a necessary exercise.

The Peace Movements in Western Europe

The peace movements that have emerged with various success in Western Europe have three characteristics: they seriously question the logic of nuclear deterrence; they correspond to the growth of a new brand of anti-Americanism, different from the old brand practised by France; and they are also the consequences of an identity crisis diversely affecting some Western European countries, partly as a result of the adverse effects that NATO has had on the development of a national defence effort. The peace movements are strongest in those countries where these three factors are present and can reinforce each other.

Nuclear Deterrence

The evolution of the balance of the forces in favour of the Soviet Union, linked to a technological revolution that makes limited nuclear war less impossible to imagine (at least in abstract terms), have exposed the political weaknesses of the 'flexible response' doctrine and therefore its relative inadequacy. One may even wonder whether this doctrine did not always presuppose psychologically that the United States enjoyed superiority and that the prospects of war in Europe were so remote as to be a complete abstraction. The moment the risks of war appear somewhat conceivable, and the extent of US protection doubtful, the entire logic of nuclear deterrence rebounds. Its rationality is questioned in the name of 'civilization'. The fear of nuclear holocaust in the name of civilization is what ultimately unifies such different messages as the 'no-first-use' proposal presented in *Foreign Affairs* by four well-established experts or the extremism of unilateralist nuclear disarmers such as E. P. Thompson in Britain

Until and including World War II, one could sacrifice one's life for the freedom of one's country. Now it may appear moral to sacrifice one's freedom for the survival of the planet. The anti-nuclear movement is particularly strong in countries where moralism is reinforced by religious or ecological concerns. Nuclear forces tend to atomize the spirit of defence. Debates among experts, once they are exposed to the public by the media in demand of explanation and sensation, can

13

only have a negative impact on populations, which understand very little and are rightly shocked by the often barbaric nature of these debates. In this context America's protection is increasingly seen as more a threat than a guarantee, and the Soviet Union less frightening than the prospect of war.

It is easy for Soviet propaganda to play on these morally if not politically justifiable fears and to denounce in particular the danger represented for the Europeans by the installation of medium-range nuclear missiles on their soil. In that sense, one can say that Chancellor Schmidt in his 1977 speech in London, Kissinger in 1979 in Brussels or President Reagan lately on many occasions, were the best Soviet propagandists. It is as if the nuclear horrors of tomorrow are obliterating the conventional horrors of yesterday both for Europe and for many non-European countries. Many people conveniently forget that Europe has been shielded from these bloody conflicts by the existence of the nuclear weapon.

Anti-Americanism
The second factor that accounts for the growth of nuclear pacifism is the birth of a new anti-Americanism. For many Europeans, the United States today combines negatively the imperial tradition of *Pax Americana* (as reawakened by the Reagan Administration) and the continuation of the incoherence of the Carter period. America appears as authoritarian and bent on pursuing its self-interest and it is the European countries that have traditionally expected the most from the United States that are the most disappointed. But anti-Americanism goes beyond the mere denunciation of American political style and political choices. There is also a rebellion against American values and models and this translates into an anti-establishment trend. By rejecting America, one refuses the model of one's parent. Ironically this rejection corresponds to an American type of radicalism. Reagan's present policy towards Central and South America conveniently rekindles the old anti-imperialist cause. Denunciation of American imperialism acts as a common denominator for both the old (political) and new (cultural) brand of anti-Americanism. Jack Lang's denunciation in Mexico of the American cultural imperialism is a perfect illustration of this new symbiosis.

The Crisis of Identity
Third, the growth of self-styled peace movements corresponds to an identity crisis that is affecting the countries of Northern Europe in various ways, nowhere with greater consequences than in West Germany.

The long-term impact of NATO's protection over countries with weak military traditions (like the Netherlands), or too strong military traditions (like the Federal Republic) could only be adverse. It is difficult in the long run to act responsibly when one does not exercise responsibilities. The fact that the US protection is above all nuclear can only accentuate that trend. What is the meaning of a conventional defence effort whose value seems mainly complementary to nuclear weapons and whose use is either linked to marginal or catastrophic scenarios?

In this context, a country like the Netherlands could easily be tempted to return to its historical tradition of quasi-neutralism and countries in the middle of a serious national crisis (such as Belgium) are also affected. But the main problem of course arises over the evolution of the Federal Republic of Germany. Symbolic demonstrations against the United States in Berlin, where Kennedy had been greeted ecstatically, and concrete governmental decisions in defiance of the American wishes on East–West matters are evidence of a change that is undeniable. This evolution evokes so much passion that it must be treated with great care and restraint. 'Peace movement' activists are only a small minority in the Federal Republic, 5–6% of the population at most. Even if the number of their sympathizers is added, they still represent as a fraction no more than the Communist (PCF) voters in France, i.e. less than 20%. If one can derive truth from polls, America is far more popular in the Federal Republic than in Britain for example – 73% against 46% (*Newsweek* poll, 15 March 1982). But the Federal Republic of Germany is not Britain. It is at the heart of Europe and it remains a divided country with a unique past. Any shift of public opinion and governmental attitudes there is significant.

The evolution of the Federal Republic is both normal and inevitable but that does not mean that it should not worry us. Integration within the West was achieved by Adenauer. Normalization with the East (and with the German Democratic Republic in particular) was achieved by Chancellor Willy Brandt. Under Chancellor Schmidt, the Federal Republic has been engaged in a policy of normalization *vis-à-vis* itself. Such a policy, while maintaining the dual heritage of Adenauer and Brandt, takes into account the interests of a middle-size power who wants to be recognized as such throughout the world.

In taking this road, the Federal Republic has been encouraged by the example of a neighbouring country that places self-interest above all. But once *Gaullisme* started to cross the Rhine, it contained within it at least the seeds of problems. Normalization in the German case means confronting a division which is bound to appear artificial. It is not the German State that is the problem but the German Nation. With the passage of years and the maturing of new generations, it was simply natural for Germany to rediscover and confront both her immediate and her remote past. In her efforts to place herself firmly in the West, the Federal Republic had to accept as normal an abnormal relation with herself. That simply could not last for ever. In a world of crises, both economic and international, leading to a rediscovery of the 'virtues' of nationalism, the problem of Germany was bound to surface. It is not simply a political or partisan problem. There ought not to be anything reassuring about scenarios that shift party politics towards the right and envisage the return of the CDU to power. It was more or less inevitable that, once the vision of an integrated Western Europe faded in the 1950s, the Federal Republic should start looking towards East Germany and towards a definition of self-interest that was more German and less Atlanticist or European. Inevitable or not, the French, by providing the example of *Gaullisme*, and the US, by disappointing the Federal Republic, have accelerated the tempo of this evolution. It is our common responsibility to limit the consequences of these changes by making the Germans feel that they are an integral part of the West and of Europe. In this task, the French (for geographic and historic reasons) have a special responsibility.

Why France is Different

That rejection of the logic of nuclear deterrence, and identity crisis and anti-Americanism are at the roots of the developments of the peace movements in Europe, can be further demonstrated by the counter-proof of France. If France appears as an island of stability and firmness confronted by the growing waves of European pacifism it is partly because the peace movement in France is largely controlled by the Communist Party and this tends to repel the majority. But it is mainly because the three factors just described above do not apply to the French case. *Gaullisme* may have made France a nuisance to her Allies in the 1960s, but it is now largely responsible for its steadfastness. The principle of an independent *force de frappe* is no longer a matter of political debate in France since, by the middle of the 1970s, the Communists and the Socialists had accepted its logic. Nor does anyone question that France should remain outside the integrated military body of NATO. This consensus – some would say on the value of bluff – has protected France from disturbing debates. Together with a fortunate geography that places Germany between France and the Soviet threat and the fact that France is not concerned with the TNF modernization decision, this lack of contentious issues explains France's relative immunity to pacifism. *Gaullisme* has helped France on two more counts. It has provided France – exaggeratedly may be – with the sense of a special mission in the world, most recently emphasized by President Mitterrand. This conviction, linked with the control France has over her defence policy, has protected her existential interrogation. France does not face a crisis of identity. Nor does anti-Americanism, as a symbol of a rebellion against the values of the establishment, apply to France as it does to Northern Europe. Thanks largely to *Gaullisme*, a certain kind of anti-Americanism has been a value shared for many years by the political establishment itself and therefore anti-Americanism cannot represent for Frenchman a way of defining oneself by opposition to one's parent. The intelligentsia which might

15

have acted as a focus for dissent, discovered the *gulag* in the early 1970s and this confirmed their dislike of the Soviet Union. When one puts all these factors together, they account for the appearance of France as a pillar of stability in the Western Alliance. This optimism should however, be tempered by four considerations. If France is not affected by neutralism it is because her strategic doctrine is largely one of neutrality. If anti-nuclear movements were to see their influence spreading in the West it would be difficult for France to remain for long unaffected. Moreover, there has been an indirect price to pay for that earlier victory of *Gaullisme*; it may – as mentioned earlier – be taking its toll in Germany today. Finally the French Government has lately been using an old brand of anti-Americanism in a new third-world guise and condemnation of US cultural imperialism may prove as detrimental to the demands of the Alliance as the anti-establishment rebellion of the Northern part of Europe.

Conclusions

The tendency of our societies to drift apart is reinforced by government policies and by the democratic nature of our political system The Reagan Administration, in its search for a policy that would weaken the Soviet Union, has so far succeeded mainly in weakening the Alliance. The European Governments in a desperate attempt to preserve what can be saved of detente, have moved dangerously towards dissociating their economic exchanges with the East from their political and military implications, thus reinforcing both the Soviet Union and the advocates of a different kind of unilateralism in the United States.

Family analogies are fashionable these days to describe the troubles of the Alliance. What is happening clearly surpasses a family quarrel but it is our common duty to prevent a progressive divorce that would be catastrophic both for the United States and Western Europe. Pacifism should not be the only highly visible force that the Americans and the Europeans have in common.

The domestic nature of our societies and the weight of electoral considerations when given priority over international concerns are aggravating the seriousness of the crisis. Anti-Americanism or anti-Europeanism cannot be allowed to compensate, in the eyes of the electorate, for the competitive failure of the French and American economic programmes.

The erosion of the Alliance and the crisis of the logic of nuclear deterrence reinforce the advocates of a conventional defence for Western Europe. Europe can no longer remain a 'civilian power'. But, the reasons that have prevented the creation of a European defence system yesterday are still present today. France, comforted in her tranquil selfishness by the way the international system has evolved, is not ready to modify her strategic doctrine. The Federal Republic cannot become a nuclear power and is neither ready nor willing to exchange an American nuclear guarantee for a French one. Moreover, the economic crisis makes *any* further defence effort a very difficult proposition. On each side of the Atlantic, there are growing frustrations with the state of the Alliance but no-one can think of serious alternatives. It is highly symbolic that, in spite of the fertile imagination of those who work in the field of international relations, we have found no word to describe the post-cold war post-detente era. It may very well be that for more than 30 years we have lived through an exceptional period. There was in the West a generous and powerful giant, there was apparently a stable balance of forces, there were prosperous economies and nationalism, as a result of two world wars, was weak. All these ingredients are slowly disappearing. European pacifism and American unilateralism are both symptoms of the resurgence of new nationalistic trends in the Western World. Shakespeare was making a prudent meteorological judgment when he observed that: 'So foul a sky will not clear without a storm'. Let us hope, at least in the case of the Western Alliance, that Shakespeare was wrong.

Deterrence, Consensus and Reassurance in the Defence of Europe

MICHAEL HOWARD

To ask a historian to look into and prescribe for the future is to invite a presentation consisting of as much past history as the author thinks he can get away with and as little prophecy and prescription as he thinks his audience will accept. Historians have seen too many confident prophets fall flat on their faces to lay themselves open to more humiliation than they can help. We know that all we can do is to help diagnose the problem or, better, expose false diagnoses. We also believe that in doing this it is helpful to consider how a situation has developed. I make no apology therefore for spending a few moments in casting a backward look over the origins and development of the Western Alliance to see how we have got to where we are now. There is little point in considering where we should be going if we do not first decide where we are starting from.

Let us go back thirty-five years, a third of a century, to the immediate aftermath of the Second World War. After the 'Battle of the Books' between the revisionist and counter-revisionist schools, a picture has now emerged over which most historians now agree. It is one of wartime understandings between the Soviet Union and her Western Allies – understandings based largely on Western illusions or at best the most fragile of hopes – breaking down within a few months of the end of hostilities. The Soviet Union moved in to consolidate, as part of her Empire, the territories already occupied by her armed forces – economically, politically and militarily. Simultaneously the United States was liquidating her wartime commitments to her European allies as quickly as – some might say more quickly than – she decently could. As a result, Western Europe in 1946–7 trembled on the verge of economic collapse, a collapse which its Moscow-orientated Communist par-

ties were fully prepared to exploit. In Germany, and especially in Berlin, democratic political parties fought what seemed to be a losing battle against strong, well-organized and confident Communist opponents who, for the past fifteen years, had been preparing for just such an opportunity. There was a widespread fear, not so much of Soviet military attack on Western Europe, but of a disintegration of the whole political and economic structure that would make any such attack unnecessary.

It was to prevent such a disintegration that the United States initiated, in 1947, the European Recovery Programme. This programme may have had an unforeseen escalatory effect in that it was perceived by the Soviet Union as a threat to their own control of Eastern Europe, and so precipitated those actions in Prague and Berlin in 1948 that were read by many in the West as clear evidence of Soviet aggressive intentions. If the Russians were thwarted in their use of political means for attaining their objectives (so the argument went) might they not use military ones – unless they were deterred from doing so by the clear perception that any such move would bring them up against the enormous latent power of the United States?

Strategic Reassurance

This was the thinking that led to the creation of the North Atlantic Treaty Organization in 1949. In Western Europe serious expectation of Soviet armed attack was still not high. It was to increase dramatically for a few months at the time of the Korean War, but even then the Europeans were less conscious of any imminent 'Soviet Threat' than they were of their own weakness, disunity and inability to cope with such a threat if one emerged. The American military presence was wanted in

17

Western Europe, not just in the negative role of a *deterrent* to Soviet aggression, but in the positive role of a *reassurance* to West Europe, the kind of reassurance a child needs from its parents or an invalid from his doctors against dangers which, however remote, cannot be entirely discounted. This concept of *re-assurance* has not, so far as I know, hitherto been a term of art in strategic analysis, but it should be, and so far as I am concerned it is now.

Whether the North Atlantic Treaty and the steps taken to implement it were really necessary to deter the Soviet Union from a military onslaught on Western Europe we cannot tell until the Soviet Union is as generous with access to her official documents as we are in the West. It is, however, improbable, given both her historical record and her political philosophy, that she would have seriously contemplated such an action unless and until a recognizable 'revolutionary situation' had developed in the West in which they could plausibly intervene to give fraternal support to the toiling masses and to a powerful indigenous Communist Party that would act as their agent in controllling the region after its conquest. These requirements seemed, in the 1940s, to be developing quite nicely. Within a decade they had disappeared. Whatever the effectiveness of *deterrence*, *re-assurance* had worked. The economy of Western Europe recovered, and with it the political self-confidence of the West Europeans. The Communist Parties withdrew from the centre of the political stage to the periphery, and increasingly distanced themselves from Moscow. Serious fears of Soviet attack dwindled and, after Stalin's death, they almost disappeared from the public consciousness. The outbreaks in Eastern Europe from 1953 onwards showed that it was the Soviet Union that was now on the political defensive. Its treatment of the Hungarian rising in 1956 led to massive defections from, and splits within, the Communist Parties in the West. In West Germany the economic miracle sucked out of the Eastern Zone by the hundreds of thousands precisely those well-qualified young people that the DDR needed to reconstruct her own economy. By the end of the 1950s Western Europe was an economic power-house

that would have dominated Eastern Europe if the Soviet Union had let it. A decade later it was beginning to rival its own protector.

During this period the success of *re-assurance* was, in some respects, an obstacle to *deterrence*. The peoples of Western Europe were so effectively reassured that they were prepared to run those military risks that have given their military leaders nightmares for the past thirty years. In 1950 there may have been serious fears of Soviet attack. Three years later, when the European statesmen came to consider the price which their military advisers had calculated, at the Lisbon Meeting in 1952, that they would have to pay for a credible deterrent military posture, such fears had almost disappeared. The re-establishment of economic stability was considered to demand overriding priority and the 'Lisbon Force Goals' went out of the window. In the judgment of the political leaders of Western Europe the danger of Soviet military attack did not appear great enough to warrant the costs involved in building up the kind of defensive forces that, on a purely military calculus, would be needed to deter it.

The Nuclear Alternative: Defence on the Cheap

It was then that thermo-nuclear weapons came to the rescue of soldiers and politicians alike, providing a deterrent that appeared militarily credible at a socially acceptable cost. The long-term implications of depending on weapons of mass destruction for national security worried only a politically insignificant minority. Governments, and the majorities on which they relied, found in nuclear weapons so convenient a solution to their budgetary problems that they were adopted almost without question. 'Conventional forces', with all their heavy social costs, could be reduced to the status of trip-wires, or at most, of shields to repel an enemy assault for the brief time needed for the Strategic Air Command to strike decisively at targets within the Soviet Union. The critiques both of the moralists and of the military specialists made no impact on those real centres of power in Western governments, the Treasuries, centres which owe their power to their capacity to reflect and enforce broadly accepted social priorities. Whatever their defence specialists might tell them about the balance of military forces, the peoples of Western Europe, so long as they remained prosperous, saw little danger of Soviet attack and wanted defence on the cheap. They remained *reassured*, though whether this reassurance came from shrewdness or from self-delusion, from confidence in American nuclear supremacy or basic disbelief in the reality of any Soviet threat, it would probably be impossible to say. In any case throughout the 1950s and the 1960s deterrence and reassurance both worked. The Europeans did get defence on the cheap, as they were getting energy on the cheap, and, thanks to the benevolent Keynesianism of the ruling economic pundits, everything else on the cheap. As one European leader remarked of his own nation, they had never had it so good.

Pleasant as this condition was so long as it lasted, it had two characteristics which in historical perspective emerge very clearly. One was that the credibility of the *deterrent* posture depended on a continuing American nuclear ascendancy over the Soviet Union, something about which I shall have more to say in a moment. The second, and perhaps more significant, was that the peoples of Western Europe effectively abandoned responsibility for their own defence. Their own armed forces, forces which have always had the social role of embodying national self-consciousness and will to independent existence, became almost peripheral, part of a mechanism of nuclear deterrence the ultimate control of which lay elsewhere. The reluctance of the British and French Governments to accept this situation and their development of strategic nuclear capabilities of their own has to be understood in these psychological terms, rather than those of the somewhat tortuous rationales which French and British officials now advance to justify their existence.

And even if these nuclear strike forces do, however marginally, enhance national independence, they are not 'popular' forces. That is, they are not forces with whose fortunes the nation can identify itself, as the British people identified themselves with the fortunes of their forces in the recent Falkland Islands campaign. To show the significance of this fact, permit me a brief excursion into history. Popular involvement in war, as all readers of Clausewitz will know, is a matter of comparatively recent origin. In the eighteenth century, wars in Europe were fought by specialists responsive only to the requirements of absolute governments, and the less the population was involved in them the better. The role of the good citizen was to pay the taxes needed for the upkeep of these specialists, to acquiesce philosophically in any incidental hardships that their operations might cause him, and to keep his mouth shut. It was the French Revolution that (after the American Revolution) made popular involvement an intrinsic factor in war, a factor that was to become of growing importance until, in the First World War, it overshadowed everything else. In that conflict popular passion rather than military skill, much less political wisdom, determined the course of the war and ultimately its outcome. In the Second World War popular participation was still an essential element, although the contribution of scientific and technical specialists was increasingly decisive. But in the nuclear age those specialists have again reduced peoples to the passive roles they played, or were supposed to play, in the eighteenth century. It is assumed that war, if it comes, will be fought for them by experts, over (if they are lucky) their heads.

The Experts and the Public

The extent to which this has occurred can be seen by considering the debates over NATO strategy that have taken place, whether in official circles or in centres for strategic studies during the past twenty years. Increasingly the defence of Western Europe has been considered simply as a problem of 'extended deterrence' involving calculations of possibilities and probabilities as abstract as those of a chess game; as a problem to be solved by various combinations and deployments of delivery systems, strategic, intermediate or tactical, land-based, sea-based or air-based, but all under American control. The expertise needed to make these calculations is shared only by small groups of specialists and officials in European defence ministries, who have seldom seen it as their duty to expound these calculations to a wider public. The efforts of

19

such bodies as the International Institute for Strategic Studies and its associates elsewhere in Europe to educate public opinion in these matters has had at best limited success. They are too abstract, too arcane. Whatever the merits of the argument, for example, that the Soviet deployment of SS–20 missiles had to be countered by the emplacement of cruise missiles and *Pershing* IIs, it did not arise out of any profound and widely held anxiety among the peoples of Western Europe. It was a debate between specialists – and specialists who did not have the political antennae to foresee that such emplacement might make people feel more vulnerable rather than less. Such specialists are like theologians. When they lose touch with the springs of popular belief, when their analysis becomes too complex and remote, their authority becomes attenuated. New teachers will arise, Martin Luthers, John Wesleys, pastors whose beliefs may be simplistic to the point of lunacy, but whose message is responsive to popular needs and who can speak in a language that everyone can understand.

This is not to say that the specialists are to blame for this failure in communication. In defence questions as in any other area of government – economic policy, for example, or finance – the layman does not expect to have to master the technical details. He employs the expert to handle them for him. In defence as in these other fields there is always likely to be a difference between expert and lay perceptions, and it is the job of political leadership to reconcile them. In the field of defence this difference appears nowhere more clearly than in the distinction I have made between *reassurance* and *deterrence*. For the expert the two are indistinguishable. He will not believe his country to be safe unless he is satisfied that provision has been made to counter every option open to every likely adversary. The layman may be less demanding, but sometimes he is more. In certain moods, for example, the Congress of the United States has refused to be reassured by the deterrent posture that its military specialists have pronounced to be adequate. In Europe, on the other hand, the peoples of the Western democracies have accepted as amply reassuring a deterrent posture that their experts have

repeatedly told them is dangerously inadequate, and if the events of the past thirty years are anything to go by, popular instinct has proved more reliable than expert fears. In spite of the repeated warnings of its military specialists, no threat has materialized. Instead, the prosperity of the West has reached unheard of heights. It is the Communist societies, those which thirty years ago seemed so psychologically as well as militarily menacing, that now appear to be on the verge of economic and political disintegration.

Changes in the International Structure

Since the system that we have adopted has proved so successful for so long, is there really anything for us to worry about? Is there any need to reassess the requirements for defence, deterrence or reassurance for the 1980s and 1990s. I must admit once more to a historian's bias, which predisposes me to assume the obsolescence of any international structure with the passage of time. The Vienna Settlement of 1814–15, for example, lasted for about forty years. So did the Bismarckian Settlement of the 1870s. The structure is bound to be transformed by the dynamics of social change, by the altered perspectives and beliefs of a new generation sceptical, and usually rightly so, about the settled assumptions of its predecessors. We must ask not only whether the existing solutions are still valid for the problems that evoked them, but whether the problems themselves remain unchanged, and whether attitudes stereotyped in the late 1940s will still be relevant half a century later.

There can be little doubt that since 1949 changes have occurred, both objective and subjective, on a scale comparable to those between 1815 and 1854, or between 1870 and 1914: changes in the relationship between Western Europe and the United States; and changes in the military balance between the United States and the Soviet Union. These have been on a scale quite sufficient to compel a reappraisal of requirements for deterrence and reassurance established a generation ago.

The various causes and symptoms of transatlantic tension have been discussed so generally and so repeatedly that I propose to focus only on that most relevant to our immediate problem, that is the degree of anti-American sentiment now so evident in so many countries of Western Europe, to say nothing of the understandable resentment this has created in the United States. Opinion polls have revealed this anti-Americanism to be far less widespread than its more dramatic manifestations may sometimes suggest but, whatever its strength and incidence, it is disturbing enough to demand an explanation and to be taken seriously into account. It indicates that, for an appreciable number of Europeans, what was once seen as the prime requirement for *deterrence*, that is the commitment of American power to the defence of Western Europe, no longer provides the political *reassurance* that once it did; in some respects indeed it provides the exact opposite. So far from the Americans being in Europe to help the West Europeans defend themselves, they are seen in some quarters as being here in order to prosecute *their* war, a war in which the Europeans have no interest and from which they will be the first to suffer.

How has such a widespread and grotesque misunderstanding come about? Obviously there is a whole complex of reasons, in which simple cultural friction plays its part. But it is at least in part the outcome of the process I have described, by which the defence of Europe has become perceived not as the responsibility of the Europeans themselves but increasingly in terms of a system of 'extended nuclear deterrence' manipulated from the United States in accordance with strategic concepts with which few Europeans are familiar. If I may return to my historical discourse, in the eighteenth century the European bourgeoisie was well content to leave the conduct of war to its specialists and enjoy the improved quality of life made possible by that division of labour. But it was precisely this divorce of the bourgeoisie and their intelligentsia from the whole business of national defence that gave rise to the first 'Peace Movements', comprising intellectuals who maintained that, because wars were conducted by monarchical states with aristocratic-led professional soldiers, it was this war-making mechanism that actually *produced* wars, and that all that was needed to abolish war would be to abolish monarchs, aristocrats and the

military profession. After that it could be assumed that the peoples of Europe would live together in peace and harmony. The wars of the French Revolution were to disillusion them, as the First World War was to disillusion another generation of peace-bred intellectuals and the Second World War yet a third. But it takes only one generation of successful peacekeeping to engender the belief, among those not concerned with its mechanisms, that peace is a natural condition threatened only by those professionally involved in preparations for war. The military become the natural target for the idealistic young. And how much more will this be the case if those military are predominantly foreign? If the decision for peace or war appears to lie with a group of remote and uncontrollable decision-makers whose values and interests do not necessarily coincide with one's own? And if war is going to involve slaughter on so unimaginable a scale? Is it not these foreigners who are actually provoking the war? Are not the bases they have established in our territories a standing provocation to attack, eroding rather than enhancing our security? So the growth of pacifism, always endemic in a society that delegates defence questions to specialists, has in contemporary Europe become associated with anti-Americanism, and derives from that a populist veneer that otherwise it might lack.

It is here that the change in the military balance comes in. I would not like to judge how far the effectiveness of American *reassurance* in the 1950s and 1960s was due to any general perception in Western Europe of American nuclear predominance. Certainly neither European nor American defence experts habitually cited this as evidence for the credibility of nuclear deterrence. One can only say that expectations of the damage Western Europe might suffer as a result of Soviet response to that American 'first use' on which NATO strategy explicitly depended led to no widespread questioning among Europeans of the validity of that strategy. It was the Americans, under Mr McNamara, who were unhappy about it, but they could find few people in Europe, outside our tiny defence community, to share their doubts. The fact that the 'Peace Movement' has become active

21

in Western Europe at the precise moment that the United States has publicly admitted Soviet nuclear parity may or may not be co-incidental. It does mean however that the 'Peace Movement' can now support its arguments with some fairly tough strategic analysis, and find more sympathy within the defence community than would have been the case twenty years ago. It is no longer only a minority of anti-militarist intelligentsia who question the validity and credibility of a deterrent posture which would, if activated, destroy everything it is concerned to defend.

The result of these developments has been a serious disjunction between *deterrence* and *reassurance*. The object of *deterrence* is to persuade an adversary that the costs to him of seeking a military solution to his political problems will far outweigh the benefits. The object of *reassurance* is to persuade one's own people, and those of one's allies, that the benefits of military action, or preparation for it, will outweigh the costs. It is true that the Europeans were reassured in the 1950s not by any careful calculation of what they would lose or gain by war, but by their perception of the reverse – of how much the USSR would have to lose and how little to gain. She could threaten, or rather her allies could threaten, such cataclysmic damage to the enemy, at such low *immediate* social cost to herself, that the risk of any comparable damage to herself was seen as remote enough to be tolerable.

This is the situation that has been changed by nuclear parity, and it is a change of which all Europeans and an increasing number of Americans have now become conscious. Defence specialists may be puzzled and scornful that people who have been under threat of nuclear attack for at least twenty years should only now be beginning to take the problem seriously, but that they have now begun to do so is a new political fact that governments will have to take into account. It is also apparent, at least in Europe, that *reassurance* cannot be re-established by any improvement in the mechanism of *deterrence*, certainly not of nuclear deterrence. Perhaps the people of Western Europe ought to feel safer when the installation of *Pershing* II and cruise missiles has made clear our capacity to counter an SS–20 first strike, but I doubt whether they

really will. Perhaps we should all feel safer if the United States did develop the capacity to carry on, and 'prevail' in, a prolonged nuclear exchange with the Soviet Union but in fact public opinion in Europe is terrified by the prospect – and so is much of it in the United States. In the calculus of nuclear deterrence both developments may appear appropriate, even essential, but such a calculus does not translate easily into the language of political reassurance and certainly not in a Europe where any nuclear exchange, on however limited a scale, spells almost inconceivable disaster. Limited nuclear options do not look very attractive if we are likely to be one of them ourselves.

The Fear of Nuclear War

Any consideration of domestic consensus on defence questions must therefore begin with the realization that in Europe the Soviet Union is very widely seen as less of a danger than is the prospect of nuclear war. I state this dogmatically and can support the statement with no evidence from opinion polls. It is an impression gained from a wide study of the press, the media, and discussion with friends and colleagues outside the defence community. It is also important to realize that the nuclear war anticipated is not seen as one arising out of a Soviet attack on Western Europe, but rather from some self-sustaining process of escalation, perhaps originating in an extra-European conflict, but essentially caused by the whole apparatus of nuclear weapons in some way 'getting out of control'. Nuclear war is seen as a *Ding an Sich* (thing of itself), unrelated to the existing political situation or to any security requirements likely to arise out of it. It is therefore against the prospect of nuclear war itself, rather than that of Soviet attack, that Europeans now require *reassurance*, and any measures taken to deal with the latter that make the former seem more likely will continue to be deeply disruptive. The explanation that any measures effective in deterring Soviet attack make nuclear war *less* likely is no longer, for many Europeans, altogether persuasive. As fears of nuclear war become detached from fears of Soviet attack, so reassurance becomes divorced from deterrence. And it must be admitted that those calculations of nuclear strategy so distressingly prevalent in the United States, which take place in a kind of empyrean realm remote from the political realities of Europe or anywhere else, have powerfully contributed to this divorce.

Reconciling Deterrence and Reassurance

How are we to deal with this problem? How are deterrence and reassurance to be once more reconciled? This is the task that will confront statesmen and strategists for the rest of this century.

The task is complicated by differing perspectives on either side of the Atlantic as to what it is that we have to deter. The difference between European and American readings of Soviet power and intentions, to which we could and perhaps should devote an entire conference, have here to be accepted as given. As European fears of Soviet aggression have waned over the past thirty years, so American fears have grown. We have too the curious phenomenon that the countries most directly threatened by Soviet military power – West Germany and France – are those most confident in their ability to handle the Soviet Union through the normal machinery of diplomatic and political intercourse, while for the most remote, the most powerful and the least threatened of the allies – the United States – the Soviet Union still bulks as a figure of almost cosmic evil with whom no real dialogue is possible. Whether the European attitude is the result of greater wisdom or merely of wishful thinking is a matter that we could debate endlessly but I believe that a significant element in this difference of view lies in the degree to which the Europeans have abandoned the primary responsibility for their defence to the United States. Europeans have come to take the deterrence provided by others for granted and now assume that the dangers against which they once demanded reassurance only now exist in the fevered imagination of their protectors. A certain American tendency to hyperbole, an attachment to worst-case analysis and some unfortunate attempts to make our flesh creep with official publications in gorgeous technicolour whose statistics have been questioned even by European defence specialists,

have not helped improve matters. Such propagandistic efforts are widely discounted, and even when they are believed they are likely to engender not so much resolution as despair.

Our first task must therefore be to get Soviet power and intentions into perspective. The exaggerated melodrama implied in the term 'The Soviet Threat' seems and has always seemed to me unnecessary and counter-productive. There is a major problem of ideological hostility, and a major problem (though one not to be exaggerated) of military imbalance between a power the size of the Soviet Union and the smaller, even if richer and more dynamic, states of Western Europe. One does not have to attribute to the Soviet Union either predatory intentions or ambitions for global conquest to persuade all but a stubborn minority that the states of Western Europe have a problem of military security that must be solved if normal intercourse with the Soviet Union is to be sustained on a basis of equality. The Soviet Union has shown herself to be no more reluctant to use military means to solve political problems, when she can get away with it, than anyone else. It is not difficult to reach consensus within most groups of West Europeans that West Europe needs defences against the Soviet Union. Where consensus breaks down is over the question whether Europe can possibly be defended by nuclear war.

The second task therefore is to show that Europe *can* be defended, and that the costs of doing so would not outweigh the benefits. These costs must be seen as twofold: the prospective costs of nuclear war, with which public opinion is chiefly concerned; and the immediate costs of an economic kind, which are what worry governments. It is easy enough to say that no price is too high for the preservation of our independence, but it does not quite work out like that. Governments are concerned with independence, but they are also concerned with social stability. Even in the darkest days of the Cold War 'the soviet threat' was seen as ancillary to, and only given credibility by, the danger of social disintegration in the West. It is still a reasonable assumption that a stable and prosperous Western Europe will not present an attractive

23

target to Soviet ambitions. Defence expenditure has therefore to be fitted in to a general framework of economic policy in which the maintenance of an industrious economy and a high level of social welfare (so far as these can be reconciled) must enjoy an overriding priority. This assumption has not altered over the past thirty years, nor is it likely to change much over the next thirty.

During the past thirty years this problem of costs was, as we have seen, taken care of by nuclear deterrence. The immediate costs were kept acceptably low, the risk of incurring the ultimate costs seemed acceptably slight. Now, although there is a far greater reluctance to incur those long-term risks, there is no greater readiness to accept any increase in immediate costs, especially during a period of recession when the danger of social instability seems greater than at any time since the 1940s. Again, it is easy to say that no price should be too high for the avoidance of nuclear war but, for governments concerned with their everyday tasks, nuclear war still remains a remote if terrifying hypotheses, while mass unemployment, commercial bankruptcies and industrial discontent are an imminent reality. A society where domestic consensus has collapsed is in no position to fight a war, nuclear or otherwise.

So where does this leave us? First, the requirement for effective deterrence remains, if only because the Soviet Union cannot be expected to observe a higher standard of conduct towards weaker neighbours than other states, whatever their political complexion, have shown in the past. Second, deterrence can no longer depend on the threat of a nuclear war, the costs of which would be grotesquely out of proportion to any conceivable benefits to be derived from engaging in it. Third, proposals to make nuclear war 'fightable', let alone 'winnable' by attempting to limit its targets and control its course, however much sense this may make in the military grammar of *deterrence*, are not persuasive in the political language of *reassurance*. And finally the problem cannot be solved by any massive transferral of resources to conventional capabilities. The immediate social costs of doing so, whether one likes it or not, are unacceptably high.

Reducing Dependence on US Deterrence

Whatever the solution may be, I do not believe that it can be found at the macro-level of nuclear deterrence. There is a point beyond which the elaboration of nuclear arsenals ceases to bear any evident relation to the real problems faced by political communities and, so far as Europe is concerned, we passed that point long ago. It must be sought at the micro-level of the peoples, the societies that have to be defended, and for whose political cohesion, moral resolution and military preparedness nuclear weapons can no longer provide a credible substitute. There has been for many years what I can only describe as a morally debilitating tendency among European defence specialists to argue that, if the reassurance provided by the American nuclear guarantee were to be in any way diminished, European morale would collapse. I do not believe this to be true and, in so far as it is true, it is as a self-fulfilling prophecy, and one that American defence analysts have taken altogether too seriously. The reassurance on which most Europeans rely is the presence among them of American troops, a presence that makes the defence of West European territory appear a feasbile proposition and has encouraged us to make greater provision for our own defence. What is needed today is a reversal of that process whereby European Governments have sought greater security by demanding an ever greater intensification of the American nuclear commitment, demands that are as divisive within their own countries as they are irritating for the people of the United States. Instead we should be doing all that we can to reduce our dependence on American nuclear weapons by enhancing, so far as it is militarily, socially and economically possible, our capacity to defend ourselves.

By 'defend ourselves' I mean defend ourselves in the conventional sense with conventional weapons. I know that this view will not be universally popular. It is often argued that no such defence is possible unless we are prepared to turn West Europe into an armed camp but that proposition would be true only if we intended to fight a total war aiming at the destruction of the Soviet armed forces and the dictation of peace in Moscow. It is also argued that, whatever effort we made, the Soviet armed forces would ultimately overwhelm us. Of course they could, if they were prepared to pay a very high price, which is why I for one would be unwilling explicitly to renounce under any circumstances the use of nuclear weapons. It has been argued that, for those exposed to it, conventional war is no less terrible than nuclear war, and indeed events in the Lebanon have shown us just how terrible it can be – especially for those who have no means of defending themselves. But terrible as conventional war would be in Europe, nuclear war would be unimaginably, unendurably worse. Modern societies recover from conventional war within a generation. Whether humanity would ever recover from nuclear war is a matter for legitimate doubt.

Let us remember what we are trying to do. It is to deter the Soviet Union from using military force to solve its political differences with the West and to deter them in a way that will be credible to their leaders and acceptable – *reassuring* – to our own peoples. It is to make clear to the Soviet Union that in any attack on the West the costs will hugely outweigh the benefits, and to our own people that the benefits of such a defence will outweigh the costs. We have to make it clear to our potential adversaries that there can be no easy military solution to their political problems, no 'quick fix'. And this is best done by showing that any attack would be met by lethally efficient armed forces, backed up and where necessary, assisted by a resolute and prepared population, with the distinct possibility that the conflict might escalate to nuclear war and the certainty that, *even if it did not*, their armed forces would suffer casualties out of all proportion to any likely gains. The object of such defence would not be just the denial of territory. It would be the infliction of damage on the attacking forces on a scale incommensurate with any political objective they could conceivably gain by their attack. The image that the West Europeans need to present is that of a hedgehog – painful to devour and impossible to digest.

This is no doubt an ideal model but I defy anyone to think of a better. The probable alternative is one of inadequate, ill-equipped and undertrained forces, fighting on behalf of a divided or an indifferent population and dependent on an American President being prepared to sanction a nuclear release that would certainly destroy all they were fighting to defend and that might very well unleash a global holocaust into the bargain. That is the prospect that worries so many of us today, and the 'Peace Movement' is only articulating, in extreme form, many widespread and legitimate doubts. To escape from this situation and move towards the goal I have suggested would mean a change of emphasis from nuclear deterrence to conventional, or even unconventional defence. It would mean a shifting of primary responsibility to the Europeans for the defence of our own continent. It should also involve a greater degree of popular participation in defensive preparations, participation the more likely to be forthcoming if it is clear that such preparations were predominantly if not wholly non-nuclear. An invitation to participate in such preparations would indeed be the acid test for the 'Peace Movement', sorting out those who were interested only in making moral gestures and those whose sympathies lie on the other side of the Iron Curtain from the great majority of thoughtful citizens seriously concerned with questions of defence.

Progress along these lines, however modest, would do much to resolve the difficulties within the Alliance and create what Professor Lawrence Freedman has called 'a more mature relationship'. It would create a defence posture acceptable to our own peoples as well as credible to our potential adversaries. It would not solve the problem of deterring a first nuclear strike by the opposition. For that, as for much else, the Europeans must continue to depend on the United States, and few Americans would wish it otherwise. But this reliance must be placed in perspective. A Soviet nuclear attack on Western Europe, or the plausible threat of one, is perhaps not utterly inconceivable. It is certainly an option that we need to deter. But it does not rank high on the list of political probabilities, and the measures taken to counter it should not be regarded or depicted as being basic to the defence of Western Europe. The necessity for such counter-measures should be fully and publicly explained, but they should be put in the context of the fundamental task which only non-nuclear forces can effectively carry out, the defence of territory. Nuclear deterrence needs to be subordinated to this primary task of territorial defence, and not vice versa

It is the reassertion of this order of priorities, this reuniting of deterrence and reassurance, that seems to me basic for the creation of consensus within the Alliance over the requirements for the defence of the West in the 1980s, or indeed for however long it may take to establish such intimate and friendly relations with the Soviet Union that defence becomes a pure formality. And in order to maintain consensus, the achievement of this relationship must be seen to be our long-term goal. I hope it goes without saying that any developments along the lines I have proposed should go hand in hand with arms-control initiatives, both to eliminate unnecessary causes of tension and to keep the costs of defence on both sides down to socially acceptable levels. But we should not allow ourselves to expect any miraculous breakthroughs as a result of such initiatives, or be unduly depressed or bitter if they fail. 'The Dual Track' is essential to effective reassurance: peoples expect their governments to provide them with adequate protection, but they also expect them to seek peace and, if they are not seen to be doing so, consensus over defence will crumble away.

Above all we must stop being frightened, and trying to frighten each other, with spectres either of Soviet 'windows of opportunity' or of the prospect of inevitable, self-generating nuclear war. Defence will continue to be a necessity in a world of sovereign states. Nuclear war is a terrible possibility that nothing can now eradicate, but of whose horrors we must never lose sight. To deal with the dilemma arising from these twin evils we need clear heads, moral courage, human compassion, and above all a sense of proportion. The main condition for consensus in the 1980s is in fact that we should all grow up. This, unfortunately, may be the most difficult requirement of all.

Broadening the Strategic Focus: Comments on Michael Howard's Paper

SAMUEL P. HUNTINGTON

On rare occasions in the history of any subject, a thinker has an insight and articulates a new concept or idea, after which everyone says 'How brilliant! How obvious! How did we ever get along before without it?' Such is the case with the concept of 'reassurance' that Michael Howard develops in his Paper. How *did* we ever get along without it? We surely will get along in the future only by making good use of it. It is the central contribution of an absolutely first-rate Paper, which is throughout original in thought, elegant in phrasing, and penetrating in analysis.

As a result, strategy must now be explicitly directed to not one but two problems: deterrence and reassurance. The solutions to these problems are related, sometimes positively, sometimes negatively. One major source of our current strategic difficulties, Michael Howard argues, is that the needs of deterrence now conflict with the needs of reassurance. That may be true. But it is also necessary to recognize that the current intensity of both problems stems from a common source. That source is the change during the 1970s in the military balance of power between the United States and the Soviet Union, particularly in the area of nuclear weapons. Perceptions of this changing balance and of the resulting relative weakness of the West are, as the public opinion polls demonstrate, widespread in both Europe and America. Weakness, in turn, generates fear. With some people the fear is of the Soviet Union, and of intensified Soviet aggression or pressure on the West. That is one version of the 'present danger', and those with this concern lobby for a greatly expanded military effort to restore a more satisfactory balance. With other people, however, the fear generated by weakness is of nuclear war and the awesome destruction that would be entailed by almost any use of nuclear weapons.

That is their 'present danger', and they debouch into the streets with 'peace' marches and demonstrations against nuclear deployments and in favour of nuclear freezes.

The current situation in the West thus bears marked similarities to that which existed in the late 1950s and early 1960s. As a result of *Sputnik* and Soviet missile developments and the apparently confident (but false) claims of Khrushchev about Soviet military prowess, feelings of weakness permeated Western societies. These resulted, on the one hand, in the Campaign for Nuclear Disarmament (CND), 'Ban the Bomb' marches, 'peace' candidates for public office, and the like. On the other hand, they also produced intense concern in the United States about the Soviet Union moving ahead in space technology and weapons, the Gaither Committee report, a 'missile gap' scare, and major efforts to push the US nuclear build-up, which took off dramatically following the advent of the Kennedy Administration in 1961. Fear of nuclear war and fear of the Soviet Union, in short, rose together from perceptions of Western weakness. In the event, some of the perceptions turned out to be misperceptions and the Kennedy Administration's efforts to expand US military power rapidly corrected the balance. The true nature of the balance was dramatically underlined by the Cuban missile crisis, after which fears of both nuclear war and of Soviet aggression declined markedly. Reassurance was re-established when it was shown that deterrence worked.

A somewhat comparable situation exists now. Reassurance will only be achieved when the credibility of deterrence is no longer in doubt. The conflict at present is consequently not so much between reassurance and deterrence as it is between short-term reassurance and long-term reassurance. Those whom weakness has made afraid of nuclear war want to be reassured that nuclear war will not happen; they seek that reassurance through nuclear freezes, 'no-first-use' pledges, nuclear-free zones, and the like. Insofar as these actions impede the re-establishment of Western military strength, as well as possibly encourage Soviet adventurism, however, they directly obstruct long-term reassurance. They treat the symptoms but not the cause of the present uneasiness in the West. That cause can only be removed by the massive reconstruction of Western – primarily US – military power to correct the effects of the eight successive years when the US consistently reduced her military strength. The first imperative, therefore both to enhance deterrence and to enhance reassurance is to rectify the military balance – particularly in the nuclear area – along the lines initiated by the Carter Administration and carried forward and intensified by the Reagan Administration.

In saying this, it must also be recognized, however, that we will never be able to recreate the levels of assurance against the Soviet threat that some right-wing extremists would like, nor the levels of assurance against the possibility of nuclear war that some street demonstrators would find comforting. We cannot escape the presences of a hostile power and of nuclear weapons, and while the appropriate military build-up can raise the levels of both deterrence and reassurance, nothing can be done to make the world reassuringly safe. We have no choice but to live with a certain level of anxiety with respect to both the Kremlin and the bomb.

Removing any doubt as to the equivalence – particularly in terms of survivability and flexible retaliatory capability – of US strategic weapons is a first priority. As has been recognized for years, however, and as was forcefully delineated by Henry Kissinger in his speech in Brussels in 1979, no attainable US nuclear capability can restore the older pattern of extended deterrence for Europe. Deterrence and reassurance in Europe require other approaches. There may be many possible ones; let me mention four.

First, it is conceivable that the existing and planned NATO military capabilities will suffice for deterrence. John Mearsheimer,

among others, has made a powerful case that the conventional balance on the Central Front is nowhere near as precarious as it is often made out to be and that Soviet commanders could only see great losses and high risks in an offensive campaign in Central Europe.[1] In the discussions of this Conference, François de Rose argued that deterrence in Europe rests not on an American *nuclear* guarantee but on an American *security* guarantee which results from the fact that the independence and security of Europe are of vital concern and interest to the United States. Consequently, any attempt to destroy them would imply the risk of a major conflict with the United States which is probably what the USSR wants to avoid at all cost. Furthermore, any prospect that conventional hostilities in Europe could not bring immediate Soviet victory would be fraught with political and military dangers for the Soviet Union in Eastern Europe. This argument parallels the stress that the Reagan Administration has placed on protracted conventional war, horizontal escalation, force sustainability, and industrial mobilization.

There is therefore some reason to think that what we have (and will have) may be enough. Yet there remain powerful arguments on the other side as to the vulnerability of NATO, particularly to a quick offensive, and uneasy doubts as to whether, even with appropriate warning, NATO would in fact be able to mobilize its forces for an effective defence in Germany. Uncertainty as to the possible outcome of a war involving the current order of battle could be enough to deter the Soviet Union but it is not enough to reassure the Allies. The current balance and current policy are precisely the sources of the feeling that we are unassured and that, hence, the Soviet Union may be undeterred.

If the existing balance is inadequate for reassurance and possibly inadequate for deterrence, what are the alternatives? That which is most widely proposed is, of course, a significant increase in NATO conventional strength. Michael Howard makes an eloquent case for such a strategy. 'We (Europeans)', he says, 'should be doing all that we can to reduce our dependence on American nuclear weapons by enhancing, so far as is militarily, socially and economically possible, our capacity to defend ourselves,' that is, 'to defend ourselves in the conventional sense with conventional weapons.' This will, he notes, require a greater European military effort. He suggests that such an effort should not be beyond the realm of possibility if its purpose is not to be able to dictate peace in Moscow but to create a situation where, if they invaded Western Europe, the USSR 'would suffer casualties out of all proportion to any likely gains,' even if nuclear weapons were not used.

Deterrence by conventional defence has a certain appeal. It has, indeed, been set forth by a variety of committees, experts and conferences, at least since the noted Lisbon NATO Meeting of 1952. After thirty years, it remains appealing, but it also remains an unreality. Michael Howard himself calls his prescription an 'ideal model', and European Governments and peoples have never been willing to implement it in practice. For years this attitude was justified on the very practical grounds that it made more sense to rely on the American nuclear deterrent. Now that the latter is no longer what it used to be, perhaps a credible European conventional defence force will begin to materialize. But the attitudes of European publics and governments are no more favourable than they have been in the past, and economic conditions are far less propitious than they ever have been in the past. The burden of proof that conventional defence is a feasible option lies on its proponents and clearly has not been met.

There are further problems with the concept itself. Michael Howard speaks of a European conventional force that would impose unacceptable casualties on the Soviet Union. What would the level of such casualties have to be? A successful invasion of Western Europe could bring the Soviet Union a total change in the 1945 settlement and in the global balance of power, the projection of their power and influence to the Atlantic coast, the subordination of the industrial heartland of Europe in the Rhine and Ruhr valleys to Soviet purposes, the dissolution of the First OECD) World as we know it and its relegation to North America, Australia and New Zealand, since Japan would inevitably have to accommodate herself to the new power the Soviet Union would be able to wield in Asia.

How many casualties would a Soviet Government be willing to pay to achieve these results? A few hundred thousand? Certainly. A million? Very probably. Two or three million? Quite possibly. What forces would Western Europe have to have to impose such casualties? What European cabinets would vote the resources to maintain such forces? Even if one assumes three or four Soviet casualties for every European casualty (ignoring, for the moment, the fact that the war would be fought in the midst of European populations), how long would European Governments and armies be willing to suffer the hundreds of thousands and probably millions of casualties that would be necessary to convince the Soviet Union to back off?

There is yet a further problem. The purpose of NATO strategy is deterrence. A purely defensive strategy is inherently a weaker deterrent than one which promises retaliation against valued assets of the aggressor. This has long been recognized to be the case at the strategic nuclear level. It is also true at the conventional level. Given the nature of modern conventional weapons and current NATO forward defence strategy, a Soviet offensive is almost inevitably going to be a partial success. Even if it does not reach the North Sea or Frankfurt or the Rhine, it will still penetrate some distance into West Germany. Once it is stopped, the Allies may attempt to pull together forces for a counter-offensive. Such would be a difficult political and logistical undertaking. Inevitably the pressures will be on all parties to attempt to negotiate a cease-fire and a resolution of the conflict. With their armies ensconced in Bavaria and Saxony, the Soviet Union will clearly have the upper hand in such a negotiation. Although they may not have gained everything they wanted, they are certainly likely to come out of the conflict in a better position than they were before they started hostilities.

On the record to date, then, a conventional defence strategy has been unfeasible politically; if it could be implemented, it would be of dubious value militarily.

Are there other alternatives? In his Paper Michael Howard points out that the Congress of Vienna Settlement and the Bismarckian Settlement of the 1870s each lasted about forty years. The fortieth anniversary of the end of the 1939–45 war is only a short time away, and hence we should ask 'whether attitudes stereotyped in the late 1940s will still be relevant half a century later'. Discussion of NATO strategy has in large part accepted the constraints of the post-1945 settlement. This is particularly marked in the extent to which the alternatives debated have been spread along a single continuum from total reliance on the American nuclear deterrent, at one end, to total reliance on a European conventional defence force, at the other. Forty years later perhaps it is time to get off that continuum and to consider other possibilities that may be more appropriate for the changed conditions of the 1980s. Many such 'off-continuum' strategic alternatives may exist. Let me mention two, which perhaps deserve more serious consideration than they have received.

First, given the problems involved in a conventional defence of Europe, is there any way in which a credible nuclear deterrent can be recreated? The answer is that there is an obvious way, if Europeans are willing to pursue it. The threat to use nuclear weapons in response to a conventional attack is most credible – and, indeed, may only be credible – when the national existence of the state attacked is at risk. No one seriously doubts that an Israeli Government, for example, would use nuclear weapons if massed Arab armies threatened to swarm across its borders and into Tel Aviv. Although it is certainly not NATO's only problem, NATO's central problem is the possibility of Soviet aggression in Central Europe. One relatively certain way to deter that aggression would be to create a reasonable-sized, invulnerable German nuclear force capable of retaliating against the Soviet Union. Such a force could be based both at sea (in submarines and on surface ships) and in a mobile form on land. It could conceivably develop out of the deployment of US *Pershing* II and GLCM (ground launched cruise missiles) to Germany. It is planned to have these weapons under purely US control. Conceivably, they could be shifted first to dual control and then to purely German control. As it developed, the German nuclear force might or might not join French and British

nuclear forces as part of a broader European multilateral (if one dares use that word in this context) nuclear deterrence consortium. The *sine qua non*, however, is that one finger on the nuclear trigger should be in Bonn; nothing less would provide a sufficiently credible deterrent against a conventional attack by the Soviet Union.

Movement in this direction would mean discarding several assumptions of the late-1940s settlement, particularly that which saw Germany as an inherently aggressive power which consequently had to forgo defence measures permitted other states. But the Federal Republic has accepted the division of Europe and of Germany. However much she may wish for a peaceful reunification, she clearly is not a *revanchiste* power. (Even if she were, it is not clear how a modest-sized nuclear force would help her to achieve her objectives.) The unassailable logic which President de Gaulle applied to the development of the French *Force de Frappe* in the early 1960s is even more relevant to Germany now, which is, after all, in the front line. While the Soviet Union might well be willing to sacrifice a million soldiers to control Western Europe, they are not likely to be willing to sacrifice Moscow, Leningrad, Kiev, Stalingrad, and much else besides to achieve that end. The damage that could be inflicted by even a modest size nuclear force would be devastating; the certainty that it would be inflicted would be as close to one hundred percent as anything can be in the uncertain world of politics and war. Deterrence would operate.

What about reassurance? Paradoxically such a strategy would probably provide a great deal of reassurance for Germans and would quite likely cut the ground from under the German anti-nuclear movements. As Michael Howard points out, the debilitating aspect of current strategy is the extent to which it makes Europeans dependent upon Americans for their security. That is not a healthy situation. A minority of the German public is intensely opposed to the deployment of American theatre nuclear weapons in their country. It is highly unlikely that the same opposition would manifest itself to German nuclear weapons. People become reassured when they feel they have some control over the critical decisions affecting their future. It is also hardly coincidental, as many have pointed out, that pacifism and anti-nuclearism have been much weaker in France, which proudly accepts responsibility for her own nuclear and conventional defence, than in other European countries which are more dependent on American protection. A German nuclear deterrent would put responsibility for the key decisions affecting German security in German hands, although it would not necessarily mean that Germany would opt out of NATO or forego the security guarantees of the United States and the other European powers. It might well, however, facilitate the withdrawal of some American troops from Germany.

A German nuclear deterrent might be somewhat less than reassuring for at least parts of the publics in other European countries. World War II, however, is now almost two generations in the past, and on this issue the successor generation may well have greater tolerance and understanding than its predecessors. In the late twentieth century it is difficult to see why France and Britain can be trusted with nuclear weapons but not Germany. One person expressed to me the fear that Germany would target Paris; if that is the basis on which opposition to a German nuclear deterrent rests, it should be brought out into the open for the ridicule it deserves. A German nuclear force could, however, raise deterrence concerns elsewhere in Europe. The certainty of increased costs to the Soviet Union for aggression in Central Europe could enhance the relative attractiveness to them of aggression on the flanks of Europe. The price of the more assured deterrence in Germany for the Alliance, could, in short, be a greater external commitment of men and resources to the defence of Norway and Turkey. I do not now recommend the creation of a German nuclear force. I do suggest, however, that the issue deserves a far fuller and more serious consideration than it has received for some while.

A much preferable alternative to such a move would be for NATO generally to adopt a conventional retaliatory strategy. Such a strategy would capitalize on the developments during the past decade in Eastern Europe and

the changed relationships between Eastern and Western Europe. Next to a nuclear attack on the Soviet Union herself, the contingency that the Soviet Union fears most must be an Allied conventional offensive into Eastern Europe. The arguments in favour of a shift in NATO strategy from flexible response to conventional retaliation are overwhelming, and I have enumerated them elsewhere.[2] Suffice it here simply to make three points.

- A politically-diplomatic defensive stance in favour of the maintenance of the *status quo* need not imply a militarily defensive strategy once the *status quo* has been attacked. This is simple common sense. In addition, of course, for two decades NATO has contemplated nuclear retaliation against the Soviet Union, in the event of an attack on Western Europe. The concept of conventional retaliation into Eastern Europe is morally far preferable and hence should be far more acceptable than one which relies on early recourse to nuclear weapons.
- A strategy of conventional retaliation would not require the massive conventional build-up needed for a strategy of conventional defence. The widely quoted axioms that the offence requires a 3–1 or 4–1 or 5–1 superiority applies not across the front as a whole but rather at the point of attack. A Soviet offensive is a real threat not because they have that a 3–1 superiority in the overall balance of forces in Europe, which they do not, but because they can concentrate their forces to achieve it at the critical point or points. NATO can do exactly the same in reverse, and the new US army 'Air-Land Battle' tactical doctrine is precisely suited to this purpose.
- The virtual certainty of the immediate movement of West German divisions into East Germany and of American divisions into Czechoslovakia and Hungary would be a major deterrent to Soviet attack on Western Europe. The Soviet Union would not and could not count on the loyalty of Eastern European forces and populations. Most importantly, neither could Eastern European governments, do so and they are likely to do everything they could to dissuade the Soviet Union from attacking the

West. NATO strategy has for too long relied on the diminished credibility of the threat to go up the escalation ladder. A conventional retaliatory strategy would make deterrence rest not on the threat to go up but on the threat to go East.

How much reassurance would a strategy of conventional retaliation provide? It would certainly provide more than a strategy that places major reliance on American nuclear guarantees, but it would also clearly require a substantial American conventional capability in Central Europe. It would be a strategy to which the Europeans could make major contributions, either to the offensive forces required for prompt movement to the East or to the holding forces required to slow down the Soviet movement to the West. To a large extent the latter should be militia and reserves derived from Michael Howard's 'resolute and angry population'. Indeed his emphasis on a more popularly-based defence of Western Europe becomes feasible and militarily useful *only* when it is combined with the threat of a rapid eastward movement by NATO regular forces. In effect, the Soviet Union would be told: 'if you go West, you will confront an organized, armed and trained population ready to make you pay a price, bearable but still heavy, for every kilometer, while we go East to encounter unreliable armies and to arouse the sullen and rebellious populations which you remember so well from 1953, 1956, 1968 and 1980–81.'

While there may be other strategic alternatives for NATO, there are, then, at least these four:

- continuation of the existing strategy and forces;
- creation of a massive conventional defensive force;
- creation of a German nuclear deterrent force;
- adoption of a strategy of conventional retaliation.

To put it mildly, there is unlikely to be an immediate consensus forming in support of either of the latter two possibilities. People will say that both ideas are unsettling and dangerous. New ideas are, however, always unsettling; that is their virtue. They are also always labelled dangerous; that is their burden. In the 1980s, however, NATO is unlikely to achieve the desirable minimum levels of deterrence or reassurance either with the current strategy, which has been found wanting because it is incredible, or with the conventional build-up strategy, which is lacking because it is unfeasible. The post-war era is over. A new strategic environment demands new strategic policies. Deterrence, reassurance and consensus require a broadening of the strategic focus and a consideration of the new strategic alternatives which are more appropriate for the conditions of the 1980s than the outworn options that have figured so long in strategic debate.

NOTES

[1] John J. Mearsheimer, 'Why Soviets Can't Win Quickly in Central Europe', *International Security*, Vol. 7 (Summer 1982), pp. 5–39.

[2] See my 'The Renewal of Strategy', in *The Strategic Imperative: New Policies for American Security*, (Cambridge, Mass.: Ballinger, 1982), pp. 21–32.

32